A

·   ·   ·

B O O K

The Philip E. Lilienthal imprint
honors special books
in commemoration of a man whose work
at the University of California Press
from 1954 to 1979
was marked by dedication to young authors
and to high standard in the field of Asian studies.
Friends, family, authors, and foundations have together
endowed the Lilienthal Fund, which enables the Press
to publish under this imprint selected books
in a way that reflects the taste and judgment
of a great and beloved editor.

The publisher gratefully acknowledges the generous contribution to this book provided by the Philip E. Lilienthal Asian Studies Endowment, which is supported by a major gift from Sally Lilienthal.

Isami's House

Isami's House

THREE CENTURIES
OF A JAPANESE FAMILY

Gail Lee Bernstein

UNIVERSITY OF CALIFORNIA PRESS

BERKELEY   LOS ANGELES   LONDON

Credits
Figures 10–22, 25–29, and 31 courtesy of Horiuchi Yōko

University of California Press
Berkeley and Los Angeles, California

University of California Press, Ltd.
London, England

Library of Congress Cataloging-in-Publication Data

Bernstein, Gail Lee.
    Isami's house : three centuries of a Japanese family / Gail
Lee Bernstein.
        p.   cm.
    Includes bibliographical references and index.
    ISBN 0-520-23974-1 (cloth : alk. paper)
    1. Matsuura family.   2. Japan—History—Tokugawa
period, 1600–1868.   3. Japan—History—1868–.   I. Title.

CT1837.5.M39B47   2005
929'.2'0952—dc22   2005005760

Manufactured in the United States of America
14   13   12   11   10   09   08   07   06   05
10   9   8   7   6   5   4   3   2   1

The paper used in this publication meets the minimum
requirements of ANSI/NISO Z39.48–1992 (R 1997)
(*Permanence of Paper*).

To Michael Patrick Sullivan

CONTENTS

ILLUSTRATIONS

MAPS

FIGURES

PROLOGUE: HISTORY REVEALED

One evening in early March 1993 I received an unexpected telephone call from Tokyo.

"Did you know my older sister is in the hospital?" Tami asked. I knew that Toyo had been hospitalized since January, but I had been led to believe that she would recover. Tami informed me, almost matter-of-factly, that Toyo was dying. Seventy-two hours later I was on an airplane headed for Tokyo.

Toyo was my "Japanese mother." I had met her thirty years earlier on my first trip to Asia. In 1963, Japan was still a long way away—two weeks by ship from California—and only a generous fellowship for doctoral dissertation research enabled me to visit, at last, the country I had been studying since my undergraduate days. I found lodging with the assistance of a fellow graduate student, who wrote to her Tokyo friend, who phoned his aunt, who contacted her friend, who agreed to take me in. The aunt's friend was Toyo, the sixth of fifteen children born to the Matsuura family, whose male householdheads had served for 265 years as headmen, or *shōya,* of a mountain village in northern Japan.

Toyo provided much more than food and shelter. She taught me conversational Japanese, cared for me when I was sick, arranged for my recreational and social activities, and introduced me to the members of her large and amiable extended family—the twelfth and thirteenth generations of Matsuura. Her twenty-year-old daughter, Yōko, was like a younger sister to me. Whenever I returned to Japan, I stayed in Tokyo with Toyo, visited Yōko, and socialized with Toyo's many siblings, nieces, and nephews, who, when they got together for family events and invited along their in-laws, could number as many as fifty. When Toyo and her husband went to San Francisco on a holiday in the 1970s, I flew to the airport to meet their plane. We exchanged New Year's cards and occasional gifts, and in January 1993, her older granddaughter, together with two friends on vacation from their American college, stayed at my home for several days.

In the late 1980s it occurred to me that the Matsuura family's size and continuity could provide a prism for viewing modern Japanese history. By narrating the life stories of family members, I hoped to put a personal face on the last three hundred years of life in Japan. True, the family was not exactly ordinary, typical, or average. By the eighteenth century, they had become members of the local governing elite and also prosperous entrepreneurs in their region, supplementing their considerable agrarian income with sake brewing and other commercial activities. In the early twentieth century, they were among the wealthiest landholders in Fukushima prefecture. After World War II, the Matsuura and others in the thin stratum of extremely large landholders, who numbered under 100,000 in a rural populace of more than 5.5 million households, became the targets of agrarian reform designed to break down their domination of tenants and to encourage greater economic equality in the countryside.[1] Despite their wealth, however, Matsuura family members' experiences in many ways paralleled and illustrated patterns in the overall history of early modern and modern Japan.

Toyo and her siblings, in the family's twelfth generation, joined the millions of other rural migrants to Tokyo in the early decades of the twentieth century, seeking advanced education, work, and a place in the emergent urban middle class. In the interwar years, many of the family's menfolk, accompanied by their wives, participated in Japan's empire by serving in the military abroad, working in overseas trading companies, or staffing the diplomatic corps. All of the family's members experienced the military occupation of their country, and in the postwar period they worked toward their own and Japan's recovery.

When I wrote to Toyo about my idea of tracing the history of her natal family, she was delighted and even offered to help. Our joint research project was thwarted, however, by my biological mother's long illness, which prevented me from returning to Japan for almost a decade. Toyo's health too deteriorated after surgery for breast cancer. I had planned to begin collaborating with her on our mutual project in the summer of 1993, but the telephone call from her youngest sister, Tami, earlier that year altered my timetable.

Toyo's twenty-seven-year-old granddaughter met me at Narita Airport, scooped up my suitcase, and led the way through the maze of train lines until we reached our destination, a hospital in the western outskirts of the city. In Toyo's private room, Yōko, wearing a surgical mask, was helping her mother drink from a straw.

Although Toyo immediately recognized me, I barely recognized her. She lay on her back, attached to tubes. Her face was sunken, her mouth toothless. But her mind was clear. She remembered our research project, and, as I stood beside her bed, she told me about the book her father, Isami, had written, and described where in her house I could find it. That night, Yōko and I located the book, and a few days later, Toyo slipped into a coma. She died within two weeks, and when I returned to Japan in the summer of 1993, it was to attend her memorial service.

Isami's ninety-one-page book, titled *Yamashiraishi mura o kataru* (Telling about Yamashiraishi Village), became an essential source for my research into the family's past. Born in 1879, Toyo's father was the patriarch of the eleventh generation of the Matsuura line, and his long lifetime spanned the modern history of Japan. His chronicle traces his family and their village from their founding ancestor in the late 1600s to his own time. The lives of the fifteen children born between him and his wife also fill the pages of his book.

Although Isami died one year before I met Toyo, his writing and his children's recollections helped reveal his colorful personality, firmly held values, and passionate commitment to the continuity of his family line. He and Toyo have emerged as the central figures of this book.

How did the Matsuura family manage to remain not only intact but also in village office for over two and one-half centuries? How did they survive numerous political changes, family crises, famines, wars, peasant uprisings, and the entire upheaval of the country's transformation to modernity? And what led to their eventual undoing as local leaders? These were the questions obviously haunting Isami, the self-appointed family chronicler and, for all intents and purposes, the last headman of his village, when he sat down in 1949 to trace "the ancestral generations of the Matsuura family who built Yamashiraishi."[2]

Isami's chronicle contains clues for understanding why his family's leadership ceased. It was not that he and his immediate forebears, as rural leaders and landlords, resisted the forces of change. In fact, they embraced the Japanese government's goal of promoting industrialization and introducing Western learning, beginning in the second half of the nineteenth century. Isami himself was an amateur inventor, fascinated with new technology and dedicated to the task of providing his many children with a progressive education. Many of the values espoused by Japan's modernizers, such as hard work, frugality, respect for learning, self-sacrifice, and productivity, were consonant with traditional agrarian values. From the very beginning of their family line, the Matsuura, like other local notables, were characterized by an entrepreneurial spirit, supplementing their rice income with a variety of business activities and public works projects that for centuries had promoted economic development in their areas.

Industrialization, with its concomitant urban culture, however, introduced other values—individualism, for one—and middle-class lifestyles that ultimately undermined agrarian life. Increasingly outmoded, the emphasis on family solidarity and continuity, self-sacrifice, industriousness, and respect for learning lived on in some of the Matsuura progeny for at least one more generation, helping them to make the transition to urban middle-class life. In the end, however, the very agrarian values and institutions that allowed the family to cohere through three centuries and also guided Isami into the straits of modernity ultimately and ironically forced its demise.

In 1975, when Toyo first took me from Tokyo to Fukushima prefecture to see the family's old house there, the trip still involved a long train ride, but the cultural distance was even greater than the physical. As we stood talking on the platform of the local railroad station, an elderly farmer approached us and stared. Pointing to me, he bluntly asked Toyo, "Is she Japanese?" Toyo laughed but did not explain. After all, what was I doing there? It was hard even for me to explain what had first drawn me to Japan and harder still to translate my personal interests into scholarship.

Whenever I was in Japan, I felt torn between the demands of my academic work and my social involvement in Toyo's family. The novel idea of merging the two had come to me one night in a "Eureka!" flash. For years I had been caught up in the lives of this family's members, who, in a number of ways, resembled my own large extended family of aunts, uncles, and cousins. Fascinated, in particular, with the women's lives and eager to talk about them, I had felt constrained by an academic agenda that, at the time, did not include women's studies or, for that matter, family history. For many years I had pushed my personal interests aside, relegating anecdotes of Matsuura family members to my journal, classroom, and conversations with friends. The evolution of new and legitimate academic topics and methods that allowed scholars to study women and also "ordinary people" and to intrude themselves, if only occasionally, into the story they were trying to tell, freed me, at last, to do what now seems to me perfectly natural: to write about people who, for forty years, have opened their homes and their hearts to me.

In Toyo's absence, her relatives and friends joined in helping to write this story of her family, as did many others whose assistance I acknowledge individually in the following section. While I gratefully thank these many generous acquaintances, I must assume full responsibility for any errors. I must also confess that, despite my best endeavors and those of others who came to my aid, I shall always feel that this book would have been better had Toyo lived to write it with me.

Gail Lee Bernstein
Tucson, Arizona

ACKNOWLEDGMENTS

Of the many Matsuura family members who contributed to this book, I should like to thank, first of all, Toyo's sister Nakamura Tami. In addition to being a consummate hostess and longtime friend, she has been a valuable informant and expeditor. Her sisters, Ishiwata Mina, Akakura Fuki, Sugai Fumi, and Tsukioka Yasu, gave generously of their time to relate their childhood memories. Toyo's sister-in-law Matsuura Masako, the widow of her brother Yūshirō, graciously hosted me on three separate occasions when I visited the family's natal village in Fukushima prefecture on research trips. Toyo's granddaughter Kazuno Reiko accompanied me on the first trip; Toyo's daughter, Horiuchi Yōko, was my guide on the second; and Nakamura Tami accompanied me on the third. Yōko often served not only as my guide but also as my hostess, informant, and research assistant, and she generously lent me old family photographs. Other family members too numerous to mention pitched in to help in ways too varied to recount. They photocopied Japanese documents, mailed books related to my research, provided relevant newspaper articles, and patiently answered my endless questions.

One of the challenging aspects of interviewing people about their lives is knowing which questions to ask. Toyo's sisters did not see how their life stories might contribute to my research, and at times I had to tease information out of them. Thinking that their roles as wives and mothers were unworthy of academic exploration, they gave limited answers at first. Once, one of the sisters began talking about how she and her children fled Russians in Manchuria in 1945. When I probed further, she seemed puzzled. "Is this what you are interested in?" she asked and then added, "If that's the case, my husband knows more about it than I do." The next day she brought me an article her husband had published on coal exploration in Manchuria in the 1930s.

On one occasion all five of Toyo's remaining sisters willingly gathered around the lunch table at her house, where Yōko now lived, for the stated purpose of answering my questions. Yōko took out family photographs to help jog their memories, but they all talked at once on different topics. One sister expressed concern that I would not be able to weave the fragments of their conversation into a meaningful narrative. Yet, they seemed reluctant to speak one at a time, perhaps fearful of hogging the limelight. My best interview material came at unexpected times—for example, when somebody who was getting ready to leave suddenly remembered a telling anecdote about her father, or when a chance comment in a restaurant led to a vivid recollection.

Information on the early history of the Matsuura family and their village derives largely from written sources. In addition to Isami's family chronicle, I benefited from the work of Asakawa township's local historian, Kawaoto Shōhei, who compiled a multivolume history of the region in which the Matsuura figured prominently. When I first met Kawaoto in 1993, he was in possession of over five hundred handwritten documents from the Tokugawa period (1600–1868), borrowed from the Matsuura family house in the village of Yamashiraishi. Matsuura materials are more numerous than those of any other family in the Asakawa area, especially for the Tokugawa period, and even include records of daily visitors to the house. Kawaoto rendered some of these documents into modern Japanese for inclusion in the three-volume *Asakawa chōshi* (History of Asakawa Township). He graciously shared information with me on two separate meetings in 1993 and in 1995.

Primary sources for Asakawa are also contained in the two-volume *Shishin shōbanshō* (History of All Memorable Events), published by the Asakawa Town Hall. For the history of Fukushima prefecture, I consulted several prefectural histories and reference works, including Kobayashi Seiji and Yamada Akira, *Fukushima-ken no rekishi* (A History of Fukushima Prefecture), volume 7, and the *Kadokawa Nihon chimei daijiten* (Kadokawa Encyclopedia of Japanese Notables), volume 7.

Written primary sources on the family for the post-Tokugawa period, in addition to Isami's chronicle, come from the published memoir of Isami's second son, Kōjirō: *Indoneshia sanjūnen* (Indonesia: Thirty Years); the memoir of his brother-in-law Ishii Itarō: *Gaikōkan no isshō* (The Lifetime of a Diplomat); and letters I received from Matsuura family members. My memories of the family, fortified by slides, photographs, and journal entries of my own during the forty-year period from 1963 and 2003, were especially useful for the chapters covering that period in the book.

Interviews with family members and with people who knew the family supplemented written sources. Kawazaki Fumio, the priest of Chōtoku Temple, the Zen Buddhist temple in Yamashiraishi, and two former Matsuura house servants were kind enough to talk to me about their memories of the family. The thirteenth-generation househead, Matsuura Tomoji, on three separate occasions allowed me to tour the family's large house, take pictures, and look through family photograph albums.

I also wish to acknowledge Toyo's longtime friend Ibuka Yuriko, who, with her husband, helped me to fill in details about Toyo's life in Manchuria, and Toyo's classmates Sugiura Sugako and Shiba Miyoko, who recounted memories of her from their school days at Freedom School.

At the University of Arizona, I relied greatly on my diligent and resourceful research assistant, Fujie Aldrich. Also providing translation assistance for difficult Tokugawa texts was Yukiko Kawahara. Additional research assistance came from Yuri Nakamura and Shizuko Radbill. The genealogical chart is the work of Tim Jefferson. Loretta Sowers read portions of the manuscript to provide feedback as an avid history buff. Millard Ladd Keith III gave me a valuable sense of audience, reading with the eyes of an undergraduate, albeit an exceptionally perceptive one. My longtime friend Carl Tomizuka, as always, served as both a sympathetic sounding board for my ideas and a source of information, drawing on his personal memories of Japan, his broadly based education, and his familiarity with contemporary Japanese society to contribute to my research.

My gratitude to Anne Walthall is immense for her close reading of an early draft of the first part of this manuscript and for her encouragement. I also profited greatly from James L. McClain's clear and concrete suggestions for revising the manuscript; he put a great deal of time and effort into the task. I also wish to thank the anonymous reader of the University of California Press for thoughtful, tactful, and sensitive comments and editor Scott Norton for his sage advice and detailed recommendations. Sheila Levine, as always, offered her special brand of encouragement, practical assistance, professional expertise, and patience.

The necessary funding for this project came from the Northeast Asia Council of the Association for Asian Studies (1993) and the American Philosophical Society (1993 and 1995). A Research Professorship from the Social and Behavioral Sciences Research Institute in the spring semester of 1995 and a research leave in the fall semester of 2003 released me from my teaching duties. Additional funding for research assistance from the Department of History of the University of Arizona was especially helpful in the later stages of manuscript preparation.

My brother, Irwin F. Bernstein, was a lifelong supporter of my work and expected to receive a copy of every book I have published. I thank him posthumously; he died days before I completed the final draft of this manuscript.

I have lost count of the number of versions of this book edited in red pencil by Michael Patrick Sullivan. His contribution in the form of editorial suggestions, technical assistance, unflagging enthusiasm, moral support, and behind-the-scenes help through all stages of this publication, and all of my previous ones as well, is impossible to repay, but I have tried to do so in some small measure by dedicating this book to him.

NOTES ON CONVENTIONS

In accordance with East Asian practice, Japanese surnames in this book precede given names. Thus, Ishikawa Toyo's surname is Ishikawa. Exceptions are the names of Japanese whose English-language works are cited and Japanese who observe the practice of giving surnames last.

Following Western practice, I calculated age, whenever possible, from date of birth. The Japanese custom of counting a person as one year old at birth and two at the beginning of the next calendar year may have caused discrepancies in cases where written Japanese sources show a person's age but not date of birth.

To pronounce the Japanese names and terms in this book, you may find it helpful to divide them into their component syllables and give roughly equal stress to each syllable. For example, Tokugawa is To-ku-ga-wa. Consonants are pronounced roughly as they are in English. Vowel pronunciation is similar to the *a* in *father,* the *e* in *end,* *i* like the *e* in *equal,* the *o* in *old,* and the *u* in *rude.* Thus, Isami is pronounced Ee-sah-mee. The diphthongs *ai* and *ei* are pronounced like *tie* and *say,* respectively. Thus, the village of Yamashiraishi is Ya-ma-shee-rie-shee and Yajibei is Ya-jee-bay. A macron (straight line) over *o* and *u* indicates that the sound should be doubled in length, so Yūya is Yuuya, and Kōemon is Koo(Koh)-eh-mon.

Japanese nouns are not distinguished as singular or plural. Hence, Matsuura could be singular or plural.

TIME LINE

DATE	EVENT	MATSUURA VILLAGE HEAD (by generation)*

1868–1912 / Meiji period continued

DATE	EVENT	MATSUURA VILLAGE HEAD
1879	Birth of Isami	
1894–95	Sino-Japanese War	
1901	Marriage of Isami and Kō	10: Yūya (d. 1937)
1904–5	Russo-Japanese War	

1912–26 / Taishō period

DATE	EVENT	MATSUURA VILLAGE HEAD
1912	Birth of Toyo	
1920	Isami becomes Matsuura househead	
1923	Great Kantō Earthquake	

1926–89 / Shōwa period

DATE	EVENT	MATSUURA VILLAGE HEAD
1931	Japan's seizure of Manchuria	
1937	Outbreak of second Sino-Japanese War	
1938	Isami becomes village head	11: Isami (ret. 1946, d. 1962)
1941	Japan's attack on Pearl Harbor	
1945	End of World War II	
1945–52	Allied occupation of Japan	12: Yatarō (ret. 1954, d. 1958)
1954	Annexation of Yamashiraishi by Asakawa	

*Ret. = Year when househead retired from village office

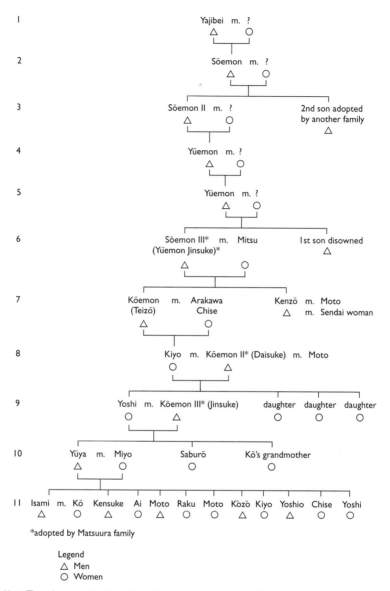

1   Yajibei m. ?
     △   ○

2   Sōemon m. ?
       △   ○

3   Sōemon II m. ?   2nd son adopted
       △   ○   by another family
                                △

4   Yūemon m. ?
       △   ○

5   Yūemon m. ?
       △   ○

6   Sōemon III* m. Mitsu   1st son disowned
     (Yūemon Jinsuke)*   △
       △   ○

7   Kōemon m. Arakawa   Kenzō m. Moto
     (Teizō)   Chise   △   m. Sendai woman
       △   ○

8   Kiyo m. Kōemon II* (Daisuke) m. Moto
     ○   △

9   Yoshi m. Kōemon III* (Jinsuke)   daughter daughter daughter
     ○   △   ○   ○   ○

10   Yūya m. Miyo   Saburō   Kō's grandmother
     △   ○   ○   ○

11   Isami m. Kō Kensuke Ai Moto Raku Moto Kōzō Kiyo Yoshio Chise Yoshi
     △   ○   △   ○   △   ○   ○   △   ○   △   ○   ○

*adopted by Matsuura family

Legend
△ Men
○ Women

Note: This select genealogy lists only family members whose names either appear in this book or are
indirectly mentioned.

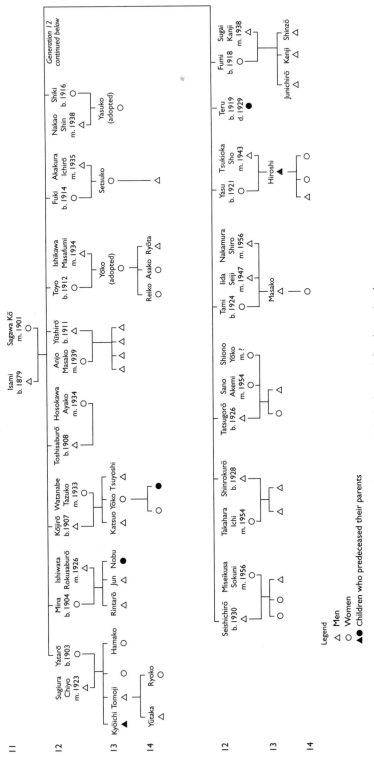

Legend

△ Men
○ Women
▲● Children who predeceased their parents

Note: This select genealogy lists only family members whose names either appear in this book or are indirectly mentioned.

CENTRAL PERSONS

Bungorō (Ishii)	Isami's uncle, a Seiyūkai politician
Chiyo	Isami's daughter-in-law (wife of his first son and heir)
Daisuke	Isami's beloved great-grandfather, eighth-generation Matsuura househead
Fuki	Isami's third daughter
Fumi	Isami's fifth daughter
Isami	eleventh-generation Matsuura househead
Isoko	Isami's granddaughter-in-law (wife of Tomoji, thirteenth-generation househead)
Itarō (Ishii)	Isami's cousin and brother-in-law, consul-general in Shanghai and ambassador to Brazil
Jinsuke	Isami's grandfather, ninth-generation Matsuura househead
Kensuke	Isami's brother
Kō	Isami's wife
Kōjirō	Isami's second son
Kōzō	Isami's brother
Masafumi (Ishikawa)	Isami's son-in-law (Toyo's husband)
Masako (Matsuura)	Isami's daughter-in-law (wife of Yūshirō)
Masako (Nakamura)	Isami's granddaughter (Tami's daughter)
Mina	Isami's first daughter
Miyo	Isami's mother and wife of Yūya, tenth-generation househead
Moto	Isami's step-great-grandmother (Daisuke's second wife)
Moto	Isami's sister, wife of Ishii Itarō

Seishichirō	Isami's seventh son
Shiki	Isami's fourth daughter
Shinrokurō	Isami's sixth son
Sōtarō (Ishiwata)	brother-in-law of Isami's first daughter, Mina, and Imperial Household minister at the end of the Pacific war
Tami	Isami's eighth daughter
Tatsugorō	Isami's fifth son
Teru	Isami's sixth daughter
Tomoji	Isami's grandson, thirteenth-generation Matsuura househead
Toshisaburō	Isami's third son
Toyo	Isami's second daughter
Yajibei	founding ancestor of the Matsuura lineage
Yasu	Isami's seventh daughter
Yatarō	Isami's first son and heir, twelfth-generation Matsuura househead
Yōko	Isami's granddaughter (Toyo's daughter)
Yoshi	Isami's grandmother, wife of ninth-generation househead, Jinsuke
Yūshirō	Isami's fourth son
Yūya	Isami's father, tenth-generation Matsuura househead

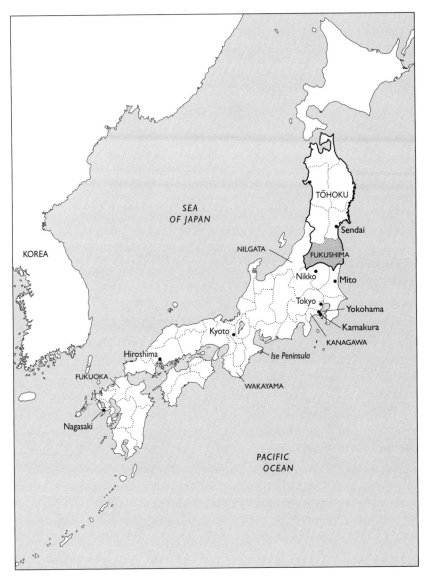

KOREA

SEA
OF JAPAN

TŌHOKU

Sendai

NILGATA

FUKUSHIMA

Nikko

Mito

Tokyo

Yokohama

Kamakura

KANAGAWA

Kyoto

Ise Peninsula

Hiroshima

WAKAYAMA

FUKUOKA

Nagasaki

PACIFIC
OCEAN

MAP 1 Modern Japan

_____

An Agrarian Childhood

IN THE SPRING OF 1890, eleven-year-old Matsuura Isami's great-grand-father Daisuke, the retired village head, took him by train on his first trip to Tokyo. Accompanying them were Isami's grandparents: Yoshi, who was Daisuke's daughter, and Jinsuke, her husband and the current village head. The family group had awakened at dawn to start the trip, their path down the mountain aided by servants hauling luggage on their backs and carrying lanterns to light the way. At the town of Ishikawa, five miles down the mountain, they hired a horse-drawn cart to carry them fifteen miles west across the rice plain to the new railroad station in the town of Shirakawa.

Members of the Matsuura family were accustomed to walking. Thirty years earlier, Daisuke had even walked to Tokyo (then called Edo) with his wife, Moto. It took them eight days to cover the entire distance, roughly 120 miles. Now, thanks to the newly opened Tōhoku line, Daisuke and his relatives could reach Ueno Station, in the nation's capital, in less than one day, hurtling through space at the breath-taking speed of twenty miles per hour. The iron rails symbolized industrialization, one of the goals set by the new Meiji government in its zeal to modernize.[1]

The three adults seated on the hard wooden benches in the train compartment had a clear mission. They were mulling over their young charge's future. In the twilight of his life, Daisuke, the eighth-generation patriarch of the Matsuura family, worried that Isami, heir to the eleventh generation, would fall behind in the world if he did not obtain a modern, Western-style education.

Tokyo was at the forefront of exhaustive Japanese efforts to learn from the West. The opening of Japan's doors to trade and diplomatic relations with the United States and Europe in the 1850s had introduced an avalanche of Western culture and technology that had undermined the value of classical Chinese scholarship, which had dominated Japanese intellectual life for hundreds of years. Negotiations with Westerners, whose treaties had forced Japanese relations with them, required a whole new body of knowledge. "Civilization and enlightenment," a popular slogan in the 1870s, called on Japanese to study all things foreign: languages, science, technology, medicine, political institutions, protocol, etiquette, law, dress, cuisine—the list seemed endless. From translating constitutions to learning how to eat spaghetti with a fork, literate Japanese tackled the task of learning all about the Occident.

Isami's father had left the early education of his firstborn son in the hands of Daisuke. From the age of five, Isami had lived with his great-grandparents in the separate retirement cottage on the family's grounds. His first four years of compulsory education were taken at the "simple, easy [village] school" that Daisuke had founded. When Isami demonstrated greater ability as a student than his father had shown, Daisuke, having, in Isami's view, a "very progressive, action-oriented personality," considered sending him to Tokyo for his higher education. Although Daisuke himself was a scholar of Chinese classics and gave private instruction to many of the young people in their area, he recognized that Chinese learning was now outmoded.[2]

While in Tokyo the family group visited a world exposition of goods and technology intended to open Japanese eyes to the so-called wonders of the modern industrial world. Daisuke also arranged to have the famous artist Nagahara Tan paint his portrait with his great-grandson. The oil painting of the pair, which still hangs in the retirement cottage on the grounds of their village home, captures the transitional nature of their era: the patriarch, with his long, pointed, white beard and his white hair, looks like a Chinese mandarin—the keeper of the old-style humanistic learning promoted in the previous Tokugawa era—while Isami, dressed in hybrid fashion with Japanese jacket, Western military-style cap, and a white scarf tied jauntily around his neck, represents the family's future.

The main purpose of the trip to Tokyo was to seek advice on Isami's future education from a man whom Isami identified in his family history as a former official in their home region.[3] Somehow this got translated into the legend (perpetuated by Isami's children) that the travelers had called on Fukuzawa Yukichi, the well-known Meiji educator and ardent exponent of Western education who later became something of a role model for Isami. Aside from this confusion, all parties agree on the advice the Matsuura patriarch received. A Tokyo education would certainly be superior to anything their home prefecture had to offer, but sending Isami to the capital city at such a young age would involve a risk, because he might not want to return to the countryside, where he was needed to carry out the Matsuura tradition of village leadership. "If he is someone who must return home, it would be better to let him finish middle school in the countryside and then, after his ideas are, for the most part, fixed, send him to the capital."[4] With their plans for a metropolitan education deferred, Isami and his relatives traveled back to their village to rethink his future.

In September of that same year, Daisuke made another trip to Tokyo, this time to visit his grandson Saburō—Isami's uncle. Saburō had already brought pride to the family by gaining employment in one of Japan's newly established modern banks. But pride was overwhelmed by grief when Saburō suddenly was stricken with cholera, which British traders had brought with them to Japan's treaty ports, newly opened since the 1850s.[5] Saburō died before his twenty-fourth birthday, and Daisuke himself, overcome with sorrow, died shortly thereafter, in his seventy-second year. One hundred twenty young men whom he had tutored over the years arranged to honor him by dedicating a stone Shinto shrine lantern to his memory.[6]

After Daisuke's death, his son-in-law and heir, Matsuura Jinsuke, relied more than ever on his own firstborn son, Yūya, Isami's father, for help in managing village affairs. The thirty-year-old Yūya had become the legal head of the household in 1887 and had been married for more than ten years to Ishii Miyo, the daughter of a village head from a neighboring county. The couple by this time had five children. Assured of the eventual assistance of his own oldest son, Isami, and of managers who helped oversee family holdings, Yūya was poised to launch the third century of Matsuura local leadership.[7]

Although not as interested in book learning as some of the earlier generations of Matsuura patriarchs, Yūya focused his energies on promoting education. As times rapidly changed in the Meiji period with the opening of Japan to the West, Yūya regretted not having pursued his own education more seriously. Daisuke had entrusted Yūya's early education to his senior assistant and then sent him to board in the home of a Chinese studies scholar, because he thought his eldest grandson needed to know the world outside his own home. The classical education that Yūya received imparted basic literacy and instilled such fundamental Confucian virtues as filial piety, frugality, loyalty to political authority, decorum, and observance of duty, but his instruction hardly equipped him to grasp the wider political world outside Japan or even outside his prefecture. Moreover, he showed no special interest in his studies. After several years at his tutor's house, where he helped care for the family's children in exchange for room, board, and tuition, he returned home in his midteens to work in the family's extensive business enterprises, which included sake and soy sauce production and rice-land holdings in several villages.

For Isami's education, Yūya chose several different public and private institutions established in their prefecture to carry out the new Meiji government's mandate of four years of education. The idea of sending Isami to Tokyo appears to have been discarded after Daisuke's death. Nevertheless, Isami did become the first Matsuura to attend modern educational institutions and to receive at least a taste of Western studies, including English-language classes. The mastery of foreign languages, preferably English or German, was deemed essential to Japan's future elite, because these languages provided access to Western learning, which had become the measure of "civilized" life in this era.

Even a smattering of Western subject matter in Isami's childhood, however, was not easily accessible. He attended upper elementary school in the town of Asakawa, two and one-half miles from the village of Yamashiraishi, but after one year there he was sent to the Fukushima prefectural preparatory school in Kōriyama, about thirty miles from his village, in order to study English, a subject not offered in Asakawa but required to pass the entrance examination for the Kōriyama middle school. Two years later he was admitted to that middle school for a five-year course of study.

Only a small percentage of male students possessed the requisite ability, ambition, and financial resources to go much beyond the four years of schooling mandated by the Meiji government at this time. Isami was one of the fortunate few.[8] His pursuit of advanced education, however, necessitated boarding in Kōriyama: commuting was impossible given the fifteen-mile distance between the nearest train station and the village of Yamashiraishi. One of Isami's lifelong ambitions became the opening of a train station closer to home in order to bridge the gap between his isolated village and the metropolis.[9]

Isami completed his formal studies in 1899, at twenty years of age. He never went to school in Tokyo. Instead, he returned to his village just in time to help rebuild the family's century-old house after it burned down in a "mysterious fire."[10]

⎯

The Matsuura family had lived in the mountain village of Yamashiraishi (the name means literally "mountain white rock") since the time of their

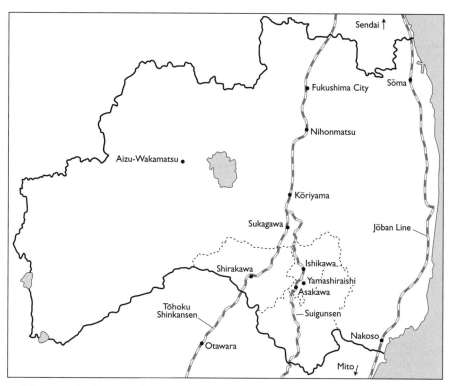

MAP 2 Fukushima prefecture

founding ancestor, the late seventeenth century. The village, in existence since the late sixteenth century, is located in the southeastern part of present-day Fukushima prefecture, one of six prefectures forming Japan's remote Northeast, or the Tōhoku region. Cold and mountainous, the Northeast was not amenable to rice farming, and yet the area was dependent on rice as a food staple and as the mode of currency in which land taxes were paid to the ruling military class.

Unlike more temperate climes to the south, where double-cropping was possible and warm summers produced healthy rice crops on flat plains, Yamashiraishi farmers, like others in the Northeast, eked out one harvest each year, if they were lucky. They worked small, scattered plots of flat land no larger than a suburban American lawn or paddies climbing up the hillsides. The village covers less than three square miles. Its 1,730 acres, including a small wilderness area, sprawl over seven hamlets separated by low-lying, tree-shrouded mountains. "Our home region," Isami wrote, "did not receive many blessings of nature."[11]

The Northeast, largely unexplored in the seventeenth century, lay far from the capital of the highest military general of the land, the shogun of the House of Tokugawa, in Edo (present-day Tokyo). It was even farther from the ancient cultural center of the emperor's court in Kyoto. A cultural and economic backwater in the eyes of urban dwellers, the rugged "deep North" intrigued—and intimidated—the renowned poet Matsuo Bashō, whose travels largely on foot through the region brought him close to Yamashiraishi, in Shirakawa domain, in the same year that the Matsuura founding ancestor became village head. In his midforties and in poor health, the poet approached his trip to the "furthermost interior" with some trepidation, fearing his hair would "turn white as frost" before he returned home—"or maybe I won't return at all."[12]

Shirakawa became the northern perimeter of the Tokugawa family's territories after they had pacified the country in 1600. The domain served as a strategic buffer between the Tokugawa and several powerful military houses to the north. The castle town of Shirakawa was the Tokugawa government's last checkpoint barrier for travelers on the highway going north, where guards carefully checked travel documents.[13]

During the Tokugawa period, from 1600 to 1868, the family's successive shoguns, even while devising strategies to maintain control of their 260 or so domains, some more loyal than others, gave each domainal military governor *(daimyō)* considerable autonomy vis-à-vis his own bureaucracy, army, vassals, and taxes. These hereditary military rulers in turn allowed the villages within their territory to govern themselves as long as they faithfully paid their taxes and preserved the peace. Village heads *(shōya),* members of the peasant class, served as the channel of communication between their villages and the military governor's local representatives, headquartered in towns scattered throughout the domains. Tax collectors, judges, record keepers, arbiters of disputes, and local boosters all rolled into one, village heads survived by walking the thin line between their fellow villagers and the military lords above them.

Obsessed with preserving its power, the Tokugawa family, through its own large bureaucracy *(bakufu),* attempted to maintain the elaborately structured political and social system. The four legally defined status groups of samurai (warrior rulers), peasants, artisans, and merchants were hereditary; foreign contacts were severely restricted; and the content of theatrical productions and literature was subject to censorship. Through sumptuary laws regulating everything from dress to deportment, house construction, number of servants, and content of theatrical performances, the Tokugawa government attempted to control the population of thirty million people, who, despite restrictions and sometimes owing to them, produced a vibrant popular culture along with diverse goods and services and gained access to education, making the Japanese arguably the most literate country in the world by 1800.

But wealth and learning were not distributed equally throughout the land. Although the Japanese were productive rice growers, when terrible famines devastated broad swaths of the countryside during the Tokugawa period, rice farmers desperately struggled to meet their tax quotas.[14] One task of village heads was to increase productivity in order to pay the land tax, which was levied on the village as a whole. Spearheading economic development and the spread of literacy and culture in the rural areas, village leaders such as the first eight Matsuura househeads in the Tokugawa period promoted rural industry and trade and contributed to the construction and maintenance of temples and shrines, even as they profited from their extensive rice lands, often simultaneously exploiting and assisting their villagers.

By the late eighteenth century, especially toward the end of the Tokugawa period, Isami's ancestors had become members of the upper stratum of the farm class and, as such, potential targets of peasant uprisings. The family's wealth and role as village heads also made them vulnerable to extra levies from domain officials in search of additional revenue sources. In the early 1860s, for example, the Asakawa government office asked his great-grandfather Daisuke for a special "donation" of three pairs of Japanese sandals per every hundred *koku* of assessed land, to give as gifts to the visiting wife and father of a high-ranking official from a nearby town.[15] In 1867, Daisuke and two other households paid three or four gold coins *(ryō)*—more than any of the other eighty-two households—as their families' share of a special tax levy.[16] Wealthy rural landowners and entrepreneurs such as the Matsuura risked losing the privileges of their special status if they refused the governing class's requests, which were made with increasing frequency toward the end of the Tokugawa era.[17]

Daisuke seemed unperturbed by these extra expenditures, which he recorded without notation in the same journal he used to itemize his travel and gift expenses in a given year. If he did not distinguish between his family budget and his official outlays, he also did not worry excessively about either exceeding his budget or meeting the extraordinary levies. Nor did he chafe at the Tokugawa regime's incompetence; he had sufficient wealth to pay off the officials without questioning a political system that was impoverishing the many and approaching collapse.

The immediate cause of the massive crisis that afflicted Japan in the last fifteen years of Tokugawa rule was an event of such terrifying proportions that it threw Japan's political system into immediate turmoil and tore apart the frayed, anachronistic political bonds that had held the country together for over 250 years. That event was the arrival in 1853 of an American naval squadron under the command of Commodore Matthew C. Perry, who brashly sailed into Edo Bay and, backed by four gunboats, demanded an end to the shogun's ban on contact with Western countries.[18]

Few Japanese had ever seen foreigners. Shogunal policy since the early seventeenth century had prevented Japanese from going overseas and had limited trade contacts primarily to the Dutch and Chinese at the port of Nagasaki, at the other end of the country from the Matsuura family's village. With the coming of Perry, this isolation policy ended. The British had already forcibly opened China's ports to trade in 1842, after the so-called Opium War. Under pressure from American negotiators and against the wishes of the emperor, the shogun reluctantly signed treaties in 1854 and again in 1858, opening trade and diplomatic relations with Americans. Similar treaties signed soon afterward with England, France, Holland, and Russia enabled European and American diplomats, traders, sailors, and missionaries to enter the newly opened ports, including Yokohama, close to the seat of the shogun's government in Edo but outside its criminal jurisdiction. According to the terms of the treaties, these foreign nationals, if accused of a crime, had the right to be tried by their own consular courts.

The firestorm of protest that followed the signing of the treaties turned the political system upside down. Although shogunal officials, in the face of the Western countries' superior military force, saw no choice but to open Japan, a group of domainal lords and samurai thought otherwise. They appealed to the imperial court to legitimize their more isolationist views. Calling for the expulsion of the "barbarians," patriotic, sword-waving samurai assassinated foreigners and Japanese advocates of foreign trade, inaugurating a decade of violence and civil war.

In 1860, the year Isami's father, Yūya, was born, a group of young extremist samurai, outraged by the treaties, murdered the shogunal official in direct control of the country as he traveled in a palanquin through a snowstorm to his office in the shogun's castle in Edo. The assassins' movement to "revere the emperor and repel the barbarians" gained further momentum in the succeeding four years, when enemies of the Tokugawa strengthened their own armies and allied with one another.

Commoners living close to Edo were politically awakened by the foreign threat and converged on the city in response to the crisis. "Suddenly everybody seemed to have an opinion on the matter and gathered in various places to argue," recalled Shibusawa Eiichi, the son of a well-to-do peasant-entrepreneur from a village fifty miles northwest of Edo. In 1861, Shibusawa had gained his father's permission to move to Edo, which he had been primarily motivated to do, he recalled, because of his "growing conviction that these were no longer the times to be a peasant."[19]

Isami's great-grandfather Daisuke, also a well-to-do rural entrepreneur, was not entirely unaware of the stormy political scene in Edo aroused by the unfamiliar, and unwelcome, presence of foreign men and women from the United States and the other four countries that had signed treaties with Japan. In fact, he might very well have described to Isami how he and his wife, Moto, while visiting the shogun's capital in the spring of 1863, had taken a side trip to nearby Yokohama, one of the newly opened treaty ports that symbolized Japan's foreign crisis, and had circled the harbor area in a rented boat to view the large oceangoing steamers and sailing vessels of the five treaty countries. The foreigners had quickly gained control of over 90 percent of Japan's trade with the outside world, and Yokohama, with its fine harbor, rapidly drew even more Western traders.[20] In late March, several English and Dutch men-of-war also arrived in the harbor.[21] In his journal Daisuke specifically reported seeing foreigners—probably the first non-Japanese he had ever encountered. Yet, his journal entries on other activities, such as pilgrimages, pleasure jaunts, and commercial transactions, were more detailed, suggesting that the seriousness of the national political and economic predicament wrought by the forced opening of Japan to foreign trade and diplomatic relations had not yet penetrated his consciousness, even though he was in the thick of it.

Shortly before Daisuke and Moto's visit in and around Edo, nearly a quarter of a million people left the capital. In the face of an anticipated war with the foreigners, the shogun had released the domain lords and their families and retainers from their longstanding requirement to maintain separate residences in Edo, so that they could return home to prepare their domain defenses. The sight of thousands of people streaming out of the shogun's capital so captured the attention of one American merchant-observer that he described the event as "a grand epoch of history" in a letter he wrote to the *New York Tribune* on February 3, 1863.[22]

Daisuke made no mention of the emptying of Edo in the journal he kept of his two-month trip with Moto to the capital and its surrounding tourist attractions. Only after the couple's return from Edo did the political consequences of the treaties finally reach their home grounds. At that point, Daisuke could no longer ignore national and international events.

In 1864, civil war broke out in the southern part of Fukushima, near Hanawa, the site of the Tokugawa office newly opened to oversee the territory that contained the Matsuura family's village. That year's revolts by a pro-emperor, anti-foreigner group were followed in 1865 by another peasant demonstration, this one in response to the economic impact the new foreign trade had on Japan. Poorer farmers, hurt by the ensuing inflation, protested the Hanawa intendant's decision to give a monopoly over the *konnyaku* trade to a group of village heads in Shirakawa domain. (*Konnyaku* is the devil's tongue plant, or konjak, of the arum family, from which an edible jelly was made.) Daisuke was drawn into the affair when he joined five other village headmen in signing a formal apology addressed to the local intendant to secure the release of the four major leaders of the demonstration.[23]

Peasant uprisings erupted elsewhere in the region and indeed all over Japan in the following year. In Shindatsu to the north, an uprising was specifically aimed at wealthy rural families.[24] One year later, in 1867, when pro-emperor forces from the southwestern domains of Chōshū and Satsuma captured the ancient capital of Kyoto and forced the resignation of the moribund Tokugawa shogunate in Edo, the violence finally threatened the Matsuura's village.

For several decades the village of Yamashiraishi, as well as the rest of Shirakawa domain, had been directly under the control of the shogun's government. The village and others nearby remained, for the most part, on the sidelines during the civil war, but not Aizu-Wakamatsu, the large domain three days' journey on foot northwest of Shirakawa. Staunchly committed to Tokugawa rule, Aizu's ruling family, a collateral branch of the Tokugawa, joined an anti-imperial alliance composed of thirty-one domains located in the Tōhoku region. After Aizu's fortified White Crane Castle fell on November 8, 1868, and the Imperial Army entered the city, many families of military officers committed group suicide. Imperial soldiers raped and looted the population, and merchants from as far away as Shirakawa came to buy and barter the war booty.[25]

Caught up in the mayhem, peasants in many neighboring domains staged uprisings. In the Asakawa area, two hundred rioting peasants trashed the property of village heads and wholesalers as the political order collapsed around them. Triggering their outburst was another poor harvest, as well as the additional and unprecedented burden of their conscription into pro-Tokugawa armies to fight in the civil war during the busy harvest season.[26] Peasants focused their anger on wealthy sake brewers, cutting open sake barrels and spilling the contents onto the ground.

Even though two years earlier Daisuke had sided with demonstrators, bailed out their leaders, and succeeded in restoring peace after the "Konnyaku Riot," this time farmers from the neighboring village of Itabashi did not spare the family. In his official report, Jinsuke described how he and Daisuke had tried to reason with the crowd at their gate, but the rioters would not listen to them.[27] They broke down the door of the sake storage house and damaged tools. They also used a wood plane to carve ugly scars into a post inside the Matsuura family's house, built seventy years earlier, after rioting farmers from the nearby town of Asakawa and environs in the 1790s had converged on the family's village.

The plane marks, reminders of communal disorder, were left unrepaired for the next thirty years, while the Matsuura family, remarkably, rode out the overthrow of the Tokugawa House and the dismantling of the entire antiquated system of rule. But the violence of the crowd shocked Daisuke, who was accustomed to thinking of himself as a benevolent village headman, and after the attack he seems to have lost the will or energy to continue in an official capacity. Having passed his fiftieth birthday, he decided to retire, turning over his responsibilities to his son-in-law Jinsuke.[28] Nevertheless, despite social and political changes of a revolutionary scale that followed the collapse of the entire Tokugawa system and resulted in the ousting of hereditary village heads elsewhere in the area, the family managed to remain in office.

Threats to the Matsuura hereditary position after 1868 no longer came from house-smashing farmers but from modernizing reformers in the new central government. The young samurai from domains in the southwestern part of Japan, who in 1867 overthrew the shogun and the entire moribund Tokugawa political system, sought to control all of Japan from a single center. They transferred the teenage emperor to Edo, which they renamed Tokyo, "eastern capital," and declared it the new capital of a unified Japan. They also declared a new reign period—Meiji, "bright or enlightened rule." Justifying their rule in the name of the supposed ancient authority of the emperor, whose reign period lasted until his death in 1912, the young new leaders quickly set about implementing administrative changes designed to increase their command over the country. The effects of their ambitious program of reform soon reverberated in Yamashiraishi, where the Matsuura struggled to retain their local political influence.

Although the Matsuura patriarchs had witnessed many administrative changes and several major political crises during the 180 years of their local stewardship before the Meiji Restoration, they had managed to survive them all. Protesting farmers had been pacified; inept intendants had come and gone. Rulers from the military class had arrived on the scene, conducted the usual greedy assessment of rice yield, extracted loans from the family, and rotated out. The village had fallen under one jurisdiction or another, but for the most part it had been left alone as long as the required tribute reached the intendant's office in Asakawa, close to the Matsuura family home. The events of 1868, however, were different. These constituted not simply change but revolution in the guise of an "imperial restoration."

In a matter of years, the new leaders succeeded in replacing all hereditary domains and Tokugawa lands with a centralized system of prefectures, whose governors owed their political appointment directly to them. Yamashiraishi became part of the new nation's third largest prefecture, Fukushima, created by combining a number of domains, including Aizu, Shirakawa, Sōma, and Nihonmatsu, along with the districts of Shindatsu and Shinobu. The new prefecture derived its name from Shindatsu's castle town, which became the prefecture's capital city, also called Fukushima. Located in the northern part of the prefecture, Fukushima City emerged as the site where local politics would thereafter be played out, at a considerable distance from Asakawa, which had been the Matsuura's closest political nexus since the days of their founding ancestor.[29]

One of many popular slogans of the era—"rich country, strong army"—reflected the Meiji government's goal of forging a strong modern nation-state capable of achieving parity with Western powers. To this end, the leaders launched further drastic reforms. Pronouncements from Tokyo came one after the other. Promoting the hitherto secluded emperor as a symbol of national unity and modernity, the Meiji government overturned Tokugawa strictures on class mobility and foreign trade and announced a bootstraps policy of economic development and military strengthening modeled on the leading powers of the day.

Japan's new leaders focused on liberating people to pursue freely chosen occupations and on educating them to achieve nationalist goals through a system of compulsory education for boys and girls. With a stroke of the pen, the new government eliminated the centuries-long samurai monopoly on arms and instead required all men to serve three years in the nation's new national army and four additional years in the reserves. To encourage industrial development and to knit the country together, the Meiji government began construction of a national railway line in one of its earliest reforms. The line that the young Isami rode with his elders to Tokyo was completed in 1887, between the capital's Ueno Station and Kōriyama.[30]

Local leaders such as Daisuke and his successors, first Jinsuke and then Yūya, faced unfamiliar challenges as they developed strategies to guarantee that their part of the country and of the prefecture did not fall behind in Japan's race to achieve "civilization and enlightenment." Daisuke, already retired as village headman, had briefly considered heeding the appeal of local literati, who asked him in the 1870s to apply for a bureaucratic post in the inspectorate (kensakan). Isami's beloved great-grandfather had forged good relations with Asakawa government officials and was admired by villagers for miles around. Like many of his ancestors, Daisuke had established a reputation as a talented man of letters, but beyond that he was admired for his powers of persuasion. He already had contacts in Tokyo, as his 1863 trip there with Moto demonstrated. In the eyes of his adoring great-grandson Isami, he was also handsome, open-minded, dignified, kind, tolerant, smart, progressive, and even elegant.[31]

Yet, not even these admirable traits were sufficient to convince Daisuke's wife that he could deal successfully with the group of young and inexperienced hotheads who had seized control of Japan. They were, after all, unknown entities. Moreover, they hardly enjoyed the support of everyone in the country. The new leaders' monopoly on power and their reform agenda produced opposition groups whose suppression and whose methods of protest were often violent. The 1870s witnessed numerous outbreaks of organized resistance. Those samurai who were not among the founders of the new government had lost their elite status and thus staged armed rebellions; farmers threatened by the new land tax and compulsory military service rampaged across the country, destroying the homes of the rich and toppling newly erected telegraph poles. Political parties, inspired by Western political practice, became yet another way of contesting central government encroachment.

These troubled times led Moto to discourage Daisuke from coming out of retirement to apply for a position in the new government. She argued that if he failed, he might harm his descendants. Sensing that her husband was not cut out for the more complex and even dangerous political battles that lay ahead, Moto persuaded Daisuke to devote himself instead to teaching the younger generation.[32] He consequently threw himself into the task of educating the young at a time when compulsory public education worldwide was still rare. Embracing the goal of universal literacy, he became a champion of popular education in his area. Daisuke contributed land for the first primary school in Yamashiraishi; it opened in 1873 on the family's property along the road below their house, with thirty students enrolled. In the late 1880s, Isami was one of the school's pupils.[33]

To represent village interests at the prefectural and national levels, Daisuke relied on his son-in-law and heir, Jinsuke, and Jinsuke's firstborn son, Yūya. Longtime village heads struggling to maintain local autonomy in the early Meiji period tended to be among the strongest promoters of the newly formed Liberal, or Freedom, Party (Jiytō). The Matsuura men, too, found themselves sympathetic, though not overly so, to the efforts of the newly formed political parties to protect local regions from the growing arm of the central government. While Yūya demonstrated a conservative, Confucian bent of mind that made him no special fan of the liberal ideology espoused by opponents of the new governing oligarchy, he appreciated the personality of Nakae Chōmin, a champion of Rousseau and an outspoken liberal ideologue, even if, according to Isami, Yūya "probably did not approve of Nakae's 'strange [i.e., democratic] ideas.'"[34]

The nemesis of the parties was the ruthless Tokyo appointee Mishima Michitsune, who was nicknamed "the devil governor" for good reason. His other nickname was "the public works governor," because his plans for road construction and other public works in Fukushima entailed poorly paid heavy labor and additional local taxes.[35] Mishima, one of the southwestern samurai who had overthrown the Tokugawa, was determined to destroy the parties. Fukushima, the center of the popular rights opposition movement in the northeastern districts in the early 1880s, became the site of bloody confrontations.

The Matsuura must have been aware of the political turbulence so close to home. They most likely knew the several activists from the nearby town of Ishikawa who clashed with authorities over their political activities. Among them was the Shinto priest who was also the Ishikawa township head and Kōno Hironaka, the Liberal Party leader in Fukushima, who was arrested for his role in opposition activities.

Still, the Matsuura, reluctant politicians with a long history of political neutrality, initially remained aloof from the Liberal Party and the outbreaks of violence in 1882 that resulted in arrests of many of its members. Prefectural assemblies, political parties, and election campaigns were among the unfamiliar Western political ingredients that Matsuura househeads encountered. The family's forte had always been conscientious tax administration and conflict negotiation—in disputes among villages over water rights, for example, and among families within their own village. Their area of operations centered on the local intendant's seat in Asakawa, a mere forty-minute walk from their village.

As late as the leadership of the eighth generation's Daisuke, the family's official status as peasants, albeit very wealthy ones and village heads, gave their househeads no official access to political affairs at the national level. Before the mid-nineteenth century, there had been no acceptable public forum for the discussion of countrywide political issues.

One way or another, the Matsuura had to learn how to work with the unfamiliar political institutions and practices that developed in the Meiji period. In particular, they had to devise strategies to guarantee that their part of the country and the prefecture would not fall behind. Their leadership role now also entailed manipulating the new political system in order to protect their region from the central government's demands. In addition, they could no longer restrict their activities to the Asakawa region; their scope had to expand at least as far as Fukushima City, the new capital of the prefecture and the site of the newly established prefectural assembly. Despite the efforts of Daisuke and Jinsuke to avoid political entanglements, the Western-influenced political institutions and practices introduced in the Meiji period virtually demanded the family head's participation if he were going to champion his region's interests.

Between 1878 and 1890 the Meiji government revamped the local administrative apparatus several times. After carving out prefectures and a new tax system, the central leadership created a single, uniform system of counties within the prefectures.[36] In 1879, Yamashiraishi fell under the jurisdiction of Ishikawa county, which had a population of almost thirty thousand.[37] Extending the county's reach even further, the oligarchs in Tokyo also mandated village assemblies to "deliberate upon matters relating to the general expenses of the locality, and upon the means of defraying expenses therein."[38] Further administrative reforms in the late 1880s finally shocked the Matsuura into political action. The Home Ministry announced a plan for the consolidation of villages through mergers, which led almost overnight to the disappearance of Yamashiraishi as a separate entity. Its new designation rendered it merely a hamlet of another village. This new arrangement cost the Matsuura their age-old village leadership position, but it did not remain uncontested.

The Matsuura men swung into action to overturn the annexation. During their seven-year-long effort to reinstate Yamashiraishi as a separate village, Jinsuke rented a farmhouse in the prefectural capital of Fukushima City, so that he and Yūya had a place to stay while they lobbied prefectural officials. Father and son also traveled back and forth by train between Fukushima and Tokyo to make personal appeals to the Home Ministry. In 1888, the twenty-eight-year-old Yūya even did a brief stint as a member of the new prefectural assembly, though not because he sought the job.

Prefectural assemblies had been in existence for only a decade, and qualified candidates were few in number when Yūya was elected as an assemblyman. To be eligible, members had to be males over the age of twenty-five, residents of the prefecture for at least three years, and landholders paying an annual land tax of ten yen or more. Only about 2.45 percent of the population was qualified to run as candidates, and only 4 percent of the population was qualified to vote for them.[39] Yūya was among that handful, and, without his knowledge, a party politician nominated him.

Serving in prefectural assemblies was often a boring and frustrating experience, and many assemblymen resigned early. The political system created by the central government was designed to draw local notables into the decision-making process at the prefectural level without actually giving them much power. Prefectural governors, appointed by the central government and under the control of the Home Ministry in Tokyo, monopolized the right to draft bills, and all assembly resolutions were subject to their final approval. They represented the state's policies, not the individual prefectures' needs.[40]

Boredom, however, was not the main problem in Fukushima. For many years the prefecture had been rife with violence, much of it centered on the despotic governor. In 1884, seven radical Liberal Party politicians from a nearby prefecture were hanged for attempting to assassinate him.[41]

The strain of political life soon took its toll on Yūya. During his one-year stint in the prefectural assembly, he proposed a plan to sell bonds to finance the purchase of national forest land in the prefecture to be used as a kind of trust fund to generate income for the prefectural school system. He also offered to donate some of his own money. The plan, however, was rejected.[42]

Within the year, Yūya fell sick with an undisclosed ailment whose symptoms sound like nervous prostration. Isami, who was nine years old at the time, recalled in his family chronicle how Yūya had become too "agitated" and had to resign, giving his seat to the person who had received the next highest number of votes, while he himself recuperated in Fukushima City under the care of a housekeeper from the Inoue family, with whom the Matsuura had longstanding ties.[43]

Despite this resignation and Yūya's departure from party politics after 1893, his and his father's political efforts ultimately paid off in that year. They succeeded in restoring Yamashiraishi's separate identity and preserving the office of village head for themselves. Over forty-four years later, at Yūya's public funeral, which the entire village attended, he was eulogized ("worshipped") as "the saint of village autonomy," in the words of his eldest son.[44]

Yūya's childhood and early adulthood paralleled the wrenching birth of the modern Japanese nation. By the time Isami came of age, on the eve of the Russo-Japanese War, however, Japan's new political order was in place. The country boasted a modern-style constitutional monarchy with a national legislative body. It was now ready to prove itself equal to the West by taking on and defeating a Western country. Awaiting Isami was the excitement of Japan's rapid transition both from a country saddled with inequitable foreign treaties to a nation recognized as a world power in possession of its own empire and from a largely rural society to an industrialized, modern one.

Isami enthusiastically embraced Japan's foray into modernity. He was especially fascinated with technology. Throughout his life he would delight in making sketches of labor-saving machinery and seek manufacturers willing to produce his inventions. But also awaiting Isami as he reached manhood was the struggle to master unfamiliar modes of politics and business practices in the new nation-state, the effort to advance his community's interests while rearing and educating his many children, and, finally, the long period of war, military occupation, and recovery.

Fortunately, Isami did not know what lay ahead for him when he completed his formal schooling. He returned home a cherished young man full of energy and confidence, rooted in family and agrarian values but at the same time forward-looking, optimistic, and receptive to change, like the new nation itself at the turn of the twentieth century.

PART ONE

Ancestors and Descendants

ONE

The House Isami Built

EARLY ONE MORNING AT THE END OF APRIL 1899, the second floor of the Matsuura sake storehouse caught fire. Flames leaped from it and quickly spread to the family's wooden farmhouse, built a hundred years earlier. The blaze also consumed a neighbor's house.

Remarkably, despite the many family members and servants living on the grounds, nobody was injured. The cause of the fire remained unknown; Isami's father, by then the househead, chose not to pursue the matter, preferring to look to the future. Fire was an ever-present danger in a country vulnerable to earthquakes and accustomed to building with natural materials such as wood, thatch, and paper, which were all readily available but also highly flammable. While the ashes were still smoldering, Yūya turned to his twenty-year-old heir and said, "This is a house you are going to live in longer than I am. Build it the way you want."[1]

The razed house had been built shortly after the Asakawa riots of 1800. At that time, rampaging peasants had destroyed the lumber the fifth-generation patriarch had planned to use to build a new house, and he had ended up building a residence of more modest size to avoid the appearance of flaunting the family's wealth in the face of angry, hungry villagers. The house bore the scars of another attack six decades later, during the civil war that toppled the Tokugawa government in 1868, when rioting villagers broke in and gouged marks into its central pillar with a wood plane.

Isami lost no time and spared no cost in rebuilding after the fire. This time modesty was not a consideration. The wood house that Isami built survives into the twenty-first century, more grandiose than any of its predecessors. Its generous proportions expose urban visitors to a sense of spaciousness almost unimaginable in today's crowded cities. Isami decided that his family's size, entrepreneurial activities, and involvement in village governance dictated a large residence with flexible space, flanked by smaller,

freestanding buildings. All together, the compound was designed to accommodate extended family gatherings, community rituals, and the village
head's business.

The Matsuura house bespeaks the wealth and prominence of the family
in its heyday. The property is fronted by a stone wall and is approached by
a steeply ascending narrow road. Eleven stone steps set into an opening in
the wall rise to the garden and the house beyond it, which sits by itself in
front of a grove of conifers. In the Tokugawa period, gates and walls were
signs of status and prestige forbidden to ordinary peasants, and the house
on the hill, until the end of the twentieth century, towered over other houses
and the road below, announcing the elite pedigree of its owners in their
prime.

Isami's architectural design, typical of *shōya* houses in the area, called for
a cavernous central living room occupying most of the south side of the
house, facing the garden, and lined with forty tatami—thick rush mats,
each about six feet by three feet—that completely covered the floor. (Typically at the turn of the twentieth century, rooms were built to contain four
and one-half, six, or eight mats.)[2] The room's dark wood ceiling was thirteen feet high. On the south side of the room, in lieu of an outer wall, sets
of floor-to-ceiling *shōji*—wood-paneled sliding doors inset with panes of
translucent paper—allowed sunlight to enter.

Despite the house's imposing size of fifty-four hundred square feet, its
interior floor space was almost entirely empty. People sat on the floor, not
on chairs. The only furniture in the central room consisted of several low
tables and cushions, a charcoal brazier for hand warming, a legless wood
desk, and a large wood chest for clothes. The *kotatsu,* a sunken footwarmer
filled with hot coals and covered with a heavy quilt, was the only other source
of heat. Portable screens helped keep out drafts in cold weather. Family members (including, in the early 1900s, Isami's numerous siblings) ate, studied,
played, and slept in the large living area. Children slept alongside one another in the middle of the room on bedding stored in built-in closets during the day and spread out on the tatami at night. Servants slept behind
them, on the periphery.

The central living room, following Japanese custom, also held a built-in
butsudan, the black lacquer Buddhist altar on which the mistress of the house
left food offerings for family ancestors. Observing well-established Matsuura
House rules, the household head and his wife always slept directly in front
of the altar.[3] Framed photographs of previous householders and certificates
of commendation for their community service, which still hang along the

north and east walls of the room, added to the sense of reverence for the ancestral line and pride in the continuity of the family name.

When Toyo took me to see the house in 1975, we slept in one of the other three large tatami-lined rooms on the east side of the house. These are twelve and one-half tatami in size and are separated from the central room by *fusuma,* sliding wall panels covered with thick paper. Facing woods, the rooms are pleasantly cooled by breezes in the summer. The room Toyo and I used, which features a *tokonoma,* an alcove for displaying art objects, had once served as a formal parlor to receive guests. Sleeping in the house was like lodging in a boarded-up hotel, emptied as it was of the many people of all ages who had once dwelled in it, their presence replaced by a lonely space, silence, and the artifacts of their past.

In Toyo's childhood, meals were prepared in a kitchen that was outside but adjacent to the west side of the house. It had an earthen floor and occupied nine hundred square feet on the ground level. Even after a more modern, smaller kitchen was installed inside the house in the north wing, this huge original kitchen, with its high ceiling to allow the smoke from the stove to disperse, was used for making special holiday fare, such as rice cakes and rice mixed with red beans, or for preparing food for large numbers of guests. Although in recent times the original kitchen was converted to a garage and storage room, it still contains a well for drawing water, a wood-burning stove with two burners, and a large wooden counter extending from the step leading up into the main living area. One room over the kitchen provided additional sleeping space for workers employed in the family's sake brewery, located on ground level to the west of the old kitchen. Along the north corridor were several toilets (some of them added later), a bath, and a room used variously for storage or as a birthing room.

In addition to serving as a family residence, the Matsuura home was a place of business. Family and business possessions required four storehouses standing side by side on the eastern edge of the garden and several more in other villages. Isami took the precaution of having these two-story structures rebuilt of clay and plaster with tile roofs and an earthen door, more fire-resistant than wood. One of the storehouses held rice; the second contained miso, soy sauce, and pickles; the third housed the family's clothing; and the fourth stored plates, lacquerware, and art objects, such as hanging scrolls for the *tokonoma.*

Until Isami's father's time, the Matsuura house also served as the village head's office, where village affairs were transacted. Farmers having business with the househead were relegated to the vestibule facing the garden on the south side of the house, where they would either stand on the stone floor in their work clothes and boots or sit on the steps. Distinguished visitors, on the other hand, were invited to remove their shoes, step up onto the veranda, and walk around the east side of the house to be received in the formal parlor. The house also sheltered more than five hundred documents that dated back to the earliest ancestors and recorded all events: the many visitors to the house over the decades; villagers' tax payments, petitions, births and deaths; disturbances of the village peace and the ensuing punishments and resolutions. For Isami these pieces of paper, miraculously rescued from the fire, formed a vital part of the precious history linking him to past village heads—the generations of his ancestors who, beginning with the lineage founder, had "built Yamashiraishi."[4]

The fire that destroyed the Matsuura family's main house spared the detached cottage *(inkyō)*, where Isami's adored great-grandfather Daisuke had lived in his later years with his second wife, Moto, and where Isami had slept as a child. Grandfather Jinsuke, the fifty-eight-year-old current village head, had lost his first wife, Yoshi, shortly after his father-in-law, Daisuke, died, and he was already looking forward to spending his retirement years in the cottage, "surrounded by his many grandchildren" and in the company of his second wife.[5] The ninth-generation patriarch planned to build a small waterfall in the garden with the help of several village youth.

The retirement cottage, separate from the house and built on top of the stone wall to the east of the gate, offered far more generous accommodations than most village elders enjoyed. Customarily parents lived with their heir and his wife, but usually not in a detached dwelling, and certainly not one as graciously appointed and meticulously maintained as the Matsuura's. Whereas the houses of neighbors resembled shacks, the Matsuura retirement cottage featured three rooms of generous size, each of about eight to ten mats. The room where guests were received even had its own *tokonoma* decorated with floral arrangements in harmony with the seasons. The sliding paper partitions separating the rooms were still in good condition, having been replaced only twelve years earlier, and artwork on the walls added to the sense of refinement.[6]

The Matsuura, like other Japanese families, observed a long tradition of caring for their elders and honoring their ancestors. Buddhist rites, Confucian ethical teachings of filial piety, and naming practices reinforced these customs. Generations of family members were buried in the village cemetery over the hill behind their property and memorialized on tablets in the Buddhist temple. Isami's father's name, Yūya, contained the first syllable of the first ancestor name, written with the same Chinese ideogram. Isami's family's history lay all around him and permeated his daily life. He grew up living not only with his parents, grandparents, great-grandparents, and, until he was eight, with his great-great-grandmother Chise, but also in the presence of his ancestors, all of whom, in one form or another, dwelled around him. And all the household members—living and dead—needed tending.

—

The first certifiable ancestor of the Matsuura family was a man known simply as Yajibei. Accompanied by his wife and mother-in-law, in 1689 he moved to Yamashiraishi from the town of Asakawa, two and one-half miles away, to assume the position of *shōya*, village head.[7] It was not an easy job.

Yajibei entered a village shattered by the previous head's corruption and decimated by economic hard times. Like other areas of Shirakawa domain, Yamashiraishi's population had been declining for decades.[8] Although it had been a relatively large village for its time, in a period of only three decades, from 1650 to the 1680s, the number of residents had dropped by one-third, from 940 to 600.[9] A serious famine in 1680 only partly explains this demographic decline. The previous domain ruler's notoriously unfair tax system also accounted for the region's failure to thrive.

In Yamashiraishi and elsewhere in Shirakawa domain, peasants barely managed to feed their families in the face of harsh weather, let alone meet their tax payments, which, in Shirakawa, amounted to as much as half of the rice harvest.[10] Unfortunately for Shirakawa peasants, domain rulers were moved around often by the shogun in order to prevent them from becoming too powerful, and each time a new military governor took over, he conducted his own survey of village landholders and agricultural production in his realm, which invariably resulted in higher assessments and justification for levying higher taxes on villages.[11] Unlike other areas, where military governors had ruled the same domain for centuries, the Shirakawa rulers enjoyed only temporary appointment to their domains, which they "treated as a piece of property . . . for their own private use."[12]

The military governor in Shirakawa between 1649 and 1681 was Honda Tadayoshi, who assessed not only each village's rice paddies but all of its land, including mountains, wasteland, and newly reclaimed rice fields. He even insisted on extracting taxes from abandoned land, and he introduced a larger container as the standard to measure volume of rice.[13] Three taxes were designed solely to compensate for the loss of rice during transportation to Honda's castle, and one of these was twice as high as a similar tax levied in territories directly under the shogun's rule.[14] Scores of other taxes and fees, from soybeans and potatoes to firewood and reeds, drained the scarce resources of the villages in his domain. Several farmers fled to avoid the taxes, leaving the remaining residents to make up the difference. Honda was so cruel and his behavior so irrational that he even executed his own retainers, and many vassals in his service resigned.[15] A man with few redeeming virtues, he possessed neither the literary bent nor the martial arts skills expected of the ruling samurai class at his time. And his son was no better.

Honda's son, who received a parcel of land carved out for him by his father in the Asakawa area, continued in his father's tyrannical footsteps.[16] Farmers who could not pay their share of taxes were tortured.[17] Impoverished peasants were so desperate, they sold themselves or their wives and children to pay their taxes, which also included a labor corvée, or they abandoned their lands altogether, leaving the remaining cultivators to meet the tax, levied on each village as a whole.

In the two decades before the arrival of the Matsuura founding ancestor, Yajibei, villagers appealed to Honda to reduce their tax burden. Landholders claimed that Honda's cadastral survey—conducted in 1651, immediately after he took over the region—had overestimated the village's rice productivity. Although Honda finally agreed to lower the assessed value of village rice land, the village head and his heir never informed the villagers; instead, this father and son continued to collect the same amount, shamelessly pocketing the difference.[18] For seven years they embezzled a portion of the rice tribute payment they collected annually from the village to transmit to Honda.

Even after a new governor from the prestigious Matsudaira line replaced Honda in 1681, one year after a serious famine, the old tax assessment remained. Ignoring a petition for a new assessment of the yield, signed by 207 village heads from 180 villages and sent directly to the shogun's bureaucracy, the new governor overturned Honda's tax reduction. He ruled instead that the villagers should receive an annual rebate, with the exact amount to be determined by the Asakawa intendant on the basis of his estimate of each year's harvest.[19] This ruling failed to satisfy the villagers of Yamashiraishi, who filed another petition with three local commissioners, but to no avail.[20] To meet the levy, they would have to open more paddies, an exhausting and expensive undertaking. In addition, they were now required to pay half in rice with the other half in gold and copper coins. Other villages in the domain also complained about unfair tax burdens. As late as the middle of the nineteenth century, Yamashiraishi continued to petition, unsuccessfully, for a new assessment of the yield.[21]

The embattled villagers eventually became suspicious of their head's scheme to cheat them and in 1689 officially accused him of illegal behavior. They persuaded the authorities to question him and his son. Domain rulers preferred to stay out of village affairs as long as peasants faithfully paid their tribute and preserved the peace. In this case, however, the governor's deputy official—the district intendant, headquartered in the town of Asakawa—agreed to launch a full-scale investigation, probably because, as Isami wrote, villagers were unsatisfied with the answers the village head gave to the intendant's initial questioning, and "there was a lot of fighting and shouting."[22] Disputes could tear apart a village—and interrupt the flow of tribute upward to the lord's castle.

While the accused father and son languished in prison, awaiting the verdict of the investigation, the village of six hundred peasants invited Yajibei to become Yamashiraishi's headman, or *shōya*.[23] Yajibei agreed to serve, probably on a provisional basis, until the intendant ruled on the criminal charges of Yajibei's predecessors.[24] Meanwhile, the case against them dragged on for over ten years while the district intendant took written testimony from plaintiffs, defendants, and witnesses. Justice may have existed in Tokugawa Japan, but it was not necessarily swift.

At long last, the intendant determined that the two men, father and heir, were guilty as charged of double-taxing the villagers. Although punishment of headmen for abuse of authority elsewhere during this time usually involved prison sentences or banishment, the guilty men of Yamashiraishi received much stiffer sentences.[25] In 1701, an executioner stepped onto the river bank in Asakawa, raised his sword over their kneeling bodies, and, with rapid flourishes of his blade, lopped off their heads.[26] Their execution was a shocking event, even in a country whose ruling military class had lived and died by the sword for centuries. The spectacular denouement of this "great scandal" was an object lesson for Yajibei and his descendants about the importance of honesty in office and the necessity of village harmony.

As an outsider, Yajibei had been in a delicate position when he was selected as headman. The village was already a hundred years old. Families had lived there for decades. Headmen in Japan were usually chosen from within the village, but perhaps this village, torn by dissension, had turned outward to seek a neutral party. Yajibei's selection had been arranged through the good offices of the Asakawa intendant but evidently approved by the villagers: ninety househeads had come out in strength to greet him on the day he entered Yamashiraishi. They viewed him as, in Isami's words, their savior.[27]

Yajibei's putative lineage and his personal qualities made him well suited to the job. His ancestors, according to one account, had been low-ranking members of the elite samurai military class. They owed fealty to a high-ranking feudal official named Asakawa Jirozaemon, who in turn had served the powerful northern military House of Date. The Asakawa clan were hereditary caretakers of the Date castle in the town of Asakawa. When the great overlord Toyotomi Hideyoshi took over the region in the sixteenth century after centuries of feudal warring, the Date and their followers retreated north to Sendai but ordered their retainers, including Yajibei's family, to stay back to tend the Asakawa ancestral graves.[28]

Although samurai status gave Yajibei a certain cachet, at the time of his generation his family's low hereditary rank scarcely qualified him for standing within this elite military group. And while he bore the rank of rural samurai, or *gōshi,* he did not own land of his own, as the rank implies. Moreover, because he was unaffiliated with any domain lord, he was officially a masterless samurai, or *rōnin,* ineligible for the annual stipend paid in rice to samurai who served in their lord's bureaucracy. In truth, Yajibei was a man of modest means who probably supported his wife and mother-in-law by working as a scribe or tutor. As the second son of his family, he would not have been entitled to any inheritance even if there was one.[29]

Given Yajibei's personal circumstances, the receipt of land and a modest salary in exchange for managing village affairs, strained though they were, must have seemed like an attractive bargain. True, his new position as village head entailed becoming a peasant within the legally fixed system of four status groups and, therefore, giving up any claims he might still have had to the higher status of warrior. This meant losing the privileges of public address by a surname, such as in official documents, and of bearing a sword, which were reserved for the warrior class. Nevertheless, the putative samurai status of his ancestors elevated him a notch above other villagers in a society where family background mattered a great deal and memory was long.

Several other advantages and traits recommended Yajibei for the position of headman. He enjoyed the support of the local intendant, also a member of the samurai class, with whom he would have to negotiate. In addition, the Matsuura founding ancestor, like most samurai by the end of the seventeenth century, was literate—a prerequisite for village heads, who had to keep tax records and communicate in writing with domain officials. More remarkable was his wife's literacy at a time when only a very small percentage of the world's female population was educated. In fact, judging from the letters she left behind, Isami concluded that she was a better writer than her husband.[30] Finally, Yajibei had a reputation for being a reliable, virtuous man.

Despite these qualifications, villagers waited ten years before giving Yajibei their formal approval. Isami sympathized with them. Because of the previous *shōya*'s dishonesty, he imagined, "the people's spirit must have been broken and their daily lives impoverished."[31] They finally confirmed Yajibei's appointment by presenting him with a legal agreement similar to the previous head's contract, which spelled out the conditions of his office in formal, Chinese calligraphy, written with a bamboo brush.

The contract explained how the villagers, after conferring among themselves, had settled on its terms. First, provisions were made for Yajibei's housing as well as for an unspecified, but probably modest, amount of farmland and woodland. Villagers also promised to pay the equivalent of an annual salary *(onengu maikin),* either in currency or in kind, which would vary from year to year on the basis of the village's rice harvest. The ninety signatories representing the six hundred villagers further pledged to help Yajibei meet all his responsibilities as village head. Finally, the contract promised that if, for any reason, Yajibei could no longer continue as head, he was welcome to keep everything the villagers had given him.[32]

This modest and tenuous bargain, struck after a decade-long probationary period, provided the first Matsuura village head with written confirmation of his status. Yajibei not only successfully fulfilled the terms of his contract until his death two decades later, but also he founded a lineage that served continuously in Yamashiraishi until 1954. More than 250 years after Yajibei became the village head, a Matsuura household head—in the person of Isami's son—was still serving as *shōya.*

Isami praised his family's founding ancestor as an enlightened man in the Buddhist sense of the word *(satori)*—selfless, without ego. Indeed, one of Yajibei's lasting achievements was to promote Buddhism in the village. With the goal of restoring the shattered harmony of the village five years after the public execution of its corrupt headmen, Yajibei arranged for a priest from the Sōtō Zen Buddhist temple in the town of Ishikawa, five miles north of the village, to establish a branch temple in Yamashiraishi. So in 1706, Chōtoku Temple was founded, and thereafter descendants of Yajibei served as patrons of the temple.[33] Alongside the temple, which still exists, stone monuments for the ancestors of the Buddhist priest and for Matsuura family heads stand facing each other in a grove of pine trees.

—

Sometime during the Meiji period, the Matsuura built a village office on their grounds, separate from the house, and it too survived the fire. During the Tokugawa period, the home and office of village heads had been one and the same structure. Now their separation symbolized the new political arrangements of the Meiji period, when village heads became more like functionaries of the central government, even though they were still chosen by their own villagers and had to build and supply their own offices.[34]

After Isami's father formally assumed the village headship in 1901, he dressed carefully for work every morning, donning a pleated skirt, or *hakama*, before walking twenty feet to the village office on the other side of the garden or to a room in the retirement cottage, which doubled as his private office. Steps from the retirement cottage led to the village office through a narrow corridor-like room that ran over the main gate and served as an infirmary, where a doctor came from Asakawa to give vaccinations to villagers. Yūya returned home for lunch and went back to work again in the afternoon. Although he did not draw a salary (Isami wrote that his father was "doing well enough and did not need a salary"), he threw himself into community projects. Described by his heir in approving terms such as *conservative, old-fashioned,* and *patient,* Yūya was "so busy, he didn't have time to change his clothes."[35]

The village head's primary responsibility in the Meiji period remained what it had always been: the collection of taxes, with the attendant compilation of census figures. Yūya's task was easier in some ways than his ancestors' had been, because the new revenue system enforced by the central government after 1873 required that land taxes be paid entirely in money rather than in a combination of currency and produce. Also, tax payments were calculated on the basis of the value of an individual household's landholdings rather than on the assessed crop yield of the communal village. Responding to these changes, Yūya revised the tax payment system for the village's 145 households, and this system became a model for other villages.[36]

Maintenance of peace and order was another important function of the village head, though the establishment of police posts throughout the countryside made this maintenance much less informal and local than it had been in the past.[37] Nevertheless, Yūya never forgot how, when he was eight, his family's house had been attacked by angry villagers at the end of the Tokugawa period, and he made every effort to avoid further disorders. In particular, he was careful not to flaunt the family's wealth.

Although the house his son built was impressive, Yūya made a fetish of frugality. Generous in his contributions to the community, he acquired a reputation as a tightwad with his own household. Clean-shaven and thin, he had an almost ascetic appearance, and his parsimonious personal habits were legendary. When a small coin fell into the crawl space under his house, he asked one of his servants to retrieve it. He used the same tea leaves all day, recycled envelopes, and washed his own loincloth when he took his nightly bath. Once he gave a teenage house servant fifty sen with orders to carry guests' bags to the train station. The servant recalled that he spent ten sen to buy a *manju* (steamed soybean bun) and brought the rest of the money back, because he knew he would have to account for his expenses.[38] One of Yūya's granddaughters, Toyo's younger sister Fuki, observed that he wanted to be remembered only as a good man in his community and not as powerful, famous, or rich. Fuki recalled that if somebody expressed envy of someone else for being wealthy or smart or lucky, Yūya would ask, "Has he died?" This was his way of saying that, until the end of a person's life, no one knew what fate held in store for him, and therefore he should not be the envy of others.

Local economic development was a major area of concern for Yūya as village head, as it had been for his ancestors. A memorial tablet erected by the village at the base of the hill leading to the Matsuura house commends him for introducing tobacco as a lucrative cash crop. (More precisely, he reintroduced it, because village sales of tobacco were recorded by one of his forebears in the early nineteenth century.) By the early 1920s, 134 households were engaged in tobacco cultivation and 111 in silkworm cultivation. These cash crops may account for the steady growth in the village's population, which, in 1907 under Yūya's watch, reached nearly eleven hundred people, its highest number up to that time.[39]

Yūya periodically shelled out "pocket money," as Fuki called it, for other worthwhile local causes, such as the construction of an office for the local branch of the agricultural association—a farmers cooperative organization—and a residence for the schoolteacher. He also donated funds for the renovation of the village Shinto shrine and paid half of the cost of rebuilding the Buddhist temple after a fire in 1913.

Village leaders typically contributed to the public weal in various other ways. After his father, Jinsuke, died in 1917, Yūya memorialized him by arranging the production of five hundred copies of a biography of Tomita Kōkei, a native son of Fukushima and a star pupil of the revered nineteenth-century agrarian reformer Ninomiya Sontaku; he distributed the books to prefectural and local offices. In 1918, in a further act of local boosterism, the Matsuura family arranged to produce two hundred copies of a book of photographs of casualties from the Ishikawa area in the Sino-Japanese and Russo-Japanese wars and to distribute these to temples, shrines, veterans associations, and town offices.

Yūya's personal style of leadership continued into the twentieth century, despite the new government's administrative reform agenda, which sought to extend the long arm of the central government's bureaucracy as far down as the village level. In its zeal to centralize rule, the government in Tokyo sought to replace the office of *shōya,* headman, with appointed officials carrying new titles, such as *kochō,* census chief, changed after 1894 to *sonchō,* mayor. Village heads in the Meiji period technically became officials "at the bottom of a bureaucratic ladder on which all the higher rungs were occupied by appointees of the central government or the prefectural government."[40] But despite changes in administrative structure, job description, and terminology, Matsuura family members have continued down to the present day to use the old word *shōya* to refer to their family's long tradition of serving as village head. If, as Isami claimed, the Matsuura built Yamashiraishi, then in a very real sense they also owned it by Yūya's time, thanks to the diligent work of their ancestors over many generations.

—

When the founding ancestor of the Matsuura family died in 1722, he left behind a healthy, literate son named Sōemon, upon whose shoulders rested the responsibility for the survival of his family line. Sōemon projected the image of Confucian virtue and especially of filial piety, which was valued in his day and thereafter.

Beginning in the early years of the eighteenth century, respect for parents was officially promoted in the 260 or so domains under the rule of the Tokugawa military house, even though scholars and military authorities did not consider ordinary peasants capable of following the complex and demanding ethical teachings originating in China. Loyal sons who were tax-paying peasants were promised as much as ten silver pieces and status privileges, such as the right to carry a sword, as rewards for their devotion to their parents. Men and women who were especially dutiful toward their parents but did not pay taxes were recognized with twenty silver pieces.[41]

Demonstrating his virtue as son and heir, Sōemon, together with his wife, lived with and cared for his parents in their old age. They had sons of their own and continued the good start Yajibei had made in building the family's reputation and landholdings. The most long-lived of all the Matsuura ancestors before Isami's time, Sōemon was over eighty when he died.[42]

The househead in the second generation proved to be not only a dutiful heir and a talented man of letters but also someone with a business sense to go along with his air of Confucian propriety. Sōemon's profit motive was inspired, no doubt, by the flexible nature of the *shōya*'s salary, as specified in the original contract his father had signed with the village. The *shōya*'s terms of office afforded a kind of bonus clause: the larger the village harvest, the more he earned. For this reason it behooved village heads to encourage greater rice productivity and even to invest their own resources in helping villagers to improve and increase their cultivated fields.[43] But, because Sōemon was assured an annual salary, even if the amount varied from year to year, he had the means to invest in other income-producing endeavors as well. In 1732, only forty years after the family entered the village and ten years after his father's death, Sōemon, like other ambitious eighteenth-century Japanese peasants of some means, began manufacturing sake in a building adjacent to the family house. This was a costly enterprise that required considerable capital. Isami speculated approvingly that Sōemon must have been a "good planner" as well as "quite entrepreneurial."[44]

Confronted with deficits, many domain officials in and after the mid-eighteenth century took steps to encourage greater rural production so that farmers could earn more and thereby meet their tribute obligations. Sake brewing was a valuable winter occupation providing secondary employment for farmers after the rice harvest. Fermented in large wooden barrels, sake was drunk on numerous ceremonial occasions, and its production required the labor of many hands.

The Matsuura brewery remained a family enterprise until 1913, when Yūya closed it down. Isami was not sorry. As much as he valued his ancestors' entrepreneurial activity, which, after all, had contributed to the family's wealth and well-being, Isami himself did not drink, and he disapproved of drunken guests in his home.

Sōemon's term of office as village head in the Matsuura family's second generation also corresponded to changes in administrative arrangements and tax burdens that increased and complicated his responsibilities even as his sake business dealings grew. In 1741, the region that is present-day Shirakawa was split into three domains: Shirakawa, Echigo-Takada, and a third domain directly under the control of the Tokugawa government but administered by Echigo-Takada. Yamashiraishi fell into this last domain.

In the following year, the new domain ruler predictably called for yet another survey of the productive capacity of his realm in order to secure more tax revenues. Also in 1742, seeking to extend his reach into his newly acquired domain, he opened a headquarters in Asakawa, at the outer edges of his domain, with the construction expenses paid by an unnamed "wealthy person in Asakawa."[45]

The new domain ruler, like others elsewhere in the country, was clearly bent on maintaining order in addition to extracting tribute. To this end, he spelled out nineteen official ordinances regulating villagers' lives. As the officials responsible for enforcing them, village headmen such as Matsuura Sōemon were held accountable for any incidents of unruliness or disobedience occurring on their watch.

One of the ordinances, still in existence in Yūya's time, mandated the organization of a system of group responsibility implemented decades earlier in other parts of the country and possibly already functioning in Yamashiraishi. Villagers were instructed to work together in mutual responsibility teams of five neighboring households *(gōnin-gumi)*, each led by a village elder who assisted the *shōya* in his official duties. These became officially recognized structures of village governance with whom the *shōya* had to work.

Another ordinance called on villagers to report suspicious newcomers to the authorities. The notice also promised to reward people who reported on Christians, though it was hardly likely that any Christian converts were secretly practicing their religion in this area. So-called hidden Christians were more likely to be found in the southwestern part of the country, near the port of Nagasaki, where Europeans had first plied their trade in the second half of the sixteenth century. Christianity had been outlawed by the Tokugawa in the early seventeenth century after the expulsion of Portuguese and Spanish missionary orders.

Firearms and tobacco, also introduced by the Iberians, had also been banned by the early Tokugawa rulers, but not alcohol. Perhaps noting the success of local sake-brewing enterprises such as the Matsuura family's, the military rulers simply enjoined villagers to refrain from drunken behavior in towns.[46]

Charged with enforcing communal morals, village heads also had to avoid the wrath of peasants, who constituted over 80 percent of the population. Lacking weapons of their own and caught between the demands of the political-military hierarchy above them and the interests of the village peasants below them, the Matsuura *shōya* always walked a thin line. Village peasants during the Tokugawa period could legally initiate lawsuits, often with dire consequences for the defendant, as the beheading of the previous village head and his son had so vividly illustrated, and they could illegally rise up in revolt. But not all headmen remembered these lessons.

In the first half of the eighteenth century, the Shirakawa area was rife with disorder. Yet, despite peasant protests, appeals, and other types of collective action directed initially at domain officials and then later against wealthy rural merchants and village heads, Sōemon's headship was not attacked in any of the four large-scale and widespread peasant uprisings between 1720 and 1742.[47]

Local disorders were serious matters. One uprising in the 1720s, for example, lasted a month and engaged fifteen thousand farmers, who railed against the "lavish life styles" of domain officials. The officials, like members of the samurai elsewhere, had grown accustomed to the great variety of goods and services promoted by urban merchants and were heavily in debt to them. Their budgetary excesses required additional taxes from the peasants. The violent explosion of peasant anger led to the resignation of one of the governor's senior advisers.

In another riot, following a poor harvest in 1723, the peasants turned their rage against both local officials and village heads. Demanding an extension on their deadline for paying taxes, rioters forced their way into the residences of village headmen and the heads of leagues of villages, whom they accused of being too ready to enforce government tax policies.[48]

Peasant demonstrations broke out again in neighboring Shirakawa in 1742, the year of a new cadastral survey. Yamashiraishi was not involved. But, as village headmen, the Matsuura househeads were perpetually caught between the authorities' expectations of them and the commoners' potential for creating massive disturbances.

TWO

Kissing Cousins

IN DECEMBER 1901, Isami wed his cousin's oldest daughter in a marriage arranged by his father, Yūya.[1] The fifteen-year-old child bride cried on her wedding day when the traditional bride's hair ornament was placed on her head. She was a student, with her "hair still in braids," when she regretfully told her school principal that she would not continue with her schooling because she was "going to be a bride." She vowed, like Isami, to give her children more education than she had.[2]

Isami's young wife, Sagawa Kō, came from a family of village heads to the south of Asakawa, in present-day East Shirakawa county. The oldest of four children in her family, she lost her parents around the age of seven, her father to typhus and her mother to heart disease, and was subsequently reared by her grandmother, who was Yūya's sister and Isami's aunt. She was two years younger than what the average age had been for brides in the region over fifty years earlier; by the end of the decade, women's average age at marriage would be twenty-three.[3] The marriage was nevertheless considered legal, as the 1880 Penal Code permitted most forms of consensual sex over age twelve.

Unlike his bride, twenty-two-year-old Isami was more than ready for marriage. After living for only one year in the house he had built, he had volunteered in December 1900 for one year of military service in an army infantry unit in Niigata prefecture. Outfitted in a dark blue uniform and round cap, he was trained in modern military combat tactics and learned how to use the long-range .26-caliber rifle. In the autumn of 1901, Isami advanced to a three-month officer-training program in another military unit in Sendai and rose to the rank of infantry lieutenant.

Isami was not much interested in military affairs, however, and by the time he had completed his term of military service and returned to Yamashiraishi, plans for his marriage were already underway. During Isami's absence, Grandfather Jinsuke's poor eyesight had finally forced him to retire at the age of sixty in 1901, and Isami's father, Yūya, replaced him as village head. The family was now ready to "receive a daughter-in-law."

Despite discrepancies in age, education, experience, and character traits, Kō and Isami turned out to be an excellent match. Isami was a slender, handsome young man with a long, thin face and a dark, trimmed mustache, while Kō, several inches shorter than her husband, had softer features and a more rounded face. After her marriage she wore her hair swept back off her forehead, and in middle age she smoked a *kiseru,* a tobacco pipe favored by women. Remembered by one of her daughters as being "very beautiful and French-looking," Kō evidently pleased her husband, who, according to his daughters and his own account, was never unfaithful to Kō throughout their long and fruitful married life. His views on monogamy and marital fidelity were influenced by Fukuzawa Yukichi, the Meiji-era popularizer of Western learning, who favored an egalitarian relationship between husband and wife and criticized the custom of polygamy.[4]

The birth of the young couple's first child and heir was registered in the household census in March 1903, fifteen months after his parents' marriage. They called him Yatarō, the first syllable of his name honoring both the first ancestor, Yajibei, and his grandfather Yūya. Destined by sex and birth order to lead the twelfth generation of Matsuura as househead and Yamashiraishi as village head, Yatarō might have assumed his responsibilities much earlier than the late 1940s if circumstances had been slightly different. For, in February 1904, within a year after Yatarō's birth, Isami was called back into military service, this time on active duty. Japan had just declared war on Russia.

Isami was drafted shortly after the Japanese navy surprised the czar's fleet in Port Arthur, Manchuria, with a night torpedo attack. Both Russia and Japan coveted Manchuria, traditionally a Chinese territory, for its mineral resources and strategic location. Japan also sought to prevent Russia from threatening its new holding in Korea, and Russia wanted the warm-water port facilities off the southern tip of the Liaodong (Kwantung) Peninsula for its landlocked navy. In this heyday of imperialist expansion, China and Japan were among the few Asian countries not yet colonized, but China was nevertheless being slowly picked apart by the more powerful nation-states, including the newly risen Japan, which had already sparred with Russia over Manchuria a few years earlier.

Although the Russo-Japanese War lasted only one and one-half years, the fierce fighting cost the Japanese side alone over 120,000 lives; for the

Russians, the toll was even higher.[5] With over 2 million Russian and Japanese troops mustered for battle by 1905, it was the largest war the world had yet seen, and Isami was in the thick of it. He rejoined his old Sendai regiment, whose mettle was tested when the men were transported to a port in northern Korea, near Pyongyang, and then crossed the Yalu River to meet up with other divisions engaging Russian troops in a massive artillery battle in southern Manchuria. This large force traversed a mountain range and destroyed a lookout post before confronting Russian troops. Isami was injured in the ensuing battle in November 1904, one month after Kō gave birth to their first daughter, Mina. The injury probably saved his life. Removed from the battlefield, he was sent home to recuperate in a hospital in Sendai and thereafter served as an instructor in military studies.

In late May of the following year, the Japanese navy, under Admiral Tōgō Heihachirō, sank the Russian fleet in a classic naval maneuver executed in the straits between Japan and Korea, and by the following autumn, the war was over. Thanks to the diplomatic offices of United States president Theodore Roosevelt, a treaty was signed in September 1905 at Portsmouth, New Hampshire, confirming the expansion of Japan's empire in East Asia by recognizing the country's "paramount interests" in Korea and its foothold on south Manchuria, where it had gained the right to build a railway.[6] Sharing in his nation's glory, Isami returned home a local hero, with a medal from the army and a bullet permanently lodged in his chest.

His military obligation dispatched, Isami had few other specific duties to perform until 1920, when he assumed official headship of the Matsuura family and their property. He did not replace his father as village head until 1938, though he increasingly helped shoulder his father's responsibilities. Income from the family's extensive landholdings spared him the immediate need for gainful employment. Largely freed of financial worries and official duties until he became householder, Isami concentrated on producing, rearing, educating, and finding suitable spouses for his children. Family maintenance was his major work.

Even by the rural standards of their day, the marriage of Kō and Isami proved remarkably fertile. In the first three decades of their marriage, the compatible couple reared eight daughters and seven sons, all of whom were born in easy deliveries in the small tatami-lined room behind the living room, some with the assistance of a midwife. After the tenth child, Kō's deliveries were so easy, she would work up until the last moment and give birth even before the midwife arrived. She breastfed all fifteen children. Only one did not survive into adulthood, a daughter who died at age ten.

Kō's long string of births was noteworthy even for her day. She joked that since the village office was adjacent to the retirement cottage on the grounds of the family's property, the clerk would run across the garden at the first sound of a newborn's crying, step up onto the veranda, walk briskly around to the north side of the house to look at the baby in the birthing room, and then run back to the office to register the birth. "It's really convenient," she said, "but at first I was embarrassed." By the time the fifteenth child was born, Kō was in her midforties and finally tired of having children. She did not like the fact, she said, that her grandchildren were close in age to her offspring.[7]

The selection of suitable names for so many children required thoughtful consideration. When the children's grandfather, Yūya, was born in 1860, the family had departed from their practice of repeating the same four or five names for the heirs and of changing names at different times in the life cycle. Besides, in the early 1870s the Meiji state prohibited the naming of children with suffixes signifying ancient court ranks, such as the *emon* in Sōemon.[8] The children of Kō and Isami bore more modern-sounding names, though still redolent with significance for their family history.

The boys' names signified, first of all, their order of birth. The *roku* in the sixth son's name, Shinrokurō, for example, was written with the Chinese ideogram for six, and the *shichi* in the name of the seventh son, Seishichirō, means seven. As in earlier times, Chinese characters selected for other parts of the sons' names alluded to desirable qualities or virtues, such as the *shin,* "sincerity or fidelity," in the name Shinrokurō and the *sei,* "prosperous," in the name Seishichirō. Kōjirō's name means "meritorious second son." In several cases, an almost pictorial weaving together of present and past generations was achieved by characters chosen to honor patrilineal ancestors and perpetuate their memory. The character for *yū,* which means "courage," in the fourth son's name, Yūshirō, formed the first syllable of Yūya and was also the character for Isami's name.

Names additionally constituted one way that parents transmitted their beliefs about gender. Isami's sisters Chise and Kiyo appear to have been named after female ancestors (the seventh-generation patriarch's wife and daughter), suggesting their parents' desire to honor female as well as male family members. His sister Moto, however, was named after a brother who died young, not after the revered second wife of Great-grandfather Daisuke.

Daughters' names were customarily entered in the household registry in the simpler Japanese phonetic syllabary rather than in Chinese characters, which conveyed a sense of meaning, dignity, and classical learning. Since her name was written phonetically, Fuki did not know what it was supposed to represent, if anything, but she thought perhaps she was named after a spring grass or flower called *fuki,* a butterbur or coltsfoot.

In their later lives, several of the daughters of Isami and Kō adopted Chinese characters to match the sound of their names. Tami surmised that her name and her sister Yasu's together formed part of a male ancestor's posthumous Buddhist name whose Chinese characters suggest "bringing order to the people," something which, Tami explained, the village head was expected to do. Mina, the eldest daughter, always wrote her name phonetically, even though she could have easily found appropriate Chinese characters for it, because her name was intended to convey the numbers three *(mi)* and seven *(na),* signifying her birth in the thirty-seventh year of the Meiji era, or 1904. Later in their lives, several of the daughters added the final syllable *ko,* meaning "child," to their names to make them sound more modern. This had become a common onomastic practice for girls' names by early decades of the twentieth century.[9]

Although the daughters' names, unlike the sons', did not mark their order of birth, throughout their lives they tended to observe that order when socializing with one another. The Japanese language itself reinforces an awareness of age hierarchy by using different words for elder and younger sister or brother. In family photographs the sisters usually lined up from youngest to oldest. The older daughters tended to travel together, while the younger formed a separate group. Even their mother unconsciously observed this awareness of birth order: she had so many girls close in age that when she wanted to summon one of her daughters, she would begin with the firstborn and call each one in order of birth until she reached the right name.[10]

Given Kō's fecundity, and the elders' longevity, the Matsuura household swarmed with people for many years. In the early Meiji period the household included representatives of five generations. Chise, the widow of the seventh-generation patriarch, died in 1887, eight years after Isami was born. Daisuke, her son-in-law, died in 1890, after the death of his second wife, Moto, and shortly before the death of his daughter Yoshi (Isami's grandmother). Yoshi's husband, Jinsuke, lived into his seventy-ninth year, dying in 1917. When his grandchildren were young, Isami's father, Yūya, was still raising his own numerous offspring. His tenth child was born three years before the birth of his first grandchild, Yatarō; his eleventh and last child, who did not survive, was born three months after Yatarō was. Yatarō and his siblings played with aunts and uncles who were themselves still children in a home that exemplified the Confucian ideal of many generations of family members living under one roof.

In addition to the numerous children swelling the household population in the first two decades of the twentieth century, young nursemaids were assigned to every child below school age, and, for a time in the 1920s, a woman schoolteacher rented a small room behind the central living room. "The house was always noisy," Mina recalled. "There were so many people, there hardly was any space. You could hear the drone of people's voices in the house even from a distance. When we were growing up, at least twenty or thirty people were living in the house. There were a lot of people coming and going."[11]

Around the time of Isami's marriage, Yūya relieved some of the population pressure in the household by marrying off his older children. His second oldest son, Kensuke, was married to the adopted daughter of a local family whose surname he assumed. Yūya's eldest daughter was married the following year, and the second daughter four years later, in 1907. By 1911, with the marriage of Isami's sister Moto to her cousin, only his seventeen-year-old brother, Kōzō, and his eleven-year-old sister, Chise, were still living in the Yamashiraishi house; four other siblings had died young. There were still many mouths to feed, numerous marriages to arrange, and much kin work to perform in order to maintain family ties that extended beyond their own village and gave them valuable social links to the world outside Yamashiraishi.

—

Kin work came naturally to Isami and his father; it was part of a long tradition of bolstering the family. The third-generation Matsuura household, who was named Sōemon, like his father, and those who followed also consciously forged familial ties with a widespread network of influential lineages.

One important avenue for enhancing family status and increasing social capital even in the seventeenth century was an advantageous marriage, arranged for the children of the house by elders, who often chose relatives for their children's spouses. Marital ties increased social contacts, which benefited village heads and their villages.

In the case of the Matsuura, wives were preferably chosen from among daughters of other village heads, like Kō and also Miyo, Isami's mother. Literate, hardworking wives sustained the household and strengthened its regional influence. Unfortunately, Isami's family history makes scant references to the family's wives and daughters until the nineteenth century. We do not know their names, but we do know that the wife of Sōemon II, in the family's third generation, was the first woman to receive notice. She was honored after her death with a Buddhist name, carved into a tablet, for a fee, by the temple priest and placed on the family's Buddhist altar to be venerated with the other ancestral dead.

Another way social networks were created was through carefully arranged adoptions of second and third sons to suitable families who lacked heirs of their own. Such instances were common in the Matsuura's region, where the birthrate was low.[12] A family could adopt a boy as their son, or if they had a daughter, he could be an adopted son-in-law.

Sōemon II's younger brother was sent to a well-established samurai family named Inoue, whose househead occupied the office of judge *(kenden)* in the local criminal justice system. The boy was given the new and aristocratic name of Ichiuemon and raised to become head of his adoptive family's fifteenth generation. Ties between the two families remained close down to the twentieth century.

Adoption was encouraged by the system of inheritance. The longstanding practice of primogeniture dictated that families bequeath their entire inheritance to only one child, usually, though not always, the firstborn son. Equal distribution among all the children would have reduced the relatively small holdings of most families to fragments too small for subsistence. Upon their marriage or adoption, noninheriting children ordinarily left the household in the hands of the heir, who remained there with his wife, children, parents, and, if they were still alive, his grandparents. This ideal family—one heir from each generation, all generations living together, ideally in harmony, under one roof—was called, in Japanese, the *ie,* or stem family.

The Matsuura family was already moving toward this ideal by the time of Sōemon II. They had grown to a creditable size for their day, with nine members: five males and four females, probably spanning three generations.[13] Sōemon II's reclamation of additional rice land enabled that many people to be fed.

Sōemon II, like his father, had an energetic entrepreneurial spirit. He opened new fields to cultivation by leveling a hilly area that had trapped water on adjacent land. The leveling created land suitable for rice growing and released the water to irrigate it. The project required access to considerable labor power, and even his wife worked on it, according to Isami. Engineering skill was also needed; among other things, Sōemon II had to over-see the construction of a sluice to channel the water's flow for irrigating the paddies. Several other families reclaimed land in a similar way, thereby in-creasing the region's capacity to pay assessed land taxes.[14]

Added wealth from land enabled landholders such as the Matsuura to sup-port larger families and to invest in new entrepreneurial or money-lending activities that further enriched them. Landholders who financed reclama-tion projects, moreover, often were rewarded for their efforts with tempo-rary tax relief in addition to title to the newly opened land, and the peas-ants who provided the manual labor for the project typically became their tenants. Farmers who could not repay their loans lost their land and also became tenants of the moneylender.[15] In 1764, two years before he died, Sōemon further promoted the family's well-being by acquiring the privi-lege of using the family surname on official documents, a distinction ordi-narily reserved for members of the elite samurai military aristocracy but given to select village headmen as a standard way of rewarding their cooperation with the authorities.[16]

Despite their wealth and status, families such as the Matsuura could fail to produce a suitable heir. Unfit, unhealthy, or simply unconceived male heirs threatened the continuity of the family and its wealth, good name, and capacity to serve as local leaders. A profligate heir could ruin a family altogether. Several examples of unqualified or nonexistent heirs apparent dot the long history of the Matsuura. In most cases the problem was dealt with by adopting a promising male from another family, either to replace the defective one or to fill in for the nonexistent one or to marry the daugh-ter of the household, assume her surname, and live in her parents' home as both son-in-law and heir. Isami's great-grandfather Daisuke and grandfather Jinsuke were both adopted sons-in-law brought into the family to marry Matsuura women.

The first case of a Matsuura adopted heir occurred earlier in the family's history, in 1800, when, in the waning years of his life, Sōemon II's grand-son Yūemon, the fifth-generation househead, had to make a difficult deci-sion affecting his only son. Yūemon's heir suffered from a leg problem that made walking difficult. His disability raised serious doubts about his fitness to serve as his father's successor, especially in a critical time following a farm-ers' uprising. Yūemon, too, had been frail in health from an early age, and every year he had frequented natural hot springs in their area in hopes of improving his physical constitution.[17]

For the first time in their recorded history, a break in the Matsuura blood line occurred when Yūemon, eager to retire from the village headship, decided to adopt a twenty-seven-year-old man from the Murakami family to make him the Matsuura's legal heir. The official paperwork for such transactions included changing the new heir's temple affiliation to Yamashiraishi. Significantly, the form, filed in 1800, refers to him not simply as an adopted son but as a *muko yōshi,* an adopted son-in-law. Moreover, at the end of the same year, Yūemon recorded the adoption of a twenty-three-year-old woman named Mitsu.[18] It seems that the disabled son was the family's only child, and to secure the family's future Yūemon recruited both a daughter and a husband for her. Such measures were part of the arsenal of strategies employed by families bent on assuring their continuity through succession by one son, whether biological or fictive.

The family now had to provide for its disabled biological son. Two married brothers could not live in the same household, and the disabled brother would not have been adopted by another family. Consequently, he was established on a separate plot of land and given a house, a wife, and, as a wedding present, the rice fields originally reclaimed by his great-grandfather Sōemon II. He was also given an entirely new surname to prevent him or his heirs from ever laying claim to Matsuura property.

While the terms of the settlement may seem harsh, the resolution was generous in one sense. Even though the young man was essentially disowned, his separate surname and property gave him status as an independent householder instead of leaving him as a branch of the main house, subordinate to the adopted brother who had replaced him as heir. Nevertheless, he did not fare well. Unable to bear children of their own, he and his wife resorted to adopting a boy and a girl. Their descendants ended up as poor cultivators who barely eked out a livelihood doing agricultural day labor.

To paper over the rift in the Matsuura family's biological continuity and to symbolize the adopted heir's complete separation from his own bloodline, Yūemon renamed the boy Sōemon, after the househeads in the second and third generations of Matsuura. Family naming customs helped to reinforce the fiction of unbroken lineage, despite the break in the genetic affinity of individual male heirs from one generation to the next.

Family heirs thought of themselves as inheriting not only a house and its prosperity but also a house name—the ancestral line, which they honored as a religious obligation. Poorer peasants who were denied use of a legally inheritable surname also observed the custom of passing down specific personal names from one generation to the next as a substitute for surnames.[19] Commoner households, and especially those of village officials, often chose the same personal name for the family head for several generations "to mark [the household's] continuity and signify its superior status vis-à-vis ordinary peasants."[20]

Wealthy rural entrepreneurial families such as the Matsuura also took other measures to preserve their household's continuity. The fifth generation's Yūemon, for example, was the first patriarch to keep a diary. This activity was not lost on Isami, who also kept a diary and whose name, like his father Yūya's, was written with the same ideogram as the first syllable in Yūemon's name. Through diaries and family histories, prominent families deliberately created a "house style" *(kafū)* that would perpetuate their household over time.

In a sense, wealthy members of the peasant class, with their hereditary claims to land and position, forged a "family ideology" that promoted the goal of family continuity. As such, they imitated the preoccupation of the elite samurai class with perpetuating family name.[21] Seen as a corporate unit, the household—its male ancestral line, reputation, wealth, and name— became a legacy, whose preservation ideally was the goal of all its members. In the case of farmers, the household's added engagement in economic activities made the goal of continuity as a corporate body all the more tangible.

Naming practices for male heirs in the early generations of the Matsuura family not only reinforced the sense of family continuity but also deemphasized the value of individual personality. The frequent recycling of personal names over the generations probably was intended to underscore the Matsuura monopoly of village office rather than to convey unique, memorable individuals.

Only four personal names were chosen for the heirs of the first nine Matsuura generations: Yajibei, Sōemon, Yūemon, and Kōemon. For generation after generation, until Isami's father, Yūya, in the tenth generation, there was always a Matsuura patriarch and village head with one of these names. Some of the Matsuura used more than one of them over the course of their lives. In their later years, for example, the second- and third-generation Sōemons changed their name to Yajibei, in honor of the first ancestor; similarly, the fourth-generation househead, Yūemon, took the name Yajibei in his retirement years. In the eighth and ninth generations, both Daisuke and Jinsuke at different times in their lives bore the name Kōemon.

As in more modern times, names did more than honor those who bore them in past generations; they also conveyed desirable qualities. The Kō- of Kōemon, for example, was written with the Chinese character for thought, while the first syllable of Sōemon meant religion.

Matsuura househeads, by generation	Wives
1 Yajibei	?
2 Sōemon, Yajibei	?
3 Sōemon II, Yajibei II	?
4 Yūemon,[a] Yajibei III	? from Yabuki village
5 Yūemon[b]	? from Shioda village
6 *Sōemon III, Yūemon[a] II, Jinsuke	*Mitsu? from Shioda village
	? from Kōriyama village
	? from Yabuki village
7 Teizō, Kōemon	Arakawa Chise
8 *Daisuke, Kōemon II, Yūemon[a] III	Matsuura Kiyo
	Moto
9 *Jinsuke, Kōemon III	Matsuura Yoshi
10 Yūya	Ishii Miyo
11 Isami	Sagawa Kō
12 Yatarō	Sugiura Chiyo
13 Tomoji	Ikuchi Isoko

LEGEND: Roman numerals = the first, second, or third time the same name appears in the family genealogy; [a] = the name as initially rendered in characters; [b] = the same name but rendered in different characters; * = adopted; ? = unknown or uncertain information concerning wives' identities. Note that the several wives listed for one man were sequential wives, not concubines.

Subsequent generations until the tenth generation's Yūya followed the practice of naming or renaming heirs, whether biological or adoptive, after previous family heads, much like the Western onomastic custom of selecting identical names for the grandfather, father, and son of a patrilineage, though without the equivalent of *Junior* or Roman numerals (used here only to help eliminate possible confusion over identity). One imagines that after a while the distinctions among the various Sōemons and Yūemons and Kōemons blurred in everybody's mind (they certainly do in the eyes of the contemporary historian trying to sort them out), but that may have been the point, for the result was not only a sense of seamless rule by one family but also the illusion of rule by one and the same person in the family.

Besides, the recycling of Japanese males' given names did not seem confusing to people at the time because given names were not necessarily used to refer to either family members or fellow villagers. Within the household, individuals might be called by their family roles (father or elder brother or grandmother, for example); within the village, by their official function (village head, intendant), much like the practice in other societies of addressing someone simply by his or her title: doctor, reverend, captain, professor, and so on. (Maids, however, were called by their given names.) Among the nine generations of Matsuura househeads who recycled the same four names, those who assumed more than one of these names over the course of their lifetimes usually made the changes in correspondence to a significant passage in their life cycles, for example, when they became househeads or village heads or when they retired from their headship position. All the househeads also received Buddhist names posthumously.[22]

Several times in its history, the Matsuura family solved the complicated problem of the unfit or nonexistent male heir with naming practices that helped conceal breaks in their biological continuity. An elaborate process of negotiating adoptions and marriages also helped preserve the continuity of the Matsuura household, if not necessarily the family genes. In subsequent generations after 1800, adoption of sons, sons-in-law, and even daughters as well as intermarriage with relatives continued to serve as strategies for maintaining the family's existence.

THREE

Father of the Village

IN THE LATE 1920S, a journalist from *Fujin no tomo* (Woman's Friend) magazine visited Yamashiraishi to interview the Matsuura for a story on "the good family." *Fujin no tomo* was published by Hani Motoko, the founder of a new, progressive women's school attended by three of the Matsuura daughters. Her magazine frequently featured articles on parenting and child-rearing. The reporter was assigned the task of determining whether the "large, multigenerational, rural, and long-lived Matsuura family" could provide clues to good parenting inasmuch as they "maintained a traditional lifestyle in old Japan, yet their children were successful in Tokyo, the heart of modern Japan."[1] The journalist's visit to the big farmhouse built under Isami's supervision thirty years earlier provided an opportunity for Kō and Isami to discuss their well-defined philosophy of childrearing.

The three secrets of successful parenting, Isami told the reporter, were a good blood line; fidelity to one's spouse in a monogamous marriage; and a healthy natural environment, with fresh air, ample sunshine, and outdoor play areas. He assumed that he and his wife had inherited the first trait, he faithfully practiced the second, and the countryside where the children grew up provided the third ingredient.

The children were encouraged to engage in strenuous outdoor activity and maintain close contact with nature. In autumn, they entertained themselves by jumping from the roof of the one-story house into piles of fallen leaves. When snow fell, the children carved skis out of the bamboo growing in the woods and skied down the slope behind the village cemetery, a half-mile behind their house. Warm springtime weather inspired hikes in the mountains, and in summertime, they swam in the narrow stream downhill from the house. Tami also recalled dancing in the August O-bon festivities and watching the annual Asakawa fireworks display from a window of the retirement cottage. Grandfather Yūya kept a horse under a tree in the garden, but when the horse ran around the garden, it frightened his youngest granddaughter, Tami, so she did not ride it.

The children's playroom in inclement weather was either the covered kitchen area outside the main house or the large living area, where they pushed aside the few pieces of furniture in the room so they could sing, wrestle, play hide-and-seek, or practice juggling bags filled with sand or buckwheat. They were also allowed to toss a ball in the room.

Isami advised parents to throw away store-bought toys. Manufactured toys were not only expensive but dangerous, he explained (many were made of glass), and they discouraged children's creativity. With the exception of drums and kites, the Matsuura children were encouraged to use their imagination to create their own toys. Playthings consisted of whatever natural objects they could find in the fields around them. Sticks became swords, a piece of bamboo turned into a horse, leaves served as bowls, and pebbles were candies.[2]

Store-bought toys and clothing for fifteen children were not only difficult to obtain and costly, but they were objectionable on ideological grounds as well. Kō and Isami did not approve of what they viewed as urban mothers' consumerism, which, they charged, produced pampered, materialistic, and ultimately unhappy children. "They put nice clothes on them, fuss over them, teach them things they don't need to know and destroy their innocence. They are proud of their creations, but the children are sacrificed."[3]

These views on childrearing reflect similar teachings of Fukuzawa Yukichi, the Meiji educator who was held in great esteem by both Isami and his father, Yūya, for his modern, "progressive" teachings. Yūya had one of Fukuzawa's poems framed and hung in the village school. It spoke of the intimate connection between natural and social harmony. Fukuzawa, too, had preached the value of physical exercise and even "rough sports" for both girls and boys, and he had advertised the benefits of country living for children: "When a child eats . . . and plays and exercises as country children do, the benefits exceed the best food of the cities."[4] Fukuzawa considered many children of wealthy urban families to be "both mentally and physically feeble," because it was the "tradition of their houses to overprotect and overfeed and overdress the children, and to have too easy a life, leading to a lack of activity."[5]

Not so the Matsuura family. Neither of the children's parents believed in coddling the young. Isami criticized the "class of educated women" who hovered over their children and laid down many rules about what they could and could not do, overreacting to the first sign of possible illness. "Throw away thermometers" was his advice, arguing that children should not be raised like greenhouse flowers. In the Matsuura home, which was sunny and let in a good breeze, every child had to bathe, even if he was suffering from a cold or she had already fallen asleep and had to be wakened. After their nightly baths, Isami played with his children, but even here the playfulness had a purpose: to develop their physical strength with exercises. He would spin the young ones around as they hung from his arms.[6] "We don't have any thermometers or *haramaki*" (wide cloth belts worn as stomach warmers), Isami told the reporter.[7] He washed cuts or wounds with an antiseptic that resembled vinegar and ministered to upset stomachs and colds with a tiny pill, called *wakamatsu,* that daughter Fuki thought was probably a Chinese herb. In the couple's opinion, their children owed their health to Mother Nature.

When the fourteen surviving children were grown and on their own, Isami conveyed his attachment to their family life and its sylvan setting by commissioning an artist friend to paint a picture of their snow-laden house and grounds in wintertime. Isami's calligraphy on the side of the painting expressed the hope that his "seven boys and seven girls" would remain healthy.

Fortunately, most of the children were hale and hardy well into old age. Only Yatarō and Teru experienced serious illness in their childhood, suffering from attacks of appendicitis, as Isami did. In 1929, when Teru was ten, her appendix ruptured before the doctor summoned from Asakawa could reach her, and she died of peritonitis. Grieving over the loss of this "clever" child, as her sister Yasu described her, Isami built a pool in her memory by constructing gates to dam the stream below the house, and he composed a haiku linking her to the reflection of flowers in the water.

Although Isami's offspring enjoyed exceptional freedom during play time, he and Kō were adamant about instilling in them the Confucian virtue of family harmony. They intervened at the start of arguments or fights, calling offenders to their side, then mediated and resolved conflicts. In this they were apparently successful. "We never have any problems due to fighting among the children," Kō told the visiting journalist. "The younger ones learn from the older ones, and the older ones take care of the younger ones."[8]

The two parents set down strict rules for respecting others. When children as young as three revealed dishonest or selfish behavior, they got a "talking to" from Kō or Isami, who tried to explain why their behavior was objectionable. If, after three incidents the child still misbehaved, the antidote was punishment in the form of spanking. The parents also followed the customary disciplinary practice of putting misbehaving children outside the house, even at night—the Japanese equivalent of sending a child to his room. Such incidents were evidently rare, though Toyo remembered being punished in this way when she caused a disruption one night by insisting that her mother, and not one of the maids, take care of her.

What is striking about these clearly articulated views on childrearing is the sense they convey of two parents operating as a team. Unlike early twentieth-century discourses on parenting, which assigned women the task of raising children and variously advised urban fathers to assert "strictness" and mothers to exercise "love," or fathers to be "loving" and mothers disciplinarians, Kō and Isami did not observe a thoroughgoing gendered division of labor in the shaping of their children's character, and both displayed a combination of affection and strictness.[9]

The two strictly enforced discipline when guests arrived at the family's house. At such times, the children were neither seen nor heard; instead, they were sent out of the room. Ordinarily five or six children at one time ate together at separate tables from their parents, with a servant dishing out the food. If the younger children became rude or unruly, the older children hit them on top of their heads or sent them to a back room.[10]

Discipline was balanced by physical closeness. Kō was a loving, if preoccupied, parent with a personality described as "simple, honest and cheerful" (akarui) by the journalist who wrote about the family. The village priest described Kō as quiet, and her youngest daughter, Tami, described her as very gentle. She carried the infants Japanese-style on her bare back under her kimono, a physical intimacy at least one of her children remembered well into her own old age. Although Kō was too busy with the babies to give the older children as much attention as they might have liked, when they returned from their Tokyo schools in the summer, her "mother's intuition," as one daughter put it, enabled her to guess how much they had grown over the year and have the right size summer clothes ready for them.[11]

Kō also showed a firm side, especially to her children. Although her husband teased her by calling her frightening (kowai), her youngest daughter described her disciplinary style as simply strict (kibishii). "Mother spoke her mind directly." She indulged the children on their first day home from school in the summer, but thereafter she expected them to do household tasks, and even when young they learned to fulfill social obligations. Mina, for example, remembered traveling with Kō at the age of four to visit Kō's ailing grandmother and receive her first lesson in the etiquette of omimai, condolence calls on the sick. By example, Kō also taught the virtues of charity, giving their old clothes to a beggar who came to the house every year.

Isami helped with the daily work of raising the children, both in educating them and in performing domestic tasks. Departing not only from the traditional Japanese male role but also from traditional Japanese fare, he baked oatmeal cookies in a large stone oven for the children's snacks. He cut their hair, bathed them when young, and otherwise assisted at night when the babysitters and servants were busy with mealtime preparations. As a hands-on father, Isami carried out the dictum of Fukuzawa Yukichi: "The father of the infant should . . . endeavor to share the labor of the infant's care."[12]

An inveterate tinkerer fond of labor-saving devices, Isami built a hand-operated wooden washing machine, to ease household work. Once he bought Kō a new device that he found in Tokyo for making *udon* (wheat noodles) from scratch by cutting the flour into thin strips. Thanks to his ingenuity, the family enjoyed the luxury of electric lights as early as 1914. After he figured out how to produce electricity from the nearby river, he built a small shed alongside it to serve as a power station for generating electricity to the family's house, the retirement cottage, and the village office. Every night at dusk Kō would call out, "Turn on the lights!" Electricity came to the rest of the village later, in 1919, and to commemorate the event, Isami and Kō chose the name Teru, meaning "shine," for the daughter born in that year.

In certain ways, Isami embodied the stereotype of the stern, authoritarian father. The househead's position was bolstered by the Civil Code of 1898, which formalized his control over his children's marriages and gave him legal superiority over his wife in matters of divorce, business transactions, and inheritance. "Father made decisions without wavering," said Tami. "Once he decided on a course of action, he did not like to change plans."

Isami balanced his firm, no-nonsense approach to parenting, however, with close attention to each child's well-being. Isami's daughters remembered him with respect and reverence; in their eyes he was authoritative but not oppressive, and he was very clear about his moral values.[13] On special occasions he wrote a commemorative poem or a letter of encouragement or moral exhortation. On the eve of his departure from home for middle school, second son Kōjirō recalled, "I received from father a long letter whose contents I do not remember but that sounded like moral instruction."[14] "When I was in college," Isami's youngest daughter remembered, "students were asked to choose a motto for themselves. I asked my father what I should select. I think he realized I always felt trapped between my older sisters and my younger brothers—who tended to act like older brothers with me. So he recommended as my motto 'Washite majiwarazu.'" The words, Tami explained, meant that she should try to get along with others but always follow her own way and think for herself.

Matsuura patriarchs were not only heads of their own house but pater-familias to their villagers as well. Over the centuries, successive Matsuura househeads had come to think of their role as village heads no longer as a contractually specific job, an elected office, or even a bureaucratic post, but as a hereditary right, a moral obligation, and indeed a natural state of affairs. The Matsuura viewed their family as coterminous with Yamashiraishi; in their minds, the village was an extension of their household, an organic cooperative arrangement, not simply an administrative unit that could be drawn on the map of a distant government official. In the eyes of the villagers, too, the Matsuura patriarch was the *oya,* or parent, of Yamashiraishi, as the village priest in the 1990s explained.[15] Former family servants described the village head as the *oyakata,* the master or patron who preserved peace and order in the village.[16]

These sentiments, of course, papered over the very real economic relationship that had emerged over time between the village head and the villagers who were in a subordinate position to him. The Matsuura family, already very wealthy by 1800, probably acquired even more land as a result of the new tax system implemented by the Meiji government. They owned much of the land in Yamashiraishi and two nearby villages, and they maintained storehouses in Shirakawa. Tenants and servants were beholden to the family, whose wealth translated into power. Nevertheless, labor relations between the Matsuura and their tenants and servants were cast in the form of mutual obligation and responsibility, typical of the Tōhoku region.[17]

Paternalistic familism ensured that in years of poor harvest, when village farmers could not pay their rent to the Matsuura, the househead laid out the money for them. In Yūya's case, his oldest granddaughter, Mina, claimed, "He never refused any request. He was a bank." Although Yūya may have charged interest for these loans, as was the practice among other village heads and large landholders, another granddaughter, Fuki, implied that he did not expect to be repaid and did not pressure debtors. She went on to explain, "You never knew when they would come with the money. Sometimes they would come late at night."

The Matsuura family also took the teenage children of poorer villagers into their home to work as servants. They became members—lesser members, to be sure—of the Matsuura household, sleeping in the same room as family members or, as was the case with the sake employees, bedding down in the loft above the kitchen. According to one of Yūya's granddaughters, the servants who worked as baby-tenders and nursemaids of her and her siblings were like older sisters. This group of servants was fed, dressed, trained, and married off by the mistress of the house in a feudalistic pattern of relationships that evolved over time and extended to other villagers who worked as cultivators or tenants on the family's land. Servants even participated in festivities honoring Matsuura ancestors during the village-wide Buddhist O-bon festivities.

When wealthy village heads neglected their obligations, or at least appeared negligent or greedy in the eyes of their villagers, the myths sustaining social harmony were broken, and the villagers rebelled. In times of natural disasters in particular, the headman was expected to demonstrate paternalistic benevolence. Such was the case in the late eighteenth century during the time of Yūemon, the fourth-generation Matsuura patriarch.

—

Throughout the summer of 1783, Mt. Asama, the active volcano eighty miles northwest of Edo, intermittently belched smoke and ash until finally, on August 4, it exploded with a horrifically loud roar. For four days the volcano spewed lava and threw up ash and rock that fell on the crops of three provinces.

The abnormal weather that followed afflicted regions as far north as Fukushima. Damaged harvests and crop failures resulted in widescale food shortages and mass starvation, the Great Tenmei Famine, throughout the remainder of the decade. The center of the famine was northeastern Japan, where it was reported that nearly half of the population died. Shirakawa domain was hit especially hard. Villagers in some areas reportedly resorted to eating bark, digging up roots, and even consuming their work animals.[18] Hungry rural populations seething with anger broke into the storehouses of the wealthy.[19] As the situation worsened, domain officials confronted a "living hell" of rotting corpses and lawlessness. Stories of cannibalism circulated.[20]

The new military governor of Shirakawa supervised a massive relief effort for his domain, which had lost nearly all its rice crop in 1783. Using his family connections with the Tokugawa main house, the governor, Matsudaira Sadanobu, bought rice from other parts of Japan and distributed it to his vassals and villagers during the famine of the 1780s. He took many other measures to assist the peasants, such as canceling land taxes and making medicine available.[21] Unlike the nearby domain of Sōma, where eighty-five hundred people perished, starvation was averted in Shirakawa.[22]

Villages near Yamashiraishi, now located in Echigo-Takada domain, were less fortunate and lost sizable proportions of their populations, in some cases as many as 30 percent. Two of the six villages in a league under Matsuura stewardship were particularly hard hit. By 1802, Itabashi's population had declined from 492 to 353, and Satoshiraishi's from 405 twenty-five years earlier to 267. The smallest village was down to only ninety-six people.

In contrast, Yamashiraishi lost only one person between 1775 and 1805. Moreover, most of its villagers were still landholders. Only 19 of the 107 households did not own their own land.[23] Isami credited the villagers' re-markable ability to survive one of the blackest times in Tokugawa history to the benevolent leadership of his family's head at the time. Yūemon, he wrote, "was a great man. He supported the village and its recovery."[24]

In the twilight of Yūemon's life, he and his heir took at least two steps to help their villagers. In response to their own domainal authorities' efforts to spark relief initiatives at the local level, the two men secured a loan of twenty *ryō* (gold coins) from Echigo-Takada officials to start a cotton weav-ing project in Yamashiraishi. Also, in 1796, five years after Yūemon's death, his heir and eighty other signatories, including other league headmen, signed a document that vowed to meet their villages' tax assessment by paying the taxes of those farmers who could not afford to cover their share.[25]

Such paternalistic benevolence seems scarcely to have diminished the Mat-suura family treasury. By the fourth generation their business activities had expanded beyond sake; they were also engaged in the lucrative manufac-ture and sale of soy sauce and other agricultural and craft products. When Yūemon died in 1791, he left a generous inheritance to his only son, who went on to become the most prosperous of the early Matsuura households. But while the Matsuura family thrived through its first four generations, the village as a whole fared less well.

Although the population of Yamashiraishi remained stable in the years immediately following the volcanic eruption, it had been dropping before the family founder, Yajibei, entered the village, and it further declined by over 15 percent in the sixty-five years afterward. By the middle of the eigh-teenth century, it was down to 521, with 294 males and 227 females.[26] And whereas the Matsuura household still had nine members, the average household in the village, as well as elsewhere in Japan in the eighteenth cen-tury, averaged only four to six persons.[27]

Isami's account of this era never considered the possibility that his ancestors were getting rich at the expense of their villagers. He attributed the population decline simply to the proliferation of various taxes levied by greedy domain governors on not only rice but also persimmons, roof thatch, rope, lacquer, and horses.[28] There was no question, however, that the fourth-generation Yūemon's prosperity had helped to solidify his family's position as members of the rural elite—large landholders as well as entrepreneurs who served as virtually hereditary headmen in the countryside and whose economic assets and lifestyles set them above the ordinary peasant.

Yūemon was the beneficiary of the wealth, status, and privilege attained by the work of the first three generations of Matsuura. He earned additional status privileges and enjoyed scholarly opportunities, which further cemented the family's rural elite standing and enabled them to emulate the military aristocracy while distancing themselves from common peasants. In his time, the Matsuura family name also became legally inheritable.[29] In addition, in 1774 domain authorities, hoping to encourage the family's continued cooperation, bestowed a sword on Yūemon, which suggested, if not honorary samurai status, then certainly "pseudo-samurai pretensions,"[30] even though officially the family remained members of the commoner class. Further status privileges came in a 1776 certification of commendation signed by three officials awarding Yūemon permission to keep two servants.[31]

More honors and responsibilities followed. In 1778, five years before Mt. Asama erupted, Yūemon became the first Matsuura to serve as league headman, or *ōjōya* (literally, "great headman"). The six villages under his stewardship, including Yamashiraishi, had a combined population of two thousand people at the time of the eruption.[32] In his father's time, another Yamashiraishi family head had served in this leadership position, which entailed channeling communication between the headmen of a number of villages and the intendant.[33]

The additional recognition of the fourth generation's Yūemon as a man of culture, learning, and literary talent further reflects the social distance that had grown between wealthy village heads and peasants by the middle of the eighteenth century. From the days of the Matsuura founding ancestor in the late 1600s, literacy had been a basic prerequisite for serving in village office and an expected virtue of village heads' wives as well. The ability to read, to write (preferably in a graceful hand), and to make arithmetical calculations was necessary for managing the extensive paperwork and record-keeping inherent in the job. Beyond mere minimal literacy, Yūemon laid claim to the sort of classical learning that contributed to the village head's prestige by enabling him to assume the cultural style of the ruling samurai class, who were not only the political and military elite, but supposedly the moral and cultural leaders as well. Book learning, mainly derived from Chinese sources and confined largely to the samurai class in the early years of Tokugawa rule, later became available to commoners who could afford it, and it contributed to their upward social mobility, if not legally, then culturally, just as formal schooling in the modern period, when fixed social classes were abolished, would carry Isami's children out of the countryside and into the middle class.

—

"Father did not like stupid children," Isami's third daughter, Fuki, recalled. Mathematics was one of his strong suits, and he made the children practice their sums every day before letting them go out to play, occasionally hitting them if they made mistakes.

The family's large living room, in addition to serving as a playground and sleeping quarters for the children, also served as a study hall to supplement their public school education. During study hours, either Kō or Isami sat on the tatami behind the legless wooden desk placed in one corner of the room and, like teachers, doled out assignments for the children to complete. The older ones might read from the writings of the agrarian reformer Ninomiya Sontaku (1787–1856), known as the Peasant Sage of Japan for his efforts to improve farmers' lives, while the younger children might practice drawing an apple.[34]

Isami's children came to respect his learning, acquired by schooling and avid reading. His daughters, in particular, became lifelong learners, taking classes, studying foreign languages, and reading well into their old age. Among Isami's interests were novels, including foreign works in translation. His eldest daughter, Mina, recalled the death of a famous Meiji novelist in 1917, when she was thirteen. "Father called out excitedly, 'Natsume Sōseki has died!' I thought it was a relative of ours." Kō, who had trouble keeping up with her husband's worldly knowledge, tried to educate herself by asking him to explain unfamiliar terms to her, such as *jury system* and others associated with Western political institutions introduced into Japan.[35]

The Matsuura children began their formal schooling in the village primary school. Modern for its day, it was a two-story wooden building with a veranda, originally built by Isami's great-grandfather Daisuke on family property near their house. Students carried their books in cloth squares, called *furoshiki,* and came to school dressed in traditional country clothing:

kimono made of indigo-dyed blue and white cotton *kasuri* cloth and wooden clogs *(geta)* on their feet.[36]

In their first five years in primary school, children learned arithmetic and the phonetic Japanese writing system. They also acquired the discipline needed to memorize the hundreds of Chinese characters required for literacy. Before leaving the classroom at the end of the day, the children had to consult a dictionary to look up unfamiliar Chinese ideographs from the day's lesson.

The public primary school was the passion of the Matsuura children's grandfather and Isami's father, Yūya, although he had been privately tutored as a child. Yūya had been an indifferent student when young, but his interest in education increased by the time he was a grown man. As village head, he presided over the annual graduation ceremonies for the twenty-five to thirty graduates.

The Matsuura commitment to educating the young even involved subsidizing the advanced education of worthy village youth and extended-family members. As Yūya assumed more of a leadership role in the 1890s, he took steps to promote educational opportunities for local youth, like his father and grandfather before him. Yūya generously contributed funds for local schools in the spirit of benevolent paternalism expected of local notables. He donated money to purchase books for a private school built by the mayor of the nearby town of Ishikawa and thereafter made annual monetary contributions to it. When the mayor took sick toward the end of the Meiji period, he asked Yūya to oversee its management, and toward the end of that period, it succeeded in acquiring official accreditation as a private middle school.[37]

Yūya and his wife, Miyo, even agreed, albeit reluctantly, to finance their son-in-law's advanced studies. Their daughter Moto's husband, Ishii Itarō, was Miyo's nephew and Moto's cousin. Despite these close family ties, neither Yūya nor Miyo was pleased with their twenty-four-year-old son-in-law's decision to quit his job with the South Manchuria Railway in 1911, at the time of his marriage, in order to study for the diplomatic service examinations. Determined to win entrance into the Foreign Ministry, he studied on his own at the public library in the Ueno district of Tokyo. Even after failing the examination on his first try, he pleaded with his in-laws to continue providing assistance. By this time he was the father of an infant son. He explained that he was at a disadvantage because the vast majority of successful candidates had graduated from Tokyo Imperial University, whereas he had graduated from Fukushima middle school and then gone to Shanghai to attend the East Asia Common Culture Institute (Tōa dōbun shoin), a school funded by the Japanese government to train China specialists.[38]

Their son-in-law's ambitious goals and the Matsuura's patience with him eventually paid off: on his second try, in 1915, Ishii Itarō became the first graduate of the Shanghai school to enter the Foreign Ministry by examination. Ishii launched a career in the diplomatic service that took him and Moto overseas to San Francisco, Washington, DC, and London in the 1920s and eventually earned him an ambassadorship.[39] For Isami, at least, the dazzling success of his brother-in-law demonstrated the value of investing in his own children's education even to the point of depleting family assets.

The way Isami handled a village scandal after he became village head illustrates the responsibility that he, too, assumed for the education and moral training not only of his own brood but of other village young as well. The scandal involved the family of the village priest, whose marriage Isami had helped arrange. This priest was the twenty-first-generation heir in a family of hereditary priests who had officiated at the Zen Buddhist temple that Matsuura househeads had supported since the days of their earliest ancestor, Yajibei. When the priest died at a relatively early age, his despondent widow, described by one of Isami's daughters as "mannish looking," developed a consuming and unrequited passion for the young, married, village schoolteacher. Increasingly depressed, she took to her bed. On the night of the summer O-bon festival, when the spirits of dead ancestors are thought to return temporarily to earth, she disappeared. Her body was found at the bottom of a well near the temple.

The woman's son, now orphaned, appeared unsure whether he wanted to continue his family's tradition as hereditary priests of the temple. He began associating with an unruly group of boys at his Ishikawa middle school, resulting in his grades suffering. Isami took the troubled youth aside and urged him, in effect, to pull himself together and be more stouthearted. His message of tough love was accompanied by concrete arrangements to have the boy study at a large Zen Buddhist monastery in Yokohama. Presumably Isami paid the costs. The boy returned to take over his father's position as village priest and remained forever grateful to Isami, whom he viewed as a surrogate father.[40]

—

The support of formal schooling was only one aspect—a more modern one—of the paternalistic role assumed by house and village heads as political functionaries. In a variety of ways, the more conscientious of the early Matsuura patriarchs had traditionally also provided an economic safety net of sorts for poorer members of the village. They made jobs available in the family's enterprises, assembled peasants' village crafts and agricultural products for the market, guided land reclamation projects, lent money, and, above all, attempted to buffer the impact of tribute exactions, often by paying extra levies with their own monies. By their acts of noblesse oblige, they had preserved the loyalty of villagers for over a century when, toward the very end of the eighteenth century, under the fifth-generation Matsuura patriarch, the situation abruptly changed.

Throughout the Fukushima area the number of peasant protests of various kinds steeply rose in the eighteenth century.[41] One major uprising in the last years of the century centered on Asakawa. This time the Matsuura were not spared. Theirs was the only house in the village attacked by the rioters. The family's increasingly visible wealth and identification with merchantlike, nouveaux-riches commerce had made them and other wealthy rural businesses the potential target of poor peasants' organized protests in times of distress.

A ten-day spree of rioting by three thousand farmers in the Asakawa area in January 1798—nine years after the French Revolution—brought a crowd to the Matsuura family's door on the morning of January 26. The fifth-generation patriarch, also called Yūemon (though his name was not written with the same characters as his deceased father's), had left with his wife and mother several days before; only family servants and a "young couple" remained at home. Rampaging peasants spilled out large amounts of the sake manufactured on the grounds of the family's compound and damaged other property as well. In Satoshiraishi—one of the villages in the league under Matsuura leadership—they damaged the home of a neighborhood group *(kumi)* leader and two households engaged in horsetrading before ending their rioting in the town of Asakawa.[42] In all, eighty-nine households and two temples were damaged by the rioters.

Peasant protestors did not harm any of the occupants, which was typical of such outbursts elsewhere as well. Destructive rampages, called *uchikowashi* (literally, "house-smashing") were directed at the goods and homes of wealthy rural families, and they had sporadically erupted in the countryside when the majority of the population, infuriated by rising prices, vented their anger at business establishments in controlled acts of violence, spilling sake but not blood. Although these rampages erupted throughout Japan, Fukushima was a particularly disturbance-prone region in the Tokugawa period.[43]

Vulnerable establishments took steps to protect themselves by hiring additional security guards to surround their house and reinforce their regular defense staff. Even women were mobilized to protect property. The wife of a samurai named Itō Jinzaemon, "a very brave woman" according to one narrative of the event, "was ready to fight with a long sword."[44] Still, the more privileged rural dwellers were vastly outnumbered by aggrieved peasants who knew how to organize their uprisings and articulate their grievances.

Nevertheless, one wonders why the Matsuura, having helped their villagers survive famine and economic hard times following the eruption of Mt. Asama in the previous decade, lost the loyalty of this turn-of-the-century generation of peasants. The family chronicler, Isami, did not bother to ask this question. Shrugging off the January 26th incident, he commented that, since the family was in the middle of rebuilding the house after a fire in the previous year, the damage was minimal. Ironically, the incident was launched by an ominous secret letter titled "Hi no yōjin" (Precautions against fire), which had been distributed to each of the twelve leagues of villages under the Asakawa administrative office.[45]

The letter accused the twelve Asakawa league headmen and numerous horse traders of "selfish, unfair and greedy procedures for collecting money" at horse markets. Pack horses were used to transport cargo and were therefore a valuable commodity; in Yamashiraishi alone there were about eighty horses at the time of the riot.[46] Private brokers handling cargo shipping by pack horses were often among the wealthiest members of their village, and their wealth was visible. Their business required a sizable landholding with storage space for cargo; a wide courtyard easily accessible for pack drivers and their horses; and a large house, where business was conducted.[47] In addition to those involved in the horse trade, the crowd attacked the houses of six officials overseeing the provision of the labor and animals needed for the post-station system, which transported official retinues and cargo on relay horses.

The Matsuura wasted little time in rebuilding after the riot, though they built their new house on a smaller scale than originally planned because, according to Isami, the rioters had sawed up the lumber that the family had planned to use. As if to minimize his family's responsibility, Isami also noted that the rioters were probably outsiders who had not come from Yamashiraishi: there were several groups of them, and they had converged on Yamashiraishi from elsewhere.[48]

Another motivation for the Matsuura to rebuild at a smaller size, however, may have been that they knew the peasants resented the way prosperous families showed off their wealth and exploited poorer farm families.[49] A contemporary account of the incident blamed the disturbance directly on greedy village headmen who "took advantage of their position and did not pay for services they received from the farmers."[50] This narrative, written from the point of view of the farmers, explains that they had to "pay all kinds of money for different kinds of unreasonable demands" made by merchants and village heads (often one and the same). "Merchants and *shōya* made all kinds of excuses to get money from peasants." Such unfair treatment, the narrative continued, placed farm households in straitened economic circumstances even before the unusually cold and windy weather of 1797 damaged their rice seeds, which led to a poor harvest. They had tried unsuccessfully to plant a second crop, but it was too late in the season and the seeds grew poorly.[51]

Desperate farmers had petitioned at least three times for the twelve Asakawa league headmen, Yūemon among them, to ask local authorities to inspect their fields in order to qualify for tax relief. Rather than siding with them, league headmen, who served in intermediate positions between the heads of several villages and the local authorities, "did not go along with the petition."[52] More infuriating, when the intendant finally came out to investigate the harvest, he told the farmers to pay "thank you" money *(myō-gakin)*, a sum given to the authorities as an expression of gratitude for being granted a privilege or special protection, often pertaining to business interests.[53] A change in the local tax commissioner at this point had given farmers hope for tax relief, but the league headmen, instead of helping them take advantage of the new official's arrival on the scene, urged the farmers not to petition again, arguing that such a request would be inopportune. In the end, the league headmen collected more rice taxes.

The object of the farmers' rage, for the most part, was not domain officials of samurai rank, however, but the village and league headmen of their own status group. The farmers were furious that village leaders, rather than protecting them, had caved in to higher-ups. In particular, the peasants claimed they had endured many injustices at the hands of "persons with the titles of league headmen." They even accused league headmen of "peasant bullying" and pocketing an extra assessment of eight hundred bales *(hyō)* of rice claimed to have been levied by the regional intendant's office but in reality "used by league headmen for their own expenses."[54]

The disturbance ended after the intendant reluctantly called out fifteen hundred soldiers from surrounding domains, who needed two days to suppress it. Several peasant leaders were executed, and domainal officials, including the commissioner, who had arrived on the scene only one month earlier, were punished with salary reductions.[55]

Nevertheless, the Matsuura survived their ordeal and emerged from the Asakawa disturbances with their leadership role bloodied but still intact. In the eyes of poorer farmers at least, the family held the ambivalent status of both exploiters and saviors, parasitic landlords and paternalistic local officials, venal merchants and wage-paying employers, lenders and leaders on whom the villagers had come to depend.

Matsuura househeads were far more elevated in status than they had been a century earlier, when the humble founder of the lineage first moved into the village at the request of its residents to serve as their head in accordance with a legal agreement whose terms they had carefully delineated. By the early nineteenth century, the Matsuura position as village heads was virtually unchallenged, the family's wealth considerable, and their power over other villagers' lives sufficient to make them seem more like domainal officials than common peasants serving provisionally at the behest of other peasants. Yet, precisely this combination of wealth and widespread social connections made them valuable spokesmen for village causes.

The Matsuura had joined the growing ranks of Japan's well-to-do rural entrepreneurs, or gōnō (literally, "wealthy farmers")—though they were not called by this term until a later date. Such "families of means" were not only large landholders and local magnates, but they were businessmen developing cottage industries and growing crops to sell on the country's expanding market.[56] Their products were especially in demand to feed a growing population of urban dwellers in cities such as Edo, the shogun's capital; Kyoto, the ancient capital where the emperor dwelled; Osaka, the country's entrepôt; and the towns that grew up around the castles of each of the 260 or so domain lords. Typically, gōnō also engaged in moneylending activities, and, of course, they had close ties with the political elite. Their local influence, connections, learning, and the knowledge gleaned from their contacts with relatives and interactions with other village heads and samurai officials proved useful to the village in dealings with higher authorities and other village heads, with whom they regularly negotiated.

One petition in the early 1790s captures the role of the Matsuura village heads as intermediaries in the chain of command between their fellow villagers and domain officialdom. A young village man requested Yūemon's permission to work at a sake brewery outside Yamashiraishi. Authorities tried to prevent peasants from leaving their land, because they depended on the rice tax for their own revenues. The young man wrote that his father was in financial trouble; both he and his brother had to find wage-paying labor because they could not survive by farming. Another petition, signed by the members of his neighborhood group, sided with the young man, arguing that his absence would not affect his family's ability to keep farming and promising to take care of his land while he was gone.[57]

Another example of the village head's role as intermediary occurred six years after the riots. Yūemon's heir, the sixth-generation Yūemon Jinsuke, attempted to present the Asakawa intendant with an appeal for tax reduction from the villages under his leadership, when two farm wives boldly bypassed their own village head and Yūemon Jinsuke and made a direct appeal to the intendant at his headquarters. He apologized on their behalf to the officials and reported that he had given strict orders to representatives of their village never again to disregard the established political hierarchy. His actions presumably saved the women from further recriminations.[58]

The village head's job also involved the sensitive task of helping to raise money in the form of donations to pay for extraordinary expenses, such as repairs of local buildings. Yūemon Jinsuke took up a collection from eighty-nine headmen and twelve fellow chief headmen to repair the intendant's headquarters in Asakawa, which had been damaged by fire, and he also collected money for repair of the Shinto shrine roof.

Other activities of an official nature seen as benefiting the villagers required the village head in 1806 to engage in local boosterism by distributing various awards and commendations. In one example, he wrote a certificate honoring a ninety-two-year-old farmer for his "ripe old age," only to submit a written notice shortly thereafter of the same farmer's sudden demise. He also wrote apologies on behalf of several village leaders and a farmer who unknowingly lent a horse suffering from a tumor to Asakawa township for mating purposes.

Further official business involved a decision to grant one villager's request to cut down 150 pine trees (woodland surrounding a village was communally owned) and to sign an appeal from another farm family who asked for permission to reduce their rice tax because their second son was "getting a wife," and therefore they would have an extra mouth to feed.[59]

Petitions addressed to the Matsuura from villagers shortly before and after the Asakawa uprisings poignantly convey the sense of dependence on the family's goodwill and their exalted position in the eyes of poor farmers around 1800. One year after the Asakawa riots, a Matsuura servant named Hanzō was expelled from the household for misbehaving. By his own account he had become drunk and unruly and had been rude to his parents.

Scolded once before by Yūemon, he had failed to reform. Worse, he had discharged a firearm. How Hanzō came into possession of the gun and used it has gone unrecorded. Although firearms were strictly regulated, most villages, especially in the north, possessed muskets, carefully guarded by the headman, registered with the authorities, and lent out for protection against wild animals, such as boar, which could destroy crops and threaten villagers as well.[60]

In his appeal to Yūemon, who was not only his village head but also his employer and surrogate parent, Hanzō promised, once again, to reform his behavior. He also apologized to his father and to the members of his neighborhood group and promised to behave like a filial son, curb his drinking, and not fire his gun. Instead of asking to be taken back into the Matsuura household, the contrite young man, supported by his father and members of his neighborhood group in separate written appeals, requested permission to go elsewhere in search of work, signaling both his contrition and deference to Yūemon's power over him by his desperate words: "I'll do whatever you tell me to do."[61]

FOUR

Strong Wives

"*TAIHEN! TAIHEN!* SOMETHING AWFUL HAS HAPPENED!" At the sound of ten-year-old Tami's cries, household members rushed out to the garden, where only minutes before, her grandmother Miyo had been weeding. In her early seventies, Isami's mother faithfully worked in the garden every morning in the summertime, just as the servants cleaned house before eating their first meal of the day. To teach her youngest granddaughter good work habits, Miyo had also awakened Tami early every morning so that she could weed before the school day began. But on this day, ignoring Isami's advice not to exert herself, Miyo had gone out on an especially hot day, and around noon, feeling ill, she had sat down on the veranda of the cottage, too weak to go inside. "Bring me a glass of wine," she said to Tami, but after taking only one sip, she toppled over, motionless. Paralyzed by a massive stroke, Miyo also became mentally incompetent and delusional, claiming to see Kabuki actors in the garden. Until her death a decade later, she was confined to a specially built bed placed in the cottage and under the care of a nurse.[1]

Seeing his wife physically and mentally incapacitated after half a century of life with her, Yūya grew despondent and died three years later, in his seventy-seventh year. "Even though he had a fever," wrote Isami, who had been in Tokyo at the time, "he insisted on taking a bath," and he contracted pneumonia. Isami had rushed back to the village after receiving a telegram reporting that his father was gravely ill, but he could do nothing to save him. His father, Isami implied, had lost the will to live without his wife.[2]

Even in her old age, Miyo had tried to make herself useful. True, she was vain about her appearance. After bathing she would carefully splash her body with an astringent made of lemon peel soaked in sake. But, as the former mistress of the household, despite its wealth, she was accustomed to work. Although servants did much of the manual labor in well-to-do farm families such as the Matsuura, the mistress of the household was the "chief," as

Tami explained, and the successful management of domestic life depended on her. She instructed servants, often not much older than children themselves, in domestic skills. Miyo had trained her daughter-in-law Kō, who now trained the oldest servant girl and relied on her to break in new house servants. The servants, children of poor village families, came to live with the family around the age of eleven, after graduating from primary school, and they needed a great deal of instruction.

Like her mother-in-law Miyo before her, Kō had to wash the servants' hair (removing the lice), supervise their morals, and teach them manners and respect for authority, which included knowing their place. They called the mistress of the house by the respectful title "*okami-sama*," and at night the servant girls massaged her shoulders. In return she provided gifts of clothing twice a year. In the summer they received a lightweight summer kimono (*yukata*) and clogs (*geta*), purchased from the itinerant *geta*-maker, who came to the house with a big pack on his back. At the end of the year they received a kimono. Servants typically stayed in the house until they married, and Kō and Isami brokered their marriages. If the mistress did not herself possess the skills and managerial talent necessary for running a large household and performing these diverse tasks, then, according to the common wisdom, the family would flounder.

Family members and their servants made most of the goods they used; living in their remote mountain village, they could purchase very little. The closest town, Asakawa, was two and one-half miles away, and the sole means of transportation was walking. "If somebody entered the village in a cart, we all came out to stare," recalled Tami of her childhood days in the late 1920s.

The work of the female servants varied and was frequently strenuous. They sewed, mended, and washed clothes; made shoes for family members (poorer villagers made their own); cleaned the house; weeded the garden; helped in the kitchen; and served food. Twice a year they replaced the rice paper in the sliding doors (*shōji*), and for weddings and other receptions, they removed the sliding partitions separating rooms to make more space for the large number of guests.

At any one time, three or four servants and an equal number of nursemaids resided with the family. The nursemaids bathed and dressed the younger ones. Young male servants grew vegetables, cultivated tobacco, and worked as porters, carrying luggage on their backs to the train station, hauling dried tobacco leaves to market, and delivering messages and running other errands.

These multiple tasks required time-consuming supervision. Kō showed the young female servants how to remake collars, seams, and other well-used parts, such as the seat, to get maximum wear out of clothes. When she could no longer repair a kimono, she made it into a jacket. Although she was the main cook in the household, she also gave cooking lessons to servant girls, who assisted her in the large earth-floored kitchen on the west side of the house. She showed them first how to light a fire under pots and then advanced to instructions for specific dishes, such as beanpaste soup *(misoshiru):* "Do not let the water boil!"

Meals, while simple in comparison with the foreign delicacies enjoyed by Isami's children in their adult years in Tokyo, were certainly more than adequate for the time: rice, beanpaste soup flavored with potatoes and vegetables, salted fish, boiled burdock, pickled vegetables, and fruits. Eggs came from chickens raised on the grounds. Kō grew watermelons and strawberries, planting them herself with the help of the servants. (The watermelons were huge, and one year, during the summer Buddhist celebration of O-bon, when villagers stayed up late dancing and celebrating, somebody stole all of them.) Kō also prepared Isami's favorite dish, *udon* (wheat noodles), and, as a special treat for the children in the summertime, she served *onigiri* (triangular or cylindrically shaped cold white rice balls) dipped in soy sauce.

In the winter months, beanpaste soup was the major staple. Kō made the soybean paste (miso) by fermenting the beans in salt and leaven for six months to a year. The miso, stored in large barrels in one of the family's storehouses, kept for two or three years, whereas miso today, as Tami remarked, keeps for only six months. Kō also preserved whole salmon by buying it fresh, thoroughly salting every part, including the innards, and burying it in the ground, where the snow kept it frozen all winter. Slices cut off throughout the winter served as a tasty supplement to an otherwise bland diet.

Family meals were also supplemented with raw potatoes and radishes, which were likewise buried and stored in a deep hole. As the snow fell, the hole served as a refrigerator, preserving a supply of vegetables throughout the winter. The children tasted fresh fish, beef, and cow's milk for the first time only after moving to Tokyo.[3]

Isami and Kō's children were drilled in the values of frugality, hard work, respect for elders, and studiousness. Although the family's sons were not required to learn farming, the daughters absorbed the lessons taught to the household servants, acquiring the same practical skills, such as how to take creases out of a blouse by patting it and other ways of caring for clothing. There was even a special way to wash, fold, and store a *yukata*. Tami recited the steps she had learned some sixty years earlier: "You washed it in a large pot set outside the house. The maids burned wood to heat a fire under the pot. When the water was hot, you washed the collar first, then the hem, then one side, then the other, and then the back part. To store it, you removed the lining and laid everything flat in a wood drawer. It lasted longer this way, and when you took it out, it looked like new." Through her domestic skills, the househead's wife was essential to the continuity of the family line and the well-being of the current generation. The househead's wife, in Tami's words, "protected the *ie*."

—

The sixth generation's househead was "unlucky with wives," wrote Isami, who considered himself a very lucky husband.[4] Isami was referring to the Matsuura family's first adopted son, who replaced the family's disabled heir and in his adult years was renamed Yūemon, like his adoptive father, with the added name of Jinsuke on official documents to avoid confusion. Judging from these documents, we can surmise that Yūemon Jinsuke was a conscientious and energetic leader and, as such, a good choice as heir in the early nineteenth century, following the Asakawa riots, when the village head's duties were becoming more complicated and time-consuming. Nevertheless, in his personal life all was not well.

Preoccupied from the very beginning of his new life in the Matsuura family with serious official duties and with the management of Matsuura lands and commercial activities, Yūemon Jinsuke was confronted with a punishing series of personal and domestic trials that tested him to the utmost in the first decade of the nineteenth century and almost led to the dissolution of his adoptive family.

First, into his thirties, Yūemon Jinsuke and his wife were childless. Couples in the Northeast typically married young—around twenty-two for men and seventeen for women—and women completed their childbearing years by around thirty.[5] However, Yūemon Jinsuke had joined the Matsuura household when he was already in his late twenties, and his wife, the niece of his adoptive mother, had entered when she was twenty-three. Either she was unable to conceive immediately after her marriage, or she miscarried. The couple's awkward circumstances—neither had grown up in the Matsuura household, and they were strangers to each other as well—may have contributed to their fertility problems. In 1807, however, at the late age of thirty, Mitsu succeeded in giving birth to a son.

Although Yūemon Jinsuke now had some assurance of a male heir, he still faced another problem, this one interfering with his ability to carry out his official duties. By a perverse quirk of fate, he developed a painful leg ailment that seems curiously similar to the disability of the disinherited heir he had replaced, although there was no genetic connection.[6] In July 1806, he filed a written request for permission to visit a specific hot springs for medicinal purposes, explaining that he was ill and naming the two people who would handle business while he was away.[7]

Yūemon Jinsuke's ailment severely limited his ability to carry out his official responsibilities. Although the village headman typically conducted business in his home, certain matters required him to travel on foot elsewhere to meet with other headmen and officials at the intendant's office in town. In the short period of three months in 1805, Yūemon Jinsuke made at least seventeen trips to Asakawa, usually staying for a few days each time. In 1806 he requested permission to travel to Echigo-Takada, the domain seat, saying he would be away for two months and asking Chōtoku Temple to handle business in his absence.[8] Even when at home, the village head had to move around the village, climbing its hilly terrain to meet with the local Buddhist priest or to oversee the rice tribute collection.

Yūemon Jinsuke's adoptive father shared some of these obligations with him, but another misfortune befell the family in 1808, when his father—the fifth generation's Yūemon—died at a relatively young age, leaving his heir, in his midthirties now, fully in charge of the household and the village. The worst blow was yet to come, however. In the same year as his adoptive father's death, his thirty-two-year-old wife died shortly after giving birth to their second son. Although a man of his stature should have been able to arrange another marriage so that he would have help in raising his infants, Yūemon Jinsuke waited eleven years before remarrying, choosing a woman whose family owned a business thirty miles away, in Kōriyama.[9]

The care of his two young sons must have been left largely to family servants or perhaps to the children's grandmother, though there is no mention of her in Isami's chronicle. Even wealthy and prominent families could not always be assured of a large enough household to carry on the work of reproduction from one generation to the next.

Meanwhile, Yūemon Jinsuke's official duties intensified when Yamashiraishi came directly under shogunal control as a Tokugawa territory *(bakufuryō)* sometime after 1808. When centralization occurred elsewhere in the region, villagers faced hardships in adjusting to new systems of tax payments enforced by the shogun's bureaucracy in Edo. Yamashiraishi must have confronted similar problems. Villages under direct Tokugawa control, for example, had to ship their rice tribute all the way to Edo instead of simply sending it to their domain's castle town. Moreover, whereas their domain lord might allow them to commute at least a portion of their rice tax to currency for ease of payment, the *bakufu* required them to transmit their rice tax in kind. This involved more expensive transportation costs.[10]

Yet another responsibility came to Yūemon Jinsuke in 1809, when he became the league headman, representing several villages and mediating between them and the local intendant, as his adoptive father had done.[11] Yūemon Jinsuke struggled to remain in office, expecting his firstborn son to replace him when he reached maturity, but as the two boys grew into early manhood, it became obvious that neither had turned out to be likely candidates for the role of Matsuura heir. The early loss of their mother and grandfather, the lack of a surrogate mother to oversee their upbringing, and the frequent absence of their father may explain the unruly behavior of the children. The older boy, Teizō, had a reputation for being *wagamama* (selfish); he merited the nickname *dada* (spoiled). In theory, Yūemon Jinsuke could have bypassed his firstborn son and groomed his younger son, Kenzō, for the headship, but Kenzō was even more headstrong than his older brother.

Yūemon Jinsuke decided to send the younger boy as an adopted son-in-law to his own natal family, which lacked a male heir. Kenzō, however, did not get along well with his adoptive family. In fact, he was so unhappy, he abandoned his wife and ran away to Sendai, where somehow he managed to win the hand of the daughter of a samurai. Before long he was "acting like a *rōnin*," or masterless samurai, instead of a peasant and talking about moving to the shogun's capital in Edo. He eventually settled down as a teacher in a Buddhist temple school on the way to Edo, and his wife taught sewing at home. His second wife probably did not know anything of his Yamashiraishi background. Estranged from the Matsuura and childless, he could hardly be of help to them in preserving the continuity of their family line, though he did redeem himself as a teacher; after his death, the local people dedicated a memorial stone tablet in his honor. As guardian of the family's reputation even into the distant past, Isami tried to persuade the prefectural officials to designate the memorial as a prefectural cultural treasure.[12]

Yūemon Jinsuke's older son proved totally unmanageable. Neither the boy's father, who was preoccupied with village affairs and increasingly disabled, nor the boy's stepmother, who came on the scene late in his childhood and produced no children of her own, could rein in the family's heir, whose undisciplined behavior failed to subside even after his early marriage, at around the age of seventeen.[13] Perhaps for this reason, Yūemon Jinsuke remained in office for seven more years after his son's marriage.

While still in office Yūemon Jinsuke fostered at least two projects designed to improve the village's economic viability. One was the introduction of tobacco as a cash crop in 1812;[14] the other, recorded in 1824, was the collection of portions of farmers' unhusked rice to store in a village public granary as security for years of bad harvest. Each of the approximately 120 households, including two with female househeads, contributed to this village savings bank.[15]

The project was well timed; in 1825 there was a bad harvest in the Asakawa region. This time village leaders petitioned the shogun's officials at the Asakawa office and, one year later, more boldly appealed directly to Edo for money loans. Six years earlier, in 1820, the long arm of the shogun's bureaucracy had reached into Asakawa, where the *bakufu* took over the administrative headquarters originally established by the regional lord of the Echigo-Takada domain.[16] Although the new administrator was "caring," as seen in his previous year's allocation of funds for child care, no significant amounts of money were earmarked for Asakawa farmers in the years following the disastrous 1825 and 1827 harvests. When two village heads, representing eighty-five villages, took the desperate step of directly petitioning one of the shogun's senior councilors *(rōjū)* on his way to the shogun's castle in Edo, they were arrested, though not severely punished.[17]

An increasingly incapacitated Yūemon Jinsuke, no longer able to cope with the duties of his office, especially during these distressing times, reluctantly yielded the headship of the family and village to his young profligate son in 1830. Barely able to walk, Yūemon Jinsuke opened a roadside retail store in Yamashiraishi, called Matsuya, which sold sundries. His second wife managed the store while his daughter-in-law was left trying to manage his son.

The village suffered further hardships in the decade that followed. The Zen Buddhist temple, built by the first Matsuura family head, burned down, and the countryside endured two more harvest shortfalls, one in 1833 and another in 1837, in the era named Tenpō. Desperate village petitions produced half-hearted responses from the shogun's local officials, who were often new to the scene. In one instance, the Asakawa intendant responded to the pleas of forty-three villages for assistance by encouraging them to help one another; to learn how to cook uncommon wild plants, such as bracken; and to eat nuts previously considered inedible, such as horse chestnuts and acorns.[18] By the 1830s the Tokugawa seemed bankrupt of money, ideas, and even common sense.

In this same decade—the waning era of Tokugawa rule—Yūemon Jinsuke's young and headstrong heir, renamed Kōemon, nearly succeeded in destroying the family's wealth and reputation, if not its very existence, by indulging almost obscenely in what Isami called his "manly tastes," which included a collection of firearms *(teppō)*. Kōemon's interest in guns was not connected to military pursuits or political ends but rather was fueled by a passion for material possessions. An inveterate collector, he also accumulated valuable furniture and artworks, including a screen by the famous sixteenth-century artist Kanō Eitoku. He indulged in other passions as well. Kōemon kept a woman companion, a rare behavior in itself, and he did not install her in his home, under the supervision of his official wife (the proper place for concubines), but kept her in the retirement quarters of the local Shinto priest.

Only Kōemon's premature death from a stomach ulcer in 1842, in his late thirties, saved the family from eventual insolvency. Even so, they came close to extinction, because he and his wife had only one child, a daughter named Kiyo. Moreover, Kōemon died in the same year as his stepmother of twenty years, leaving his father, Yūemon Jinsuke, alone and hobbled by his own medical problems.

Fortunately, before his death, the otherwise feckless Kōemon had arranged the adoption of a young man who would live with the Matsuura family, marry his daughter, assume the family surname, and become their heir. The boy destined to become the head of the Matsuura family's eighth generation was dispensable to his own biological family, who already had two sons, but essential to the survival of the Matsuura family line. Born in 1818 and named Daisuke, he was five years older than his wife, Kiyo. Daisuke became Isami's beloved great-grandfather and the first ancestor he came to know well.

Although Daisuke entered the Matsuura family as their son-in-law and heir, he was so badly treated by his father-in-law—the self-indulgent and hot-tempered Kōemon—that on several occasions he ran back to his own family in Sukagawa, twenty-four miles to the northwest. What helped Daisuke to tolerate his situation and persuaded him to stay was apparently the kindness of his mother-in-law, Chise, and her intervention in his behalf.[19]

Chise emerges as the earliest female member of the Matsuura family to be described in the family history with more than a few words and to be clearly identified by her surname (Arakawa) as well as her given name. She was born in 1807 in a village in present-day East Shirakawa county. Married at the age of fifteen and widowed young, she never remarried and continued to live in the family's household, evidently well treated, until her death in 1887, when Isami was eight. Her son-in-law, Daisuke, was probably the source of Isami's stories about her. One story narrates an incident that occurred in Daisuke's early days in the Matsuura household. One wintry night, after returning from his natal home, he discovered that he had lost a portion of the thirteen gold coins he had received from his family. Scolded by his father-in-law, the young man was rescued by Chise, who took him to the back of the house, where she replaced the coins with money from her own purse.[20]

Chise's access to money of her own despite the squandering tendencies of her husband raises intriguing questions about the position of women in the wealthy farm families of this time. Like other women who married into well-off farm families in her day, Chise probably arrived with a substantial dowry of clothing, hair ornaments, sewing equipment, other items of daily use, and coins that belonged to her even after her marriage.[21] Given her husband's poor health and equally poor character, it made good sense for her to side with her young son-in-law, who was only eleven years younger than she was and who would some day become head of her household and village head—as indeed Daisuke did, sooner than he expected.

In 1841, at the age of twenty-three, Daisuke was asked by villagers from Yamashiraishi and the neighboring village of Satoshiraishi to take over as their village head when Kōemon became seriously ill. After the death of his father-in-law the following year, Daisuke assumed Kōemon's name, and he immediately set out to revive the family's declining fortunes. With his wife's grandfather Yūemon Jinsuke as his mentor, he paid off debts by selling some of the household possessions and artwork that his father-in-law had acquired, though he chose not to sell the collection of guns, and he could not get the price he wanted for the Kanō screen.

Daisuke freed Yūemon Jinsuke to look forward to his retirement years with equanimity. The older man managed to find a compatible woman of his age and enjoyed "a relaxed life" with her on the grounds of the Matsuura property, without bothering to form a legal marriage bond. He pursued his literary and artistic interests, playing his *shamisen* (a three-stringed lute) and reading books from the bookshelves he had built in his earlier years, when he had dabbled in carpentry.

Meanwhile the popular adopted Matsuura heir, Daisuke, had good reason to feel satisfied with his life. An amiable, unaggressive man with a literary bent, Daisuke got along well with others, including Asakawa government officials. According to Isami, he "revived the offices of both village headman and league headman."[22] In his adoring great-grandson Isami's recollection of him, Daisuke had great powers of persuasion. In a nonthreatening manner he could "deal successfully with difficult problems and get people to agree."[23]

Daisuke certainly faced difficult problems. Not only famine but nationwide epidemics had contributed to a mortality crisis that reduced Japan's population by over 4 percent between 1834 and 1840.[24] Only seven households, in addition to the Matsuura, were listed on official village records as paying the annual tax on rice land in 1847.[25] The rest either no longer owned land or, if they did, simply could not come up with the rice and gold coins required to pay the tax. Another possibility, however, is that Daisuke came to the assistance of his distressed villagers, either by lending them money or by reducing their rent payments. These were typical practices expected of wealthy landlords in times of peasant distress, especially in the Northeast.

Even Kōemon, for all his faults, had aided the villagers in the final years of his life by somehow helping them to adjust to the new debased copper coin issued in great number by the Tokugawa government following the devastating period of crop failures in the 1830s.[26] The flood of new coins, along with other coinage debasement, reduced the value of copper coins, which were popular among peasants because they came in values small enough (roughly like pennies) to buy less expensive items without the need of cutting up and weighing silver ingots. The drop in the value of their money, as well as the poor rice harvests in the 1830s, left farmers scrambling to pay for necessary goods, such as cooking oil and services, like funeral ceremonies and the shipment of their rice to market.[27] In gratitude for Kōemon's assistance during this era of widespread rural unrest, villagers overlooked his faults and paid tribute to him on his tombstone.[28]

With the worst of the famine years behind them and Kōemon gone, the two villages under Daisuke's headship "settled down," according to Isami.[29] Daisuke looked forward to a peaceful life. The Matsuura household in the late 1840s contained eight people spanning four generations: the sixth generation's patriarch, Yūemon Jinsuke, and his woman companion; the widowed mother-in-law, Chise; the young househead, Daisuke, and his wife, Kiyo; and the young couple's three children. Although Kiyo was only twenty-six, she had already borne three healthy daughters, and in 1848 she was pregnant again. Yet, Kiyo's wifely virtues—fecundity and diligence—led to another totally unexpected family tragedy that once again threatened the survival of the Matsuura lineage and its role in village leadership.

Only three days after giving birth to the couple's fourth daughter in August 1848, Kiyo went out on a hot day to help with farmwork in the fields. It is unlikely that her physical labor in this *shōya* family was necessary so soon after giving birth. After all, she had the luxury of living with her own mother rather than with a demanding mother-in-law. Isami commented only that she "took a chance" or "acted unreasonably," as his own mother, Miyo, had done.[30] At any rate, she overexerted herself and, while drying grass for hay, to everyone's horror she suddenly collapsed and died. Like her paternal grandmother—Yūemon Jinsuke's first wife, who had also died soon after giving birth—she left behind young children and an older generation in need of care, as well as a grieving husband.

Kiyo's death nearly destroyed her thirty-year-old husband. Distraught and inconsolable, Daisuke began drinking heavily, and for the next few years the Matsuura family and the village of Yamashiraishi once again faced uncertain times at a perilous moment in Japan's history.

In the final stage of the long Tokugawa era, with civil uprisings and even foreign war looming over the land, the disconsolate Daisuke found another spouse. She turned his life around and helped him to ride out the revolutionary political challenges that lay ahead.

Daisuke's second wife was Moto. She was the ex-wife of Kenzō, the restless younger brother of Daisuke's deceased father-in-law. It was Kenzō who, unhappy as an adopted son-in-law in her family, had run off to Sendai and married the daughter of a samurai. Moto was the woman he left behind. She was therefore Daisuke's aunt, but only by a complex pathway of previous adoptions and marriages.

Eight years older than Daisuke, Moto helped raise Daisuke's four daughters "strictly," according to Isami, and, therefore, well. She also accommodated Chise, the grandmother of the girls and the mother of Daisuke's first wife. Chise, only a few years older than Moto, would live in the household for over three more decades. In the eyes of Isami, Moto "had a good head and fine character." By rescuing the grieving Daisuke, managing the household, and providing advice that helped him to become "a highly respectable person," Moto saved the Matsuura line and their position as village heads on the eve of the Tokugawa family's own demise as rulers of Japan.[31]

Ironically, neither Moto nor Daisuke was a blood relative of the Matsuura, and both had been victimized by Matsuura men of the preceding generation. Moreover, the man they chose to become their heir and the ninth Matsuura patriarch was, like themselves, not of Matsuura blood. Nevertheless, they were dedicated to the Matsuura family as well as to each other.

With four daughters and no son, Daisuke, in the late 1850s, decided to secure the continuity of the Matsuura family by selecting an adopted son-in-law for his second daughter, Yoshi. He bypassed his oldest daughter, because Yoshi's personality traits most resembled his own.[32] The young man picked as her husband and the Matsuura family's heir apparent was Daisuke's nephew and Yoshi's cousin, Jinsuke, renamed Kōemon, the third Matsuura patriarch to bear that name. He was the oldest son of Daisuke's second older brother, who owned a nail-making business in which Jinsuke had worked. The birth in 1860 of the young couple's first child, Yūya—Isami's father—assured the continuity of the family through the tenth generation and into the twentieth century, well beyond the destiny of the Tokugawa family, which was fighting to preserve its hereditary rule at the national level.

The marriage of Daisuke and Moto spanned the last years of the Tokugawa period and the first decades of Meiji. They had been married for about ten years when Moto accompanied Daisuke on their two-month sojourn to Edo, the seat of the shogunate in the waning days of Tokugawa rule. Although Daisuke had business to transact in the shogun capital in 1863, he and Moto were mainly traveling for pleasure, as though taking a delayed honeymoon or celebrating a wedding anniversary.[33]

There was a striking degree of compatibility between husband and wife in this marriage, the second for both. First and foremost, they both enjoyed good health, which was a prerequisite for making the trip to Edo. Travel in Japan in the 1860s was physically demanding, and all the more so in the Tōhoku region. The hardy couple—Daisuke was forty-five and Moto fifty-three—had to travel on foot (the country lacked wheeled carriages), occasionally renting horses during the eight-day trip. Leaving home in late February, they encountered frequent rainy days and a snowstorm that forced cancelation of sightseeing excursions along the way. Accompanied by a man named Tokusaburō, who was probably a servant, the three covered as many as seventeen miles on good days; in bad weather, ten. Once they traveled twenty-seven miles in one day. Their straw sandals *(waraji)* took such a beating that every few days each had to purchase another pair. Daisuke joked that he felt "bested" by Moto, who did not have any blisters, whereas he had twenty or thirty. At night in the inns where they stopped along the way, he asked her and Tokusaburō to massage his red, burning feet.

In addition to good health, the couple shared an interest in sightseeing.

On route to Edo, Daisuke and Moto lingered in Nikko for a day to view the ornate memorial-shrine dedicated to the first Tokugawa shogun, who had moved to Edo in 1600 and received his title from the emperor in 1603. Edo in those days had been a sleepy fishing village overlooking a natural bay and built around the site of the shogun's huge, moat-encircled castle. Over the years of Tokugawa rule, it had expanded to include the families and retainers of the more than two hundred overlords, required to maintain separate estates there under the nose of the shogun as part of the Tokugawa regime's elaborate system of controls. Merchants catering to the needs of the samurai class and to their own class's tastes in popular culture further swelled the population rolls and added to the liveliness of the city. By 1863 it was the world's largest city, with a population of one million.

Daisuke and Moto, though residents of the remote Tōhoku, were not exactly country bumpkins. After arriving in Edo, they enthusiastically toured many of the city's attractions. Their circle of friends and acquaintances included members of both the merchant and samurai classes, and they were invited to stay in the homes of several different people. One day the couple visited the home of an intendant who was hosting a friend of theirs. The friend's daughter entertained them with a Japanese harp *(koto)* performance— a mark of high breeding for young women. By the time of Daisuke's generation, the Matsuura households apparently felt comfortable hobnobbing with wealthy urban dwellers, including officials, and they drank appreciatively of urban culture, a taste they would pass on to their great-grandson Isami.

Popular entertainment was especially alluring to Moto. She and Daisuke trooped off to attend Kabuki and puppet theater performances, strolled around the Shinobazu pond in the Ueno area, and visited an acquaintance in the Asakusa region—a boisterous amusement quarter with a carnival atmosphere. When Daisuke was busy with his commercial dealings, Moto was independent enough to tour on her own or attend a theatrical performance with Tokusaburō and acquaintances they had met at inns along the way.

Included in the itinerary was a two-week pilgrimage to several well-known sites in the Sagami region—a walk of about three or four days along the Oyamadō, a major highway originating in Edo. Public pilgrimages to sacred places were a long-standing feature of Japanese life, and the sight of women on pilgrimages was common by the end of the Tokugawa period. In fact, one of the sacred places Moto and Daisuke visited was a shrine dedicated to the female deity Benzaiten. Moto's presence, however, was noteworthy at another site: Mt. Oyama, known for its Shingon Buddhist temple and summer festival of the Sekison Shrine. Few references exist to women visiting this mountain, and women were not allowed to climb to the Sekison Shrine at its summit, which was, at any rate, open to pilgrims only in the summer.[34] For these reasons, Moto and Daisuke limited themselves to paying homage to the popular Buddhist protector deity, Fudō, who was enshrined at Oyama, among many other places, and has been especially revered by travelers.

Pilgrims drew various benefits from the sacred mountains they visited. They shared a sense of community with other Japanese who visited sites associated with distinctively Japanese gods. A pilgrimage to a sacred mountain might involve a "purifying austerity," a spiritual renewal and cleansing.[35] Pilgrims might also seek blessings from the Shinto gods thought to dwell there. Daisuke mentioned none of these benefits or experiences in his journal entry, which may have lacked focus on spiritual renewal and cleansing because the trip was more about sightseeing than pilgrimage, judging from his observations.[36]

In the lively popular culture of the day, pilgrimage graded into tourism, with all the attendant complaints. Daisuke reported, for example, that the couple's hike was interrupted by a brief but heavy squall, during which Moto found it difficult to walk. But afterward, the sky cleared and they walked almost five miles to the Matsuya Inn, where they spent the night. He added that a party held at the inn prevented them from getting a good night's sleep. He failed to note any impressions of the temples, much less religious feelings connected with the pilgrimage, but he did record the amount of money he dropped—one *ryō*—in an offertory box at one shrine.

Within another year or two, pilgrimage would take on another purpose, when hoards of unruly pilgrims flocked to religious sites, and especially to the Ise Shrine complex in central Japan, to vent their anxieties in an era of increasing disunity and confusion.[37] But Daisuke and Moto seemed oblivious to the imminent demise of the Tokugawa system.

More typical of the matters occupying the couple's minds were their daily expenses. These Daisuke meticulously recorded in his journal. The young man whose father-in-law once scolded him for losing a few gold coins was now a middle-aged househead and *shōya* scrupulous about keeping track of his money, even if he was not necessarily frugal about spending it. Entries included one *ryō* for a two-day stay with Moto and their servant at an inn, with food included. Daisuke even dutifully noted the cost of a gift of hair combs—seven *ryō*—purchased for him by the Asakawa intendant Watanabe Hironobu, whose advice on Isami's education he would solicit twenty-seven years later, when he took his young great-grandson to Tokyo for the first time. Daisuke and Moto also splurged on purchases of gifts for family members and household items, including ten soup bowls and a dagger costing eleven *ryō*. Clearly, they had enjoyed their trip, though they spent more than they had intended, which Daisuke noted in his journal with a proper nod to the virtue of thrift.

The relationship of Daisuke and Moto served as a model for Isami's own companionate marriage. He learned a lesson early in life and never forgot it: a hardworking, sensible, intelligent, cultivated, compatible wife of strong character was absolutely essential to the well-being of her husband and household. In his account of Moto, Isami quoted a Japanese saying to the effect that a wise, older woman was like a treasure who can make a man great.[38]

Going Out into the World

FIVE

Urban Studies

ONCE A MONTH ISAMI MADE THE LONG TRIP from the countryside to Tokyo to check on his children's progress. Around the age of ten, they were all sent to Tokyo for schooling. "In those days," Tami reflected, "you couldn't have pursued education otherwise, but these days no mother would live apart from children who are only ten or eleven years old." Fuki and Mina remembered how their father would appear unexpectedly in their classroom or at school concerts. "He was an original," they agreed. "He never imitated anybody." Unusual even among urban middle-class fathers for his attention to their schooling—a responsibility usually allocated to mothers in contemporary Japan—he was a "*kyōiku papa,*" his daughters quipped: an "education father."

Deprived of the privilege of attending school in Tokyo among the vanguard of modernizing Japanese, Isami went to extraordinary lengths to assure a Tokyo education for all of his children. In 1920, he even embarked on the costly enterprise of building a home, or as he jokingly referred to it, a "relocation center" or "asylum" *(shūyōjo)* in Nishigahara, the northeastern outskirts of the city, to house the children during their Tokyo school years.[1]

Nishigahara still retained a rural flavor in the 1920s and 1930s. The family's wooden house was surrounded by rice paddies, and the garden had six cherry trees. A framed picture of Kō and Isami, taken at the time of their marriage, and a painting of the family's village house hung in the living room to remind the children not to forget their parents and to observe appropriate behavior. Isami also hung the portrait of himself and Great-Grandfather Daisuke that was painted on his first trip to Tokyo in 1890, when he was eleven and Daisuke was inquiring about educational opportunities for him in the capital.

One or two maids were on hand at all times to cook, do the laundry, and mend clothes. Usually women in their early twenties, they served as surrogate older sisters, while the older siblings served as substitute parents. In the absence of a father figure, however, the children tended to become unruly, so Isami decided to make monthly visits to check on his brood. At first, he notified them in advance of his arrival, but then he started acting more like a "health inspector," he joked, and he would arrive unannounced. Of course, the children would pass the word around—"Father is here!"—and rush to rehang the picture of their parents, which they hid when he was away, because Kō was such a young bride (she had dropped out of school to marry Isami) they felt embarrassed to have friends see it.[2]

Kō shared her husband's educational goals and, like him, hoped to give her children more schooling than she had received. To this end she set up an education fund, where she put the ten thousand yen in "child support money" (yōiku hin) she was given, probably by her father-in-law, each time she gave birth. The couple estimated they would need around one hundred thousand yen to finance their fourteen children's Tokyo schooling: eight thousand yen for each boy and five thousand for each girl.[3] Influenced by generations of his ancestors, Isami greatly respected book learning, but, more important, he and Kō recognized that the children's futures depended on their formal schooling. Both understood that, in the new Japan, education was the key to social advancement.

Opportunities abounded even for members of the old peasant class and especially for its wealthier male members once class boundaries were cleared away in the early Meiji period. "Country gentlemen" such as the Matsuura, who had spearheaded economic development at the local level even before the modern period, emerged as the nation's new middle class. By the turn of the century, the scions of local notables from Japan's large farm class dominated the nation's middle and higher schools on their way to becoming white-collar workers in government and private corporations, replacing the samurai as the new backbone of Japan. In early twentieth-century Japan, self-made men replaced the hereditary samurai elite as the popular culture heroes.[4]

Admission into the nation's leading educational institutions would give the Matsuura boys the necessary credentials to enter the growing ranks of urban, salaried workers, who by 1920 constituted about 20 percent of the workforce.[5] The competition for admission into institutions of higher learning, especially the top-ranked schools, had become stiffer by the third decade of the twentieth century because an increasing number of students in the Taishō period (1912–26) sought the academic degrees needed to secure professional or managerial careers. For this reason, middle-class fathers, especially academics and other professionals, increasingly took an interest in their children's education in the 1920s and worried about their ability to gain admission into good schools.[6]

Isami was especially keen on having his boys become doctors, but he recognized that women too needed advanced schooling to qualify for marriage to urban professionals. Like many politically aware men of his time, including government policy makers, Isami supported the higher education of his daughters as well as his sons. He believed that well-educated women would benefit the country by raising intelligent and healthy children. The builders of the new nation assigned this important role to mothers in the drive to achieve "civilization." Since the time of the Sino-Japanese War, at the end of the nineteenth century, a discourse of home and womanhood had directed feminist goals to nationalist ends. "Father believed that women, too, needed to be *erai* [important or great]," Fuki recalled. It would not help the country to educate men alone.

Isami's goal of educating his daughters may have reflected the influence of Moto, his wise step-great-grandmother and Daisuke's second wife, and most certainly it conformed to the wishes of his wife, Kō, but it was also resonant with the teachings of Fukuzawa Yukichi, the leading popularizer of Western learning in the late nineteenth century. An exponent of women's education, Fukuzawa was much admired by Isami and his father. Attention to women's education also reflected the slogan "good wives, wise mothers" *(ryōsai kenbo),* which had guided official thinking about women's role since the turn of the century. The well-educated middle-class mother, according to this view, was essential to the rearing of children trained in the virtues and skills required by the country in its push to build a "rich nation and strong army"—another slogan trumpeted by the founding fathers of modern Japan.

The education of the Matsuura girls in the period during and after World War I coincided with a drive to reform urban family life and dwellings, with the wife at the center of domestic arrangements. Household management was becoming a specialization requiring appropriate training. Architects, journalists, and women educators joined forces to invent a new style of domesticity for the emerging middle class and especially for women in the smaller nuclear families of urban Japan.[7]

Despite the rhetorical attention paid to educating women in the 1920s and 1930s, when the Matsuura daughters attended the equivalent of women's colleges, the women enrolled in college were mainly from upper-class families. The women who were actually afforded a higher education accounted for only 10 percent of the students enrolled.[8] These women numbered about fifteen thousand out of a total population of sixty-five million. Moreover, among political leaders, women's education remained secondary to the task of educating men, and its purpose was to enhance their roles as competent homemakers. Still, Isami's dedication to his daughters' higher education, if not to future careers for them, was, in their words, truly progressive.

Isami was convinced that quality education was possible only in the nation's capital. Tokyo boasted the best schools and offered the most modern and Western cultural opportunities. To be modern was to live in a city, and, in the words of one popular song of the day, Tokyo was "the pride of civilization."

By 1919, Japan's capital city was already swelling with an influx of rural immigrants seeking a place in the expanding industrial economy. Most of its population of over two million crowded onto trains every day en route to jobs, schools, and stores. New sites of entertainment especially popular with young people, such as cinemas and cafés, also drew crowds. "Tokyo is famous for its packed trains," said another popular Japanese song of the day. "No matter how long you wait, you cannot get on. When you try to get off, there's a life-or-death struggle awaiting you."[9]

Ever since Great-Grandfather Daisuke had taken Isami by train to the capital when he was a boy, Tokyo had spelled progress to him. True, he and Kō were critical of the way middle-class urban mothers pampered their children, and they preferred to raise their own brood in the fresh air and natural beauty of their own village. Nevertheless, the capital city was the center of political and intellectual life, the seat of modernity, the site of the new middle-class lifestyle, and the major receptor of Western learning. Whenever he was in Tokyo, Isami rode the Ginza subway line to Nihonbashi, the city's commercial center (where Daisuke also had conducted business), and shopped in the Mitsukoshi department store for Western goods such as butter to bring back to the village. "He was a very modern man," Tami reminisced as we strolled past the same department store on a shopping trip in the spring of 2003.

Not even the Great Kantō Earthquake, on the first day of September 1923, altered Isami's resolve to educate his children in Tokyo. The Nishigahara house, while damaged by the tremor, survived it. At its epicenter it measured 8.3 in magnitude on the Richter scale, killing 140,000 people—the second deadliest earthquake of the twentieth century. Half of Tokyo and most of Yokohama were destroyed either by the earthquake or by fires that broke out and raged for three days, burning 465,000 wooden dwellings.[10]

Fuki was nine years old and in the third grade when the earthquake struck. She was the youngest of the children living at the Tokyo house and the only one there when the tremor struck; none of her older siblings had arrived yet from Yamashiraishi, as their school semester started later than hers. She had been pushed out of the nest earlier than Toyo, who, though two years older, was held back a little longer because in her early years she had tended to be timid and dependent; when her parents had tried to send her to Tokyo, she had clung to one of the house pillars, crying that she did not want to go. Because Isami on his visits to Tokyo felt lonely without a young child around, he sent Fuki to the city after she had completed only the first grade in the village school. "I was considered a 'good child,' quiet and obedient," Fuki said. Busy tending to four younger children, Kō did not have much time for Fuki anyhow; during summer vacations the little girl slept in the retirement cottage with her grandparents, Yūya and Miyo. She fondly remembered how, following Japanese custom, Isami had slept beside her "under the same futon" on the tatami when he stayed at the Nishigahara house.[11]

Over sixty years later Fuki vividly described how, when the ground beneath her feet first began shaking on that warm, muggy early autumn day, she had clung to a swaying fence in the garden where she had been playing. That night she slept in the garden beside the maid and her uncle Kensuke and his wife, who lived in the house next door and had also fled outside when the eastern portion of the city went up in flames. Uncle Kensuke had carried his wife on his back because she had difficulty walking. From the garden Fuki watched the horrifying scene of Tokyo's Nihonbashi district burning. Whirlwinds of fire incinerated as many as thirty thousand people who had sought safety in a park near the east bank of the Sumida River.[12] The fires remained visible even from Yamashiraishi until dust covered the sky, but still Isami did not call the children home. Their education was too important.

By the time Tami, the youngest of the eight girls, arrived in Tokyo in the early 1930s, few of her siblings remained in the house. A sister-in-law living in Tokyo was assigned to supervise her homework. Tami was so lonely she wanted to return home, but one of her older sisters reprimanded her by asking, "Why did you come to Tokyo if you are not going to study?"[13]

Most of the children had to spend their first year at a neighborhood school doing remedial work in mathematics and Japanese to make up for their less advanced rural education. Thereafter, the boys went to public schools that put them on track for the elite universities, such as Tokyo Imperial or Keiō University. Tokyo Imperial University, the nation's preeminent school of higher learning, was the gateway to secure, prestigious jobs in the government bureaucracy or in such well-established modern companies as Mitsubishi. Keiō, founded by Fukuzawa Yukichi, the pioneer advocate of Western learning, boasted a noted medical school. One of the Matsuura's seven sons, fourth-born Yūshirō, as well as three sons-in-law, graduated from Keiō University Medical School. The fifth son studied to become a veterinarian. The heir, Yatarō, graduated from Tokyo Imperial University's College of Agriculture, and the next oldest son, Kōjirō, a brilliant student who gained admission into the Humanities Division of Dai-ichi Kōtōgakkō (First Higher School), Tokyo's top preparatory school, was accepted by Tokyo Imperial University's most respected division, the Faculty of Law. Toshisaburō, too, graduated from Tokyo Imperial University, and the seventh son, Seishichirō, from Keiō.

Isami favored private schools for his daughters because he believed the public education system was not innovative enough in its curriculum for women. The girls were enrolled in elite women's schools, which he handpicked for them after interviewing their directors and examining their curricula and educational philosophies.

The oldest daughter, Mina, spent five years at Atomi Girls' School, which was not only one of the earliest private academies for women but one of the most prestigious women's schools of the time. It had been founded in 1875 by Atomi Kakei, the thirty-five-year-old daughter of a scholar, who was still principal during Mina's years as a student there during the World War I period. By that time Kakei had managed to raise enough money from her wealthy alumnae to construct new buildings. In 1912 she was honored by the Japanese Imperial Household for her work on behalf of women's education.[14]

At Atomi, Mina, a country girl, rubbed elbows with the daughters of aristocrats and wealthy industrialists. Her admission to the school reflected well on the family, for Atomi investigated the family background of every applicant, looking closely at property holdings and lineage. A graduate of the school in 1910 remarked proudly that Atomi did not admit girls from "just any old farm family."[15]

Atomi Girls' School's students were expected to work hard and live simply. The education of these socially elite young women contained a large dose of subjects considered appropriate for aristocratic women: calligraphy, tea ceremony, sewing, flower arranging, painting, and even dancing to the music of the *shamisen*. One student's graduation exercise in 1910, completed after weeks of work, consisted of a "large elaborate floral design in water color, each flower identified with a little poem."[16] Students also studied the Japanese language, Chinese classics, and arithmetic.

Mina emerged from the school with an elegance and an air of cultural refinement that set her apart from the fast-talking, go-getter personalities of several of her younger sisters and also qualified her shortly after college to marry into a distinguished family. At the age of ninety she continued to enjoy the tea ceremony and to demonstrate beautiful penmanship as well as a sharp mind.

Despite the luster of the Atomi school, by the time the younger daughters arrived in Tokyo, Isami looked elsewhere for their schooling. Atomi did not believe in encouraging Western learning or even, for that matter, Western dress. In search of a more modern educational institution, Isami chose Christian mission schools in most cases (though he himself was not Christian), because they pioneered in educating women in Western studies, including English. Isami himself had boarded in Kōriyama after primary school, precisely in order to study English.

The two youngest girls, Yasu and Tami, attended Women's Sacred Learning Academy (Joshi Seigakuin), a Christian mission school established in 1905. Following Western styles of the day, their hair was cut short in the fashionable bob, and they dressed in navy blue uniforms with middy blouses. They received five years of precollegiate education at the academy, including seven hours a week of English. Conversation was taught by American or English teachers, who, from the first day of class, greeted their students and gave them instructions in English, such as "open the window."

Sacred Learning Academy's facilities were impressively modern for late 1930s Japan. The school's Western-style flush toilets puzzled Tami at first: she did not know what they were or how to use them. The bathrooms also had tampon dispensers. Other schools used kerosene stoves for heating, whereas the Christian mission school featured the luxury of steam heat.

At the college level, the Matsuura daughters attended one or the other of two schools founded by Christian converts: Japan Women's College (Nihon Joshi Daigakkō) and Freedom School (Jiyū Gakuen). Japan Women's College was established in 1901 on spacious grounds donated by the Mitsui family, who were wealthy industrialists. Its founder and first president was Naruse Jinzō, a Christian convert who had studied for several years in the United States at the Andover Theological Seminary and Clark University. Naruse considered the main purpose of education to be the same for both men and women: the development of "complete human beings. . . . There should be no distinction between the sexes."[17]

Four of the Matsuura girls attended Japan Women's College from the 1920s to the early 1940s. Yasu was one of them. She had hoped to study music, but Isami frowned on the behavior of the boys he saw in the music school he visited. Despite Naruse's avowed educational philosophy, only Mina, who majored in English literature at the college in the early 1920s, had a strictly liberal arts curriculum. Yasu, Tami, and Fuki majored in home economics, a field that had been established in the United States as recently as the post–World War I years and was earmarked for women.

The home economics curriculum of Japan Women's College was not merely cooking and sewing classes. In fact, the term for their major course of study in Japanese, *kasei rika,* translates more closely into "the science of household management," with an emphasis on science and efficiency geared to making students knowledgeable about health and hygiene matters. The young women, for example, studied the chemical properties of various laundry soaps to determine which was the best. In one science course that Tami remembered, students dissected small animals. But although the curriculum was demanding—"It was nothing but studying" according to Tami's memory of her college years—the home economics major clearly pointed young women in the direction of a domestic role and did not put them, like their brothers, on track for a career or even a job. They were trained to become professional, urban housewives or home managers, a specialized role that was now thought to require special instruction with a heavily Western orientation.[18] Even Naruse justified his emphasis on education for women in terms of their future domestic role: he sought to strengthen women physically for childbearing. By the time the Matsuura girls enrolled, the school had acquired a reputation as a finishing school for upper-class women.[19]

Nevertheless, Japan Women's College produced a number of famous women activists, including Hiratsuka Raichō, who, after graduating in 1906, went on to found *Seito* (Bluestocking), the feminist literary journal, in 1911. In 1919, she and the famous feminist Ichikawa Fusae founded the New Woman's Association to champion women's political rights. By the time Tami entered college in the late 1930s, however, the totalitarian political atmosphere in Japan had made popular democratic agitation of any sort impossible. Japan was at war, and the heightened patriotism had produced a revulsion against Western learning. Foreigners from the West, except for Germans, were unwelcome, and language teachers were scarce. Unlike her older sisters, Tami could not study English in college.

For the college-level education of Toyo, Fumi, and Shiki in the 1920s and '30s, Isami selected Freedom School, a small, residential, elementary through postsecondary women's school founded in 1921 by the nation's first newspaperwoman, Hani Motoko. In 1917, in her own monthly magazine, *Fujin no tomo* (Woman's Friend), she had announced her intention of establishing the school. Dissatisfied with traditional Japanese education, in which "knowledge was crammed into children's heads without letting them understand why certain things are so," Hani, according to her nephew, "wanted to start a new school where children would learn through experience and govern themselves."[20]

After reading about the school in magazine articles, Isami had Toyo's oldest sister, Mina, visit the campus and speak to Hani about the advisability of placing the thirteen-year-old Toyo there. Mina was sufficiently impressed to recommend the school to Isami. At the same time, Hani was impressed enough with Mina to offer her a position as an English teacher.[21] Toyo entered the Freedom School's junior division in April 1925, while Mina, in 1926, entered into the marriage Isami had arranged for her.

The original class at Freedom School had only 26 students; by Toyo's time the enrollment had already grown to over 150. Every applicant had to pass an entrance exam, which included an interview with Hani herself, who was then in her fifties. Arriving for her interview, Toyo was still a country bumpkin in the eyes of her future classmates, who were mainly the daughters of upper-middle-class families. She was the only student in kimono; all the other girls wore Western clothes. Timid as a child, Toyo was transformed into an energetic "modern woman" by the time she graduated seven years later.

Freedom School's building, which formed a U shape on a broad lawn and was located in the suburban Mejiro section of Tokyo, was designed by the American architect Frank Lloyd Wright. It was Wright's only school project and one of only two structures that still stand completely intact out of the twelve he designed in Japan between 1916 and 1922.[22] Freedom School and the Imperial Hotel in downtown Tokyo both survived the Great Kantō Earthquake: Wright took pains to account for temblors. Constructed of wood, mortar, and *oya* stone (lightweight lava), the main hall boasts twelve-foot-tall windows set in a peaked roof.

Even though Wright was already committed to designing the Imperial Hotel along with ten other projects, he agreed to Hani's request for his architectural services because he was impressed with Hani's socially progressive educational philosophy. The modern and Western-style architecture of Freedom School symbolized Hani's own innovative ideas about women's education and the role of the middle-class woman. She believed in training her well-to-do charges in self-reliance and practical skills, and to this end she added to the strictly academic requirements a variety of chores that were performed on a regular basis. Not only were students responsible for cleaning the school (there was no janitor), but they also cooked, gardened, and worked in the office. It was a long day for the Matsuura sisters, who commuted by train from their house and then walked fifteen minutes from the station to the school. "I was so busy all the time," Fumi recalled." We had to start the day by cleaning the classrooms. I remember running from the train station to the school to arrive on time at 7 A.M."

Hani evidently believed that students learned by doing—and by making mistakes. Each day the two hundred students and staff members ate a hot lunch prepared by a rotating group of thirty students in the basement kitchen, a large room with a stone floor, huge black iron pots for cooking rice, and a stone sink that ran along one wall. Not surprisingly, when the youngest class prepared the meal, it was not always edible; one American teacher, Eleanor Hadley, remembers spitting out squid so tough she could not chew it.[23]

The academic program of study at Freedom School gave Toyo and her classmates solid instruction in Japanese language and literature, English, history, mathematics, and science. Foreigners were invited to the campus to give guest talks and to teach English. The young women learned other course material through a hands-on method of instruction that emphasized practice rather than memorization. They produced plays by Shakespeare and Chekhov, learning their lines in English.[24] They studied music by participating in the chorus, and all day Saturday was devoted to arts and crafts— drawing pictures, dyeing fabrics, weaving on a loom. "There were many fine teachers," Toyo's friends recalled, "though at the time we did not realize what a privilege it was to have such fine teachers paying so much attention to our education."[25]

In addition to conventional women's subjects—sewing and cooking— the students learned bookkeeping for management of household budgets, a new role for middle-class women. The content of these homemaking courses showed the Western influences that guided Hani's educational philosophy. She organized a systematic program of instruction in sewing Western women's clothing, because she believed kimono were too heavy and uncomfortable (though she herself always dressed in Japanese clothes). Students began with simple hemming and gradually learned how to make blouses, skirts, and even coats. Each student sewed her own white graduation dress. By commencement the girls could cook not only Japanese food but, remarkably enough, French and Chinese cuisine as well. In this sense, the domestic arts taught at Hani's school represented a modernized, more cosmopolitan and professionalized version of what Kō taught her servants back home in the village.

Hani also introduced Western sports. Women's participation in sports was generally not encouraged in Japan before Hani's time, in contrast to public schools in the United States, which, by the turn of the century, had begun offering physical training for both sexes. By the 1890s, most American women's colleges had begun to promote athletics, including biking, tennis, and basketball, so that the "New Woman" who emerged from these colleges was physically active.[26] Emulating this trend, Hani's school offered activities such as biking, and her husband helped pioneer tennis on the campus's four tennis courts.

Among the Freedom School's lasting influences on Toyo was instruction in Christianity. Hani opened the school day with a thirty-minute assembly consisting of Bible reading in English and a discussion of what Hani called the Christian spirit. She had been exposed to Christian teachings and baptized while a student at a private Protestant school. Many of her students came from Christian families or had converted to Christianity.

Hani absorbed mainly the ethical teachings of Christianity as they applied to individual behavior. She also paid close attention to the development of her students as individuals and to their feelings and inner life. One of her students remembered how she not only encouraged the young women's creativity and independence, but she also listened closely to their spiritual or emotional problems *(kokoro no nayami)*. She would encourage students to talk about their concerns and to show compassion and sympathy for their classmates' troubles. The girls were organized into six residential groups, called families *(kazoku)*, and group members were urged to work together and become close friends.[27]

Hani's emphasis on basic work skills, certain rational habits of mind, and communication among family members helped shape Toyo, who was entering womanhood at a time when middle-class values were being formed. College women, freed from farming or factory work, were destined to live in smaller urban homes, where they would be in charge of household management. They could not assume they would have servants or elders to help them, as their parents did. Even if they did have servants, those from the countryside could not be expected to know how to cook French cuisine or shop for a two-piece wool suit, let alone make one. A staunch exponent of the "rationalization" of daily life, Hani urged her students to "think, plan. When you go shopping, make up a budget. Schedule your activities. If you straighten up the house before going to bed, in the morning you can more quickly cook breakfast. Wash your *tabi* [Japanese socks] as soon as coming home. Don't waste time."[28] Such practical instruction, with an emphasis on problem solving and intellectual independence, was lacking in the public schools, which tended to emphasize rote learning. The Freedom School became known as Japan's only progressive education school.[29]

For the Matsuura girls, who started life as a farmer's daughters, albeit wealthy ones, Hani's curriculum constituted preparation for their future destiny as urban middle-class wives. It was designed to make them "modern," which, in those days, meant Western in their fashion sense; practical-minded; efficient; familiar with Western etiquette, nutrition, and standards of cleanliness; and capable of earning their own living or of living overseas should their husband's job send them abroad. In the 1920s, the late Taishō period, when well-to-do urban housewives used elegant silver cream pitchers for guests and the Mitsukoshi department store sold glass cups and saucers with metal handles, the kind that one could also find on Fifth Avenue in New York City, the Freedom School provided, among other things, access to "Taishō chic."[30]

But more important than consumer savvy, Hani Motoko's curriculum aimed to give young women a sense of self-reliance and creativity through holistic training that nourished body, mind, and soul. Hani did not favor a strictly domestic role for women. She disagreed with the idea that a woman should listen to her husband and never answer back or that she should use all her energy for her husband and children. By efficiently tending to their housework, they would have time left over for themselves. Hani advised women to keep track of their time and to note what they did in every hour of the day in order to leave time for themselves to read and write.[31] Hani also urged women to work outside the home and to develop their own interests and opinions. In the 1920s a small, but increasing number of middle-class women were indeed entering the workforce, combining jobs as teachers, nurses, office workers, and telephone operators with family duties.[32] Hani herself was the mother of three children as well as co-publisher (with her husband) of her magazine, *Fujin no tomo,* and founder of Freedom School. She was a visible shaper of new gender identities for women.

Even at the early age of thirteen, Toyo seemed ready to absorb everything Hani had to offer. Although she had been judged less independent than her next younger sister, Fuki, and had been kept home in the village even after Fuki had left for Tokyo, Toyo seemed to come into her own under Hani's tutelage. In her first year, it is true, she struggled with her English language classes, but during summer vacation, she borrowed one of her brother's textbooks, tutored herself, and did better the next year.[33] Healthy and talented, she soon developed a reputation among her classmates as a good cook ("her hands were fast," recalled one of her classmates), and the preparation of a variety of international cuisines remained one of her lifelong pleasures. She also learned to play basketball and tennis. Having arrived on campus in kimono, she was soon knitting sweaters that were the envy of her friends. Once she returned to Yamashiraishi with two classmates and tried to teach village women how to improve their lives. They gave instructions in sewing Western clothes. Toyo's youngest sister, Tami, was no more than seven or eight years old at the time, but in her later years she distinctly remembered a friend of Toyo's who stayed at their house and "dressed like a flapper." In a family photograph taken in 1926, Toyo and her younger sisters were already wearing Western fashion, Yasu and Teru in middy blouses and Shiki and Fuki with braided hair and white dresses. Only the married women in the picture wear kimono. In the late 1930s, even Kō had her hair cut short in the new style.

The Freedom School made its mark on Toyo in other ways as well. The school chorale's rendering of "Ode to Joy," from Beethoven's Ninth Symphony, introduced to Japan in the World War I era, became one of her favorite works of music. Sermons by guest ministers and the daily reading of the Bible laid the foundation for her eventual conversion to Christianity. Kashiwagi Church, the Tokyo church she joined over two decades after graduating, was founded by Uemura Tamako, who had taught English at the Freedom School and was the daughter of Hani's religious mentor, Uemura Masahisa. Several of Toyo's best friends throughout her life were classmates; she and eighteen other graduates attended the sixtieth reunion of their class.

Toyo's sisters fared less well at the Freedom School. Shiki, who was more fashion conscious than studious and was also headstrong, got into an argument with one of her teachers and dropped out to get private instruction in French. Fumi lasted for four and one-half years until a life-threatening abdominal infection, actinomycosis, whose cause she later attributed to the stress of her college days, forced her to drop out too.

By the time she graduated in 1932, Toyo was determined to become a writer for Hani's woman's magazine. Many of Toyo's classmates, after graduating, did pursue careers. At twenty, her friend Morikawa Miyoko, the daughter of a famous photographer who did formal wedding pictures, became editor of *Fujin no tomo* and stayed on in the job for almost fifty years,

FIG. 1 Oil painting of Isami and Daisuke, 1890.

FIG. 2 The ninth-generation
Matsuura househead, Jinsuke.

FIG. 3 The eighth-generation
Matsuura househead, Daisuke.

FIG. 4 The road leading to the Matsuura family compound in Yamashiraishi
village. Atop the fronting wall is the retirement cottage (on right side of the
structure) and the village office (on the left). The main house and garden can
be seen beyond the gate in the wall.

FIG. 5 The front of the Matsuura main house, facing the garden.

FIG. 6 The storehouse (white structure at center) and part of the retirement cottage (at right front of photo) in the Matsuura compound.

Fig. 7 A room in the retirement cottage in the Matsuura compound —the one with the *tokonoma,* the alcove that displays art objects, as mentioned in chapter 1. Also, the oil painting of Daisuke and Isami (see figure 1) can be seen in the upper right corner of the photo.

Fig. 8 Matsuura family members visit the ancestral cemetery in Yamashiraishi village.

FIG. 9 The tenth-generation
Matsuura househead, Yūya.

FIG. 10. The Matsuura family in 1926. In the bottom row, from left to right:
Yatarō, Kyōichi (Yatarō's firstborn child), Chiyo (Yatarō's wife), Yasu, Yūya,
Miyo, Teru, Ishiwata Rokusaburō (Mina's husband), Fumi, Mina, and Shiki. In
the second row, from left to right: Fuki, Toyo, Kō holding Tami, Isami holding
Tatsugorō, Kōjirō, Toshisaburō, and Yūshirō.

FIG. 11. Newspaper clipping of an article about Isami and Kō, showing photographs of them and their seven remaining daughters and seven sons, appearing from top to bottom by descending age, 1937. Source unknown.

FIG. 12 Toyo and her sisters in 1937. Bottom row from left to right: Shiki, Fuki, Toyo, Mina. Top row: Tami, Yasu, Fumi.

FIG. 13 The entering class of Freedom School in 1925. Toyo is seventh from the right in the second row. Hani Motoko, wearing a kimono, is in the center of the second row.

Fig. 14 Toyo at age twenty in 1932.

FIG. 15 The formal wedding picture of Toyo and Ishikawa Masafumi, 1934.

FIG. 16 The wedding of Toyo to Ishikawa Masafumi (seated at the center of the front row), photographed with guests in front of Nogi Shrine, 1934. Kō and Isami are seated in the front row, second and third from the right, respectively.

FIG. 17 Toyo in Qingdao, mid-1930s.

FIG. 18 Toyo's husband, Ishikawa Masafumi, in Qingdao, mid-1930s.

FIG. 19 Toyo with her husband and an unidentified friend (in front) in Qingdao, mid-1930s.

FIG. 20 Toyo with Yōko, 1944.

FIG. 21 The Matsuura family in Yamashiraishi village in 1945 with five soldiers who helped Isami make fuel from pine trees. Top row, from left: Tami, Yasu holding Hiroshi, Shiki, Mina, Hamako (Yataro's daughter), Chiyo (Yatarō's wife) holding Hamako's daughter, Tazuko (Kōjirō's wife), Kōzō's (Isami's brother's) son. Middle row: Fuki holding Setsuko (her daughter), Kō, Yōko (Kōjirō's daughter), Isami, Rintarō (Mina's first son), Katsuo (Kōjirō's older son). Front row (on laps of soldiers): Tomoji, Seiji (Yūshirō's son), Jun (Mina's second son), Nobu (Mina's daughter), Tsuyoshi (Kōjiro's younger son).

FIG. 22 The Matsuura family, 1947, at the time of Tami's first marriage. Tami and her husband stand behind Kō and Isami (seated in the center).

FIG. 23 Isami's heir, Yatarō.

Fig. 24 Isami in his last years.

FIG. 25 Some of the twelfth-generation Matsuura and their children, 1955. Photographed indoors in the photography studio of the Mitsukoshi department store shortly before Toyo, Yōko, and Masafumi left for Brazil. The family members all wear Western clothes, and the women have permanent waves. From left to right, top row: Seishichirō, Shinrokurō, Tami, Akakura Ichirō (Fuki's husband), Yōko (Toyo's daughter), Tatsugorō, Setsuko (Fuki's daughter). Bottom row: Fumi, Shinzō (Fumi's third son), Shiki, Yasuko (Shiki's daughter), Toyo, Masako (Tami's daughter), Fuki, Hiroshi (Yasu's son), Yasu.

FIG. 26 Toyo (center) touring Kamakura with Yōko (on the right), her nephew Shinzō (Fumi's third son), and the author, 1963.

FIG. 27 Toyo and her siblings' families at a Tokyo restaurant in 1963. Toyo is seated in the front row, holding a child in a plaid shirt on her lap. Yōko is person on the left in the back row. Author stands in the center of the back row, with Fumi's oldest son to her right.

FIG. 28 Toyo, her surviving sisters, and her sister-in-law Masako visiting their natal home in Fukushima: 1991. From left: Tami, Mina, Masako (Yūshirō's widow), Yasu, Toyo, Fumi, Fuki.

FIG. 29 Matsuura family members at Toyo's funeral service, Kashiwagi Church, Tokyo, 1993. Seated in the center of the front row, from left to right are her sisters Tami, Fumi, Mina, and Fuki, and her sister-in-law Masako; standing in second row, beginning with the third person from the left, are her grandchildren Reiko, Asako, and Ryōta; her daughter, Yōko; Tsukioka Sho, the husband of her sister Yasu; and Yasu.

FIG. 30 Clockwise from bottom-left: Mina, the author, Fumi, Yōko and her daughter (both standing), Tami, and Tami's daughter Masako.

FIG. 31 Toyo's surviving siblings at the home of Toshisaburō and his wife, 1995.

SIX

The Marriage Pipeline

ISAMI SUBSCRIBED TO THE TRADITIONAL VIEW that parents were responsible for arranging their children's marriages, and he had definite views on how to go about doing so. Progressive in his views on education, he was conservative in his control over the timing of his children's engagements and the choice of their spouses. Isami's first rule of marriage arrangement was to observe order of birth, which he did in all but Yūshirō's case. In Toyo's case, four of her older siblings, including her oldest sister, were already married, and five younger sisters were waiting in line behind her; Isami reasoned that people would wonder what was wrong with her if a younger sister married ahead of her, and he would be unable to make a suitable match for either her or them.

Isami's second rule was to avoid pairing children with close family members, as had been the custom in Isami's own family. Even though he himself was happily married to his country cousin, Isami preferred to cast a wider net for his sons and daughters. Seeking their spouses from the newly emerging middle class, he looked for well-educated young men and women whose families were neither too rich nor too poor.

As always, it was important to acquire in-laws whose backgrounds would enhance the status of the Matsuura family as a whole. Well-to-do relatives by marriage could advance the interests of the family by broadening its social network and creating new and potentially valuable contacts. Indeed, information on relatives was commonly advertised in marriage discussions. Socially prominent in-laws furthered the marriage prospects of all the remaining unmarried siblings. A brother-in-law who was a doctor or university professor, for example, strengthened the credentials of siblings looking for marriage partners. Conversely, a ne'er-do-well damaged his relatives' marriage chances. Concerned about the family's image, Isami had discouraged his fourth-born son, Yūshirō, from following his heart and going to music school to train for a career as a professional singer. Isami argued that singers had a bad reputation; they were associated with the "water trade"—theater people, popular entertainers, prostitutes. He feared that Yūshirō would endanger his sisters' marriage prospects if he entered the entertainment world. Yūshirō complied with his father's wishes and went to medical school instead.[1]

Although marriage was a serious business for the Matsuura family, it was not necessarily a lucrative business. The children's marriages, like their education, were a drain on household resources. Even so, late into the 1930s Isami and Kō continued to allocate generous amounts of their income to promoting the best possible betrothals for both daughters and sons.

Isami's considerable investment in his daughters' education provided them with the credentials they needed to qualify as wives of good providers. Befitting the social class aspirations of the family, his daughters typically were married to college graduates in ceremonies that took place in Tokyo, with receptions at a famous catering establishment in the upscale Ueno section of the capital. They received from their parents the bride's traditional trousseau of a sewing box, a chest of drawers *(tansu)*, and a mirror made of paulownia wood from Aizu, at a total cost of sixty *man yen* (roughly six thousand dollars). Brides also gave gifts to all members of their husband's household, including the servants. To save on costs, not all the bride's siblings attended the wedding reception; in some cases only the sister closest in age to the bride was invited. The sisters' custom of each wearing the same wedding kimono for good luck further reduced expenses. But because the receptions were held in Tokyo, a second party, incurring further expense, was held in their village home for the new spouse to meet the local people.

In the 1920s, the family's investment in marriage seemed to be paying off. In 1926, the eldest daughter, Mina, married Ishiwata Rokusaburō, the third son and fifth child of a Tokyo family with samurai lineage and a stellar record of scholarship and public service dating back to the Tokugawa period. Ishiwata ancestors had served as naval advisers to the Tokugawa military government. Rokusaburō's paternal grandfather, Eijirō, was an early scholar of Dutch navigation and shipbuilding techniques, and his father, Bin'ichi (Toshikazu), was a legal expert who held a PhD in law and had helped to write modern Japan's new criminal laws in the nineteenth century. A graduate of Japan's preeminent Tokyo Imperial University, Bin'ichi was chosen by the Ministry of Education in 1886 to study in Europe. His career résumé included stints as public prosecutor for the Tokyo Appeals Court and chief secretary for the first cabinet of Prime Minister Saionji Kimmochi; he was also a member of the House of Peers. Among the father's close friends was Konoe Atsumaro, a member of one of the most prominent aristocratic families in Japan. Rokusaburō's oldest brother, Ishiwata Sōtarō, also a graduate of Tokyo Imperial University, was already on his way to a distinguished career in the Ministry of Finance, thanks in part to Konoe Atsumaro's patronage. Sōtarō and Konoe's son Fumimaro were only a few days apart in age and had been classmates in high school.[2] Rokusaburō himself had graduated from the prestigious Peers School and had studied under the well-known economics professor Kawakami Hajime at Kyoto Imperial University.

Given his family's distinguished background, Mina's husband frankly admitted he never would have considered marrying her, a mere country girl, had she not graduated from a Tokyo women's college. Her ties with Atomi Girls' High School had helped as well. The couple's match had been initiated through Mina's Atomi school friend, whose brother was a friend of Rokusaburō. There was no doubt that Mina's Tokyo education, combined with her family's wealth, had boosted her eligibility for marriage into the Ishiwata family. Isami was so pleased, he bestowed a diamond ring on his firstborn daughter for her wedding gift.[3]

Despite careful investigation of prospective spouses' backgrounds, marriage arrangements were not always successful, even by Isami's own criteria, and throughout their lives he and Kō stepped in to help their married children weather stormy times by providing money, advice, maids, and housing, as needed, and occasionally by directly intervening to save troubled marriages. The marriage of a child, whether son or daughter, did not mean simply "one less mouth to feed," as poorer farmers may have viewed it; it meant more relatives to interact with and, at times, to rescue. Although a married daughter had no legal claim to an inheritance from her natal family and was expected to serve her husband's family with total dedication, Isami and Kō watched over all their offspring long after their wedding ceremonies. The legal right of the househead to authorize his children's marriage entailed, in Isami's case, a lifelong sense of responsibility for the success of the match.

It was not only the Matsuura daughters whose marriages were closely scrutinized. The sons also had to marry women of suitable education and family background: either college-educated women, or city-bred women, or, ideally, a combination of the two. For Kō and Isami, their eldest son's marriage, in 1923, was the most important one. Following Japanese custom, they expected their firstborn son and heir, Yatarō, and his wife to live with them eventually in Yamashiraishi, care for them in their old age, and assume the long tradition of Matsuura village rule. Their first daughter-in-law, Sugiura Chiyo, however, was ill-suited to her assigned role. The daughter of parents who possessed barely a minimum education, Chiyo herself lacked a college degree. Moreover, she was not a country girl, having been born and raised in Odagawa (Kanagawa prefecture), about a two-hour train ride from Tokyo; she was too "citified" to serve as the wife of a future village head.

It is unclear why Kō and Isami agreed to such an unwise union. Perhaps they were still lacking experience in the intricacies of matchmaking. The match was arranged by Isami's sister Moto, by then the wife of Ishii Itarō, a member of the Foreign Ministry and, therefore, supposedly someone with access to a good selection of available brides. Moto narrowed down the choices to several young women, whose photographs she showed to Yatarō, and he chose Chiyo.[4] Isami and Kō, determined not to select a country girl, settled instead for a woman who would be miserable living with them and would make their lives miserable in turn. They did not realize this for a while, however, because the young couple spent their first two decades together in Tokyo, where Yatarō helped manage Isami's various business enterprises.

The next two sons married women whose education was equivalent to that of the Matsuura sisters. Second son Kōjirō, the family's most academically and, eventually, most financially successful son, was married in 1933 to Watanabe Tazuko, a graduate of Mina's alma mater, Japan Women's College, and one year later, Toshisaburō married another graduate of that college, Hosokawa Ayako.

In 1934, Isami deviated from his children's birth order when he arranged Toyo's marriage ahead of her older brother Yūshirō, who was still in medical school. Isami chose a man who, in the eyes of society, was an excellent catch.[5] Toyo's fiancé, Ishikawa Masafumi, had graduated in engineering from Tokyo Imperial University and, like her brother Kōjirō, was employed in the Mitsubishi Trading Company. Assigned to the company's branch office in Shanghai, he had been hastily called back to Tokyo along with his fellow employees in late January 1932, after a Chinese boycott of Japanese businesses escalated into violent confrontations between Chinese and Japanese in the so-called Shanghai Incident. Masafumi's recall made him available just when Toyo was coming through the Matsuura marriage pipeline.

Not only had the young man chosen for Toyo graduated from the right college and taken a job with the right company, but also his family background was impressive. Masafumi's ancestors were samurai. His father, Ishikawa Masayoshi, was a career army officer and a military hero, killed in 1920 in the Siberian Expedition. Although there had been little popular support for Japan's ill-fated attempt to strengthen its position against Russia in northern Manchuria and eastern Siberia, Masayoshi was memorialized in his home prefecture of Yamagata, where a stone tablet was erected in his honor. Isami arranged the match through a friend in the military who had known the groom's father.

The couple appeared to have much in common. Both Masafumi and Toyo had enjoyed the kind of elite, Western-oriented higher education available to only a small percentage of young Japanese men and women in their day. They shared a fondness for Western popular culture, especially for Western clothing and furniture styles, team sports, and social dancing. Masafumi was a stylish dresser with expensive tastes; on his days away from work he liked to wear fine, imported wool sweaters and hats, just as Toyo had a special fondness for Western cloche-style hats. During their one-year engagement, the couple attended rugby games together and even held dance parties at the Nishigahara house. Couples dancing was considered risqué in pre-World War II Japan; although it had been taught in the schools in the 1920s, it was virtually banned during wartime. Nevertheless, Masafumi was an excellent dancer whose repertoire included the Argentine tango. He played the mandolin too.

Toyo had no legitimate grounds to oppose marriage to such a well-educated, cosmopolitan man who was also a white-collar employee of a prestigious company. True, she was disappointed that she could not fulfill her wish to work for the *Fujin no tomo* magazine after her graduation. Isami had denied her permission, with the explanation that, as the oldest child living in the Nishigahara house, she was needed to watch over her younger siblings. One year later, with her older male siblings married off, Toyo was her father's focus in matchmaking. Toyo had no choice but to acquiesce; once her father decided on a course of action, he was unbending, and he believed he was acting in her best interests—and the best interests of the siblings who came after her.

Toyo and Masafumi were married on February 24, 1934, two days after Masafumi's twenty-fourth birthday, in a ceremony attended by family members on both sides and several uniformed army friends of Masafumi's father, including the official go-between. This was a period marked by war fever, as excited Japanese continued to celebrate the 1931 takeover of Manchuria, the "jewel" in the empire's crown. In fact, the couple posed for their formal wedding photograph in front of the Shinto shrine dedicated to General Nogi Maresuke, the hero of the Russo-Japanese War. Regarded as an embodiment of traditional samurai spiritual values, General Nogi, distressed by the Meiji emperor's death in 1912, had chosen to end his own life on the night of the state funeral, and his wife had loyally followed, stabbing herself in the heart. In the 1930s, as Japan pressed forward with its expansion policy on the Asian continent, popular journalism touted the ultranationalist values that the general symbolized: military valor and loyalty to emperor and country.

The bride and groom, despite their setting, reveal nothing of this growing patriotic fervor in their wedding photograph, which shows a demure Toyo in the red kimono worn originally by Mina and later shared by almost all the Matsuura brides alongside a dapper Masafumi, dressed in striped pants, vest, and black tails and carrying white gloves. Isami, with his trademark mustache, and Kō, elegant and still youthful-looking in her late forties, her hair swept back off her face, stare quietly at the camera, while Uncle Kensuke stands in the back row with Toyo's two oldest siblings, Yatarō and Mina, and their spouses.

Five daughters and four sons were still unmarried in the middle of the 1930s as Isami and Kō, now middle-aged, struggled to meet their financial obligations. In 1935, with their youngest child only five, they tapped the family's resources for the marriage of their third daughter, Fuki, to Dr. Akakura Ichirō. They held the wedding reception at their Tokyo home in Nishigahara, with the oldest daughter, Mina, helping her mother with the preparations.

Fuki met her husband through her brother Yūshirō. The two men rowed in a regatta club at Keiō University Medical School and went on hiking trips with Fuki, her younger sister Shiki, and others in their group of friends. Like other women in their social circle, Fuki was attracted to Akakura Ichirō because he was good-looking. Fuki was, in her own words, the most obedient and *jimi* (plain) of the daughters.

Isami and Kō, always watching over their brood, had come to the family house in Tokyo to inquire about the young medical student's intentions. When Isami asked the suitor, who was accompanied by his mother, how he felt about Isami's daughter, Akakura assumed they were talking about Shiki, the most *hade* (flashy) Matsuura daughter, to whom he was more attracted, and he immediately asked for her hand in marriage. True to his principles, Isami replied that Fuki, his third oldest daughter, was next in line, and if Akakura wanted to marry a Matsuura woman, he would have to follow birth order and marry Fuki. He agreed.[6]

Despite the new son-in-law's excellent educational and professional credentials, the marriage involved a compromise of sorts for the Matsuura, as Fuki later realized. Akakura family members were born and bred in Tokyo—a mark of status—but they were mostly from the merchant class, *chōnin* (i.e., commoners, and lowly ones at that), not descendants of the samurai, as the husbands of Mina and Toyo were. For decades they had resided on the eastern edge of Tokyo, in the Asakusa district, where shopkeepers lived cheek-by-jowl with prostitutes and chorus-line dancers. Known as a consumer playground offering inexpensive entertainment, the district boasted fourteen movie theaters, other theaters featuring live performances, and all-night restaurants that drew crowds from all over the city.[7]

In Fuki's eyes, Asakusa was *gehin* (low-class or vulgar). But from the perspective of the Akakura family, Fuki was "marrying up"—from the countryside to the capital. The neighbors came out in full force to greet her when she stepped out of a taxi on her wedding day and walked through the neighborhood, meeting the barber, the *geta* maker, and various other shopkeepers, but she suspected they were surprised at her plainness. "They expected somebody more *hade*, showy," Fuki recalled, perhaps somebody like her stylish sister Shiki. "They expected me to have a permanent wave or curls. Before my marriage I was still wearing braids. But I liked my husband so much, I didn't care if others found me *jimi*." Her mother-in-law also apparently found her too plain, objecting to her wedding dress—the one her two older sisters had worn, with a pattern of pine cones and cranes—because it was not splashy enough. Fuki ended up wearing it anyhow but then she changed to something more colorful to please her husband's mother. The incident was a foreshadowing of troubles to come.[8]

Accustomed to living on the outskirts of Tokyo or in the spacious family home in rural Fukushima, Fuki wept when she saw where she would be living with her in-laws. The houses were so close together that when she opened a second-story window of her new home she found herself looking right into the barber's dining room (he cut hair on the ground floor). Shocked, Fuki closed the window.[9]

Fuki had another shock when she learned more about her new family's social background. Her mother-in-law was the granddaughter of a brothel owner, and she had lived with her grandmother in the brothel during part of her childhood after her own mother had divorced. Mrs. Akakura's grandmother had placed her in a girls' school after primary school. The mother-in-law's relatives were famous Kabuki actors.

Fuki's father-in-law, though a physician descended from Kanazawa samurai, deferred to his lower-class wife because he had entered into their marriage as an adopted son-in-law, assuming his wife's surname and moving into her house, which was presumably purchased with funds supplied by her entrepreneurial grandmother. Akakura *pere* practiced medicine in the family home, and many of his patients came from the Yoshiwara, the pleasure quarters of licensed prostitutes where his wife had grown up, north of Asakusa. Mrs. Akakura managed all the money. Every night, Yuki's father-in-law handed his cash receipts to his wife, who not only counted the bills but also ironed them.

Fuki's mother-in-law was "strange" in other ways as well. She took baths in the morning instead of at night, a custom learned in the brothel. She also insisted on taking Fuki to beauty shops in the Yoshiwara, where her hair was done by male beauticians; still in her early twenties, Fuki was uncomfortable being touched by strange men. She was also uncomfortable when taken to visit the grandmother in the brothel, which she owned as late as 1941. Fuki retained a vivid memory of the prostitutes lined up for potential customers' viewing.

Isami had not known the family's background until he interviewed their neighbors. He chose not to divulge the information to Fuki. In fact, he had moved more quickly than Fuki wanted; she had graduated from Japan Women's College with a degree in home economics and a teaching certificate and, like Toyo, would have preferred to work for a year or two before marriage. Nevertheless, Isami had promoted the marriage because Akakura was, after all, a doctor, and Fuki was taken with him. They knew that Fuki, though obedient, was determined not to marry a man she did not like. Struggling to pay for the marriages of their many children, Fuki's parents opted for a well-to-do, if socially dubious, family, putting Fuki's attraction to her husband ahead of other considerations and figuring that the medical credentials of her husband, in terms of his social status and economic potential, would outweigh her mother-in-law's background and give Fuki a financially secure future. "Where my parents got money for my wedding I do not know," Fuki mused, sixty years later. "Probably they sold some rice or even rice land." Indeed, the following year, Isami professed to "feeling good" after having succeeded in repaying a bank loan by selling more family land in the nearby village of Onoda.[10]

Money was evidently not a problem for Fuki's in-laws. Her mother-in-law, said Fuki, "did whatever came into her head." More specifically, she indulged in the new popular culture that had swept over Tokyo since the 1923 Kantō earthquake. The construction boom following the earthquake introduced a more modern and Western-looking city, with wide boulevards in the downtown area, steel-reinforced office buildings, large movie houses, cafés, a sprawling railroad system, and numerous *sakariba* (bustling places), where crowds shopped and otherwise enjoyed themselves, Fuki's mother-in-law among them.[11] She went shopping every three days at large department stores such as Mitsukoshi. She went to a beauty parlor to have her hair done in the short, curled style known as the permanent wave and identified with modern femininity. She attended New Year's Eve parties at the new Imperial Hotel, designed by Frank Lloyd Wright. Two female servants and male helpers handled the housework while Fuki's mother-in-law enjoyed the leisure-time activities favored by the urban consuming masses.

Although the Akakura family's wealth freed Fuki from domestic responsibilities such as cooking, she fell almost entirely under the rule of her bossy and unpredictable mother-in-law, who treated her like one of the several servants and expected her to clean her room and do laundry for herself and her husband. In fact, her mother-in-law specifically ordered her not to make use of the servants. Once she summoned Fuki to the second floor by clapping her hands, as she did to call the servants, and when Fuki came, she ordered her to take down something from a shelf. Wondering why her mother-in-law could not get it down for herself, Fuki began to cry. Her mother-in-law warned her not to tell her husband about the incident.

Another Akakura son and his infant child lived with the family while the child's mother was confined to a tuberculosis sanitarium. Fuki, who at twenty-four still had not conceived a child, was assigned the task of caring for her nephew, which she did, faithfully, for the next five years, until the boy entered primary school.

Fuki's fondness for her husband and his lifelong devotion to her, despite his initial preference for her sister, carried her through the difficulties of the first decade of her marriage and sustained her even during wartime, when he was drafted into the army and sent to Manchuria. She comforted herself with the words of a popular prewar song, which she recited sixty years later: "If the moon were a mirror, when your lover looked at the moon, and you looked at it, you could see each other." Her father-in-law became her ally. After her mother-in-law began intercepting the letters Ichirō sent from his army camp, he addressed them instead in care of his father, who passed them on to Fuki. The father occasionally took Fuki out to a movie on the fashionable Ginza, joining crowds of other Tokyoites drawn to the bustling downtown area considered "the place to be."[12] Afterward they would stroll past the multistoried department stores and drinking spots along the Ginza and eat tempura at one of the many restaurants catering to urban consumer tastes.

Fuki also had the companionship of several young men her age, platonic friends whose families owned *kissaten* (neighborhood tearooms or small restaurants) and with whom she would sip tea and share her domestic problems. Oddly enough, at a time when the totalitarian, military-dominated government was attempting to strictly regulate the dress, hairstyles, and behavior of both single and married women, even to the point of discouraging permanent waves and closing down cafés, it was not considered strange for the young wife of a soldier to fraternize with other men, perhaps because Asakusa mores were looser than anywhere else in Japan or, in Fuki's case, perhaps because she always had her nephew on her back. Once she even drove as far as Kamakura with one of her platonic male friends. "Nobody criticized me for this. They knew that when I watched the baby, he never got hurt, not even a scratch."

It was more difficult for Fuki to socialize with her parents, because her mother-in-law, unlike the in-laws of her older sister Mina, would never leave them alone when they tried to visit, and afterward she would ask the maids to describe the presents Isami and Kō had brought for Fuki. As a result, Kō did not like to visit. In contrast, Mina and her husband lived on their own, thanks to an office job with a tobacco company in Fukuoka prefecture, which her husband had secured with the help of his well-connected oldest brother. When she and her husband visited his parents in their country home in Nasu, Kō and Isami would meet them there, and the senior Ishiwata would discreetly slip away to give Mina and her husband an opportunity to visit alone with her parents. Mina's in-laws, as she often reminded her sisters, were *interi,* intellectuals with a distinguished lineage and presumably better manners. Also, as Mina explained, "they respected the individual."[13]

Meanwhile, Fuki's next younger sister Shiki, disappointed that she could not marry Dr. Akakura, agreed to a match with another doctor, Nakao Shin, who hailed from Nagasaki. Her marriage in 1938 followed years of rebellious behavior and strained relations with her father. Isami was dismayed when she dropped out of Freedom School and furious when he discovered that she had sent a photograph of herself to an advertising company that offered her a modeling job as the "sweet girl" for Morinaga chocolate, one of its clients. Given her lively personality and her passion for shopping and eating out in Tokyo restaurants, it was not surprising that the marriage arranged for her turned out poorly. The man chosen for her, like many men of his generation, was preoccupied with his work. Adding to Shiki's unhappiness was her inability to conceive.[14]

Fumi also married in 1938. By then she had finally recovered from surgery to treat the serious stomach infection that had produced hard, painful, purulent swellings. She was matched with Sugai Kanji, who was six years her senior and an alumnus of Tokyo Imperial University. Sugai, who bore a strong resemblance to the reigning emperor Hirohito, had spent the last five years searching for coal and wood fuel in Manchuria as a geologist for the Manchuria Mining Development Company. Fumi, who was known as the most beautiful of the Matsuura sisters, explained years later why she had agreed to a match that would require her to live so far from home: "I had a big scar from stomach surgery, and he was already living in Manchuria, so we each had a flaw."[15]

It is true that Japanese men who went abroad in the late 1930s, especially those in military service, often encountered problems in finding marriage partners, and even Yūshirō, equipped with his impressive medical degree, was turned down by the first woman the family approached when the woman's father learned that he was an army surgeon stationed in Manchuria. A certain pioneer spirit was required to live in the country that the Japanese viewed as their colonial frontier. The nineteen-year-old woman who eventually became Yūshirō's bride cast aside any qualms she may have had about leaving the home islands after seeing a photograph of him in his army uniform. Nine years younger than Yūshirō and the oldest daughter of a Mitsubishi employee, Anjo Masako had just graduated from a coeducational high school in Tokyo and completed a course at a cooking school there. She found the Matsuura's fourth son handsome enough to lure her away from the comfortable cosmopolitan world of the capital and take up residence in an army camp in the northern reaches of Manchuria.[16]

Masako met Yūshirō in person for the first time when he came home on a furlough, and she saw him every day for two weeks. Thereafter, the Matsuura family launched a full-scale campaign to win Masako's hand. Eager to match his fourth-born son to this refined, city-bred young woman, Isami worked hard to persuade her. He wrote a long letter describing the family in detail, beginning with their origins in the late seventeenth century and including a list of Yūshirō's siblings, his schooling, and his current position in the army. Isami even mentioned his numerous inventions. Mina and Fuki reinforced their father's efforts by visiting Masako's family several times to speak on behalf of their brother. Only Kōjirō expressed reservations. The letter he sent from Australia, where he was working for Mitsubishi, advised against the marriage on the grounds that, as the daughter of a Mitsubishi employee, Masako would be a "luxury"—too expensive to maintain because she was probably accustomed to a life of wealth.

Ignoring the advice of their second son, the Matsuura family persisted, and finally their entreaties led Masako's father to consider the proposal. He visited Yamashiraishi to look at the Matsuura family gravestones; their number and proper upkeep signaled family continuity and respectability. He also made discreet inquiries of the neighbors. Isami then went to visit the Anjo family grave sites in Tochigi prefecture, which, like the Matsuura's, demonstrated a long and stable lineage.

Masako's father's investigation, however, turned up disturbing information that almost sabotaged the marriage. He learned that the Matsuura heir, Yatarō, was a "playboy" who idled away his time in the trendy Ginza. Isami managed to beat back opposition to the match. He promised that he would ask nothing of Masako in the future; as the wife of his fourth son, she would have no obligation to live with him and Kō and care for them in their old age. Eventually the Anjo agreed to the betrothal, setting aside their doubts about Yatarō—doubts that, within a decade, would prove prophetic in regard to his role as the Matsuura heir apparent and the effect his inadequacy would have on their daughter and Yūshirō. Masako and Yūshirō were married in Tokyo in June 1939; it was the last family wedding before the Pacific war engulfed them all.

On the eve of their departure for Manchuria, the couple was given the customary reception in the Matsuura family home so that villagers could meet the new bride. The sliding doors were opened to create enough space to accommodate all the village people, who were served what was considered a feast by the standards of the countryside in that day: octopus, tofu, and whatever seasonal fruit was growing naturally in the area. For the June reception it was silverberry. Masako followed the tradition of presenting gifts to each member of the household, including the servants. She knew even then that, despite their prosperous facade, the Matsuura had very little income left.[17]

SEVEN

Frugality and Fancy Schemes

ALTHOUGH WORRIED ABOUT THEIR DWINDLING FINANCES, Isami and Kō could not resist attending the 1934 wedding of close and prominent relatives in Wakayama, in the southwestern part of the main island. The bride was Isami's niece, the oldest daughter of his sister Moto. Her paternal grandfather was Isami's uncle Ishii Bungorō, a Seiyūkai Party politician; her father, Ishii Itarō, whose studies had been funded by Isami's parents, was consul-general in Shanghai. He, too, was strapped for cash to cover wedding costs and complained that the Japanese diplomatic corps in China was poorly paid.[1]

Despite their own money anxieties, Isami and Kō decided to splurge by extending their trip to include a visit to the Ise Shrine and the ancient capital Kyoto. They left their youngest children with family members in Tokyo. Like Isami's great-grandfather Daisuke, who, almost exactly seventy years earlier and also in middle age, had splurged on a long trip with his wife, Isami and Kō returned home with many happy memories but having nearly exhausted their household finances. They admitted, "In later years we sometimes became teary-eyed thinking about it."[2]

The effort to pay for the education and weddings of his many children led Isami over the years not only to sell rice land acquired by over ten generations of his forebears but also to devise other schemes to subsidize the family's agricultural income with entrepreneurial ventures. Involvement in diverse business operations was typical of Matsuura househeads; the family had a long tradition of entrepreneurship, beginning with the second generation's Sōemon, who launched the sake brewery in the first half of the seventeenth century. Isami's ancestors, however, had shown themselves to be shrewd businessmen, whereas he, to his chagrin, enjoyed only limited success in the business world.

Isami wrote admiringly, perhaps even enviously, of Sōemon's son, who not only opened up new rice land to cultivation but also, like his father, "proved adept at making money."[3] Authorities were so impressed with this early Matsuura ancestor, they gave him a monetary award in recognition of the way he had "used his brains on economic activity that benefited others in the village," according to what Isami wrote.[4]

The fourth-generation househead, heir to his father's successes, bequeathed extensive holdings to his son Yūemon. In addition to sake and rice, the family was marketing beans, wheat flour, firewood, and lumber as well as folk crafts and household wares by the 1790s. These products were produced by villagers in their employ, who benefited from Matsuura income-generating activities as clerks, cultivators, craftsmen, and household servants. Yūemon expanded the family business to include soy sauce manufacture and opened a retail store in Asakawa to sell the family's products.

In the sixth generation, Yūemon Jinsuke further expanded economic activities by introducing tobacco as a cash crop, and after retiring from the village headship, he opened another retail store. By the time of Isami's great-grandfather Daisuke in the eighth generation, if not sooner, the family's business dealings extended as far as Edo.[5]

Daisuke's meticulous accounting of his business transactions and travel expenses conveys the extent of his involvement in the domestic commercial economy; clearly the Matsuura family in the middle of the nineteenth century was peasant only in official class designation. In fact, they were landlords, entrepreneurs, and consumers whose close attention to the price of goods and services was typical of the profit-oriented, coin-counting city shopkeepers satirized in popular Tokugawa-era short stories.

Well before Isami's time, Matsuura househeads were accustomed to dealing in hefty sums. The substantial amounts of gold coin *(ryō)* that Daisuke handled reflected not only Matsuura wealth and business savvy but also the highly developed money economy of his time. Much of his business was transacted in Edo's major commercial district, Nihonbashi, where the streets were lined with the substantial warehouses and two-story specialty retail shops of well-established merchant houses. (In one dealing there, Daisuke lamented, "I could not do well even though I tried.") During his sojourn to Edo in 1863, Daisuke borrowed five hundred *ryō* from a tobacco warehouse *(tonya)*. In another shop, called Naraya, he received twenty-five *ryō* and elsewhere expended twenty *ryō,* either to repay a loan or to make a purchase.[6]

In truth, part of what accounted for these substantial amounts of currency was the inflation that had occurred in the short period of time since the opening of Japan's ports to foreign trade, which raised commodity prices and reduced the value of the *ryō* by as much as 40 percent. Aware of the country's lack of military preparedness, Edo townsmen hoarded staples, further driving up prices.[7] Nevertheless, even after 1863, one *ryō* could buy enough rice to feed a man for six months, purchase seventy-two liters of sake, or pay a day laborer for forty days' work.[8]

The considerable wealth of the Matsuura family was preserved by Daisuke's adopted son-in-law (and Isami's grandfather) Jinsuke, who presided over the family's land and business holdings into the ninth generation, well beyond the overthrow of the Tokugawa. The family's ability to survive the economic disruptions caused by the opening of Japan to foreign trade and the dismantling of the old political system is unusual, for there was a high rate of failure among the rural elite during the Meiji period. Many Tokugawa-era rural businesses failed to overcome the burden of new taxes that the Meiji government placed on brewery industries. In fact, in 1913, under the headship of the tenth generation's Yūya, the Matsuura family did finally have to shut down its sake industry, in part because of these increased taxes on brewers.[9]

The reasons for Jinsuke's success in weathering the volatile Meiji era escaped his grandson Isami's scrutiny. It is safe to assume that Jinsuke was a conscientious household head who continued to nurture the family's ties with relatives and other rural elites that had always been important for promoting business operations. Then too the new, more uniform and efficient land tax system introduced by the Meiji government in 1871 benefited wealthy landholders and village heads such as the Matsuura, because it eliminated the forced loans and contributions to officials they had encountered under the Tokugawa. At the same time, the new tax, levied on individual households rather than on the calculated yield of the village as a whole, adversely affected some farm families, who, if they could not pay their taxes, were forced to borrow from wealthier farmers like the Matsuura or to become their tenant farmers. It is likely that, as a result, Matsuura landholdings increased even more during this period. Nevertheless, despite a particularly bad harvest in Yamashiraishi in 1877 and rural uprisings over taxes throughout the country in the 1870s, villagers in Yamashiraishi remained quiescent, and the population even grew.[10] By 1887, Jinsuke reported a jump in village population to 800 people in 138 households.[11]

After his retirement in 1901, Jinsuke dabbled in new business schemes, an inclination his grandson Isami inherited. Most of Jinsuke's business ventures, however, were of dubious value. He gave up altogether after he lost a thousand *ryō* on an ill-fated plan to ship rice from Sendai to Tokyo and oil from Tokyo to Sendai. He learned from the experience, Isami wrote, that "you should always have something in reserve."[12] His losses, however, did not shake the foundations of the family's wealth, and Isami's father, Yūya, inherited a great fortune.

Yūya presided over the family in its heyday. By his time, in the tenth generation, the Matsuura family's holdings totaled two hundred *chō*—almost five hundred acres—a huge amount in a country where for hundreds of years the average farm household owned one *chō,* or two and one-half acres. Although mountain woodland not amenable to cultivation accounted for 150 acres of Matsuura family property, another 135 or so represented income property cultivated by tenants, who generally turned over one-third of the harvest as rent. This amounted to an annual rent income of between two thousand and three thousand *hyō* (straw bales of rice), each weighing sixty kilograms and worth twenty thousand yen. Three managers *(bantō)* handled the family's entrepreneurial activities, which, even after Yūya and Isami decided to shut down the sake brewery, included other lucrative endeavors such as soy sauce manufacture and tobacco cultivation. "Their income," said the Asakawa local historian, "was tremendously large." In 1919, the year before Isami became legal head of the family, the Matsuura were not only one of the top eight taxpayers in Fukushima prefecture but the wealthiest in the Asakawa area.[13] Yet, on the eve of World War II, as Isami's daughter-in-law observed, that wealth was almost all gone.

After becoming legal head of the family, Isami had immediately embarked on a number of entrepreneurial ventures with only limited success, and the family's fortune suffered. "Because of my strong determination to do what I thought was right," Isami confessed in his later years, "I spent a lot of the family's wealth."[14]

One of Isami's few successful business ventures was the production of oatmeal, a new food in the Japanese diet, using a propeller-like device that he invented and patented. Isami purchased a factory in Tokyo to begin producing and selling baby food. Under the management of his firstborn son, Yatarō, the factory operated at a profit during the 1930s, after Isami had snared a special contract to supply oatmeal to the army.[15] The company did well until wartime, when government rationing of staples made it difficult to get the oats and other necessary materials. Faced with the imminent weddings of Shiki, Fumi, and Yūshirō in the last half of the 1930s, after marrying off six of his older children, Isami worked on several other schemes to raise funds.

A less successful business investment was the Nakagawa Electrical Manufacturing Company. After the owner suddenly died in 1920, the company's management had fallen into Isami's hands—probably because he was a principal investor—whereupon it began to lose money. Bad luck hounded Isami's efforts. He tried to improve the company's profits by signing a contract to patent a rice husker invented by a man named Tokunaga, who also died suddenly, as did another company associate. Isami attempted to improve Tokunaga's invention, correcting its weak points, and he spent many more years trying to get his own patent for it and looking for a manufacturer to produce it. He also drew up plans for a washing machine, but had trouble developing and marketing it.

In the 1920s Isami and Yatarō had also explored investment opportunities in a hydroelectric power project in Aizu, in the western part of Fukushima, but they could not raise sufficient capital. Another project, a silk-reeling company in Asakawa, folded.[16] Isami had greater success with a hydroelectric power plant that he sold in 1938 to an electric power company in Niigata prefecture for eighteen thousand yen.[17]

Isami's zeal for inventing and investing reflected his commitment to technology and the modernity it implied. Intellectually engaged and possessed of a natural talent for designing and drawing (he also enjoyed doing architectural sketches), he nonetheless had little experience with the modern industrial business world that he struggled to enter. Undaunted by either inexperience or failure, Isami persisted in experimenting with one business deal after the other. Demonstrating a confidence bordering on pigheadedness, he had even changed the motto on the house seal to read "Even if countless numbers of people oppose me, I will go my own way."[18]

This passion for new technology may have constituted merely intellectual play, as his daughters later conjectured. Nevertheless, Isami oversaw or promoted several projects, such as waterworks, electricity, and irrigation, in the tradition of his forebears, intending them to benefit his home village in one way or another. Other of his projects probably reflected his desire to secure the family's income by not relying entirely on their agricultural land, especially since the 1920s witnessed increasingly troubled times for farmers. There was a widening gap in income, standard of living, productivity, and lifestyle between agrarian areas and the more industrialized and Westernized cities. Ever since the Russo-Japanese War, investment in modern industry and commerce had been more profitable than farmland, because landlords' income was taxed more heavily, among other factors. Landlords such as Isami increasingly turned to investment in industry and also entrepreneurial and managerial activities in the early twentieth century rather than accumulating more farmland.[19]

Unfortunately, Isami's entrepreneurial efforts often, though not always, drained the family's wealth rather than enhancing it, according to his own observations, as well as the impression his youngest daughter expressed many years later. Moreover, the family's oldest son, despite the benefit of a college education, proved unreliable. Isami set Yatarō to work at one or another of his enterprises but was always anxious about his managerial skills, and his reputation as a playboy did not help matters.[20]

Adding to the outflow of money were several real estate transactions outside Fukushima. In 1917, Isami had a large house built in the Nippori section of Tokyo, which he originally intended to use for the children's lodgings when they moved to the city for schooling but rented to an artist instead. In the same year he built a campsite *(tenmaku)* at Nakoso, on the coast east of Fukushima, where the family could stay in tents on summer vacations. In 1920, he bought more land in Tokyo, this time for the Nishigahara house that became the children's residence during their school years.[21]

Although the Tokyo houses were built in the Japanese style, of simple wood construction, without central heating or plumbing and with minimal kitchen facilities and furnishings, they required an amount of money that few Japanese possessed. Only a small number of urban residents owned their own homes in the 1920s. Urban homeowners tended to be wealthy industrialists, politicians, and members of the aristocracy; the vast majority of city dwellings were rentals.[22] Luckily, both of the Tokyo houses survived the 1923 Kantō earthquake, though another house owned by one of Isami's companies burned down in the conflagration following the earthquake. As befitted his social status, if not his financial standing, Isami was quick to send a monetary contribution to the nation's Earthquake Relief Fund.

With money tied up in various properties and investments, Isami was caught short by the nation's bank moratorium in April 1927, two years before the Great Depression. Even Fukushima banks closed. Although heavily in debt, somehow he managed to "resolve things," though he did not say how; most likely he renegotiated a bank loan or perhaps he sold off more rice land.[23] Somewhat chastened by this close encounter with bankruptcy, Isami "reflected deeply on his life course," and, as if to reinforce a resolution for greater frugality in the future, he had the character for virtue *(toku)* carved into the household seal.[24]

In the year following the bank moratorium, however, Isami threw a big party in Tokyo to celebrate the golden wedding anniversary of his parents,

Miyo and Yūya. By 1929, Isami's second son, Kōjirō, had graduated from Tokyo Imperial University and secured a job with Mitsubishi, which helped support his brothers and sisters while the country felt the full effects of the Depression. Isami correctly sensed "many problems" and hard times ahead in the world.[25]

Throughout the 1930s the Japanese countryside roiled with ferment. Rural areas had been especially hurt by the Depression. Unemployed urban workers returned to their family farms, swelling the rural population and magnifying its problems. Adding to the crisis in the Northeast were the devastating crop failures caused by bad weather in 1933 and 1934. In desperation, many Fukushima farmers resettled in Manchuria, where land was more plentiful.[26] A nationwide agrarianist movement pressed government elites to help ease the plight of farmers by providing public works, price supports, tax relief, and other benefits, while tenancy disputes dramatically increased in number, putting further pressure on local elites.[27]

Unrest in the countryside reverberated in the capital on March 15, 1932, when nineteen members of a farm cooperative movement from the Mito area, northeast of Tokyo, joined junior army and navy officers in attacking government officials. They claimed to be acting on behalf of impoverished farmers, whose suffering they attributed to the evils of Westernized city life and capitalism. In that same year, Isami's younger brother Kōzō, an army battalion commander stationed in Hamamatsu, southwest of Tokyo, suffered a nervous breakdown and had to be escorted home by his mother, Miyo, and another brother, Kensuke. He remained in Yamashiraishi for the next three years. While Isami did not provide the details of Kōzō's collapse, one can well imagine the conflict of loyalties he must have felt as both a junior officer and the son of a landlord in an era of insurrections by military peers espousing the plight of the rural poor.[28]

Insights into the bewildering political currents of the time came from Isami's third son, Toshisaburō (called Saburō for short), who became a journalist with the *Nichi nichi* newspaper in 1932, after graduating from Tokyo Imperial University. Closely following contemporary events, Saburō's reports to Isami were not optimistic. The political situation seemed ominous. The assassination of Prime Minister Inukai Ki, a Seiyūkai Party politician, marked the end of prewar party cabinets; prime ministers thereafter, with only a few exceptions, were high-ranking military men. Saburō's older brother Kōjirō concurred with this gloomy assessment. He felt there was a danger that Japan would soon enter into a war.[29] The economic situation was grim as well. There was talk of devaluing the Japanese currency.

Isami heard that financial support for the schools and local government services would be affected. When a mutiny of over fourteen hundred soldiers in February 1936 temporarily paralyzed the government in Tokyo, the sense of insecurity intensified. The attempted military coup was quashed, but not before assassination squads murdered three high-ranking officials. The disorderly times were "scary," Isami later recalled. "Everyone was uneasy."[30]

The Matsuura, as always, managed to ride out the worst of these crisis years. While all around them in the countryside, desperate farmers, unable to pay their land rents, had sold their daughters into prostitution or migrated to Manchuria, the Matsuura had paid school tuition for their daughters and sons alike and had prepared expensive dowries for the daughters' marriages. If Isami's daughters remembered correctly, Isami, like Yūya, had also assisted poorer farmers in the village and allowed his tenants to postpone rent payments, though later events suggested they had not done enough to appease their villagers.

One of Isami's major preoccupations throughout the 1920s and 1930s was to get a railway line built closer to home. His life had been tied to trains ever since Great-Grandfather Daisuke took him on his first trip to Tokyo in 1890. He had traveled by train to boarding school in Kōriyama and to his children's schools in Tokyo. More than anyone else Isami recognized that a nearby rail line could spur economic development by making schools, jobs, and merchandise in surrounding cities more accessible and by bringing the culture of the metropolis closer to the provinces.

Extensive politicking was required to get the central government's financial backing for new rail lines, but Isami, like his forebears, was a reluctant political activist. In fact, after his military service at the turn of the century, he had deliberately tried to keep a low profile. Although viewed as a war hero and envied by other men in the area for the awards he had won during the Russo-Japanese War, Isami, in his own words, had "tried to act humbly."[31] Nevertheless, in 1919 he had agreed to endorse a Seiyūkai Party candidate from Ishikawa, precisely because the party was known to support the construction of many new railway lines to service rural areas. In 1923, he had even agreed to run as a "sacrificial candidate" in a local election and, predictably, lost.[32]

In 1928, Uncle Ishii Bungorō's election to the Diet as a Seiyūkai candidate gave Isami a valuable political ally. Isami's maternal uncle also came from a *shōya* family, but, more drawn to national politics than the Matsuura men were, he had chosen to sell his family's land to pay for his campaign, and once in office he helped open doors for his nephew. The December 1931 national elections offered even greater encouragement to the local railroad boosters in the area of Ishikawa and Asakawa, for it gave 304 seats to the Seiyūkai, including one to the candidate from their area, and through him, Isami and a few other area leaders were granted an introduction to the railroad minister.[33]

Their plan called for building a train line running through their community and connecting with the cities of Kōriyama to the north and Mito to the southeast. At Mito, travelers could transfer to the Jōban line and reach Tokyo in two to three hours, giving the populace of the hinterland much greater access to the capital. After years of effort, Isami and other local leaders finally succeeded in getting approval for the construction of the single-track Suigun line, which could take passengers from the small station at Ishikawa to Mito in two to three hours. Isami rode that distance for the first time in 1934.

With the Suigun line in operation, travelers no longer had to board the Tōhoku line at the train station in Shirakawa, fifteen miles away from Ishikawa, as Isami and his older children had done whenever they went to Tokyo. But even after a station opened at Asakawa, as Tami recalled, travelers still had to get up at four in the morning to walk the two and one-half miles—about forty minutes—in time to catch the early train. Also, since there was only a single track running along the edge of rice paddies, a train heading in one direction had to wait for an oncoming train to pass before proceeding. Still, the new stations considerably reduced the ordeal of traveling to Tokyo. The Suigun line still operates, but at Kōriyama, a forty-minute ride from Ishikawa, it now connects with the high-speed Shinkansen, which carries travelers to Tokyo in a mere ninety minutes more.

Isami and Kō participated in the celebration marking the official opening of the new train station in Ishikawa in 1935. They attended "as a couple," Isami wrote, and "with great happiness and relief."[34] A plaque recognizing Isami's efforts still hangs in front of the station.

With the coming of the railroad line to their area, Isami determined that at long last he could leave political battles behind him and concentrate on his business schemes. While he had exerted himself for over ten years on behalf of his many civic projects and business enterprises, his children had grown and "advanced in their desired directions," and he had been almost too busy to notice the life around him. In his characteristic way, he wrote a poem to express his feelings at the time:

> Without realizing it ten years passed
> and I did not notice the flowers and the autumn leaves.[35]

But Isami had little leisure time to savor the flora in the countryside. Two years later, at the end of 1937, the family's financial circumstances became a matter of public scrutiny following the funeral of Yūya. Isami naturally assumed that the village assembly would automatically choose him to succeed his father as village head. Instead, to his shock, members of the village assembly launched an investigation of charges of fiscal irresponsibility on the part of both Isami and Yūya. After ten generations of Matsuura stewardship, a scandal affecting father and son, reminiscent of the cause célèbre that had brought their founding ancestor to the village 248 years earlier, threatened to blemish the Matsuura name.

The issue, as spelled out by the deputy village head, involved the way one of the Matsuura's longtime business managers had handled the family's rural enterprises. The implication was that Isami, too, might be guilty of wrongdoing. The charges revolved around the selling of rice the family had received as payment from tenant farmers renting their rice land. The investigation dragged on for two months into February 1938, but before any proof of wrongdoing was uncovered, the village school burned down as a result of a student's carelessness. The school, originally built by Daisuke in the early 1870s, had been rebuilt twenty years earlier with Yūya's financial help.

The day after the fire, village representatives called a meeting and asked for nominations for village head. Somebody nominated Isami, who archly replied that he could not serve until he knew why they had held up his selection for two months. He then took out a framed poem by the Meiji-era educator Fukuzawa Yukichi, which Yūya had placed in the school many years earlier. Only the day before the fire, Isami had gone to the school to remove the poem, perhaps irked by the long delay in nominating him. He now read it aloud to assembled village representatives and explained its meaning to them in a patronizing voice.

The poem linked changes in nature to human society. Human affairs were the source of natural events. In this instance, the selection of the village head was an example of human affairs, and the school's fire was an example of a natural event. The delay in choosing the village head, Isami implied, caused the fire, because it was the responsibility of the village head to keep everyone mindful of the dangers of fire in the wooden structure, as his father had faithfully done. But with Yūya no longer in office, and no other village head to replace him, Isami charged, they had all become lazy and careless.

Isami offered to accept the nomination only if village representatives apologized on the grave of his father. The assembled villagers rose in unison and walked silently through the snow to Yūya's grave. Isami then accepted the appointment.[36] Despite the resolution of the incident, he was still angry over it fifteen years later. He attempted to explain away the charges by accusing the deputy of hankering after the village headship office. The deputy was ambitious for political office, Isami wrote, because as Yūya's assistant, he had often gone in Yūya's place to meetings of village heads. He had become known and gained experience, and now he was smearing the Matsuura name so that he could become village head in Isami's place.

Despite its resolution, however, the incident did not mark the end of Isami's financial problems; at this point, he still had eight more children coming through the marriage pipeline. Nor did the incident bode well for his political problems; his term as village head, begun inauspiciously under a cloud of suspicion, continued under a cloud of war. Before long, a lot more than the school would be lost.

PART THREE

Empire, War, and Defeat

EIGHT

Outposts of Modernity

TOYO'S MOTHER-IN-LAW AND SISTER-IN-LAW Ikuko arrived in the charming port city of Qingdao (Tsingtao) in the summer of 1935 to spend a one-month holiday with Toyo and her husband shortly after Masafumi's employer, Mitsubishi, transferred him there to work in a branch of its import-export trading company. Ikuko relished the "free feeling" of the city so much that she returned again in 1941. She recalled Qingdao as an exciting city, filled as it was with the people and culture of many different nationalities. Foreign couples strolled arm in arm, White Russian shopkeepers plied their wares, and theaters showed foreign films.[1] The Germany brewery that made Tsing-tao Beer at the time was one of the city's most famous industries.

Qingdao life was "bountiful" as well as cosmopolitan, at least in Masa-fumi's sister's memory of it. Of course, she mainly met the people in her brother's "high-class" social circle. Living the life of a "privileged interloper,"[2] as did other representatives of imperialist powers in China, India, the Dutch East Indies, French Indochina, and elsewhere in Asia, Masafumi socialized with Japanese Army officers and Mitsubishi company officials at all-male parties, with the exception of the Chinese house servants and the hostesses, who added to the men's comfort and sense of superiority.

Qingdao and other port cities in China evoked the ambience of Europe. Located on the Shandong (Shantung) Peninsula, facing Jiaozhou (Kiao-chow) Bay, Qingdao was developed originally by Germany, which seized the territory in 1897 and won rights to lease it for ninety-nine years and to construct rail lines. Railroads and leased territories were governed and po-liced by the foreign powers that held them and were administered like quasi-colonial areas.[3] Thanks to German urban planners, who laid out public parks and extensive green spaces, Qingdao became one of the most desirable places to live in the whole of China. The skyline facing the harbor resembled a German city on the Rhine river. Two-story houses with red or green roofs were nestled between low mountains and the sea. Beautiful beaches and accommodations for travelers turned the city into a seaside resort area, known as the Riviera of the Far East by the early 1920s.[4]

Although the Germans lost their leasehold on the Shandong Peninsula in 1914, a strong German architectural influence remained. The Chinese city's Western atmosphere and amenities delighted its Japanese residents, Toyo and Masafumi among them, for they still looked to Europe as the model of civilization. Unlike drafty wood residences in Japan, the stone house that Toyo and her husband rented, a mere ten-minute walk from the sea, featured central heating, with coal supplied by Masafumi's company. The young couple were captivated by the architecture of the Handelsbank and the Gothic-style church as well as by the main street of Qingdao, paved, tree-lined, and traversed by horse-drawn surreys and rickshaw. Overnight they had become part of a social elite, the semicolonial ruling class of foreigners. They photographed each other lolling on grassy knolls, strolling along the strand, and riding in surreys, seemingly unaware that, by 1937, Japan and China would be at war. In fact, with the exception of Toyo's older brother Kōjirō, who was in the Netherlands East Indies (present-day Indonesia) in the mid-1930s, and her aunt Moto's husband, Ishii Itarō, who was consul-general in Shanghai, the Matsuura siblings and related family members revealed very little political awareness of their place in the larger picture of Japan's imperialist aggression in China. Unintentional exploiters, they too would soon become victims of war.

Masafumi's sister remembered her homeland in the ominous period of the late 1930s and early 1940s as "dark" and oppressive in contrast to Qingdao. After seizing Manchuria outright in 1931, Japan became diplomatically ostracized by the Western powers, and its military-dominated government closed itself off to Anglo-American influences. As part of the reaction against "excessive Western influences," couples dancing was proscribed and cafés were closed down. Under these circumstances, the opportunity to experience life abroad in more prosperous European-style enclaves was exciting to the relatives of Isami and Kō.

The Qingdao years from 1935 to 1941, however oppressive for the Chinese, represented a liberation of sorts for Toyo. Her move to China was made possible by the intervention of her father, who stepped in to rescue her from a marriage that from the very beginning, in her youngest sister's words, was a disaster. The young couple began married life in the home of Masafumi's widowed mother, Sen, who, though gentle, was demanding, and Masafumi was even worse. After the loss of his father when he was only twelve, Masafumi had presided over the household, which also included Masafumi's three sisters. (One of his brothers had died around the time the couple became engaged, and another was a college student in Kyoto.) Heir to the family headship and coddled by his mother, who never remarried, Masafumi had become a little prince and a petty tyrant. Treated like the stereotypical put-upon Japanese daughter-in-law, the new graduate of Freedom School was worked like a servant, while the others in the family deferred to her husband as though he were a feudal lord. If he did not like the taste of the rice, he insisted that Toyo make it again or he threw it away. He wanted special foods. He criticized her cooking and her housekeeping and compared her invidiously with other men's wives.[5]

Two months after her marriage, Toyo contracted an ear infection, caused, she thought, by not having had time to dry her hair after washing it on a cold day. The infection was serious enough that she required surgery. Fortunately, Fuki's husband helped to arrange for the operation. According to both Toyo's youngest sister, Tami, and her daughter, Yōko, Isami was sufficiently worried about Toyo to intervene on her behalf by asking Masafumi's supervisors at Mitsubishi to send him back to China, where he had been assigned before their marriage.

Their move to China freed Toyo considerably. Although Masafumi continued to send money to his mother, Toyo no longer had to serve his family members on a daily basis. Instead, she had her own Chinese house servants as well as a Japanese maid, sent by Isami, who worried that Toyo had not yet fully recovered her health. Toyo's social circle soon expanded to include the many Japanese affiliated with Mitsubishi's import-export activities.

Overseas life for Masafumi represented a step up the ladder of advancement in the enormously powerful Mitsubishi *zaibatsu,* a cartel of several businesses controlled by one family. "When we were in China," one of Masafumi's colleagues reminisced, "we were working for only one branch of Mitsubishi—import-export. We didn't realize how big Mitsubishi was. When we returned to Tokyo, we realized it for the first time. Mitsubishi and Mitsui were the two biggest Japanese companies."[6]

A well-established conglomerate by the 1930s, Mitsubishi was one of the government's "chosen instruments for economic development."[7] Its bank was one of the five largest in Japan. Masafumi's future and, indeed, his very identity were tied to the fortunes of Mitsubishi, whose growth was further fueled in the 1930s and early 1940s by Japan's mobilization for war, first in China and then against the Allied powers.

For Toyo, the China years were a mixture of stimulating social life and unresolved marital problems. She and Masafumi were a popular couple among the many other Japanese in the city, which had over 350,000 inhabitants.[8] The more than 14,000 Japanese nationals living there warranted the establishment of the Qingdao Japanese Residents' Association and separate schools for Japanese children.[9] Thanks to her training at Hani Motoko's Freedom School and the help of her servants, Toyo acquired a reputation among resident Japanese as an accomplished hostess and cook whose dinner parties featured elaborate hors d'oeuvres. She and Masafumi became known for their kindness to newly arrived Mitsubishi employees and their families and for their generosity as hosts. When their friends were preparing to return to Japan, Toyo sent food to their house and frequently invited them to dinner. Toyo was regarded as an "ideal" wife by friends in China; indeed, many of the men were attracted to her.[10]

Masafumi, too, had many friends and admirers within the close-knit Japanese community. A dashing young man with a dazzling smile and the good looks of a movie star in the Humphrey Bogart mold, Masafumi impressed associates with his warmth and kindness. His friend remembered that he did not talk much, but he went out of his way to help people. He was amiable, sincere, honest: a "courteous gentleman." But that was only one side of him; the other was a restless, unfaithful husband. Everyone connected with his company, including Toyo, knew about Masafumi's Japanese girlfriend, a woman who worked in his office. Ibuka Yuriko, the wife of Masafumi's friend, described her as *heibon* (common) and related how Toyo insisted that he end the affair. Masafumi wanted a divorce, but in those days, Yuriko added, you did not get divorced. Indeed, when Kō heard that Masafumi wanted to marry his girlfriend, she angrily confronted him. His own mother also opposed the divorce, and he backed down.[11]

Adding to the tensions between the couple was Toyo's failure to become pregnant. "Toyo loved children," Yuriko recalled. "The families of Mitsubishi employees would gather at her house, and she would help take care of the children."[12] Toyo was eventually diagnosed as having closed Fallopian tubes, the same medical condition that also prevented her older sister Fuki from becoming pregnant. Her younger sister Shiki, too, was unable to conceive.

—

Other Matsuura family members who made their way to China, Indonesia, Australia, and even as far as the United States in the late 1930s and early 1940s also attempted to start their own families, though in an increasingly hostile overseas environment of boycotts, strikes, and protests against Japanese-owned factories and businesses. But like Masafumi and his colleagues, most Matsuura family members abroad—men and women in their twenties and early thirties—only dimly perceived their role in the larger design of empire and war.

The overseas empire that Japan began securing in the last decade of the nineteenth century called for an increasing number of personnel to operate abroad, especially in Asia. The nation's leaders deemed empire essential to the maintenance of Japan's position as a world power. Whether they were abroad furthering trade and investment in China, developing Japan's newly seized Chinese territory of Manchuria (renamed Manchukuo in 1932), administering Japan's colonies in Korea and Formosa (Taiwan), or searching for raw materials throughout Southeast Asia and the South Pacific, Japanese citizen-subjects of the emperor, long accustomed to living on the home islands, where foreigners were rare, found themselves in new situations requiring special social, technical, and foreign-language skills. Here, too, Isami's promotion of modern education paid off. His sons and in-laws became part of the new colonial elite—economic, diplomatic, and military warriors engaged in promoting Japanese trade interests and territorial ambitions abroad in competition with Western imperialist powers.

One of the few Matsuura family members who grasped the larger picture of imperialism and colonialism in Asia was Kōjirō, the first of the Matsuura children dispatched overseas. Shortly after their marriage, Kōjirō and his wife moved to the Netherlands East Indies. Their three children were born on Java in the mid-1930s while Kōjirō was employed at a Mitsubishi branch office in the city of Surabaya, home to the largest contingent of Japanese in the East Indies. A colony of the Dutch, the East Indies was a paradise, in the opinion of the Japanese consul in Surabaya.[13] Kōjirō found it "more modern than Japan," and he marveled at the beautiful Dutch residences. As soon as he laid eyes on the port, in fact, he was seized by the feeling that the place held great significance for his future. He was right. Recognizing the trade potential of the islands and the value of their abundant natural resources to Japan's economy, Kōjirō hired a tutor, and within six months he could communicate with Javanese in their language.[14]

Kōjirō's arrival in the East Indies in 1933 coincided with a critical turning point in Japan's relations with the rest of the world. The League of Nations had just condemned Japan for its takeover of the Chinese eastern territory of Manchuria, and the United States had announced a policy of

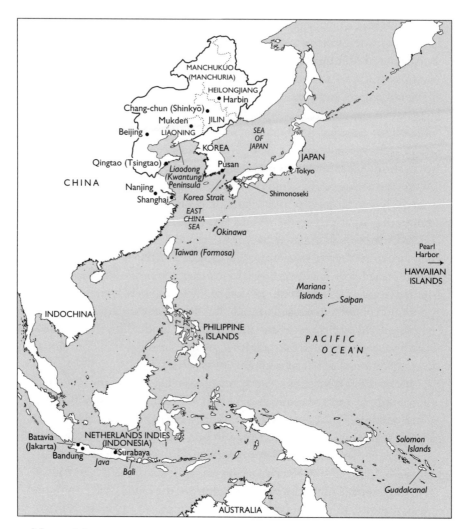

MAP 3 Asia ca. 1942

"nonrecognition" of the new puppet state of Manchukuo. Japan angrily withdrew from the league. In light of growing tensions with other world powers, the Japanese Navy was keen on promoting a strategy of southward expansion toward Indonesia's treasure trove of war materials: oil, rubber, and bauxite. Weak in natural resources, Japan depended on imported oil, purchased primarily from the West Coast of the United States but a significant 20 percent from the Indies.[15]

Even earlier, in the 1920s, the Indies had become increasingly important to Japan's economy. A steady stream of migrating Japanese merchants, fishermen, and prostitutes sought their fortune in the European colony south of the Japanese islands. For the first time in 1933, more than 30 percent of Japan's imports came from the Netherlands East Indies, while Japanese textiles and other cheap manufactures flooded the colony's markets. The sudden economic "overpresence" of Japanese goods led the Dutch colonial government to impose tariff regulations. The Dutch also imposed restrictions on Japanese immigration in 1933, after the number of Japanese living in the Indies reached almost seven thousand.[16]

If Kōjirō understood the growing value of the Dutch colony to Japan's economic expansion, his stint in the East Indies in this decade also gave him a firsthand understanding of the plight of colonial peoples. In the same year that he went to the East Indies, Indonesian nationalist leaders Mohammad Hatta and Achmed Sukarno visited Japan, where they pleaded for direct trade between Japan and native Indonesians. "Economic independence is the foremost goal of us Indonesians," Hatta said. The "exploitation by the whites frustrates us immensely."[17]

The exploitation was readily apparent to Kōjirō. As a Japanese resident, he was in a unique position in the social class system enforced by the Dutch colonial government. At the turn of the century, as a result of strenuous diplomatic negotiations, Japanese there had acquired legal status as "honorary whites" equal to Europeans. As modernizers possessing their own empire, Japanese were seen as separate from, and presumably superior to, the other "foreign Asians" in the Netherlands East Indies as well as the native population there.[18]

There was a great gap in the standard of living between the Dutch rulers and their native subjects. Dutch colonialists attributed the differences to congenital weaknesses in the Indonesian population. They viewed Indonesians, in one scholar's words, as "children under the tutelage of the West"; they were "creatures occupying a lower rung on the evolutionary ladder, waiting to be educated by their Dutch tutors."[19] Some Dutch colonial residents went even further, explaining the widespread illiteracy of the Javanese as a reflection of the native population's innate inferiority. Kōjirō confessed in his memoirs to sharing similar views at first. "I had neither knowledge about nor respect for the subject peoples."[20]

As Kōjirō made friends with foreigners of many different nationalities or ethnic groups living on the islands—Dutch, Arabs, Indians, and Chinese—

as well as with the Indonesian population, he came to grasp the significance of colonial status distinctions. He eventually realized that it was poverty, not genetics, that prevented Indonesians from acquiring an education, and discrimination that hampered their chances of overcoming their social handicaps. Not only did Dutch residents earn much more than the Indonesians, but also racial divisions, Kōjirō observed, were enforced even in movie theaters, where he was permitted to sit in the European section while the native population was relegated to a separate part of the theater.[21]

Firsthand experience with Dutch colonial rule remained imprinted in Kōjirō's memory and shaped his life and thought in unexpected ways years later, when he became a champion of the Indonesian independence movement and worked to promote Indonesian trade with Japan. His stay in the East Indies in the 1930s was interrupted, however, by a company transfer to Australia in 1938. In Australia, Kōjirō once again feasted his eyes on Western architecture and urban modernity. Seeing the "famous and beautiful port of Sydney, with its English-style boulevards," he recalled, "I felt as if I had come from Japan to Europe." While Japanese citizens were numerous in the East Indies, in Melbourne they were so rare that, on the day he arrived, Kōjirō was interviewed by a local newspaperman (whose Australian English was difficult, at first, for him to understand).[22] Before long he developed ties with Australians, ingratiating himself with the local population and expanding his international education and business contacts so successfully that, even in the aftermath of the brutal Pacific war, he would manage to reunite with and work with his country's enemies.

As Asians who had modernized, Japanese such as Kōjirō still viewed the civilization of the Western imperialists as the model to emulate, even if that emulation had meant becoming imperialists themselves in Asia. Standing somewhere between Asia and the West, they confronted difficult challenges even into the 1930s as they made their way into a world dominated by Western standards. Although Kōjirō had sympathized with colonized peoples in Asia, in his post–World War II memoirs he noted that after World War I Japan could not have criticized the Western powers for their colonial policies because Japan had been their ally—one of the "victors" in that war—and had itself colonized Korea and Taiwan.[23]

Another Matsuura relative in the 1930s also negotiated his—and Japan's—place between Western powers and their subjugated Asian peoples. Ishii Itarō, the husband of Isami's younger sister Moto, had been trained in Shanghai as a China expert before World War I. In the 1920s he was posted to the United States, first in the Japanese Consulate-General in San Francisco and then in the Japanese Embassy in Washington, DC, where he took the measure of America's power. In his first hour in San Francisco, while sightseeing along Market Street, he remarked to Moto, "Japan is twenty-five years behind." He soon corrected himself: Japan was "more than twenty-five years behind."[24]

The sight of tall buildings and opulent hotels was not the only reason Ishii viewed Japan as trailing the United States. The Japanese on the West Coast were definitely not treated as "honorary whites," the way they may have been in the Netherlands East Indies. Like his nephew Kōjirō in the Indies, Ishii witnessed efforts in the United States to halt an increase in Japanese population and economic expansion. From his first day in San Francisco, when he and Moto found that local residents would not rent homes to them because they were Japanese, Ishii observed discrimination against his countrymen. The inferior status of Japanese in the United States was vividly manifested in signs reading "No More Japs Wanted Here" and in boatloads of "picture brides" whom Ishii watched arriving in San Francisco's ports to meet their husbands for the first time. United States restrictions on immigrants—a major preoccupation of the Japanese Consulate-General—had produced such drastic countermeasures as the long-distance marriages of Japanese women to Japanese male immigrants in the United States, who otherwise would not have been able to find wives.[25]

After a stint in London, Ishii garnered the prestigious but difficult position of consul-general in Shanghai in the mid-1930s. Here, unlike his experience in the United States, he enjoyed Japan's prominence among the other imperial powers. In port cities such as Shanghai, the Japanese consulates-general were like small embassies, for they represented the strong presence of Japanese commercial interests backed by military power. Ishii worked in an imposing three-story stone and brick building situated with its Western counterparts along the city's waterfront only a short walk from the Japanese quarter, dubbed Little Tokyo. The "ponderous design" of the Japanese Consulate-General in Shanghai, as one historian wrote, symbolized the "scale and permanence of the Japanese commitment in China."[26]

Ishii was at first comfortable with his life in the diplomatic corps, though like other new recruits he felt intimidated by the aristocratic airs of senior Japanese diplomats, with their knowledge of fine wines and cigars and their mastery of the formal Western apparel they were expected to wear.[27] Before long, however, he too had learned how to don morning coats and top hats or three-piece suits and ties when appropriate. He also learned to play golf, which became a "hobby" he could easily enjoy with foreigners.[28] His foreign language studies gave him an advantage, too; he had studied Chinese while in school in Shanghai and had started learning English while in the United States. Ishii's conversion to Christianity also facilitated his cultural assimilation into the club of Western imperial powers.

Ishii and his wife, Moto, like other Matsuura relatives, were unwitting imperialists—the men sent abroad by their employers or conscripted into military service, and the women, at least in their own eyes, merely wives, not purposeful intruders. Yet, their very positioning in Chinese society set them apart, marking them as elite foreigners in their host country in an era of growing hostility to Japan's presence and suspicion of its designs. The women had little inkling of the political significance of their presence as Japanese nationals on Chinese soil, however. What they valued about their overseas life was the chance to savor the West, if only indirectly, through the culture carried to Asia by European and American traders, diplomats, and missionaries and to feel, however fleetingly, a part of the modern world represented by Western civilization at the forefront of modernity.

For Moto, the effort involved in socializing with Western diplomats and their wives wasn't enjoyable; it was troublesome. Unlike her nieces—Isami's daughters—she had not been exposed to a Western-oriented curriculum. In a scant decade after her marriage to her country cousin, Moto had been catapulted from a remote village to the wider world abroad. Unfamiliar with the languages and social customs of the Western world, and especially those of the diplomatic corps, she preferred to stay away from the endless round of receptions, but fearing that "people would notice if she did not attend," she reluctantly went along with her husband and "studied socializing."[29]

Apart from the social scene in Shanghai, the couple also were challenged by their financial plight. Two of their children attended a primary school for Japanese children, and their oldest daughter was of marriageable age. As luck would have it, they received a good marriage proposal for her, but they worried about how to pay the costs of the wedding in Japan. With the Japanese economy struggling to recover from the depression and a devaluated yen, members of the Japanese diplomatic corps in Shanghai were not earning as much as typists in the German Embassy there.[30]

While the Matsuura relatives in the diplomatic corps or on the home islands were hard pressed in the 1930s to maintain their comfortable standard of living, those employed in Japanese companies in Manchuria found their more bountiful, modern lifestyles an improvement over life in Japan. Most Japanese viewed Manchuria as "at once remote and essential" to their country's economic recovery.[31] Historically a part of China, Manchuria had begun to feel the presence of Japanese after the Russo-Japanese War, when Japan won a leasehold on the Liaodong Peninsula (called the Kwantung Peninsula in Japanese) and the right to build a railroad line in south Manchuria extending from the tip of the peninsula to Mukden. Occupied by soldiers of Japan's Kwantung Army after 1931 and renamed Manchukuo, the area was soon swarming with employees of the Japanese-run South Manchuria Railway and various other semiofficial companies seeking to exploit the resources of this Chinese land, which by the 1930s many Japanese had come to think of as their home away from home.

Fumi followed her new husband, Kanji, to Manchuria in 1937. The couple lived in central Manchuria from 1940 to 1945, while Kanji, a geologist, explored for coal. Married life was relatively easy for the fifth daughter of Isami and Kō. She remembered Manchuria as a "spacious" country with plenty of food—"more food than there was in parts of Japan."[32] As large as the combined area of France and Germany, Manchuria produced staples such as soybeans, wheat, and barley and yielded valuable minerals such as iron and gold.[33] For travelers so inclined, hunting, fishing, and mountain climbing beckoned. Under Japan's administration, the territory also offered tourists the allure of golf courses, horse-racing tracks, ski resorts, beaches, and hot springs.[34]

Fumi and her husband lived in the thoroughly modern city of Changchun. Emulating Western imperialist powers, the Japanese city planners in the 1930s had carefully planned and developed Changchun, which they renamed Shinkyō (meaning "new capital"), as a European-style city, with hotels, plazas, elm-lined boulevards, and tall office buildings befitting the capital city of Japanese-controlled Manchukuo and suiting a nation bent on showing the other world powers how thoroughly modern and progressive it was. Shinkyō was the first city in Asia to provide water closets in all residential, commercial, and industrial buildings. It also boasted botanical gardens, a zoo, and parks offering more green space than Japanese residents and visitors were accustomed to in their cities back home.[35]

The high modernist style of the new capital was intended to project "the power of the colonial state as the agent of modernity," as one historian pointed out.[36] Architecture also was designed to convey, and therefore legitimize, the seemingly more progressive, public health–conscious, scientifically managed, and even benevolent Japanese rule, which had brought world standards of urban life to what had been a small, walled trading town on grazing lands of the Manchurian frontier.[37] Germany, Russia, France, and England had also followed utopian plans for developing the Chinese cities they dominated. In fact, officials charged with directing the development of Shinkyō even before the 1930s urged architects to create impressive buildings that would overshadow their Russian competitors in Manchuria. To this end, the main administration building of the South Manchuria Railway, built in 1910, was equipped with steam heat and flush toilets.[38] In the 1930s Frank Lloyd Wright's Japanese associate, Endō Arata, moved to Manchukuo to design the Manchurian Central Bank Club in Wright's prairie style and other structures showing the American architect's pioneering modernist influence.[39]

In the year Fumi and her husband arrived in the showcase city of Shinkyō, the Japanese population swelled to over 101,000 persons—nearly one-fourth the total number of residents.[40] Living with her husband in company housing among the many other Japanese affiliated with Japan's important mining and railroad activities, Fumi never considered learning Chinese, because in her limited social circle "everyone was Japanese." Avenues with familiar names such as Fuji Dōri and Nihonbashi Dōri, a large Shintō shrine in the residential area, and the Yamato Hotel evoked home away from home for Japanese abroad. Their children attended separate schools established for Japanese children. To Fumi's eyes the native population of Manchurians and Chinese was invisible. In her later years, she would ask in puzzlement, "Why did we bother to build all of that only to lose it?"[41]

Developed cities in Manchuria offered the good life for Japanese expatriates as late as the early 1940s, and for Fumi that life was made sweeter still by the birth of three sons in rapid succession. Her parents sent a village girl as a maid to help her—"a luxury in those days." Neither Fumi nor Toyo seemed much affected by the ongoing Sino-Japanese War, which had finally broken out in North China in 1937. They were protected by large numbers of Japanese military and naval forces, who poured into Qingdao, Shanghai, and Tianjin (Tientsin) in northern China, "militarizing," in one historian's words, "the hitherto civilian cast of the Japanese presence there" and giving the Japanese "a truly intimidating position in those three cities."[42]

Despite fighting between Japan and China elsewhere, Manchukuo remained safe and relatively prosperous for the middle-class Japanese nationals living in the larger cities, and Japanese tourism flourished there throughout the 1930s and into the early 1940s, even though continental travel was expensive. "Well into the [China] war," writes Louise Young, the Japan Travel Bureau "poured resources into promoting travel in Manchuria," and as late as 1941 it opened four new Manchuria-Korea travel service centers in Japan.[43]

Remote northeast Asian outposts, such as the army camp in Manchuria where Yūshirō and his bride were stationed, however, proved hard on families. Still, as late as 1941, Toyo's sister-in-law managed to visit her and Masafumi a second time in Qingdao, though by then it was heavily militarized and train tickets were harder to buy. Even after the December 1941 attack on Pearl Harbor brought Japan into open conflict with the United States throughout the Pacific, Matsuura family members continued to travel between Japan and Manchukuo and to visit North China. Mina visited her husband several times in Beijing (Peking), and Shiki was able to join her husband in Liaoning, Manchuria, in 1942. The trunk lines of the South Manchuria Railway were not considered dangerous for civilians, because the Japanese military occupied the Japanese colony of Korea as well as Manchuria.

Of course, the residents of Manchuria were not oblivious to Japan's military engagements in China. Beginning in 1940 mass demonstrations in the Shinkyō plazas and other carefully orchestrated public ceremonies generated support for Japan. Then, too, wartime shortages forced changes in daily life. By 1940 gasoline shortages reduced bus service in Shinkyō, and the fifty buses remaining in operation switched to charcoal gas or alcohol. The wartime pinch was soon felt in food rationing policies as well. Starting in Shinkyō in December 1941 such staples as rice, cooking oil, salt, and cotton cloth were in limited supply.[44]

Still, for Japanese residents like Fumi these problems at first did not impose undue hardships. Preferential treatment in the rationing system gave Japanese citizens more goods and of better quality than the Chinese and Korean residents received.[45] Resourceful city transportation planners in 1941–42 even built a streetcar system operated on cheap electricity from a dam, which eased the problem of gasoline shortages at least temporarily.[46]

A more serious problem might have been the opposition of the city's native Chinese population, some 507,000 strong by 1942, who experienced Japan's semicolonial occupation as "humiliating subordination, no matter how modern Xinjing [i.e., Shinkyō] was as a city."[47] Unlike treaty port cities in China proper, where conflicts with Chinese required constant vigilance on the part of Japanese residents, Shinkyō's Chinese population had no choice but to remain passive in the face of the overwhelming force of Japan's Kwantung Army stationed in Manchuria. Anti-Japanese resistance elsewhere in Manchuria resulted in harsh counterinsurgency movements backed by military force.[48] In fact, as early as 1932, Isami's brother-in-law Ishii Itarō had clashed with Japanese Army officers over their brutal treatment of local Chinese authorities when he was consul-general in Kirin. At the army's request, he was temporarily recalled to Tokyo. The experience left the career diplomat and China expert "resolved to maintain a steadfast attitude of passive resistance toward the army."[49]

Precisely because the Japanese Kwantung Army was in control, Shinkyō was still a safe tourist destination for homeland Japanese as late as 1943. Fuki's desire to travel there was thwarted only because her dominating mother-in-law would not allow her to go. After the attack on Pearl Harbor in 1941, sweeping victories in Southeast Asia created a heady, though brief, sense of euphoria on the home front and among Japanese in the expanded empire, even despite the stalemate in China. In August 1943, nineteen-year-old Tami felt few qualms about traveling alone to visit her two sisters in Shinkyō. By that time Toyo and her husband had been transferred there from Qingdao. "There were Japanese soldiers all over Manchuria," Tami recalled of her two-week holiday. To safeguard her security, however, the family asked a contact in the military to arrange for a soldier to accompany her on the long train ride through Korea and Manchuria.[50]

Once in Manchuria, Tami found herself in a shopper's paradise. The two hundred yen her father had given her for travel money was more than the average middle-class Japanese tourist spent for a two-week, second-class package tour of Manchuria.[51] When she and her sisters went sightseeing in Harbin, northeast of Shinkyō, they were surprised to find shoes selling cheaply at a time when, in Japan, "nobody was selling shoes anymore" because of the war effort. She used a portion of her travel allowance to buy four pairs.[52]

While Manchuria's cities may have been fun for a young Japanese woman to visit, daily life on the home islands was another story. Despite official propaganda celebrating the military's triumphs in the Pacific and northern China and enjoining patriotic support for the "Greater East Asian War" and the "Holy War," the more observant Japanese on the home front, Isami among them, sensed that the conflict was becoming less distant, the government more intrusive, and the times more difficult and dangerous.

NINE

Isami's Children in Harm's Way

KŌJIRŌ AND HIS YOUNGER BROTHER YŪSHIRŌ met for the first time in nine years over a relaxing dinner at a Bandung hotel in May 1942. Both had been drafted into military service immediately after the Pearl Harbor attack, and by coincidence both had been sent to the Netherlands East Indies. Neither was enthusiastic about serving in the war. Better educated and more worldly than many of his countrymen, Kōjirō, in particular, was immune to the patriotic excitement sweeping over Japan in the wake of their country's successful attack on the American naval base in Hawaii. His company had transferred him from Australia to its branch office in Osaka only three months before, and he was home eating breakfast when he heard the news. "This is terrible," he recalled thinking. "There is no way Japan can win."[1] Within two months he was wearing the uniform of the Japanese Imperial Army.

Yūshirō, too, was upset. He had just returned to Tokyo after finishing his first tour of duty in Manchuria, and his wife had recently given birth to their second son. Life in Manchuria had not been easy, even for an army surgeon and even though his wife had been with him, and both Yūshirō and his wife were relieved to be back in Japan.

After his marriage in 1939, Yūshirō's young bride, Masako, had accompanied him to his army base in the town of Songo, northeast of Harbin and close to Manchuria's eastern border with Russia, in Heilongjiang province. According to Masako, the camp housed many of the nearly fourteen hundred rebellious soldiers who had participated in the unsuccessful army mutiny against the government in Tokyo, the notorious incident on February 26, 1936. While nearly all the noncommissioned officers and ordinary soldiers were pardoned, they were chastised, she claimed, by being sent to this distant outpost, an army town set on a broad, cold, open plain whose expanse was relieved by only a few trees, still leafless as late as June.

In the winter, when it snowed and the temperature dropped below zero, Masako wore a fur coat, and she and Yūshirō both pulled fur hats down over their ears.[2]

The military base, not surprisingly, lacked the cosmopolitanism of Chinese and Manchurian cities developed by one or another of the imperialist powers. Its one attraction was proximity to Harbin, known as the Paris of the East. Built on the eastern banks of the Sungari River, Harbin's broad boulevards and European-style buildings and cafés reflected the early influence of the city's large population of Russians, who, by the middle of the 1930s, numbered eighty-one thousand—one-third the number of Chinese and far more than the mere forty-seven thousand Japanese, whose country then ruled Manchuria through the Japanese Kwantung Army.[3]

The Songo army base, for all its starkness, at least enjoyed the advantage of sturdy brick buildings. Moreover, Yūshirō's status as a married army doctor working in the military hospital qualified him to use lower-ranked soldiers as house servants, who heated the couple's bath and delivered their coal.[4] Still, an army base in northeastern Manchuria, and especially Songo, was a dangerous place to raise a family. Just how dangerous it was the couple never knew.

In the middle of the 1930s, a hitherto unknown epidemic disease, dubbed Songo fever, afflicted Japanese soldiers in the area.[5] They were treated in the military hospital in Harbin around the same time that Masako gave birth to the couple's first child in 1940 in the military hospital in nearby Songo. Her mother traveled from Tokyo to help her through labor and to accompany her and her newborn on the long journey by rail and ship back home, while Yūshirō stayed on alone for another year.

At the end of that year, a biological warfare research unit employing medical scientists was established in Songo, one of several sites in Manchuria designated for developing and testing of diseases such as Songo fever (later identified as hemorrhagic fever) on human subjects. A subunit of the infamous Unit 731, the Songo facility participated in secret medical experiments, performed mainly on Chinese soldiers, intellectuals, and suspected spies or agitators but also on Russian soldiers and even women unfortunate enough to fall into army researchers' hands.[6] Unit 731's war crimes were publicly exposed only well after the war's end. Masako and Yūshirō left Songo just in time: their memories of Japanese army life in Manchuria were mainly of the cold, not the fiendish cruelty. Masako never heard of Songo fever or Unit 731 then or later, and if her husband did, he never told her.

Yūshirō may have had an intuition that he would be drafted again as an army surgeon, because, in the months after returning to Japan, he had restlessly moved his family from one house to another in the Tokyo area, going to live first in the Nishigahara house and then staying at the homes of his sisters Yasu and Shiki. Isami, in his typical role as family disciplinarian, had even written a letter urging him to "settle down." When he telegraphed his parents with the news that he was called up for a second time, Kō interrupted her trip to a hot springs to see him off in Tokyo.[7]

For Kōjirō at least, military assignment in the Netherlands East Indies represented a nostalgic return of sorts to the country where his three children had been born and where he still had contacts from his days there in the 1930s as a Mitsubishi employee. The war was going well for Japan when Kōjirō arrived in the central island of Java in March 1942. Like Indochina, Singapore, and other colonial holdings of Western powers in Asia, the Dutch colony had quickly fallen to the Japanese military after the Pearl Harbor attack. General Imamura Hitoshi's Sixteenth Army had established order in Java using a minimum of force and had taken the islands' former colonial rulers as prisoners of war. Kōjirō met Imamura in Batavia (present-day Jakarta), the political center of the colony, shortly after arriving and immediately went to work as paymaster with the rank of lieutenant, helping to procure needed war materiel for the army.

Much as Kōjirō decried Japan's war against countries in which he had cultivated friendships, he viewed the Japanese military engagement, at least in the East Indies, in idealistic terms: an opportunity for the subjugated peoples to free themselves from their European colonial masters. Remembering how the Dutch had enforced discriminatory policies against the native population, he sympathized with Indonesians' nationalist aspirations. Kōjirō saw the Japanese military in the Indies as "anti-imperialist and pro-nationalist liberators, promising to remove European overlords," an operation that proved, he later recalled, "astonishingly easy."[8] Such a view was furthered by Japan's wartime rhetoric of liberation. A Japanese naval official in Java even described himself as "the foster-father of Indonesian independence."[9]

At first, the native population of the East Indies had shared this vision of the emancipatory role of the Japanese army. According to one account, in "almost every town and city where the Japanese troops made their triumphant entry, crowds of local Indonesians lined the streets, greeting the victors with Japanese . . . and . . . Indonesian flags."[10] Japanese media further promoted this impression of liberation. Radio Tokyo, for example, broadcast the "Indonesia Raga," known as the nationalist anthem.[11] Feeding the fervor of the Indonesian nationalist movement even more, General Imamura, in one of his first acts as military ruler, released the Indonesian nationalist revolutionary leader Achmed Sukarno from prison, though Imamura frankly told Sukarno that he did not have the authority to promise independence for the native population.[12] After the war, elements of the Japanese army who sincerely espoused the cause of Indonesian nationalism joined the Indonesian nationalist movement on the island of Bali; those who died fighting the Dutch were buried alongside fallen Indonesians.[13]

The Japanese army marched into the Indies and other Western colonies under the banner "Asia for the Asians." They appeared to offer a non-Western, alternative model of modernity. As one Japanese civil official put it, "The Eastern virtues which the people of Indonesia originally possessed disappeared during the long Dutch regime. We are . . . attempting to make the Indonesians once again conscious of these old virtues."[14]

Not too long after the Japanese takeover, however, Indonesians realized that they had not been freed from the colonial yoke; their control had merely been transferred from one colonial power to another. In practice, Japan had no plan for liberating the area, let alone modernizing it. The Japanese military government considered the islands a vital source of war materiel and bluntly said as much in a cabinet decree: "Economic hardships imposed upon native livelihood as a result of the acquisition of resources vital to the national defense and for the self-sufficiency of the occupation troops must be endured."[15]

The result was disastrous for the Indonesian population. Cut off from the international market, the occupied peoples suffered from lack of food and textiles for clothing. The death rate drastically increased with economic deprivation as well as with the impressment of adult males into forced labor, including three hundred thousand Javanese who were transported overseas to other islands under Japanese occupation.[16] Women too were forced into labor—as prostitutes for the occupation army.

Ironically, Japanese military authorities observed racial distinctions with even more fervor than the Dutch, whose soldiers had themselves sexually exploited Indonesian women.[17] They were especially mistrustful of persons of Dutch Indonesian descent, whom they could not assume would oppose Dutch rule. On islands administered by the navy, Eurasians as well as Europeans were interned, though on Java most Eurasians were left alone.[18]

Kōjirō did what he could to help all sides during the war. He rescued a wealthy Indonesian Chinese merchant's property from confiscation by speaking in his behalf to a former Mitsubishi colleague who was serving as the head of the Economics Bureau in the Surabaya Military Administration. Kōjirō similarly aided a Swedish ball-bearing company whose inventory had been seized by the army, and then he used this contact to buy ball-bearings for the army.

Remarkably under the circumstances, Kōjirō also won the lifelong gratitude of two British Commonwealth captains, one English, the other Australian, who were taken as Japanese prisoners of war. He argued against the Japanese army's misbegotten plan for him to befriend the men in order to turn them into spies. Kōjirō knew the scheme was impossible; the men loved their countries. He brought them tobacco and whiskey instead. After Japan's surrender, he was the one who went to the house where they were being held and told them the war was over. "They looked at me and burst out crying. 'For you,' they said, 'the war's ending in this way is sad.'" The three men then embraced. One of them, a Captain Nichol, survived the war to become vice-head of the Victorian State Legislature. In 1951, he placed an advertisement in a Japanese newspaper seeking to locate Kōjirō and thank him. A lawyer who saw the notice brought it to Kōjirō's attention. The two men resumed contact, and in 1976 Kōjirō and his wife, Tazuko, hosted Nichol in Japan.[19]

While Kōjirō remained in the relative safety of the Japanese-held East Indies for the duration of the war, Yūshirō was less fortunate. In October 1942, he found himself in the tropical Solomon Islands, the setting for a half year of fierce jungle fighting with Americans on Guadalcanal, which would cost twenty-three thousand Japanese lives, almost all of them lost to disease and hunger.[20]

Yūshirō came close to being one of the fatalities. Weak with malaria contracted while treating Japanese soldiers under siege, he was evacuated in February 1943, when the Japanese military finally agreed to retreat. One of the military men who drew up the daring evacuation plans was General Imamura Hitoshi. Summoned to Tokyo from Java, he had been brought before the emperor, who beseeched him to retake the island. Imamura quickly recognized the hopelessness of the situation, however, because Japanese troops had been living on grass roots and water for the last month.[21]

In one of three evacuation sections during the first week of February, Yūshirō was "fished out of the water" by Japanese sailors in PT boats that crept silently to the beach, having been launched from destroyers less than a thousand yards from shore. In all, thirteen thousand men were evacuated, some too weak even to climb the rope ladder to the destroyers. The rest, dead or nearly so, were left behind on the beach.[22]

Yūshirō was taken to the Japanese colony of Formosa. There he managed to find a friend who was able to elude censors and send a letter to his parents saying that, although Japan had lost the battle of Guadalcanal, Yūshirō had survived and was coming home. Wartime censorship prohibited any mention of lost battles, and Guadalcanal represented the first wartime loss of Japanese territory to the United States. Although the letter made it through to Isami and Kō, the police heard about it and questioned Kō. Feigning innocence, she coolly claimed she did not know who had sent the letter. By the time Yūshirō arrived home, in July 1944, he could hardly stand and had to be hospitalized in Sendai.[23]

Other Matsuura family members living overseas in one capacity or another similarly confronted increasingly dangerous environments beginning in the late 1930s when they, too, were conscripted for military service. Saburō, the journalist, had been drafted and sent to central China in 1936, the same year that his brother Yūshirō, the physician, and his sister Fuki's husband, also a physician, were drafted and sent to Manchukuo.

The morally, militarily, and politically untenable situation of the Japanese in China was well understood by Isami's brother-in-law Ishii Itarō, who, as consul-general in Shanghai in the turbulent 1930s faced serious, if not insuperable, problems. Although in his memoirs he claims he "enjoyed Shanghai," on many occasions his career, if not his life, was threatened, and toward the end of the 1930s, he tried to resign from the diplomatic corps. Earlier in that decade, the political situation in Shanghai had been tense enough for Mitsubishi to send home some of its employees, including Toyo's future husband. Ishii's family stayed through the turmoil, however, while he tried to defuse political tensions between China and Japan and head off war.[24]

Chinese protested the Japanese army's 1931 seizure of Manchuria by boycotting Japanese merchants, and in 1932 this escalated into open violence in the Shanghai Incident. The conflict pitted Chinese against the militarily superior force of Japan's navy, marines, and bombers and resulted in nearly seven thousand Chinese dead and over ten thousand missing. Eventually Japanese troops withdrew from the city, but local Chinese continued to refuse to sell to or buy from Japanese.[25]

Increasingly resented during the 1930s as capitalist exploiters, imperialists, and aggressors, residents of Japanese settlements and their property in China became targets of violence, and Japanese businesses became the objects of strikes and boycotts. In response, Japanese communities, described in one report as "constantly on edge," took various preventive measures to protect their property and defend themselves while living in "prolonged states of siege."[26]

During that decade, Ishii closely assisted the Japanese foreign minister in dialogues with the Chinese government.[27] Like the Japanese foreign minister who, upon his arrival in Shanghai, said frankly that Japan's military takeover in Manchuria was "going too far," Ishii tried "heroically," in one historian's words, to offset military moves and find diplomatic solutions to growing strife between Japan and China. His efforts were not appreciated by radical military elements, and both he and the foreign minister received many poison-pen letters.[28]

As a China expert and, later in the 1930s, as chief of the Asian Bureau in the Foreign Ministry in Tokyo, Ishii understood better than most other Japanese on the scene the force of rising Chinese nationalism. Awakened patriotism marked the beginning of the inevitable end of the colonial era for all the imperialist powers, yet Japan still had, in Ishii's words, a "get-what-you-can-before-the-other-fellow-does" attitude.[29] After hostilities finally broke out between China and Japan in 1937, his ardent efforts to avert war motivated him to write a long memorandum to the newly appointed Japanese foreign minister in which he passionately urged mediation to negotiate a peace settlement with Chiang Kai-shek. The Chinese nationalist leader, he argued, "commanded the reverence of the Chinese people." Ishii bluntly called Japan's motives in China domination and exploitation.[30] Although he did not suggest returning Manchuria to the Chinese, his sensitivity to the nationalist aspirations of the Chinese echoed his nephew Kōjirō's sympathies for the plight of Indonesians under Dutch rule.

Once war broke out in 1937, Japanese armies quickly seized China's major cities, looting, raping, and bombing their way through the southern city of Nanjing (Nanking) in the process, but China showed no sign of surrendering. More Japanese troops poured into China; in 1937, there was a general call-up of eighty thousand men. Isami's brother Kōzō, a career army officer who had risen to the rank of battalion commander, was assigned to Nanjing, arriving in the obliterated city in March 1940. Mina's brother-in-law, Ishiwata Sōtarō, also served in Nanjing in the late 1930s, but in a civilian capacity as an economic adviser for the Japanese Ministry of Finance. He encountered a scene described by another eyewitness of the time as "acres of complete devastation . . . with 300,000 refugees too poor to leave, empty government buildings, and razed homes."[31]

Although the Japanese army controlled Manchuria and areas of North China, the vast hinterland remained outside Japanese control, and Japanese civilians in South China and the Yangtze River Valley were evacuated.[32] Stymied, Japan's Foreign Ministry officials, Isami's brother-in-law Ishii Itarō among them, sought a way out of a quagmire that was quickly absorbing large numbers of men and resources and necessitated the rationing of food staples in Japan.

Ishii's warning that Japan risked becoming bogged down in a protracted war with China proved prophetic. One of Japan's most knowledgeable and outspoken China experts and a burr in the side of the military, which dominated Japan's government by this time, Ishii was rewarded for his efforts and expertise in this crucial period in East Asian history with a transfer to an inferior, though safer, position outside China. Caught in power plays among factions of the Foreign Ministry and the army during a period of increasing resistance by the Chinese, Ishii was finally consigned in 1938 to the Netherlands as legation minister without portfolio and in 1940 to the post of ambassador to Brazil, far away from the war front and well out of the way of the Japanese military's designs for China.[33]

As the war with China and then with the Allied powers dragged out, at least ten male relatives of Isami and Kō were overseas in one capacity or the other, as were daughters Toyo and Fumi and their children. The husbands of Shiki, Fuki, and Yasu were in the army, while Mina's husband was working for the semiofficial North China Development Company (Kitashina Kaihatsu Kaisha) in Beijing. Saburō remained in Beijing to work for Beijing Airlines, and his wife joined him there in 1939, even while the Sino-Japanese War was in progress. Where the Japanese army prevailed, as in North China and Manchuria, the lives of Japanese were relatively safe until war's end, though even when not in combat the men in uniform, especially those who were not doctors, suffered a spartan regimen, with a minimal ration of food and discipline meted out by harsh army officers.

The Matsuura in greatest potential danger was the family's sixth son, Shinrokurō (called Shin for short), who volunteered for military service in the last year of the war. He was one of the teens whom teachers, pressured to fill quotas, had mobilized to volunteer as youth pilots. They would visit a student's home, one Japanese historian relates, and "get his parents' tearful approval."[34] Shin was only seventeen when he became the fourth and youngest of the family's sons to wear a military uniform in the 1940s. With only one year spent at naval preparatory school before enlisting, he received training to fly Japan's famed Zero planes. At the start of the Pacific war, these one-man, Mitsubishi-built fighter planes, the best in the Japanese arsenal, had ruled the sky "like eagles," as they were commonly described, but by the end of the war they were outgunned by American B-29 superfortresses, making the young Shin's military assignment far more treacherous than glamorous.

TEN

Hard Times on the Home Front

IN A POEM WRITTEN IN 1944, in the midst of a war with the Allied powers that he knew his country could not win, Isami described almost elegiacally the mass urban exodus of people, mainly women, in search of food and the tranquility and plenitude of the countryside:

> Carrying edible plants in abundance to the people who have come from the capital, the older sister sees them off.
> Thinking about their son and husband on the battlefield, mother-in-law and daughter-in-law sew *tabi*.

Isami felt a certain pride in taking in relatives from the capital and showing them the "prosperity of the mountainside."[1] The reality of feeding and housing his many family members and villagers, however, was far from idyllic; there was no prosperity in the mountains or even on the rice plains.

In 1939, food shortages appeared in some parts of Japan.[2] Entering into the second year of the "Holy War" with China and with no end in sight, the government began to ration such key staples as rice, salt, and soy sauce in the cities and to regulate the production and sale of major agricultural products in the countryside. In Yamashiraishi authorities requisitioned three hundred bales of unhusked rice for the war effort. In early 1941, to meet quotas for crop deliveries to the government, Isami turned over one of the family's storehouses to the village cooperative for use as an office and storage area. He also agreed to serve as president of the local branch of the Veterans Association, receiving for his efforts an award in 1940 from none other than General Tojo Hideki, prime minister one year later when Japan bombed Pearl Harbor.

When Japan's attack on Pearl Harbor plunged the nation into war with the United States and its allies at the end of 1941, the larger scope of military operations forced further belt tightening for the emperor's subjects. By late 1942, Tokyo residents were willing to "pay anything to fill [their] stomachs, so inadequate was rationed food."[3] Political cartoons urged greater sacrifice to achieve the national goal of increased economic self-sufficiency in the face of reduced imports.[4] With food scarce and their menfolk abroad, one after another of the Matsuura women returned with their children to their natal home in the countryside, closer to the source of agricultural produce. For the time being, they were safe, though their menfolk were not.

As early as April 1942, Isami had begun worrying about the outcome of the war. In that month, the first ever air-raid attack on Tokyo brought the war directly to the home islands. The capital and several other cities were struck by sixteen American B-25 Mitchell bombers under the command of Lieutenant-Colonel James H. Doolittle, taking off from the carrier *Hornet,* six hundred miles away. Although the physical damage was negligible, the psychological effect of the raids was considerable: Japan no longer was invincible. Two months later during the first week of June 1942, after the country lost four carriers in the Battle of Midway, the heart of the country's striking force had been destroyed, and Japan's empire thereafter was on the defensive.[5] By the summer of 1942, despite strict wartime censorship and rosy reports in the newspapers, Isami was privately criticizing the cabinet of General Tojo for its incompetence. The government, he charged, was "like two wheels not turning in tandem."[6]

Mina's husband, too, questioned government propaganda assurances about the military's ability to protect the home islands from the Allies. Still employed in Beijing, he had access to American newspapers that gave him a more accurate view of the war than people in the home islands could obtain. In August 1942, acting on his advice, Mina and her son abandoned Tokyo for Yamashiraishi, where they joined the wives of their second, third, and fourth brothers, who had moved in with Kō and Isami immediately after Pearl Harbor.[7]

As the war continued, the Matsuura household expanded to shelter even more uprooted family members. By the summer of 1945, some thirty-five Matsuura relatives, mainly women, children, and the elderly, overflowed the family compound. In addition to their children and grandchildren, Kō and Isami found housing in the village for Fuki's in-laws after they lost their Asakusa house to fire and for Yasu's in-laws, who feared they too would be bombed out of their home in the western outskirts of Tokyo.

Villagers worked hard to meet their government-imposed quotas of rice production. In 1943, a photograph taken of nine village functionaries commemorated their success in that year. Yatarō's wife, substituting for her father-in-law, Isami, who must have been away that day, sits in the center of the picture surrounded by the vice-village head and staff members from the post office and the agricultural cooperative.[8] The shortage of rice created by government requisitions led all the farmers in the village to plant buckwheat for making a noodle called *soba* to supplement their diet.

The village contributed not only rice but also soldiers to the war cause. With able-bodied men conscripted at increasingly younger ages, the Matsuura family could no longer rely on male servants for farm labor. One faithful house servant, who had lived in the house for eight years before the war and among other jobs had cultivated the vegetable fields, was drafted into the army and served in China for five years.

In place of male servants, women of the household grew food for the table. Isami himself, now in his sixties but still vigorous, planted a small vegetable field, tended by some of the female relatives, and Kō weeded. Members of the household also cut down trees for firewood. In 1944, in order to pay off a longstanding debt, Isami reluctantly cut down a grove of cedar trees and sold them to the navy for lumber.[9] Even Kōjirō's city-bred wife, and Fuki, who had gone to school in Tokyo at an earlier age than her siblings, got down on their hands and knees to grow food. "We did not know farming until the war," Fuki recalled. "I used to wonder what farmers were doing when they weeded."

The Matsuura family fared better than the average Japanese civilian, who, at war's end, consumed fewer than fifteen hundred calories a day and rarely ate white rice as a staple.[10] Matsuura family members ate rice twice a day, as well as vegetables and *misoshiru* (beanpaste soup), rich in protein, but despite their comparatively ample diet, the standard practice was for the maid carefully to dish out each rice portion, weighing it on a scale to make sure there would be enough for everybody—a "light *misoshiru* bowl's worth," recalled one of the daughters, not a heaping bowl. In the final months of the war, an acquaintance asked Isami to house him and his 110 chickens, together with incubators and feed. By accommodating him in one of the storage houses, the family gained an additional source of food. Still, a photograph of them from the final year of the war shows thin arms and gaunt faces.

Those who could not farm, such as Yūshirō's city-bred wife, Masako, who was pregnant with their third child, helped with the cooking and other household chores. Although she said everyone got along well, Masako described this period as the unhappiest in her life. She explained, "I had to sit by their [her parents-in-law's] side and sew old kimono with everyone else, even though father [Isami] had promised, before I married, that I would never have to be a 'daughter-in-law' [i.e., substitute in the role that should have been fulfilled by the eldest son's wife]. I had never done that kind of work before." Masako insisted on returning to her parents' home in Tokyo to give birth to her third son, and Kō accompanied her.[11]

Self-sufficiency in all matters, including health, was the order of the day. When Masako noticed a growth on her arm, Isami removed it himself with a knife. Only a grandchild with scarlet fever was taken to the hospital for treatment. Isami himself remained remarkably hale during the wartime ordeal, though throughout his life he suffered on and off from flare-ups of an inflamed appendix—the ailment that killed his sixth daughter in 1929 and also afflicted his oldest son. Shortly before Pearl Harbor, after complaining for several months of stomach pain whose cause doctors could not determine, he was finally diagnosed with intestinal parasites. Medicine cleared his intestines of five huge worms.[12]

Kō fared less well in wartime. She was not only busy feeding her extended family, but in the wintertime she also helped supplement the diet of poor village children by preparing a stewlike *misoshiru* soup enriched with carrots, taro, daikon, and burdock and cooked in a large cauldron. The village was even singled out for praise by government officials for providing nourishment to its young people. Kō was also head of the village women's association. By the end of the war, the strain on her showed: a 1945 photograph no longer depicts a youthful-looking, round-faced, elegant middle-aged matron, but a haggard old woman.

Despite wartime disruption, instruction of the young continued. Anticipating Japan's defeat, Isami argued that in the postwar period the Japanese would have to learn how to work even harder; they could not be lazy. He expected Mina's oldest son, wrenched from his Tokyo home, to farm in the mornings and to study in the afternoon. Although Rintarō hated his studies, the teenage boy obeyed his determined grandfather, and after lunch, when others were napping, he studied in the main hall of the Buddhist temple, where it was quiet. He was tutored by his aunt Yasu's father-in-law, who had been a Tokyo middle school teacher but lived in the temple with his wife during the war. Isami was known to be impatient with *deki no warui ko* (children who did poorly or were unaccomplished students), and he was especially strict in the disciplining of Rintarō, his eldest daughter's first-born child. When Mina asked why he always picked on her boy, Isami tersely replied, "If he feels resentful, he will fail." When Rintarō was admitted into Tokyo University a few years later, nobody was more elated than his grandfather.[13]

The family tradition of educating the children in Tokyo proved impossible to continue in wartime. The youngest three sons belonged to the "Shōwa single digit" generation, those born between the first year of Emperor Hirohito's reign in the Shōwa era (1926) and the ninth year (1934). Their generation grew up knowing little but economic depression and war. Their youth disrupted and their education interrupted, these last-born Matsuura sons would have the most trouble adjusting to postwar society.[14]

Tatsugorō, the fifth-born son (known as Tatsu for short), remained in the capital until 1940, when at fourteen he began to manifest increasingly disturbed behavior. Toward the end of 1940, Isami tried switching him from his private middle school to a public one in Tokyo, but when the boy decided, without permission, to live with his tutor, Isami scolded him and ordered him home. Instead of returning directly to the village, Tatsu stopped off in the city of Shirakawa. Lost or confused, he seems to have had some kind of nervous breakdown. To help him recover, Kō accompanied him on a walk every morning before dawn for one month. They went past the small, unpainted wooden Shintō shrine behind their house and through the bamboo and cypress woods to their ancestral grave sites. Whether it was his mother's company, the daily exercise, or the message about family responsibility conveyed by their seeking the presence of the ancestors, Tatsu "calmed down," and he returned to school in Tokyo, this time living with his sister Shiki and her husband in Chiba and commuting to classes until Shiki's husband, too, was drafted in February 1941. Frequently despondent and adrift, Tatsu was a constant worry to his parents.[15]

Shin, the sixth-born son, was a pilot somewhere in the Pacific, but the last-born son, Seishichirō (known as Sei), stayed in the family's home prefecture, entering middle school in 1944 in Shirakawa, where Isami arranged for him to live in the local Buddhist temple during the week. Over the weekends he and a group of friends visited the home of his cousin who lived nearby. Inviting one of the cousin's two daughters to join in, they escaped the strains of wartime by talking about literature. Sitting a little behind the serious group of teenagers, the cousin's younger daughter, ten-year-old Kuniko, would listen quietly to their conversations, not knowing at the time that one day she would become Sei's adoring wife.[16]

The youngest daughter of Isami and Kō remained in Tokyo, living with the in-laws of her older brother Yūshirō while she finished college. "In Tokyo during the war," Tami said, "we ate mainly pumpkin and potatoes and a little rice." Her senior class in their last semester was required to work part-time in a war-related factory, testing bulbs made for army planes.

Wartime did not deter Kō and Isami from their goal of making good marriages for their children, though it certainly made the project daunting. In 1943, they arranged a match for their second youngest daughter, twenty-two-year-old Yasu, with Tsukioka Sho, a Tokyo-bred graduate of Hitotsu-bashi University. The couple went out together only once in the two months between the start of marriage arrangements and their wedding. Although Yasu managed to conceive the couple's first and only child, Hiroshi, almost immediately after her marriage, by the time he was born in 1944, his father was fighting in North Asia. Yasu stayed with her parents but did housework rather than the fieldwork done by some of the other women of the household, because she was reluctant to turn over the care of her infant son to the village children, who traditionally worked as baby-sitters. They were inclined, she said, to leave their charges untended alongside the paddies, as their poor farming parents did while working in the fields. The Matsuura women, even in wartime, preserved some of their middle-class standards.

Although the family, under Isami's resolute guidance, continued to foster the education of the children and to promote marriage ties as well as they could, wartime conditions and other factors impeded the married children's ability to carry on the work of procreation. Separation from spouses was only one obstacle to childbearing; infertility among the sons and daughters of the fecund Kō and Isami was another.

Toyo and Fuki, born two years apart, suffered a similar reproductive problem, diagnosed by x-ray as narrow Fallopian tubes, while their brother Toshisaburō had a low sperm count, possibly caused by a high fever in childhood, and he and his wife remained childless. Their sister Shiki, born two years after Fuki, also failed to conceive. Yasu and Tami in their lifetimes bore only one child each. Fuki eventually managed to become pregnant two years after her husband, the army doctor, had been home on leave and had given her a daily injection of vitamin E for thirty-one days, which, she claimed, helped bring on menses, but she too had only one child. Toyo tried the injections to no avail; her tubes were completely closed. Desperate, in the fall of 1943, at the age of thirty-one, she temporarily returned to Japan from Manchuria to execute a daring scheme. She would adopt an infant, and not even the Pacific war could stand in her way.

Toyo turned for help to Ibuka Yuriko, the friend she had made in her Qingdao days. Mrs. Ibuka's inquiries turned up news of a baby girl born eight months earlier in Sendai to a twenty-eight-year-old alumna of Freedom School who had died shortly after giving birth. The infant's father, who was a faculty member at Tōhoku University, could care for neither her nor her two older siblings, because the woman who had agreed to marry him had proclaimed, "I am your wife, not the mother of your children. I didn't marry you to raise your children." The couple arranged to have the older children's paternal grandmother raise them, allowing them visits to their father in the summertime, and a maternal aunt brought the baby to her home in Tokyo.[17]

The aunt had hoped to keep her infant niece, but with four children of her own and wartime rationing of milk, she worried that she would not be able to provide for the extra child. At first, with the help of the rice delivery man, she located two neighborhood women willing to take turns nursing the infant, one for morning feedings and the other for night. When the baby was around six months old, the aunt turned to Freedom School founder Hani Motoko for help in finding a suitable home for the infant.

The famed educator and journalist remembered the baby's mother. A member of a wealthy Tokyo family, the woman had been active in theatrical performances while at the college. Hani located a number of women willing to nurse the baby and even to adopt her, so she was passed around among a group of volunteer wet nurses. By the time she reached the hands of her adoptive mother, the baby's face was "fatter than Toyo's," according to one Matsuura relative who saw her. Among those eager to become the infant's mother was a rich and famous novelist whom Hani did not personally know. In the end, Hani chose Toyo, assuring the baby's aunt that the Matsuura's second oldest daughter, who had graduated from Freedom School only two years after the biological mother had, would take good care of the child.

Before leaving Tokyo, Toyo took her new daughter, Yōko, to the grave site of the biological mother, where she vowed to dedicate herself to the child's well-being. She then brought the baby to Yamashiraishi to introduce her to the family and to add her name to the Matsuura family registry. The relatives all agreed to keep the adoption secret and to treat Toyo's child no differently from the other children in the family. Isami even tried to register her without mentioning the adoption, but he was unable to get around legal requirements.

Having become a mother, Toyo found a purpose for living and a reason to preserve her marriage despite her husband's infidelities and stormy temperament. Returning to him in Manchuria in January 1944, she strapped the infant Japanese-style on her back, and they began the long trip, traveling by ship across the Korea Strait from Shimonoseki, on the southwestern tip of the main island, to Pusan, Korea—the same route her father had taken as a soldier forty years earlier—and thereon by train through Korea to Shinkyō, in Manchuria. By this time in the war the trip was perilous, and the ship was in danger of being bombed; however, Toyo was not worried, because, as she told her adopted daughter many years later, she believed the baby's biological mother would protect them from her grave. Despite the mounting perils of wartime, the baby's biological parents had named her Yōko, meaning "Pacific girl," a popular name among parents of the day who still believed, or at least hoped, that Japan was winning the Pacific war. But, of course, they were wrong.

In May 1944, one hundred more Yamashiraishi village men were drafted. Despite the government's heavy censorship, Isami clearly recognized the hopelessness of Japan's war situation by the following July if not sooner. Early in that month, Saipan, in the Mariana Islands south of Japan, fell to the Americans, bringing the home islands within bombing range from land. The more clear-headed government officials understood that further fighting would be futile, and they moved to oust General Tojo Hideki from the premiership as the first step toward arranging a peace settlement. Tojo's cabinet had officially started the war with the United States by authorizing the bombing of Pearl Harbor; now, three and one-half years later, many people were "shocked into anger by what they believed to be the incompetent conduct of the war," and Tojo became "an object of intense hatred."[18] With the country braced for air raids, Isami wrote, "you could hear the voices of desperation."[19]

After Tojo agreed to resign, a Matsuura relative close to the seat of power emerged to help form the new cabinet. He was Mina's brother-in-law, Ishiwata Sōtarō. A career bureaucrat and a member of the House of Peers by imperial appointment in 1940, Ishiwata had remained in government service throughout the late 1930s and early 1940s. In 1937, he became chief of the Tax Bureau in the Ministry of Finance, and after several other stints in key positions, he became minister of finance under Tojo and two other prime ministers between 1939 and 1945. Having survived several cabinet changes and other ministerial shifts and purges while the "war situation," as it was euphemistically called, deteriorated, Ishiwata, in his capacity as minister of finance, now emerged as one of the central figures trying to reconstitute the cabinet.[20]

Ishiwata contacted the lord keeper of the privy seal Kido Kōichi and asked him to join the cabinet. As the emperor's chief political adviser and "quintessential backstageman,"[21] Kido had pushed the nomination of Tojo to head the cabinet in 1941, and he now declined Ishiwata's suggestion. Nevertheless, the two men continued searching for a new prime minister who could form a strong national cabinet. Neither Kido nor the emperor was willing "even to consider an early peace effort." Both continued to support the pro-war factions of the army and navy.[22]

The solution, though not much of one, was a coalition cabinet led by a general and an admiral. The general, Koiso Kuniaki, personally feared the war was lost.[23] A measure of his sense of desperation was his decision, made shortly after assuming the premiership, to begin arming the entire country with bamboo spears. The general also discussed with the emperor whether His Majesty should be evacuated from Tokyo for his safety. The emperor refused, though the crown prince had already been sent out of the city to live in a hotel in Nikko.[24]

Isami, too, was concerned about his family in Tokyo—its dead as well as its living. In late 1944 he went to the capital to collect the remains of his uncle—the young bank clerk whose sudden death from cholera had precipitated the death of his great-grandfather Daisuke in 1890—in order to transfer them to Yamashiraishi. Also for safekeeping, he removed from the Nishigahara house one of his most prized possessions, the portrait of himself and Daisuke done in that same year on his first trip to Tokyo, and brought it back to Yamashiraishi, where he hung it in the retirement cottage. Toward the end of 1944 and just in time, Isami called home all his remaining female kin, including his youngest daughter, Tami. Tokyo had become a major target of Allied air attacks on the home islands. The war was coming to Japan, and all its people were mobilized and threatened.

In this final phase of the war, thousands of American B-29s, taking off from Saipan, began saturation firebombing of Japan's densely populated cities. When Isami returned to Tokyo again in January 1945, the city that had always drawn him like a magnet "was mainly burned out." Although the family's Nishigahara house was miraculously still standing, the home of an acquaintance had burned down, he reported, as had the Taira train station and the Kannon statue in Asakusa, a Tokyo landmark. There was no food in the stores. The city's "endless gruesomeness," Isami wrote, "was impossible to describe." Tokyo had become "a city of men only."[25]

Critical of the government and pessimistic about the war's outcome, Isami nevertheless continued to do his duty to his country. Hearing that metal had become a precious war commodity, Isami gave all of Kōjirō's academic gold medals and trophies to the government to melt down for the war effort. On March 9 and 10, two months later, 130 American B-29s flew over Tokyo at night and dropped incendiary bombs, which fell like rain throughout the city. The bombs ignited firestorms that killed over a hundred thousand residents and destroyed twenty-three thousand homes.[26] Tokyo was an inferno, with 40 percent of the city reduced to ash. One observer described the capital as "a blazing hell." Others remembered the smell of burned flesh.[27] Asakusa, the district where Fumi had lived with her in-laws, "was filled with so much smoke it was hard to keep one's eyes open."[28] Bodies of people who had tried to flee the fires floated in the Sumida River, reminding eyewitnesses of the Great Kantō Earthquake twenty-two years earlier. Still, the bombing raids continued, and still the Japanese government refused to surrender. On April 15 the Matsuura family received a phone call informing them that their Tokyo house had burned down, as had their oatmeal factory. Mina's house was gone as well.[29] The several relatives living in the Nishigahara property managed to escape "wearing their pajamas and carrying just their pillows," Tami said. "They still laugh about it."[30]

Not even the family's village was spared the threat of air raids or the requirement of military training. Members of the Yamashiraishi Women's Association, headed by Kō, began training in bamboo spear fighting to prepare for the anticipated invasion of Japan. "Only the military," Fuki recalled in her seventies, "didn't seem to know we were losing."[31] But her brother Kōjirō, stationed with the Japanese army in the Dutch East Indies, knew better. Fluent in English, he was secretly tapping into American wireless broadcasts from San Francisco.[32] One day in April 1945, Isami observed a formation of nine American B-29 bombers fly over the village, drop their load of bombs on Kōriyama thirty miles to the north, and "fl[y] back with confidence." For Isami, "the color of defeat was visible."[33]

Despite his pessimistic forecast, Isami now drew on his passion for invention to aid the war effort by devising a way to make a primitive form of aviation fuel. Two million other Japanese were similarly employed, digging up the roots of pine trees to extract pine oil, from which the fuel could be distilled.[34] Petroleum oil was virtually gone from Japan.[35] Using the school playing field as his laboratory, Isami successfully produced enough refined pine oil to fill two big iron pots. Shortly afterward, around the time that word of Germany's surrender reached the village, he sold eleven drams of pine oil, boasting later that his oil had been declared "the best in the county or possibly even in the prefecture."[36] Indeed, Isami proudly reported that several soldiers were quartered for a few days in the family's house in order to help make the ersatz aviation fuel. While recognizing that Japan's defeat was inevitable, Isami continued to think up new ways to rescue an essentially hopeless situation. Ever the amateur inventor, he derived at least a certain amount of satisfaction from his ingenuity.

Another one of Isami's schemes for coping with wartime scarcity was harvesting sea salt. Like other rationed staples, salt was in short supply. Isami sent Yatarō with several of the village boys to the family land in Nakoso Beach in April and directed them to begin constructing a salt field. As the family heir, Yatarō had been spared the draft, and until April, when the Nishigahara house burned down, he had been living in Tokyo to manage family business. With his wife and children now back in Yamashiraishi, he joined others in filling big bottles with saltwater and then boiling the water until it was thick enough to use for cooking.

While women, children, and the elderly of the Matsuura family waited out the end of the war at home in the village, others of its members participated overseas in the "Greater East Asia War." Among these were the military men: Isami's three sons, three sons-in-law, and brother, Kōzō, in the army, and another son in the navy. Working in a civilian capacity overseas were the husbands of Fumi, Toyo, and Mina. Their lives were all in jeopardy, as was the life of Mina's brother-in-law, Ishiwata Sōtarō, who remained in Tokyo.

In early June, with Tokyo under aerial attack, Ishiwata was appointed Imperial Household minister, in charge of handling all matters related to the imperial family. The previous minister had just resigned, "feeling keenly," he professed, "the responsibility for the destruction by fire of the Imperial Palace and the Empress Dowager's palace."[37] These and numerous other buildings on the palace grounds had caught fire following an American bombing raid of nearby districts on May 25. In the previous month the prime minister, General Koiso, had also tendered his resignation, and Germany had signed unconditional surrender documents on May 7 and 8. The Third Reich, in the words of historian William L. Shirer, "simply ceased to exist."[38] Japan alone remained in the war.

The question now facing the Japanese government was how to end the war. On June 8, four days after Ishiwata's investiture as Imperial Household minister, Privy Seal Kido warned that the battle then raging over Okinawa would "result in a miserable fiasco." Kido recommended trying to negotiate for peace through a "mediating country."[39]

As Kido predicted, on June 22, 1945, Okinawa fell to the Americans after nearly three months of horrendous fighting. The struggle for Okinawa provided a terrifying forecast of the savagery that lay ahead for soldiers and civilians alike in the anticipated Allied invasion of the home islands. Taking Okinawa had cost Americans dearly. Their casualties numbered a staggering 49,000, but the toll in Japanese lives was even greater: 107,000 dead, 25,000 sealed in caves, and 11,000 taken prisoner. In addition, almost one-quarter of the civilian population on Okinawa was killed.[40]

Throughout June and July a peace faction within the Japanese government tried to interest the Soviet Union in mediating surrender negotiations with the Allies. Although the Soviets were not officially at war with Japan, their leader, Josef Stalin, had promised the Allied powers that they would enter the Pacific war after the fall of Germany, and his foreign minister rebuffed Japanese entreaties for help. The Soviets planned to attack Japan through Manchuria.

In the final weeks of the war, although Toyo and her family had returned to Japan, Fumi and her husband and three sons were still in Manchuria. No longer isolated from the home front's suffering, they too struggled merely to survive. For the past year Fumi had been selling household possessions, including Japanese clothing she had acquired for her trousseau, to buy food. As Japan's military need for fuel became more urgent, Fumi's geologist-husband stayed away from home for as long as three months at a time, searching in the mountains for coal. When he returned, his three sons, unable to recognize their unshaven, long-haired father, would hide behind Fumi's back.[41]

In early August 1945, Fumi and her family, noticing Russian troops streaming into Manchuria, realized that Russia's entrance into the war against Japan was imminent. Hungry Russian troops were already entering Shinkyō, and they took whatever they could find, even Fumi's last few kimono. They also tried to take Japanese women. "The soldiers were common [vulgar]," Fumi recalled. "They grabbed one of my friends, but a neighbor saw what was happening and banged on buckets to sound an alarm. The soldiers ran off."

Fumi was unaware of the war crimes committed by her own country's soldiers in Indochina, China, Manchuria, and elsewhere in Asia: the use of Korean and other native women as prostitutes for the military, the medical experiments performed on Chinese, the mistreatment of prisoners of war. Her opinion of the Japanese army in later years was shaped by two facts: they had lost the war and they had deserted her and her countrymen in Manchuria at war's end. When her memory faded toward the end of her life, she asked, "What finally ended the war?" But her memory of fleeing Manchuria remained vivid.

On a morning in early August, when Russia finally and officially declared war against Japan, the Japanese army in Manchuria headed south, evacuating officers' dependents and leaving civilians and reservists to fend for themselves.[42] Hearing the news of Russia's entrance into the war, Isami wrote, "I felt the danger to our country."[43] The danger to his relatives was much more immediate.

Fumi and her family gathered with other Japanese residents in the center of Shinkyō to receive final instructions for evacuation. Fearing the wrath of their longtime rival in northeast Asia, Japanese officials distributed poison to give to the children, if necessary. One of Fumi's friends, whose nine-year-old child was too sick to travel, administered a fatal dose. Others, who for one reason or another could not take their children along, entrusted them to Chinese acquaintances, never to see them again, though over thirty-five years later some of the children returned to Japan in search of their biological families.

The escaping Japanese, Fumi and her husband and three sons among them, left behind all their remaining possessions. They managed to board a Chinese train that slowly wound its way south to the port of Korotō (Haludao), in Liaoning province. It took them three weeks to reach the waiting rescue ship. They would ride for an hour and then pool their money to pay the conductor for the next hour's ride. At night they slept outside under a tent. Food consisted of one daily cold rice ball per person. Infants who died were thrown out the train windows. The boat trip across the Yellow Sea to Kyūshū, the southernmost of Japan's four main islands, took five days. And from there Fumi's family slowly traveled by train to the northern part of the main island to reunite with her husband's parents in Niigata shortly before American occupation forces began pouring into Japan. The empire no longer existed. Fumi and her family joined the millions of other unemployed and homeless refugees from the continent converging on Japan at war's end.[44]

ELEVEN

Surviving Hiroshima

ON AUGUST 6, 1945, when the world's first atomic bomb exploded without warning 1,870 feet over the center of Hiroshima, Toyo and her family were at home, less than two miles from the nucleus of the blast. Together with other Mitsubishi employees, they had made their way back from Manchuria to Japan in the waning days of the war. A number of Masafumi's relatives, including his mother, were among the city's population of 350,000, and his company's office was located in the downtown area. Although Hiroshima was the seventh largest city in Japan, it was one of only three major urban centers left unbombed by American B-29 planes; the other two were the ancient capital Kyoto and the port city Nagasaki. The Americans had other plans for Hiroshima and Nagasaki.

It was fifteen minutes past eight in the morning, and Masafumi was a little late for work because he was planning to take Yōko to his office in the center of the city. Toyo needed to work on a fire brigade that morning and was getting Yōko ready to go with her father. Her work team was assigned the task of demolishing a wooden house in a cluster of houses in order to create a fire break as a precaution against a possible conflagration. For weeks air raid sirens had been sounding as the American B-29 superfortresses flew over the coast near Hiroshima to bomb other cities, and it had been difficult to sleep at night. Over sixty major cities had already been heavily bombed in the past year. But the morning was pleasantly quiet and sunny as Masafumi hastily dressed. He was pulling on one trouser leg when the impact of the bomb's explosion blew off the door of the house.

To the pilot who dropped the atom bomb, the ground below looked like "a barrel of tar" under the rising mushroom-shaped cloud.[1] To firsthand observers on the ground, a "sheet of sun" seemed to have cut across the sky, and everything flashed white.[2] The heat melted granite. Soon burn victims, their skin hanging from their faces and hands, began walking silently toward the several interlacing branches of the Ota River like a procession of ghosts. Before long, hundreds of burned bodies floated down the rivers dividing the city. Standing on the hill that overlooks the city, a survivor was shocked by the sight: "Hiroshima didn't exist—that was mainly what I saw— Hiroshima just didn't exist."[3] A twenty-one-year-old American soldier was also unprepared for what he saw several days later: nothing. "No birds. No people. No buildings. No trees. No life. Outlines of human bodies burned like negatives in cement. . . . The city had vaporized."[4] On August 9, another atomic bomb was dropped on Nagasaki.

The Matsuura clan, gathered in the countryside well to the north of Hiroshima, first heard about the atom bombings of both Hiroshima and Nagasaki from Emperor Hirohito's surrender announcement on August 15. He had secretly recorded it around midnight the night before in a room of the Imperial Household Ministry building, located in one corner of the palace grounds. Only a few men were present; one of them was Mina's brother-in-law, Imperial Household Minister Ishiwata Sōtarō.[5]

Involvement in the surrender announcement had placed Ishiwata's life in immediate danger. The surrender document itself had already been signed by the emperor and his entire cabinet and transmitted by cables to the two neutral nations Switzerland and Sweden, but court officials feared that military men unwilling to capitulate would steal the phonographic recording and disrupt the government's plans to surrender. As a precaution, the officials had made two sets of two ten-inch recorded disks and placed them in separate cardboard containers wrapped in a cotton bag. They then hid the bag in a small safe on the second floor of the Household Ministry.[6]

As feared, a group of insurgents opposed to Japan's capitulation took over the Imperial Guard Division early in the morning of the 15th. Hearing the news, court officials assumed they were looking for the phonograph records and would come after the Imperial Household minister and the emperor's close adviser Marquis Kido, whose office was also in the Imperial Household building. Kido was resting on the floor of his office with the radio on to listen for air raid announcements when a court chamberlain burst in around 3:30 in the morning to inform him of a "riot." The insurgents had taken over the communication facilities of the Imperial Household Ministry. Kido tore up his most important documents and threw them into the toilet before he and Ishiwata, guided by court chamberlains and "with barely time to spare," fled the rebels to hide in the great vault in the basement.[7] As they entered the stifling room, Kido said to Ishiwata, "We don't know when we may be discovered and killed together, but history has already changed its course. Even if we are killed now it won't matter, for the war is being brought to an end."[8]

At noontime on that same day, the emperor announced Japan's surrender in his high-pitched, reedy voice, broadcast from staticky radios and loudspeakers throughout the country to people who had never before heard their god-ruler speak and could barely understand his formal language.[9] Still, "everyone was struck dumb" by his words, according to Isami's recollection, because many people were expecting him to announce a declaration of war against the Soviet Union.[10]

Listeners among the Matsuura family members understood that, although the emperor had not actually said as much, he was agreeing to a surrender, and they sensed that it was the atomic bombs that had forced an end to the war.[11] The enemy, the emperor said, "has begun to employ a new and most cruel bomb, the power of which to do damage is indeed incalculable, taking the toll of many innocent lives. Should We continue to fight, it would result not only in an ultimate collapse and obliteration of the Japanese nation, but also it would lead to the total extinction of human civilization."[12]

These chilling words, summarized in everyday language by radio announcers immediately afterward, led the family to try to contact the main office of Mitsubishi in Tokyo to inquire about the fate of Toyo and Masafumi in Hiroshima. Fifth son Tatsugorō and grandson Rintarō (Ishiwata Sōtarō's nephew) were dispatched to Tokyo, where they found the capital a charred wasteland—an "ashen landscape," with only clusters of buildings still standing and its population shrunken from seven million to four million. Where once a vibrant city had stood, there was now only a "vast and blackened plain."[13] The palace area remained, in the recollections of one firsthand American observer, an anomalous "oasis of green within its ancient moat."[14]

Fortunately, the two young men were spared the need to see, with their own eyes, the damage done by the atomic bombing, because they learned from Mitsubishi officials in Tokyo that Toyo's family was not among the approximately one hundred thousand persons who had perished on the day the bomb had exploded over the center of Hiroshima. The two young men returned home on August 19 to report the good news.

Toyo and her family considered themselves lucky. While whole neighborhoods had been wiped out, Toyo's house did not burn down, though a piece of its bamboo wall fell on two-and-a-half-year-old Yōko, puncturing her wrist, and her face turned black from the blast. The skin around Masafumi's exposed knee was burned and peeled off, and later tumors appeared on his leg. Although the tumors disappeared, the skin never fully healed, retaining a furrowed appearance. Exposure to radiation, he claimed, also left him impotent. Had he been in his office closer to the center of the blast instead of pulling on his pants at home, however, he would not have survived.[15]

Masafumi managed to bring Yōko to a hospital, but others were much more badly hurt, so he could not get treatment for her. He cleaned the puncture wound on her wrist by himself, yet it, like his knee, never fully healed. At the puncture site, the skin remained slightly dented, and a permanent mark remained around it in the form of brownish discoloration, like iodine. After a while, however, normal skin grew back on her face.[16]

Other residents of the city were less fortunate. All the office workers in Masafumi's company were killed. People either perished in the firestorm, which consumed five square miles of the city, or, like tens of thousands of others, they succumbed months later to radiation sickness, leukemia, and other ailments caused by their exposure to the bomb.[17] Toyo's mother-in-law died of lung cancer three years later.

In all, close to three million Japanese military personnel and citizens were killed between the official outbreak of the war with China in 1937 and Japan's surrender in 1945.[18] Yet, miraculously, all fourteen of the Matsuura children and their spouses and children, including the Zero pilot and the malaria-afflicted army surgeon, were alive at war's end. Even Mina's brother-in-law survived, hidden in the vault of the Imperial Household Ministry.

During the war, the only deaths that occurred among family members were of the elderly: Isami's mother, Miyo, who had been incapacitated for many years from a stroke and died in 1941; and the fathers-in-law of Fuki and Yasu, who had sought refuge in Yamashiraishi. All three were buried in the Matsuura family cemetery, where Isami had memorial stones erected for each one. Otherwise, the extended family remained intact, though just barely, as the succeeding years would reveal.

Following the emperor's surrender announcement and even before the official start of the military occupation of Japan, village heads such as Isami braced for the imminent arrival of the victorious Allies. In late August 1945, Isami called a meeting of village functionaries to impress upon them the urgent need to prepare for the return of hundreds of overseas villagers, including repatriated soldiers. He was especially worried about food shortages: starvation was already reported in the poorer mountain communities. A few days later on August 26, 1945, when he attended a meeting of the Ishikawa county assembly, however, he was disgusted to hear everybody merely "voicing beautiful, flowery words."[19]

Without waiting for others, Isami swung into action with his usual assertiveness. He hatched a scheme for growing barley on a nearby mountain and made several trips to investigate the site. On September 9 he submitted a proposal for the project and an estimated budget to the prefectural government through the Ishikawa local office, but even before obtaining official approval he took steps to launch the project—and just as well; the official approval, with a budget allocation, came fifteen months later, and by that time the village population had swelled to the most it had ever been: 1,423 people.[20] In the meanwhile, Isami had bought a horse from the army for 120 yen, acquired wagons, and lined up ten volunteers to plant the barley. Work began on November 7, 1945. Isami even staged a groundbreaking ceremony. Construction of a small dam, a project for which Isami later received an official commendation, began about one year later.[21]

Among those people whom Isami worried about feeding were his own adult children and their families, who were to stay in the village for several years after the war. Most of them had no other place to go. With sixteen square miles of Tokyo flattened, the capital was devastated. Bombed-out cities were experiencing serious food and housing shortages. Millions of homeless Japanese were living in shacks or abandoned trolley cars and sleeping in subway tunnels. The poor rice harvest in the fall of 1945 contributed to the nation's plight.[22] With its merchant marine destroyed in the war and its currency of no value on international markets, Japan could not import food and raw materials to ease the desperate situation. Incidents of death by starvation were reported in urban newspapers. The six million repatriated Japanese soldiers and civilians streaming back to Japan, some of Isami's children among them, further added to the crisis in the cities; they overflowed repatriation centers, which were unable to muster sufficient food to stave off malnutrition.[23] Isami could hardly expect his children to return to Tokyo when city dwellers were leading an "'onion existence,' peeling off layers of heirloom kimonos" to exchange for whatever food they could find from farmers.[24]

Isami's brother, Kōzō, was among the millions of repatriated soldiers, and he and his family returned to the village in late August 1945. With his career as an army officer quashed by the occupation's plans to dismantle the entire Japanese military establishment, a demoralized Kōzō had no choice but to relocate in the countryside, and he settled on family land in the nearby village of Fukisaku. "He had to swallow his disappointment," Isami wrote. "His life was nothing."[25]

One by one other overseas family members found their way back to Yamashiraishi, swelling the house Isami had built forty-five years earlier to over thirty-five occupants. Shinrokurō, the Zero pilot, also returned in late August, and in early September, Yatarō's in-laws sought shelter in Yamashiraishi and were given the front room. Later in the same month, Yūshirō finally returned from Sendai, where he had been hospitalized for malaria. In early October the family received telegrams from third son Saburō and from Mina's husband, both in North China, saying they were safe and on their way back to Japan. Toyo reached Yamashiraishi from Hiroshima in December and stayed for a short time. Fumi and her family arrived in early 1946.

Two family members remained overseas after the war's end. To the consternation of those back home, Yasu's husband, captured by the Russians along with over 1.5 million other Japanese in China and Manchuria at the end of the war, was held in a Siberian labor camp, his fate as a prisoner of war uncertain. Second son Kōjirō also failed to return home immediately after the surrender. He had agreed to stay in the Dutch East Indies to serve as a paid interpreter for the war crimes trials convened by Dutch military forces in Jakarta.

With or without all the menfolk, the work of recovery had to proceed, and it rested first of all on Isami and Kō's ability to feed and shelter family members and, in several cases, to nurse them and to help the able-bodied adults find employment. The work of caring for so many additional family members finally took its toll on Kō, who had also been preparing food for the village schoolchildren and leading the village women's association. Emaciated, she took to her bed at the end of 1945, suffering from an undiagnosed illness, which family members at first thought was malnutrition.

The housing pressure in Yamashiraishi eased only after the early 1950s. By then, most of the children of Isami and Kō, as well as their children's in-laws, had managed to pick up some of the pieces of their fractured former lives. Those who fared best were the family's older sons and sons-in-law, who had launched careers well before the Pacific war as physicians or managerial-level employees of large companies such as Mitsubishi. Despite the occupation's reforms aimed at destroying prewar *zaibatsu* (Japan's giant cartels), they survived in altered form in the postwar period. Although Toyo's husband lost his job with Mitsubishi, he found employment as branch head of a subsidiary trading company formed when the occupation forced the cartel to reorganize. It was a drop in status for him, but a decade later, Mitsubishi hired him back to head its new branch office in Brazil. Fumi's geologist-husband entered the Survey Bureau of the Ministry of Commerce and Industry in Tokyo soon after the family's return from Manchuria, and

Fuki's husband resumed his medical career in Kanagawa. Shiki's husband, with financial help from Isami, began construction of a medical clinic, but for several months in 1947 while his clinic was being built, he and Shiki lived in Yamashiraishi.

Even those with jobs could not easily return to Tokyo. Food shortages continued well into the late 1940s, despite food shipments from the United States, and the housing shortage in the cities lasted well into the 1960s. The only way for the Matsuura children to resume their former lives was with the assistance of relatives.

Mina's family was among the first to leave Yamashiraishi. Her husband's brother, Ishiwata Sōtarō, offered them the land on which his father's house had stood in the Komagome section of Tokyo, and they built a house there in 1947. Sōtarō himself had stayed on in the Imperial Household Ministry in the early postwar days, helping to draft occupation-mandated democratizing reforms that abolished the House of Peers, of which he and his father had been members, and reduced the size and importance of the Imperial Household Ministry, transforming it into an administrative agency of the palace, with its head no longer holding a cabinet portfolio. Interrogated during the Tokyo War Crimes Trials of 1947–48, Ishiwata escaped the fate of the Lord Privy Seal Kido Kōichi, who was jailed as a war criminal, and General Tojo Hideki, who was executed, but he died shortly thereafter in 1950, just before his sixtieth birthday.[26]

Yasu's widowed mother-in-law was also among the earliest family members to return to Tokyo; fortunately, her house, on the western outskirts of the capital, had been spared in the bombing raids. Yasu chose to remain in Yamashiraishi with her three-year-old son, awaiting the Russians' repatriation of her husband from Siberia, but when her mother-in-law became seriously ill in November 1947, she left the boy with her parents and went to Tokyo to take care of the older woman.

Family members continued to help one another resettle for several years after the war's end. The Matsuura land in the Nishigahara section of northeastern Tokyo gradually became the site of four new residences to house the families of Fumi, Fuki, Tatsu, and Seishichirō. Fumi's was the first house to be built on the property, thanks to the services of a carpenter who came from her husband's home prefecture of Niigata. Fuki's husband, Dr. Akakura, afterward paid a sum of money to Isami to purchase a small parcel of the Nishigahara property on which to build their home, and when they moved in, Fuki, bereft of servants for the first time in her life but still living with her elderly mother-in-law, started cooking on her own. Isami used the money from Dr. Akakura to pay for seventh son Seishichirō's college tuition at Keiō University. Money and resources thus circulated within the extended family network to help family members recover from the war.

Not all the children returned to Tokyo or to their old careers. Third son Saburō, who had been a journalist before the war and served in the army in China during the war, settled in the countryside near his parents in a family-owned house in the town of Ishikawa. With money borrowed from his older brother Kōjirō, who was still in the Dutch East Indies, he ran unsuccessfully for prefectural office. Winning in his second effort, this time as an "unofficial candidate" of the Liberal Party, his career in politics was nonetheless short-lived, and he became a local high school teacher before eventually working his way back to Chiba, outside Tokyo, where he taught tennis. "He never made much of his life," said his youngest sister, Tami, suggesting that more had been expected of him.

Yūshirō, too, stayed close to home. In the hard economic times of the late 1940s, the family's fourth son opened a medical office with attached clinic in Ishikawa, in an old rented house next door to his residence. He purchased surgical equipment in Tokyo with money Kōjirō had sent home and teamed up with several other doctors to share costs.

Yūshirō's refined, Tokyo-bred spouse, Masako, had not expected to be a country doctor's wife, but she recognized that the war had irreparably changed their lives. They could not afford to open a practice in Tokyo, and, besides, Ishikawa lacked doctors. Assisted by a maid and baby-tenders to watch over her four sons, for the next twenty years she helped to run the clinic and cooked breakfast for the four nurses and as many as fifteen patients, preparing the food in her kitchen and carrying it next door.

Masako also had not expected to take care of her parents in their old age, but the war had changed family roles as well. In prewar days, this role was typically filled by the eldest son, just as the eldest son was typically the recipient of the entire inheritance. But Masako's younger brother abdicated his responsibility for their parents and refused to live with them in their Tokyo home. Angry with him, Masako, the oldest daughter of her family, took her parents in and cared for them until their deaths, at which point all the siblings, taking advantage of occupation-guided changes in family law, agreed to divide the inheritance among themselves.

The youngest daughter of the Matsuura family, Tami, remained in the village until 1948, when she moved to Kyoto with her new husband, Iida Seiji, whom she had not met until her wedding day in the previous year. Marriageable men were scarce in the early postwar years, and, living back in the village, Tami did not have an opportunity to meet men of suitable background. During the war, when she had been living in Tokyo with her sister-in-law's family, it had been different. Even with the military draft, there had been many requests for Tami's hand. One came from a doctor in the northernmost island of Hokkaidō, but Tami's oldest sister, Mina, opposed the match, arguing that the man lived too far away. The husband eventually chosen for Tami was the brother of Mina's friend. He had been spared the draft because he was a medical student at Kyoto Imperial University. Later Tami learned that the Hokkaidō doctor had died young.

Although the family could no longer afford the extravagant weddings of the 1930s, Tami was married at the Meiji Shrine in Tokyo, and afterward there was a party at the family's village home to introduce Tami's new husband to the villagers. Tami wore the traditional bridal kimono with her hair done up in the classical hairstyle. To her approving father, "she looked like a doll." For her trousseau, she split the usual assemblage of Matsuura brides' expensive furniture with her next older sister, Yasu.[27]

Within a year, Tami returned to her crowded natal home to give birth. With the help of a midwife, a baby girl named Masako was born in the corridor-like room connecting the retirement cottage to the village office. Kō took care of the infant along with Yasu's child when Tami required surgery for infected mammary glands. Around the same time, Yūshirō's medical equipment finally arrived, and he x-rayed his mother, who was still ailing. The x-rays revealed bad news: Kō had contracted tuberculosis in one lung. She was among the 560,000 Japanese patients diagnosed with tuberculosis by the time the disease hit its postwar peak in 1951.[28]

Kō was immediately moved to Ishikawa, and the family arranged for a live-in helper to care for her in a house they owned next door to Saburō's house; it was on a wooded hill and within walking distance of Yūshirō's clinic. By the end of the year, Yūshirō obtained the new drug streptomycin and began a series of injections that reduced his mother's fever. Seeing his wife's appetite return, Isami hoped for a miracle.[29]

Before long two other Matsuura women also contracted tuberculosis, though their cases were less intractable. Nevertheless, Fuki's condition required surgery, performed by her doctor-husband, who had to remove several ribs, and Yasu required a special corset.

In 1949, Yasu's husband was finally repatriated, weak and emaciated from four years of forced labor in Siberia, and he too came to Yamashiraishi to recuperate. Sho spoke very little about his Siberian ordeal then or later, saying only that prisoners had existed on bread crusts and snakes. In Yamashiraishi he ate ravenously until his stomach became so bloated that Kō warned he would get sick if he did not stop stuffing himself, but for the rest of his life, though he retained a hearty appetite, he remained thin. Adjustment to the relatively normal family life of postwar Japan after years in a foreign prison camp proved difficult at first. Sho was hard on his five-year-old son, whom he had never really known. Once Kō intervened when she saw him hitting the boy and chided him for being too strict.[30]

The sons of Kō and Isami and at least one of their nephews encountered problems that were not so much medical as work-related and psychological. Almost all of the boys had difficulty finding places for themselves in postwar Japanese society. The three youngest sons, their education still incomplete, confronted a demoralized, impoverished postwar society and a ruined capital that held out little in the way of career opportunities or glamour. Occupied by a foreign military establishment for the first time in its history, a defeated Japan in the late 1940s offered little hope to teenage boys from the countryside, and Isami, by this time, lacked the resources to lavish on his youngest sons and other family members. Anxiety about the future of the younger men in the family intensified when the oldest son of Isami's brother, Kōzō, the former career army officer, also contracted tuberculosis. He had suffered a nervous breakdown during the war while his father was in China, and now his health problems became more than he could bear. Believing that he could not find a marriage partner or a job and would always be a burden to his parents, he stole his father's gun and ended his life.[31]

To survive economically the Matsuura needed to create new sources of income other than land. Isami's business ventures in the postwar period no longer represented, if they ever had, the dabbling of the idle rural rich. He seemed to be trying to establish a family enterprise that he could turn over to those sons whose education had suffered during the war or who, for whatever reason, could not make their way on their own in Tokyo. Commercial enterprises over the centuries had added to the family's fortunes. But the business schemes of the aged eleventh-generation patriarch were no longer financed by tenant rents from vast landholdings, and whether they would succeed in the postwar period was another question altogether.

TWELVE

Missed Fortunes

SHORTLY AFTER HIS WIFE KO'S COLLAPSE, Isami abruptly resigned from his position as village head. "People were starving" was the only explanation he offered for his unexpected decision to quit office at the end of January 1946. He added that he wanted to serve as campaign manager for a candidate from the local area running for a seat in the Lower House of the Diet. Presumably the candidate was concerned, as Isami was, with the problem of how to feed the population, and, if elected, he might acquire the power to do something about it.[1]

Given Isami's previous reluctance to engage in politics and his lack of familiarity with campaigning, his sudden resignation from village office for the stated reason was out of character for him. He mentioned later in the family history, however, that in 1951 he organized a society of former village heads who had been forced out of office as a result of the American occupation's political purges.[2] Perhaps Isami had anticipated being caught in the broad net cast by American reformers as part of their plans to bring grassroots democracy to Japan. Ordinances passed at the same time as the purges prohibited mayors from succeeding themselves in office.[3]

Whatever his reasons, Isami's resignation represented a historic moment for the Matsuura family. Isami himself was convinced that the family's uninterrupted monopoly of village office had come to an end, for he felt certain that the village assembly would not elect his heir to office. Yatarō, after all, had not lived in Yamashiraishi for over twenty years. Besides, Isami had long held misgivings about his firstborn son's abilities.

To Isami's surprise, however, and possibly even to his consternation, the village assembly voted five to one to elect Yatarō for a four-year term of office. Succeeding his father as village head, Yatarō moved back to Yamashiraishi from Nakoso Beach, where Isami had sent him during the war to manage the salt business on family-owned beach land. Meanwhile, Isami's candidate for the Diet lost, having proven too conservative for this first postwar election. Winners tended to be supported by liberal voting elements, such as women's associations and tenant unions; the former were enfranchised and the latter strengthened as a result of occupation political reforms. Japan's defeat changed the political "climate of opinion," undermining members of the old guard, like Isami himself, whose autocratic leadership style lost way to values such as *demokurashii,* espoused by Japan's victors.[4]

Silenced politically, the sixty-seven-year-old Isami concentrated on the task of supporting his large brood of adult children and helping them return to normalcy. This goal grew increasingly difficult to reach after January 1947, when occupation officials pushed through further reforms, this time aimed at large landholders, who constituted the power elite in the countryside and whose land had tended to be cultivated for a hefty rent by tenants under their sway. One political aim of the occupation was to redistribute land so that tenancy would be eliminated and an independent class of farmers could emerge to serve as the backbone of democracy in rural Japan.

Land reform forced the Matsuura to sell most of their remaining rice lands to their tenants at a fixed low price. Inflation in the early postwar years, together with the urgent demand for food in the cities, gave tenant farmers sufficient income from the marketing of their agricultural produce to buy the land at the legal purchase price, which was set on the basis of the rental value in 1938.[5] Committees of local farmers in each village were formed to oversee the land's reallocation, further undermining the authority of village heads, who tended to be the major landlords, as in the case of the Matsuura. Identified with the failed war cause and with undemocratic tendencies in general, local leaders saw their authority evaporate. Reformers were not necessarily "attentive to the rights, or plight, of those defined as landlords."[6]

Because Isami had been cashing in the family's holdings over the years, the approximately five hundred acres he had once owned had dwindled to considerably less. Exactly how much land the family owned at the end of the war is difficult to say. If Isami's estimate of about seventy acres is correct, the family would have received a significant rental income by early postwar Japanese standards. However, both the village Buddhist priest and the town historian agreed that in his family history Isami grossly exaggerated his wartime holdings. His daughter-in-law Masako, when she married Yūshirō in 1939, had already concluded that the family had scarcely any land left. Whatever the Matsuura owned in 1945, after land reform they were left with slightly less than two acres, just enough, according to the eldest daughter, Mina, to support immediate household members.

Mina and her sister Fuki recalled that their father was unperturbed by land reform. He told family members that even if they fought the reform, they would lose anyway. "He wore an unworried face," Mina said. "He put all his wealth into his children's education," Fuki recalled. "He said that, although they can take away your land, they can never take away your education." Isami described himself as fortunate in the sense that he had been selling off his land well before the occupation period, so land reform did not take much away from him.

Nevertheless, Isami's own written account of these times reveals a man close to seventy who, scrambling to raise money for his children, engaged in petty squabbles over ownership of whatever remaining land he possessed. He feuded with a village woman over ownership rights to one *tan* of land (1,185 square yards). "She would plant the land, and I would rip out her plantings. Whatever I planted, she would rip out." Although the village Young People's League sided with her, Isami fought back—hardly the behavior of an unperturbed, dignified, former village head. "In the end," Isami wrote, triumphantly, "she couldn't plant on the land." Shortly thereafter, Isami erected a property marker. Another conflict over landownership went to court and dragged on for three years before Isami won on appeal.[7] These court cases suggest that Isami was less sanguine about losing his land than his daughters realized.

In the period following Japan's defeat, Isami continued to seek alternate sources of income. One tactic was to locate manufacturers willing to produce his inventions. In the spring of 1952, a friend procured entrée for him to a Tokyo confectionery, where he described his propeller-like device for manufacturing oatmeal, but company representatives decided it was too complicated. He also tried to find a manufacturer for his rice husker.

A second tactic was to establish his own business. Small ventures, such as a poultry business in Ishikawa, proved too much trouble, and more ambitious undertakings required more capital and technical know-how than he could muster. The rock quarry company he tried to launch in the 1950s is a case in point. Isami's idea was to extract rock from a nearby mountain and sell it, presumably for paving roads. He first visited the site of the quarry in 1953 and learned the project would be viable if he could acquire various equipment, including a special drill to break up the rocks before transporting them on wheeled carts. He enlisted the help of his third son, assigning him the task of raising money for the venture. Saburō thought at first he could buy discarded rocks cheaply from a company in Shirakawa, but the scheme fell through. His younger brother Shin then joined him in his money-raising efforts, and so did the fifth-born brother, Tatsu, briefly. The men eventually acquired partners and several investors, but they encountered technical as well as financial problems.

Isami and his sons had to figure out how to move the carts carrying the stones over wheel tracks in the road. The trouble was that one of the tracks was higher than the other. Isami arranged to spend three nights with Shin at makeshift lodgings on the site, confident that they could find a way to solve this "cancer."[8] Inexperienced in both business and road building and probably intimidated by his father, Shin came close to a nervous breakdown and quit, and Isami temporarily closed the business. One of the partners also quit, but another, a man named Nikaidō, persuaded a friend who had his own company to take over as manager, and before long they were realizing a modest profit.

But then Nikaidō himself quit because he had to defend himself against election fraud involving his support of a candidate for political office. When a meeting of the principal investors was called, Nikaidō failed to show up. Isami then asked a friend of Fumi's husband, who was in the mining industry, to evaluate the project, and the friend advised them that the rock quarry was not a good project.

Before Isami could pull out, however, his difficulties mounted. Although the professional manager had left the company, Nikaidō came back on board and desperately asked Isami for money to fix the wheeled carts. Isami gave him the money, only to learn that Nikaidō had lied to him about the real purpose of the loan. Fortunately, Isami had put its terms in writing. He forced Nikaidō out, but after Nikaidō resigned, the Bureau of Labor Standards launched an investigation. More workers were brought in to fix the road, and once again the company started to make a profit, which, though small, enabled Isami to hire another professional manager to replace Saburō, who had been so anxious about the company's debts, he had lost weight.[9]

To add to his problems at around this same time, Isami inexplicably ran afoul of the law in 1953 when he attended a banquet at the invitation of a political group. The police suspected him of buying votes, when in fact he had gone merely to show his face, in his phrasing. He hired a lawyer, spending a lot of money for no benefit.[10] He was jailed in Shirakawa for twelve days before police dropped the charges. In the summer of 1954, Isami happened to meet an old acquaintance in Tokyo, a businessman he hadn't seen in over twenty years, who articulated the disturbing thought that a man of Isami's talents and intelligence should have achieved respectable middle-class status as a salaried employee of a major corporation by this time; he bluntly remarked, "A Matsuura like you should have been working for Mitsubishi."[11]

With a trace of envy, Isami cited the village's "most successful man," who had succeeded in launching a profitable business in contrast to Isami's own shaky investments and visionary schemes. The man had acquired a patent from Italy to make a carburetor. During the war, the army had encouraged him to develop it, and after the war, he expanded production to include iron tools. At his death, his factory employed three hundred people. "He had only one son," Isami wrote ruefully, "and inheritance went smoothly."[12]

Nothing went smoothly for Isami in the postwar period. He lost his land, his village office, and his influence, and most of his business enterprises yielded modest returns at best. He was engaged in lawsuits and had to counter criminal charges. His wife was ill; and his sons, a disappointment.

That Isami was disappointed with his sons, though proud of the long family line, was revealed in critical remarks scattered throughout his family history. He frequently mentioned the successes of his sons-in-law, especially the doctors, in contrast to his own male progeny. He was "very pleased" with Dr. Nakao Shin's new clinic, for example, but was always worried about Yatarō's management of family holdings. Saburō's first effort to launch a political career by running for a seat in the prefectural assembly had failed (even though he had garnered much support from the Ishikawa Youth Organization, his siblings, and other volunteers) because, according to his critical father, he had become "overly confident" and "maybe even careless."[13] Isami was not tolerant of failure.

Still, Isami never gave up. With Kō incapacitated, he struggled largely on his own to promote the careers of his three youngest sons. To the great dismay of his parents, fifth son Tatsu seemed to fail at everything he tried. At one point in 1946 he received a contract to sell charcoal to a contact somewhere in Tokyo. In 1949 he borrowed money to start a business raising pigs, only to watch all of them die, one after another, and Isami had to pay off the loan with money he had set aside for his own purposes—to buy wool from China, presumably to sell it in Japan. Next, Tatsu went to Tokyo to look for work, but in the late 1940s, with the country suffering a severe recession that had left thirteen million people unemployed, all he could find was a temporary job writing calligraphy on Shintō shrine banners. When his unemployment benefits ended, he briefly considered looking for work in the East Indies, where his older brother Kōjirō was still living, but instead returned, dejected, to Ishikawa. Kō, bedridden and spitting up blood, tried to encourage him, and Isami, sensing he was having a "life crisis," assigned him odd jobs to do around the house. Sympathizing with their most delicate child, Kō and Isami tried to keep up his spirits while they worried about their *rōnin,* a term that had come to be used in the postwar period to refer to men either awaiting college admission or seeking employment. Within one year, Isami succeeded in using his contacts to get Tatsu a job as an outside sales canvasser with the Pacific Company in Tokyo.

Tatsu's job greatly boosted his self-esteem. In fact, his father found him a bit cocky; he was "swaggering," as Isami put it. Ever the watchful autocrat, Isami advised his son he was acting too confident. But Tatsu continued to do well and even landed a large contract. By the early 1950s Japan's economy was showing signs of recovery, stimulated in large part by the 1950 outbreak of the Korean War, which had brought millions of U.S. dollars to Japan for military procurements. Basking in the newfound optimism of the country, the family's fifth son, for long their most troubled member, appeared ready at last to settle down. In 1954 he agreed to a marriage arranged for him with Sano Akemi, the niece of Iida Seiji, from whom Tami was now separated with a divorce pending.

Once again, the family contributed its share to help stage an impressive wedding reminiscent of the glory days of the mid-1930s. At a cost to Isami of about one thousand yen each, over forty Matsuura relatives attended the reception in the Shinjuku district of Tokyo. Recorded in Isami's family history was the illustrious name of the go-between—Matsudaira, bearer of a famous Tokugawa-era surname and possibly a descendant of the military house that had once ruled part of Fukushima prefecture. Following the latest trends in marriage, Tatsu and his bride departed on their honeymoon, riding in the special "romance car" of a train that took them from Tokyo to a popular seaside resort. Upon their return, they had Fumi's Niigata carpenter build a house for them on the Nishigahara property, making the down payment with money Isami had saved from the sale of another parcel of land to Fuki and her husband and taking out a mortgage for the rest.[14] Within a year, Tatsu's wife gave birth to their first child.

The last-born son, Seishichirō, also settled in Tokyo. In 1952, soon after graduating from Keiō University with a major in French literature, he found a job with a company that manufactured farm equipment. He landed the job with the help of the intricate web of family contacts; the man who put in a good word for him was the older brother of the wife of his brother Saburō and was also married to the sister of Toyo's husband. Within four years Isami started looking for a wife for his seventh son. Violating his practice of not marrying his children to relatives, Isami showed Sei pictures of several available brides, including Miseikusa Kuniko, the granddaughter of Isami's oldest sister, whom Sei had known since his teenage days. Perhaps Isami knew that Sei had spent time with Kuniko even after he went off to college in Tokyo. Sei gladly chose his country cousin—"I was something like his sister," Kuniko explained—and the couple built the fourth and last home on the Nishigahara property.[15] The Matsuura siblings were together again, ensconced in Tokyo and, at least in their father's eyes, back on the right track, like Japan itself.

Fifth son Tatsu's apparent worldly success, however, was short lived. "He could never work for others in an office," his youngest sister, Tami, explained. The dedicated, hard-driving "salary man" of Japan's postwar economic recovery was a masculine role model Tatsu refused to follow. Like his father, he demonstrated more of a flair for invention than for business. In the early 1950s he designed an automatic potato slicer that made the thin slices favored by restaurants and housewives. The Yukijinushi Company bought the patent and successfully manufactured the machine, but afterward Tatsu ran up debts on his other inventions, and his sister Toyo and other siblings had to bail him out. "It was very *kuyashii*" (vexing), said Toyo's daughter, using a Japanese word that can also mean mortifying.

In the wake of Tatsu's financial distress, his wife walked out on him and their two young children. Once again, family members came to the rescue of a sibling in distress. His sister Fumi, who lived next door, helped to care for the children, but after Tatsu fell behind on his mortgage payments, he had to give up the Nishigahara house, and he moved to Yokohama to look for work. Within two or three years after his divorce, he married a woman he met on a train. Eventually he and his second wife resettled in an apartment outside Tokyo. The couple was childless. Estranged from his siblings in the 1990s, he was earning a living by driving a taxi.

Tatsu became the black sheep of the family, embodying the opposite of everything his father admired. Tami, who stood for many of her father's values, including loyalty to family members, had little sympathy for either him or her third oldest brother, Saburō, in part because they had violated Isami's example of maintaining a wide network of family ties and helping each other. "He wants nothing to do with the family" described perhaps the worse sin any family member could commit in Tami's eyes, and both Tatsu and Saburō were guilty of it. In addition, these two brothers as well as the two youngest brothers "lacked direction," in Tami's analysis. On more than one occasion, her second husband remarked that the "Matsuura sisters were winners," an indirect way of saying that the brothers were losers. Her sister Fuki, more sympathetic, said simply that the brothers were "victims of the war."

The sixth-born son, Shin—the former navy pilot—also floundered in postwar Japan. While enrolled in veterinary school, Shin fell in love. Fearful that his son was making a premature commitment and unfamiliar with "love marriages," Isami, who had initiated most of his children's marriages up to this point, wrote Shin a letter explaining why, as a parent, he disapproved of the relationship. These were new times, however, and notions of romantic love, like democracy, were in the air, a product of American occupation reforms geared to promoting freedom and individualism. When the girlfriend sent Isami a letter describing her feelings for Shin, Isami was conciliatory; he invited both of them to Ishikawa, where Kō was living, to discuss the matter. Isami asked them to live apart for a year, and if they still felt the same way about each other at the end of the year, he promised he would reconsider.[16] Isami's stratagem failed, and in 1954 he reluctantly agreed to the marriage. Shin never became a veterinarian. Instead, he became another *rōnin*, this time a married one.

The marital, health, and employment problems of their children naturally distressed Kō and Isami. They had heavily invested in their children's future financial security as members of the urban middle class. They had spent generously on education and weddings to promote the well-being of daughters and sons alike. The unspoken assumptions were that their children's lives would be secure and they themselves, in their old age, would be comfortably cared for by their heir and his wife. But few of their dreams would be realized. Still, they soldiered on, trying to fix relationships and recover from economic losses the way they had always repaired and even rebuilt their houses, replanted the cypresses, and tended the grave sites.

Fortunately, Isami remained vigorously healthy, except for the flare-ups of his inflamed appendix, which were followed in one instance, in 1954, by a ten-day case of severe stomach catarrh that left him emaciated. He was nursed back to health in Ishikawa, but it was half a year before he fully recovered. Approaching his seventieth year, in 1949, he complained of feeling old. His powers waning, Isami found it increasingly difficult to take care of Kō, who was confined to bed, where she passed the time practicing calligraphy. Instead of enjoying their retirement years, they were scrambling for money for themselves and their younger children, relying on infusions of cash sent by the elusive Kōjirō in the East Indies, and dependent on medical care provided by their fourth son, Yūshirō, and two sons-in-law. Even some of the daughters, whose husbands had reestablished themselves, sent money on occasion to pay for a train ticket to Tokyo for Isami or to cover his property taxes.

In addition to promoting his quarry company and inventions, Isami took charge of household maintenance projects, overseeing the many repairs and purchases required for their several homes. He arranged to replace the sixty-six-year-old paper sliding partitions in the retirement cottage and decorated them with the words of a Chinese Tang dynasty poet. He fixed the roof on Kō's residence in Ishikawa before the rainy season and installed pipes to draw water away from the retirement cottage and redirect it down behind the school to avoid landslides in the monsoon season. Receiving fifty cedar cuttings from an acquaintance, he planted them himself directly into the ground—"they rooted nicely"—to replace the ones he had reluctantly cut down during the war.[17]

These tasks, like his social and ritual obligations—attending funerals and weddings, paying calls on sick family members, arranging proper marriages for relatives, ordering ancestral grave markers—filled Isami's days and were duly recorded in his family history. This was the business of maintaining the family, the steady work associated with the upkeep of property, human lives, social relationships, and reputation. Kin work competed with income-generating business for Isami's attention and frequently took up as much or more time.

The Matsuura heir obviously did not share his father's dedication to the ancestors, his commitment to the village, or his love for their rural property. Above all, Yatarō had not inherited Isami's creative energy, sense of duty, and caretaking zeal. He and his wife proved to be another great disappointment to Isami. In all of Isami's references to his children, Yatarō received only brief and usually disparaging mention, and Chiyo, his wife, even less mention.[18]

The problem was that neither Yatarō nor Chiyo was cut out for country living. Yatarō had been given the education denied to Isami, and the result was exactly what Isami's forebears had been told would happen if they educated Isami in Tokyo: he could not go home again to village Japan. Accustomed to big city life and known as a playboy since the 1930s, if not earlier, Yatarō steadily undermined his health by heavily smoking and drinking, habits Isami deplored; he himself had given up tobacco in 1916 after smoking for twenty years.

Not only was Yatarō's wife out of her element in rural Japan, but also she came from a family that had not been particularly studious. Her father, for instance, had only a primary school education. Although Toyo praised Chiyo's cooking, Chiyo did not know how to farm or to manage a large home in the countryside. Chiyo thus lacked both the skills of a country girl like her mother-in-law and the education and breeding of a Tokyo-born woman like her sisters-in-law. Moreover, in Tami's memory of her, she was slovenly and untidy, as epitomized by her kimono, which always looked loosely tied. Tami thought the marriage was a big mistake. "Yatarō should have married an *inaka* [country] person—somebody who could protect the *ie*, somebody who knew how to grow spinach."

One of Chiyo's responsibilities as wife of the first son was the care of her mother-in-law, Kō. Indeed, as we've seen, Isami sealed the marriage of his fourth son in 1938 by assuring the prospective bride that she would never have to care for him and Kō. But, as it turned out, their heir's wife spent very little time performing her filial obligations. The wives of the third and fourth sons in Ishikawa bore the brunt of nursing Kō. The female caregiver hired to care for Kō in Ishikawa was overseen by Saburō's wife, and Yūshirō, whose clinic was nearby, regularly examined his mother and gave her injections and vitamins. His wife, Masako, ended up helping, and nobody in the family then or thereafter had another kind word to say about Chiyo.

Despite family tensions, Isami stayed on in the Yamashiraishi house with Yatarō and his family instead of moving to Ishikawa to live with Kō, because Saburō's wife, though childless and unemployed, did not feel she could cook and care for both of her elderly parents-in-law. No longer comfortable in his own home in Yamashiraishi and eager to keep Kō company, Isami traveled the five miles on foot back and forth like a latter-day King Lear. Masako remembered that the climb up to the house from Ishikawa was so steep that she would be close to tears when she came with her child on her back, and somebody would be sent from the house with a bicycle to meet her. On one occasion in December 1953, after staying in Ishikawa with Kō for the month, Isami trudged up the mountain in the snow to find that Yatarō had moved into the retirement cottage, claiming he hated the main house because it was too large. Finding the cottage dirty and unkempt, Isami stayed only one night and then returned to Ishikawa.[19]

There was little Isami could do to discipline his heir at such a late age. Even the proud and strong-willed Isami could not completely disguise his sense of discouragement, if not humiliation. Isami blamed himself for his heir's failures, suggesting that perhaps he and Kō had been too easy on their firstborn child and had allowed him too much freedom. According to Isami's analysis, Yatarō "married early and afterward enjoyed a lazy life, pursuing pleasure." He thought perhaps that his heir's delicate health as a child may have also contributed to his lack of a strong will to succeed. In his early years, "he had a good head. He was kind and amiable. He was third in his class when he advanced to his senior year of middle school. However, he needed surgery on his nose and then suffered an attack of appendicitis." These ailments caused Yatarō to fall behind in his studies. Sick as a child, "he became delicate and nervous. He lost confidence . . . and by middle age, he always failed." When Yatarō died at fifty-six from cancer of the larynx, Isami, sounding more angry than grief stricken, wrote that his firstborn son, "in his later years, had even lost his will to live."[20]

Yatarō had begun drinking heavily after completing his second term as village head in 1954, the year Yamashiraishi was annexed by Asakawa. By the time doctors diagnosed his illness, it was too late to help him. Yatarō had avoided going to his brother Yūshirō's clinic. "He was a drunkard," was Masako's explanation for why her brother-in-law did not seek advice from any of the doctors in the family. The doctor he did consult when he noticed his voice was changing told him he was low in energy and advised him to take vitamins. Finally, when he was close to death, he went to the city of Kōriyama to see a doctor, who advised him to enter a hospital.

By then his wife, too, seems to have given up on him, just as the Matsuura family had given up on her. The story even the discreet Masako volunteered is that, instead of doing her accustomed wifely duty and helping to nurse her husband night and day in the hospital until the moment he died—as his sisters would eventually do for their husbands—Chiyo went to stay at their daughter's house, complaining that she could not get a good night's sleep at the hospital. Assuming Yatarō would be in the hospital for a while, she also decided to skip a day of visiting him in order to get her hair permed at the beauty parlor. Yatarō died the next day.

Isami likened his firstborn child to the dissolute heir of the seventh generation—his great-grandfather Daisuke's father-in-law. He wrote that, after Kōemon had died in the mid-nineteenth century, "others said if he had lived longer, he might have lost the entire Matsuura fortune."[21] But for Yatarō, there was no longer any fortune to lose in postwar Japan, nor was there a future for him or his descendants in Yamashiraishi. The family's land was gone, and their hereditary role as village heads was also over. Yatarō's election in 1946 and, four years later, his reelection for a second term constituted a vote not for him, whom villagers scarcely knew, but for the long legacy of Matsuura rule. His selection may have symbolized a final act of

THIRTEEN

Making History

AFTER YATARŌ'S DEATH IN 1958, his son Tomoji became Isami's fragile hope for the family's future. Twenty-seven years old when his father died, the new head of the Matsuura household, however, was poorly educated and, in his Aunti Tami's words, "without a plan." In contemporary American English parlance, he was clueless.

Tomoji was actually Yatarō's second-born son, as the *ji* in his name conveys; the first son died at the age of five. Isami had tried to supervise Tomoji's education after Yatarō moved his family from Tokyo to Yamashiraishi toward the end of the war. To nobody's surprise, the boy had turned out to be a poor student, and he left college before graduating. Tami blamed his mother's side of the family for his academic problems. "Genes are important," she said. "That house was not good at studying. His maternal grandfather didn't go beyond primary school." The fact that Tomoji's mother was a poor household manager and his father an alcoholic did not help matters either. Besides, Tomoji had no motivation to apply himself to his grandfather's goals of reinvigorating the family leadership.

Isami tried to assist Tomoji financially by asking his thirteen surviving children to renounce their legal claims, acquired under the occupation, to a share of the inheritance. They agreed, so what little was left went to Tomoji, who had to pay taxes on the family property. Isami also ordered three of the four storehouses he had built on the family grounds in 1899 torn down to avoid paying the taxes and upkeep on them.

Long before making all these efforts in Tomoji's behalf, however, Isami seems to have recognized the futility of depending on male heirs with Matsuura genes; by the late 1940s he had already pinned his real hopes for the House of Matsuura on finding a bride for Tomoji, someone who could help revive the family line. There was, of course, scarcely anything to offer prospective heirs and their spouses. Still, Isami's spirits were lifted when

Ikuchi Isoko, a country girl but a schoolteacher, agreed to marry Tomoji, an indifferent student and a college dropout. Following longstanding family custom, Isami hosted a reception to introduce the new Matsuura spouse to family and village members.[1] Six hundred guests—many of them drunk, Tomoji recalled—attended the two-day wedding party.[2]

Regardless of what Tomoji or his parents thought of the woman his grandfather had chosen for him, Isami himself was so smitten with this educated, ambitious young schoolteacher that he felt inspired, in the same month as the couple's marriage—December 1949—and in the same year as his seventieth birthday, to set down in writing his "thoughts, wishes, and experiences" in order to transmit them through Isoko to his descendants. This was, he wrote, his "desperate wish."[3]

When, less than a year after her marriage, his muse gave birth to a daughter, Ryoko, Isami was elated. He happened to be traveling near his granddaughter-in-law's home village, to which she had returned for the birth, and he immediately went to see his first great-grandchild. Afterward, he wrote out in calligraphy a sentiment that captured not only his feelings at the time but also the family ideology that had guided his entire life.

The words conveyed the Confucian ideal of three generations of family members living together in harmony, like the natural harmony of mountains and rivers. There were actually four generations of Matsuura living in the big house in Yamashiraishi in 1950—Isami; his son and daughter-in-law; his grandson Tomoji and Tomoji's bride, Isoko; and the baby—but they were not exactly all living in harmony. Still, Isami framed his calligraphy and hung it in the family's house, where it was still hanging when I last visited, in 2003.

The birth of his great-grandchild inspired Isami to begin work on the family's history. In November 1950, he opened four large chests that contained family documents dating to the Tokugawa period and began tracing the record of his ancestors, somehow trusting that, with the help of his able and educated granddaughter-in-law and her children, the Matsuura line would continue in Yamashiraishi.

Isami was acutely aware of his place in the family's long history. In his family chronicle, he referred to himself and previous family heads by their generational affiliation rather than by their names. His own name appears as "the eleventh generation Matsuura Isami," for example, and he wrote of his father that "the tenth generation . . . had forty grandchildren."[4] The family house with its framed awards and commendations and its Buddhist altar dedicated to the ancestors, the village Buddhist temple with the ancestral tablets, the cemetery with its grave markers—these physical embodiments of family and village history surrounded him as he began to write.

But if artifacts of his family's history, collected and preserved through the ages, lay all around him, why did Isami feel the need to devote the waning years of his life to setting down that history in writing? The answer lies in his pained perception that the traditions and values of the past had come to an end. Crises, bewildering change, and endings often serve as the impetus to write history as opposed to simply collecting and preserving material objects and documents. Throughout his life Isami had faithfully performed his duties as "preservationist"—tending to the upkeep of the family's house, graves, and woodlands and performing Buddhist memorial rites for his ancestors. Toward the end of his life he also became a narrator, seeking to explain the meaning that lay behind the artifacts he had inherited and preserved. No longer confident that these would be cherished after his death, he felt the need to fix his own understanding of what was disappearing before his eyes—the values of the past—and to transmit these to the generations that followed him. When memory is lost, history begins.

The family chronicle was the work of his "declining years," Isami wrote in the preface, and by the time he had finished it, his wealth was gone, his firstborn son was dead, and his village had been absorbed by Asakawa. When he began compiling his account, five years after the end of World War II, Japan was still under foreign occupation. The country's cities lay in ruin and, in the countryside, a program of land reform launched by General Douglas MacArthur, the supreme commander of the Allied powers, was about to challenge the very foundations of local rule and landholding that had long buttressed the authority of local elites such as the Matsuura family.

The prospect of witnessing the disappearance of his family's leadership role and the village that the Matsuura had helped to perpetuate haunted Isami as he probed the reasons for previous generations' survival and prosperity and for the village's "marked achievement" in a difficult terrain and through many desperate times.[5] It was his hope that, despite the decline of his family's position in Yamashiraishi and of the agricultural population in general, the agrarian values of the past would endure. Nevertheless, he recognized toward the end of his life that the long history of Yamashiraishi as a separate entity was over and so was "the long and peerless tradition of rule as one family," which Isami called unique.[6] Significantly, Isami titled his chronological account of his ancestors and his own life *Yamashiraishi mura o kataru* (Telling about Yamashiraishi Village), suggesting his tendency to conflate the history of the Matsuura family with the history of their village. In his mind, the Matsuura and the village were synonymous.

In the final pages of Isami's family-village history, he tried to explain why two and one-half centuries of vigorous Matsuura governance in rural Japan had come to an end. That tradition, for all intents and purposes, had died with Isami's departure from village office in 1946. Lack of steadfast Matsuura heirs alone was not to blame, he argued; American influence had also contributed to their demise, by introducing new political institutions and values and reforming landholding. "The Matsuura came boldly from Asakawa to lead the village, indeed to build it," he wrote, and thanks to them the village became wealthy. Now the land was "liberated." The results were lamentable: Farmers received plots too small to support themselves. Some recipients of land had never farmed before and did not know how. "We can only sympathize with their troubles."[7]

To make matters worse, Americans had promoted individualism and democracy—values inimical to both ancestor reverence and prosperity. "American-style society throws away the feudal family system," Isami wrote, whereas in his opinion it was the duty of everyone to "protect the realm of the ancestors." In place of the values of thrift, savings, hard work, and village cooperation, which had enabled the village to prosper, Isami saw postwar households run "according to individual desires." In contrast, "under the Matsuura, the whole village had become like one family."[8]

What was the meaning of the much-vaunted term *democracy* (in Japanese *demokurashi* or *minponshugi*)? Isami wondered. He expressed doubts about the new election system, which had enfranchised women, made the prefectural governorship an elected office, and otherwise broadened political participation among small farmers. He thought that Americans placed too much emphasis on rights and not enough on morality. Under the new political system, people were getting too involved in the bureaucracy; they were talking too much about the new system and not getting enough work done. Moreover, Isami worried about the future of morality in the village. "Everyone is becoming individualistic. Lacking in public virtue, they are too concerned about money and profit and pay too little attention to duty and obligation."[9]

Yamashiraishi had not only lost its cohesiveness; it had also lost its identity. Postwar administrative changes had turned the village of over thirteen hundred people into a hamlet annexed by Asakawa township. Isami described what he saw as the results: "We lost self-rule and the concept of loving our own village. . . . Yamashiraishi's traditional spirit and beautiful traditions are lost. . . . Our ancestors put a lot of effort into this village, and we must keep this spirit alive. There is no doubt that this tradition was the key in the past and will be in the future."[10]

These sentiments served as something of a farewell speech for Isami. Sounding like a general at his retirement ceremony, he appeared to be addressing the villagers rather than his family members when he wrote at the end of his slim volume, "My final request for coming generations . . . my one appeal . . . is that our villagers will protect and spread our values to Asakawa."[11]

Isami tended to attribute his family's staying power to the honesty, intelligence, and paternalism of the patriarchs who served as family and village heads. His account also pays tribute to the agrarian values of frugality, diligence, and communal cooperation practiced by the villagers. "The village was built by the energies and cooperation of the whole village as one family."[12] This explanation owes much to the Confucian notion of an intimate relationship between the benevolence and moral example of the ruler and the well-being of the ruled. If the leader behaved like a benevolent parent, then the people would thrive and harmony would prevail. The behavior of domain rulers in the Tokugawa period suggests that such teachings were not necessarily followed by the military elite, and Isami had little use for these feudal types or for the "bad *shōya*" who preceded his ancestors in Yamashiraishi.

Isami viewed his ancestors, by contrast, as having been both moral exemplars and economic leaders.

> As league headmen, my ancestors controlled a number of villages. There were difficult times. Some people left. This is natural. It isn't easy to work with so many people. . . . Our ancestors put a lot of effort into this village. They had to mediate household disputes and disputes over land. It is said that they banned gambling . . . and lectured against drunkenness, telling people that alcohol could lead to domestic problems. . . . As economic leaders, they introduced tobacco, encouraged straw crafts, and assembled village products for shipment to market. . . . The Matsuura advised and led the village. From the outside, the village may not have looked wealthy, but it was "spiritually prosperous." . . . Our beautiful traditions were key to our village.

Isami added, perhaps giving way to exaggeration, "It's hard for other villages to find girls from our village to marry because they are so desired as brides."[13]

Isami's moral framework colored his interpretation of history and guided his own life as well. In his historical treatment of his ancestors, he revealed his own preference for the hierarchical village society of the past, which, historians have argued, was a society that held the many in servitude to, and made them dependent on, the few and created great gaps in wealth and power. Isami's rendition of his wealthy and influential family's history casts the Matsuura patriarchs—with one exception, which he duly noted—as kind but firm parent figures, much like his image of himself, presiding over a village that was like one big, though unequally structured, family. His prideful and idealized interpretation obviously does not give a rounded picture of the Matsuura, whom Marxist historians would consider members of the "parasitic landlord class," but it is the only interpretation their loyal son, for all his intelligence, earnestness, and moral sensibilities, could make.

Isami never fully resigned himself to the loss of Matsuura leadership, even though the hopes he had pinned on Isoko, his grandson's college-educated wife, proved unrealistic. She was not in any position to help resurrect the family's position, as Isami thought his great-grandfather Daisuke's second wife, Moto, had done one hundred years earlier. While the daughters of Isami sided with Isoko over their own blood kin, they could not rescue her from either her husband or Chiyo, her mother-in-law.

Isoko had hoped to resume the job she had held as a schoolteacher before she married, but Chiyo made her help Tomoji's sister, whose husband, a bank employee, was frequently transferred to different branches in Fukushima. Once, while Isoko was away at her sister-in-law's house, the local school called her house to offer her a job. Chiyo took the call but did not immediately relay the message to Isoko, and by the time she returned home, the school had offered the job to someone else.[14]

Isoko put up with her mother-in-law's unkindness because Tomoji, for all his faults, was gentle. Still, the Matsuura sisters attributed her early death from cancer to her hard life and specifically to Chiyo's cruelty, which, they argued, had weakened her body. When Isoko died, one of Tomoji's aunts implied that she and her sisters would have preferred to see Tomoji dead in her place.

Tomoji never made an effort to run for mayor and thereby became the first Matsuura patriarch in thirteen generations not to serve in a leadership role. He inherited only the now-tarnished Matsuura name and the large farmhouse. As a courtesy to the Matsuura family, the man who did become mayor of Asakawa—a doctor's son—hired Tomoji as Asakawa treasurer, a position three steps down from the mayor's, even though the mayor personally disliked him and he was not qualified for the job. He was assigned mainly routine tasks in a town hall office.[15]

In his final years, Isami looked to the daughter, not to the son, of Tomoji and Isoko for the salvation of the family line. He dreamed of his great-granddaughter becoming a doctor and marrying a man who would take the Matsuura name and become its heir—an adopted son-in-law of the sort who had rescued the family line several times in the past, much like his beloved great-grandfather Daisuke. "He will find work," Isami fantasized, "and she will protect the family line."[16] Isami died before his great-granddaughter was married, but had he lived, he would have been disappointed: she married a local tatami salesman and stayed home to raise their children. Her brother took a sales job in a nearby town.

⸺

Two pieces of unfinished business remained as Isami approached his eightieth year. One was the publication of the family history, which he financed with his own money. Although he completed the first draft as early as 1951 and the final draft in 1958, after Yatarō's death, he purposely delayed the release of the book until May 12, 1961, in order to pay tribute to Kō's memory. As he duly noted at the back of the book, the publication date coincided with an important Buddhist death rite: the "day of the seventh anniversary of my wife Kō's death."[17]

Isami's clinical account of Kō's slow physical deterioration from tuberculosis in the family chronicle belied his deep affection for her and his close attention to her medical care. She was still spitting up blood and running a fever, he wrote in one entry in 1950, but after receiving a series of streptomycin injections, her appetite returned. Isami "hoped for a miracle, like the one that cured Fuki." In July 1950, he noted that Kō was feeling a little better, and the miracle he had hoped for had occurred. One day he reported that her energy had returned and she could wash her hair.

Isami hatched various schemes to entertain Kō during her long illness. To celebrate their fiftieth anniversary, in 1951, for example, the two decided to write their memoirs in poetic form. Isami asked Kō's nurse to draw a picture of a pair of masks of an old man and old woman to illustrate the memoirs. For diversion he also had Kō teach him traditional folk songs and dances, using an old record player—"the kind you wind up to play"—but he confessed that at his advanced age he had trouble remembering the words and steps. Isami also made his wife a sewing box, because, occasionally, when she felt well enough, she wanted to perform domestic chores, such as mending his underwear.

Isami demonstrated his feelings for his ailing wife with concrete deeds. He continued to visit her regularly, even if it meant walking the five miles between Yamashiraishi and Ishikawa in several feet of snow. When her brother lay dying and Kō herself was too sick to travel, he went to see the man's granddaughter, who was successfully managing a beauty salon on the outskirts of Tokyo, and then visited his brother-in-law to bring him good news about the young woman's accomplishments. He supervised the maintenance of Kō's house in Ishikawa. He had a Tokyo Buddhist temple make mortuary tablets for both his parents and hers.

Poems that Kō and Isami wrote in 1950 to congratulate a friend on the birth of his grandson capture their different ways of handling their feelings as they approached the end of their long life together. Isami, ever the optimist, wrote:

> Holding a child in one's old arms,
> one builds a harmonious family
> and devotes oneself to the country.

As if replying to Isami, Kō wrote, with melancholy,

> Whenever I hear about the birth of a baby boy
> in my sickbed,
> I feel sad because I cannot hold him.

Two years before she died, and despite severe back pain, Kō told Isami that she wanted to vote in the upcoming April 1953 election. Female suffrage was still new to Japan; having gained voting rights in Japan during the occupation, women voted for the first time in 1946. Tuberculosis had left Kō in no condition to walk, so Isami arranged to have her wheeled to the polling place on the back of a bicycle.[18]

Isami refused to give up hope that his wife would get better. In March 1955, despite her complaints of back pain, he told himself that "it was not so bad." The injections and vitamins that Yūshirō provided failed to reverse Kō's decline, and she complained of pain in her spine and hips as the tuberculosis spread. Finally, in May 1955, when the tuberculosis had spread throughout her body and she began hemorrhaging internally, he agreed to hospitalize her. He wrote, "Even Yūshirō thought there was no more we could do for her."[19]

In the hospital Kō asked for a Buddhist priest to give a formal reading of sutras in front of her parents' new mortuary tablets, but Isami understood that she wanted to hear the sutras for herself, too. He arranged for the priest's reading on May 11, and the next morning Kō died of a blood clot in her lung. At her funeral in Yamashiraishi, the priest from Chōtoku Temple broke down and wept in the middle of chanting prayers.[20]

The other piece of unfinished business that now awaited Isami's attention was the manufacture of one of his earliest inventions, the mechanical rice husker. To the end of his days, Isami traveled frequently to Tokyo, staying at one or another of his children's homes, and, with Tami's daughter in tow, made the rounds of manufacturers who might be willing to produce his invention. At long last, the countryside in the 1960s was mechanizing rice production, but Isami was told that his husker was already out of date. It was at a Tokyo factory in 1962 that he suffered a stroke and collapsed. After a week in the hospital without regaining consciousness, he died. He was eighty-three years old.

Isami's body was returned to Yamashiraishi and buried without cremation alongside Kō in the family section of the village cemetery. The village priest, whose training Isami had assisted, wept at the funeral as though he had lost his own parent. He also chose the posthumous Buddhist name for Isami, whose Chinese characters pay tribute to him: "The great Isami, who ruled by following a straight and narrow path and working hard."[21]

The eleventh Matsuura village head left behind thirteen well-educated adult children, almost two dozen grandchildren, several great-grandchildren, a newly published family history, and a large country home. But despite his best efforts, Isami had been forced to oversee the end of the long tradition of hereditary Matsuura leadership in rural Fukushima prefecture and to witness the decline of the Matsuura family's landholdings, lineage, leadership, and reputation after nearly three centuries of supremacy.

The very forces of modernity that Isami revered—education, technology, industry, middle-class urban living—had undermined the agrarian basis of the family's continuity. Landed families with long lineages had grown obsolete, replaced by the more typical small, city-dwelling families whose members commuted on trains and worked in office buildings. Ironically, Isami himself had subscribed to the century-long program designed to make Japan a modern, strong nation with a large urban population focused more on the future than on the past. American occupation reforms had merely provided the final push.

—

In the 1990s, some thirty years after Isami's death, local leaders in the Asakawa area tried to save the material heart of the family—the hundred-year-old house he had built. The mayor approached the current househead, Isami's grandson Tomoji, with the idea of renovating the historic farmhouse and turning it into a tourist attraction or a summer resort for children or the elderly—revenue-enhancing activities that would contribute to the region's economy while also paying for the house's upkeep. Isami would have been pleased. Near the end of his family–village chronicle, he expressed a deep regret: "Because of the new [political system], there is no way to use this huge house, but there should be. This is a historical tragedy."[22]

The taciturn Tomoji, in his sixties and living like a recluse with his senile mother, Chiyo, refused to cooperate with the mayor. His behavior, as described by others, resembled not so much the village leader as the village idiot. His aunts bemoaned Tomoji's failure to order a proper gravestone for his deceased first wife, Isoko, and he had neglected to thin the cedar trees that Isami had replanted after the war. Without sunlight, Mina explained, the grove succumbed to worm infestation, and all the trees had to be cut down.

Worst of all from the perspective of his Tokyo aunts, the last Matsuura heir refused to have any contact with family members after they had criticized him for casting out his second wife. He had been married to her for almost a decade when she was diagnosed with a medical problem. He literally kicked her out, locking the main house and posting a sign saying "Do Not Enter." The wife moved into the retirement cottage for a time but then moved elsewhere and took him to family court for alimony.

During the divorce proceedings, several of his aunts arrived to urge him to reconsider. Calling their behavior "unforgivable," he sent each of them a formal letter ordering them not to enter the family house or to telephone him. Once, when his aunts arrived on their annual visit to the family grave sites, he refused them access to the house, even after Masako, his uncle Yūshirō's widow, who lived close by, murmured, "Father [i.e., her deceased father-in-law, Isami] would be happy if his daughters could enter the house." This was her polite way of saying "Isami must be turning over in his grave." Despite Tomoji's refusal, he was no match for the combined will of the Matsuura sisters that day. His aunts, unlike Tomoji, were well educated and raised under two strong and conscientious family heads—their grandfather Yūya and their father Isami. Imbued with a sense of obligation to family ties and to the Matsuura legacy, they would not take no for an answer. Claiming they had to use the toilet, the women, in their seventies and eighties, barged in for a brief inspection.[23]

Regardless of their strength and conscientiousness, Tomoji's aunts could only stand by helplessly while he divorced his second wife, neglected the family property, and ignored the mayor's entreaties. At their father's postwar request years ago, they had waived their newly acquired legal rights to the property. "Even the Buddhist priest," Tami reported, "has given up on him." Two former family servants, who had met and married in the big farmhouse and continued to live in a small house nearby, could only shake their heads sadly when discussing the distressing decline and virtual disappearance of the family. All the hard work that Tomoji's grandfather and his long line of ancestors did in the service of family and village continuity was now undone.

In the years after Isami's death, the model *shōya* house that he built in 1899 became, in his youngest daughter's words, a ghost house, nearly empty of furnishings and devoid of the many household members who had filled it with life. But it still contained the framed letters of commendation from past government officials, which hung next to photographs of family heads on the walls of the large living room, screens decorated with Isami's calligraphy, and an antique wall clock purchased from the United States in the late nineteenth century. The house also contained dusty photograph albums and the more than five hundred handwritten documents handed down from the earliest Matsuura househeads that Isami had used to write his family-village chronicle.

In the early 1990s, Asakawa local historian Kawaoto Shōhei persuaded Tomoji to lend him the family documents for one year for the town's research project on Asakawa history. The Matsuura materials are more numerous than any others in the area, especially for the Tokugawa period. Kawaoto pored over the old handwritten items, using a dictionary to look up unfamiliar Tokugawa-era words; it took him a whole day to read three pages. Eventually he chose representative documents which he translated laboriously into modern Japanese. These include samples of official communications between Matsuura village heads and domainal military officials, which are scattered throughout several published volumes. In one volume, two pages apiece were devoted to biographies of Yūya and Isami, with accompanying photographs.

Several years later, at the turn of the twenty-first century, Fukushima helped mark the centennial anniversary of the house Isami built by designating it a prefectural cultural treasure. Although it was the oldest standing residence in the village, it was no longer the tallest; newcomers to the village had built bigger, more modern ones. Tomoji still lived in the old house, all alone except for his dog, but a little less reclusive. As the head of one of the two senior citizen clubs in the village, he permitted meetings to be held in the house, and a reconciliation of sorts had occurred with his aunts, two of whom accompanied me on my visit in 2003. There was some talk of his fifty-year-old son, who worked in a department store, returning at an unspecified time to live there, but even at that late date the topic was too delicate to broach.

In the eight years since I had last seen it, the retirement cottage had been stuffed with piles of cartons and a varied assortment of curious objects—a guitar case, a box of dolls, a white upholstered club chair, tables turned onto their sides—whose purpose and ownership remained a mystery, because his aunts did not feel comfortable asking. Tami viewed the scene with dismay. The condition of the guesthouse, she confided, was embarrassing.

At the village cemetery, we lit incense sticks and placed several on each of the ancestral stone monuments, which dated back to the eighth generation's Daisuke. We also noticed that another, unrelated family named Matsuura had erected an imposing stone marker with their name engraved in large characters, and it was placed close to the graves of Isami's ancestors and descendants, as if to crowd their markers out. The Matsuura lineage founded by Yajibei in Yamashiraishi in 1689 was nearly extinct. Researched and memorialized, it had become history.

PART FOUR

Love and Other Forms of Compensation

FOURTEEN

Absent Husband

KŌJIRŌ PEERED OUT THE WINDOW as his plane sped through the evening sky on its final approach to Tokyo's Haneda Airport. The bright lights of the capital city below enthralled him. Coming from Indonesia, where "the light from electric bulbs was so dim, it was hard to read the newspaper at night," he had the feeling that he "was returning to modern civilization from primitive times." It was 1960, and he was entering his native country for the first time in eighteen years. The customs inspector looked at him suspiciously after glancing at his passport; no entries had been stamped since the day he left Japan in 1942, wearing the uniform of the Japanese Imperial Army.[1]

If Kōjirō was a foreigner to his countrymen, he was no more familiar to the members of his household, who gathered dutifully at the airport to greet him. Lined up alongside representatives from his company who had also come to meet his plane were his daughter, his two sons, and his wife, Tazuko. The older son had been seven when Kōjirō last saw him; he was now, his father observed, a "*sararī man* [a white-collar worker] dressed in a business suit." The younger son, four when his father left, was a university student. Although Kōjirō saw signs of aging in Tazuko's face, he thought he perceived in her eyes the "strength of the wick that had continued to wait earnestly during the eighteen years of [his] absence." Standing in guilty silence as his four family members bowed to him, Kōjirō reflected, "Those who had suffered more than anyone from my selfish behavior were my wife and children."[2]

What brought Kōjirō home, after almost two decades in Indonesia, was the deterioration of his health. Preoccupied with lucrative but strenuous business negotiations, Kōjirō fell seriously ill with an ailment at first diagnosed as an intestinal problem. His discomfort was severe enough to lead the family to send his twenty-two-year-old daughter to Indonesia in 1958 to cook Japanese food for him. Two years later doctors diagnosed a mild case of tuberculosis and advised him to return to Japan to convalesce.[3] As soon as he regained his health, however, he resumed his peripatetic lifestyle as a Toyota sales representative, which required him to make three trips each year to Indonesia. His was a phantom marriage.

In the late 1940s, Kōjirō had agreed to serve as an interpreter for the defense team of General Imamura Hitoshi in the war crimes trials staged in what was then the Netherlands East Indies. The Dutch trials constituted one of approximately fifty military tribunals in various Asian locales, including Tokyo, between 1945 and 1951.[4] Only 55 of the 1,038 Japanese tried for war crimes in the Indies were acquitted.[5] General Imamura was one of them.

Imamura owed his acquittal, in part, to what Kōjirō told the Dutch judge about him. The judge, himself a lieutenant-colonel, had misgivings about leveling blanket accusations against the Japanese military high command, and he approached Kōjirō for his frank assessment of Imamura. Kōjirō described how the general's comparatively benevolent treatment of Dutch prisoners during the Japanese occupation had been criticized by his own subordinates and had angered General Tojo.[6] "He saved Imamura's life," his oldest sister, Mina, declared of her brother.

At the end of the trials, Kōjirō thanked the judge for conducting a fair hearing. The judge was sufficiently impressed with Kōjirō to write to him in 1952 after returning to Holland and finding himself criticized by the Dutch military over his conduct of the trials.[7]

Though Kōjirō knew and admired General Imamura, his reasons for joining in the general's defense had less to do with sympathy for him than with avoiding repatriation. To the great disappointment of his family, Kōjirō refused to return home after the trials. Sympathetic with the Indonesian nationalist movement, he saw a future for himself as a broker in the emerging Indonesian nation's economic development. When elements of the seventy-thousand-man Japanese army in Java discussed crossing over to the Dutch side and cooperating with them in putting down the Indonesian independence movement in exchange for guarantees of the army's safe passage home, Kōjirō was among those who argued against the idea.[8]

Kōjirō's extraordinary ability to cultivate good relationships with people of many nationalities, including citizens of countries that had been at war with one another and with Japan, was one of his greatest assets in promoting his own fortunes in Indonesia. Aided by his foreign-language skills, his experience living in the East Indies and Australia in the 1930s, his business background, his excellent education, and his diverse contacts, he had good reason to believe he would succeed, even as a Japanese and even in uncertain times.

It was true that, before their repatriation, defeated Japanese troops had faced hostile treatment from both the Dutch colonial rulers, whom the Japanese had imprisoned during the war, and the native population of Indonesians, who wanted all foreigners out of the country. During 1945 and 1946, Indonesians attacked Japanese soldiers in their prison cells, and the Dutch put Japanese troops to work as coolies repairing the Batavia airport and hauling Christmas mail from airplanes.[9] Kōjirō was protected, however, by his many contacts.

On numerous occasions in the wartime and postwar period, Isami's second son had demonstrated his mediating skills by brilliantly negotiating the separate interests of Japanese, Dutch, and Indonesian nationals, managing to retain influential friends in all three camps. Despite the harshness of Japan's occupation of Asian countries during the war and the chaotic political scene in the East Indies after the war, Kōjirō had succeeded in preserving ties with friends from many parts of the world and from the entire political spectrum of the country soon to achieve its independence from the Netherlands. Valuable connections to the Indonesian Chinese population, including the merchant whose property he had rescued from confiscation by the Japanese army during the war, added to Kōjirō's ability to operate safely in Indonesia. The Indonesian Chinese merchant became a high official in the Jakarta police force and vouched for Kōjirō's character, giving him freedom of movement that other Japanese were denied.[10]

Beginning in the interwar years Kōjirō had recognized Indonesia's potential to develop as an independent nation. His own island country, guided by visionary political leaders and pioneering entrepreneurs, had undergone a dramatic metamorphosis in the face of Western imperialism in the late nineteenth century. Kōjirō anticipated a similar development in Indonesia, but one that would not imitate Japan's own reckless imperialism in Asia. Peaceful foreign trade was the course he recommended. Kōjirō hoped to use his business experience and contacts to help promote that trade. He believed he had more of a business future in the nascent nation of Indonesia than in his own defeated country. "If Indonesia becomes independent," he thought, "there is a lot I can do for them."[11]

With good reason, then, Kōjirō wrote idealistically about serving as a "bridge" between Japan and the other countries of Asia. He was intellectually and temperamentally suited to the task. But his ambitious goals required turning his back on his family.

Eagerness to forge a new and more idealistic life for himself in a foreign land came at the expense of Kōjirō's sense of familial obligation. His internationalist spirit and business energies won out over his duties as son, husband, and father, and no amount of pressure from Isami could bring him home. "Of course, I did not forget my Japanese family," he wrote in his memoirs. "But . . . although my natal home was rural, they were fairly wealthy and so I did not worry too much."[12] The family—his wife and children as well as his parents—worried about him, however, and missed him grievously.

Kōjirō's achievements as a young man had always delighted his father. "One of my few joys," Isami had written of his second son in the early 1920s, "was Kōjirō's success in school." Isami had saved Kōjirō's school trophies and faithfully recorded the boy's every milestone: his admission into Tokyo's First Higher School, his entrance into Tokyo Imperial University, his job with Mitsubishi, and even the bonus he received in 1932 that he used to take Grandmother Miyo on a trip to several hot springs for "a very happy time."[13]

Kōjirō was the model son and grandson who had gone to the right schools, secured employment with the right company, and married the right woman— a graduate of a Tokyo women's college. But now Isami found that he had no leverage over his independent-minded pride and joy. When Kōjirō wrote to his wife in December 1949, without making his intentions clear but telling her to move with their children from his parents' home to Tokyo and arranging to send money to her there, Isami wrote back, virtually ordering him to return home immediately. Kōjirō tersely replied that he would return the following spring. He never showed up. Although Kōjirō's wife received financial support, neither she nor his parents had much direct contact with him. At one point Isami heard indirectly that, for reasons unknown to them, Kōjirō had asked a friend in Japan to send him three copies of the family's household registry. On another occasion they heard that he was planning to return soon, but the rumor proved false.[14]

Around 1950, Kōjirō tried to divorce his wife and bring his Dutch-Indonesian woman companion back to Japan with him, because after Indonesia's declaration of independence from the Dutch she was forced to leave the country. Kōjirō's marital situation became an ongoing topic of conversation and, at times, a heated debate among family members. Counting on Kōjirō to help with the family's finances at least until his thirteen other children were independent, Isami was inclined to let Kōjirō have his way and divorce Tazuko, if that was what it would take to bring him home. According to Isami's oldest daughter, Mina, Isami was reluctant to incur his second son's wrath at this critical time in the family's fortunes.

Most of the other family members also sided with Kōjirō. Although they had lived with his wife in their natal village during and after the war, the family's sympathy for Kōjirō's needs and interests outweighed issues of marital fidelity. At least one of his sisters was glad that he had found somebody to "comfort him" during his many years away from home. Kōjirō's companion, according to one family member's account, was a secretary in his company. "She was probably more his level, smart and capable," whereas Tazuko was "slow at everything she did." A friend of one of Kōjirō's brothers-in-law happened to meet Kōjirō's companion and described her as a "wonderful woman."[15]

For the most part, the Matsuura family approved of the Eurasian woman who had made Kōjirō's life easier, and they were grateful to Kōjirō for sending funds to family members. Thanks to him, his wife and children were well off on a material level, and that was the level that counted the most. Fuki thought Kōjirō's wife should have been more understanding. "They could have worked something out. He could have gone back and forth—his work required it—and kept the mistress." Mina's husband suggested offering Tazuko a financial arrangement equivalent to alimony and child support.

Mina herself objected to the divorce. She spoke her mind clearly and, in so doing, angered Isami, an experience so painful that she still remembered it in her ninetieth year. She told her father that Kōjirō and his wife should resolve their difficulties on their own. "After all, Tazuko [a graduate of Mina's alma mater] had faithfully waited for Kōjirō. She had lived with the family during the war and helped grow vegetables, even though she was not a farm girl. The villagers all liked her; some were amazed to see her working in the fields."[16]

Tazuko steadfastly refused to acquiesce in her husband's wishes, and she stood up to her father-in-law when he asked her to agree to a divorce. During her many years of separation from her husband, she had been befriended by a foreign Catholic priest who had converted her to Catholicism, and she appeared to have become a fervent believer in the religion, which prohibits divorce—though one of her sisters-in-law cynically suggested her Catholic religiosity was a ruse to prevent Kōjirō from divorcing her.

The family heard infrequently from Kōjirō after 1950. His wife and children moved to Tokyo, but Kōjirō stayed in Indonesia. Desperate for news about his second son, Isami once dragged third son Saburō along with him to the Imperial Hotel in Tokyo in 1952 to question members of a group of

Indonesians who were seeking wartime reparations from Japan. They found a Japanese-speaking Indonesian who told them how to contact Kōjirō's secretary, who was in Japan at the time. The woman said Kōjirō had been sick for a month with food poisoning that he contracted from fried crabs and had stayed at her house while recovering. She assured Isami that his second son was "highly placed" in Indonesia, talked frequently about his children, and kept a picture of his daughter on his desk.[17] Although she thought he might return to Japan in the following year, this did not happen.

At first, Kōjirō's entrepreneurial efforts were successful, and he had faithfully sent funds home to help the family through the occupation years. In addition to supporting his wife and children, his salary helped pay for the tiling of the roof of the Yamashiraishi house, the opening of Yūshirō's clinic, Saburō's political campaign, and the refurbishing of the village temple, whose elaborate gold-threaded brocade drapings over two interior pillars were a gift from him.

The money came from the Indonesian Chinese trading company that Kōjirō helped establish in 1949. His partner was the brother of the Indonesian ambassador to West Germany, and one major investor was an Indonesian Chinese merchant-friend of Kōjirō's. Most of their business came from the Mitsubishi trading company, through Kōjirō's prewar contacts. With Kōjirō serving as general manager, "M company," as he referred to it in his memoirs, initially prospered.

Before long, however, Kōjirō discovered that his Indonesian business partner had betrayed him by skimming money from the company's bank account to purchase houses and cars for his own use. Without that money, he could not pay Mitsubishi for the purchases M company had made. Kōjirō resigned from the company. Even though Mitsubishi affiliates were willing to employ him in Japan, he now felt too ashamed to "show his face" before his associates and decided not to return to Japan. "This was the most humiliating time in my life."[18]

Kōjirō's business and personal fortunes waxed and waned over the next decade. He no longer trusted Indonesians as business partners; they were, he concluded, "fundamentally different from Japanese." Yet, he could not open his own business. Not only did he lack capital, but also new laws designed to protect native economic development prevented foreigners from getting import licenses or from owning their own firms. Still, Kōjirō held on to his dream of promoting Indonesian economic development, even while declining job offers from his "many rich Arabic and Chinese merchant friends."[19]

For several years Kōjirō rented a small, simply furnished room from an Indonesian family and survived on loans from friends, among them a Dutch Indonesian farmer. Finally, in 1954, the Indonesian government sought his help in purchasing fishing nets from Japan. He arranged a sale through Nishin Trade Company, an affiliate of Toyota. Soon he was serving as a middleman for the sale of a wide range of Japanese products in Indonesia, from parachutes to textile machines to equipment that manufactured matches. The company offered to support his wife and children in Tokyo and also gave him a monthly salary of four hundred dollars and a sales bonus.[20]

In 1957 Kōjirō began working as a sales representative for Toyota trucks and cars in Indonesia. He accepted the job reluctantly; he needed to earn a living, but the job forced him to abandon his dream of helping to develop Indonesian businesses. At the time, the Indonesian market for foreign cars seemed unpromising; foreigners still could not acquire import licenses, and an Indonesian "knock down" policy required foreign cars to be assembled in that country.[21] Nevertheless, Japan was about to become a major car seller to the world, and Kōjirō would be part of his country's economic success.

Through good luck and valuable contacts, in 1957 Kōjirō succeeded in selling the first Japanese car in Indonesia—a Toyota Land Cruiser. After Indonesia and Japan reached a settlement over wartime reparations in 1958 and Toyota gained authorization to sell to government agencies, Kōjirō's sales commissions grew. Using his well-placed Indonesian connections, Kōjirō persuaded the national police to purchase several thousand trucks, whose presence on the streets of Jakarta helped to advertise Toyota's name.[22]

By helping to promote the overseas sales of Japanese automobiles, Kōjirō contributed to the economic strategy that produced Japan's dramatic recovery from defeat. Of course, he had hoped to promote Indonesia's foreign trade, not Japan's. In the late 1950s he did manage to link up with an Indonesian company that owned a license for importing foreign cars and was selling a poorly made Czechoslovakian model. Kōjirō signed a contract with the company for importing Toyotas, marking the first authorized opening for Japanese car sales to the Indonesian general public.[23]

After returning to Japan in 1960 to regain his health, Kōjirō stayed on in Tokyo, living with his wife when he was not in Indonesia on business trips. His wife was so angry, however, that she scarcely spoke to him. Feeling unwelcome in their home, he often went to a local coffee shop to read the daily newspaper. Mina, his oldest sister, quoted the Bible to his wife about the virtue of forgiveness, but to no avail. Tazuko became angry with Mina, too, for borrowing money from Kōjirō. The two sisters-in-law ended up estranged.[24] Kōjirō's work, however, continued to flourish.

In 1961, Kōjirō managed to meet Indonesian president Achmed Sukarno. His introduction to the flamboyant leader of the nationalist movement occurred through one of his many Japanese acquaintances, who had himself assisted in Indonesia's liberation from the Dutch. Learning that Kōjirō had played a role in General Imamura's war crimes acquittal, President Sukarno confessed that, if Imamura had been convicted, he would have personally tried to rescue him, because in 1942, after the Dutch colonial administration surrendered to the Japanese army, Imamura had ordered the release of Sukarno from a Dutch prison.[25]

With Sukarno's support, Kōjirō obtained more sales contracts in Indonesia. In the next few years, after Kōjirō succeeded in obtaining reluctant Japanese approval of the Indonesian president's request for a delay in making payments, he sold Sukarno a thousand vehicles for the military regiment that supplied him with his bodyguards. Prospering along with Japan in the 1960s, Kōjirō regained his health. In pictures taken during the war crimes trial period he had been a thin, youthful-looking, unsmiling man who pulled his belt tight around his waist as if to hold up loose-fitting pants; in 1963, he appeared robust and prosperous in his dark two-piece business suits when he posed for photographs with Sukarno. Well into his fifties, he still had a full head of black hair, and his round face, beaming and confident, bore little resemblance to his younger self.

Kōjirō sold several thousand more cars and trucks to various branches of the government before the 1965 coup d'état, which overthrew Sukarno, interrupted Japanese car sales in the country.[26] After a military regime under General T. N. J. Suharto was installed, Toyota resumed sales, but Kōjirō grew increasingly disenchanted with the Indonesian economy and his role as facilitator of Japanese business profits rather than as promoter of native Indonesian capitalism. Although he helped a Toyota vice president set up a business partnership in Indonesia to allow car manufacturing in that country, Kōjirō was frustrated by the Indonesian Ministry of Industry's conditions, which required the inclusion of an overseas Chinese partner as well, so he resigned from Toyota in 1970.[27]

Shortly before his retirement, Kōjirō seems to have effected a form of reconciliation with his wife. Returning together to Indonesia on a sentimental journey in 1968, the couple drove by the three houses they had lived in during their stay there thirty years earlier and even visited the Catholic hospital where their children had been born.[28] In 1975, Kōjirō fulfilled his promise to take Tazuko—still a devout Catholic—to Italy, where they toured famous church sites. At one small church dedicated to St. Francis of Assisi, he himself converted to Catholicism. "I prayed for the cleansing of sin from my heart," he wrote, "and I vowed to devote the remainder of my life to meaningful things."[29]

Toward the end of his life, Kōjirō's mental health deteriorated. After his retirement, there was no longer a place for him either in Indonesia or in Japan. Suffering from depression and possibly even experiencing a nervous breakdown, as several other male relatives had before him, Kōjirō began taking a variety of drugs, which he obtained from doctors at several different clinics. In the preface to his memoirs, published in 1977, shortly before his death, he wrote regretfully of the pain he had caused family members.

Although Kōjirō had been an absent father and husband, he had provided very well for his family's material needs. In the early 1960s, his daughter socialized with the children of ambassadors on skiing vacations in the Japanese Alps while waiting for a suitable marriage proposal. Her nails were polished, and her clothes reflected the latest in Western fashion, but she lacked the ambition and, judging from my brief time with her, the friendliness of her aunts and cousins. She also lacked their sense of responsibility. Kōjirō's daughter eventually married a physician, but the couple proved incompatible. They arranged to live on separate floors of the same house until they finally separated altogether, with the husband agreeing to take custody of one of their two daughters, even though he was diagnosed with cancer and the daughter was mildly retarded. Two generations of the family had experienced the most tenuous of marriage ties, and the tensions spilled over into the third generation—Kōjirō's grandchildren.

A successful marriage was arranged for Isami's retarded granddaughter, but her sister fared less well. An intelligent and sensitive young woman, she was distressed by her parents' strained relations and the tensions she had witnessed over the years between her grandparents. Shortly after being admitted to college, she fell into a depression. One night she had a long talk with her father, who thought he had comforted her. He was mistaken. After leaving the house, she committed suicide by jumping in front of one of Japan's new, ultramodern, high-speed Bullet Express trains.[30]

Kōjirō's was hardly the only troubled family in the postwar years. The strain of wartime and the immediate postwar years, which involved frequent health problems, relocations, and separations, undoubtedly explains some of the difficulties the adult children of Isami and Kō experienced. Husbands and wives who had married as strangers had been torn apart and then thrown back together in unfamiliar, trying circumstances, and nobody had either the time or the inclination to grapple with the psychological effects of the nation's long war, defeat, occupation, and reconstruction on individual lives, marital relationships, and fathers' contacts with their children. Economic survival was uppermost in everybody's minds. While Kōjirō's long absence represented an extreme case, absent husbands and fathers and strained marital relations were not unusual among the twelfth and thirteenth generations of Matsuura. Isami's children struggled with marriages vastly different from his own.

FIFTEEN

Couples and Uncouplings

IN OCTOBER 1950, after nursing her mother-in-law through the terminal stage of cancer, Toyo collapsed. Isami dispatched Tami to Hiroshima to assess the situation. Tami suspected that the source of Toyo's distress was a combination of exhaustion and malnutrition, but she also suggested that Toyo's husband may have contributed to her poor health. Masafumi had been drinking heavily and behaving irrationally. "He complained that the house was dirty," Tami said, "and he set fire to the drapes with his cigarette lighter." Tami vaguely remembered dousing the fire with water.

The family arranged for Tami to bring Toyo and her young daughter, Yōko, to the sanatorium in Kanagawa, outside Tokyo, where Fuki's physician-husband worked. He delivered a disturbing diagnosis: Toyo, like her mother and two sisters, had contracted tuberculosis, though she had a curable case and responded well to medical treatment. While Toyo recuperated, Yōko attended a nearby school, and Masafumi stayed on in Hiroshima with an older woman who had been hired as housekeeper. Toyo's marriage seemed destined for dissolution.

Discharged from the sanatorium after eight months, Toyo took Yōko with her to the clean country air of Ishikawa and placed herself in the care of her brother Yūshirō, who was already treating their mother. She then moved to her sister Fumi's house in Tokyo. In his wife's absence, Masafumi had calmed down and become more gentle, according to Tami, who had returned to Hiroshima to check up on him. But for the next three years Toyo and her husband lived apart.

The marriage of Toyo and Masafumi remained stormy until the end. When Masafumi was transferred to Brazil in 1955, Toyo only reluctantly agreed to accompany him. Facing a long journey to an unknown country with a husband she could not trust, Toyo drew closer to Christianity, which she had first encountered at Freedom School. In that religion she sought a way to ease her anguish and to protect herself and her teenage daughter from misfortune. Shortly before returning to Japan from Rio de Janeiro four years later, she was baptized.[1]

During their stay in Brazil there were so many fights between Toyo and Masafumi that Yōko once advised her mother to get a divorce. For Yōko's sake, however, Toyo was determined to preserve the marriage. The reasons underlying the enduring conflict between Toyo and her husband—two well-educated, well-liked, responsible, and hardworking people—are not hard to fathom. One of the publicly acknowledged problems was Masafumi's heavy drinking, which contributed to the tension between them, despite his being an excellent provider.

Yōko did not remember her father ever hitting her mother, but she did recall that when he got angry he would sweep all the dishes off the table with his hands. Once, when she and Toyo were in the bath in Brazil, he came home drunk; furious because Toyo did not greet him at the foyer, he walked up to the bathroom with his shoes on—a profoundly disturbing act in a household where everyone followed the Japanese custom of removing shoes immediately upon entering the house.

When he was drunk Masafumi would also deprecate Toyo in front of their daughter, saying Toyo was "the worst wife in the world." Once, however, when young Yōko repeated his invective, saying, "Mother is inferior," he immediately corrected her, saying, "Your mother is *saikō*, the tops." Whenever Masafumi behaved badly at night, he apologized to Toyo the next morning. He also tried to make up for his behavior by buying her rings and taking her out dancing when they lived in Brazil.

Yōko had idolized her father as a rich, handsome, cosmopolitan, and successful man, as someone with "good taste." He was kind to her, but she never forgot that he had a violent temper when drunk. When she was young, she thought she was the cause of the fights. "I thought perhaps they wanted a boy. Fortunately, I didn't know I was adopted. Otherwise, I would have thought that was the problem."

Yōko also had vivid memories of her parents' good times together, when they seemingly achieved the ideal of the modern couple. She recalled trailing behind them as they walked down the streets of Rio de Janeiro holding hands. One day, two or three years after the atom bombing, her parents had pushed aside the furniture in their house in Hiroshima, turned on the record player, and danced together, while Yōko danced around them. A romantic man, Masafumi believed in companionate marriage, or, as his daughter put it, "he thought a wife should be somebody with whom a husband could go to the movies" and not simply a housekeeper. At the time of Yōko's own marriage, her father advised her to be more than a housewife; she should be a companion to her husband and keep herself attractive. On one of her birthdays, he and Toyo urged her to go out with her husband while they took care of her children. "We went dancing," Yōko recalled. "I enjoyed it, but I don't think my husband did. He would have preferred to watch a baseball game."

In her own middle age, Yōko speculated that her energetic mother with her Freedom School training in self-reliance and competence may have been too strong for her father. He once complained that Toyo, unlike her docile sister Fuki, was not a good listener; she did not wait to hear all he had to say before she interjected, often finishing his sentences for him. She moved fast and spoke fast. Masafumi was drawn to attractive, well-groomed women who appeared young-looking, helpless, and dependent—qualities that made him feel more manly. Much as he admired Toyo, he "liked to make pets of people," Yōko said. "He liked to protect people."

After the family returned to Japan, Masafumi resumed his job with Mitsubishi in Hiroshima while Toyo lived with Yōko in Tokyo. When I lived in their house in 1963, we saw very little of Masafumi. In those years he was completely occupied with Mitsubishi business. The first time he returned home after I had entered the household, he introduced himself as "Mitsubishi's Ishikawa." His was the dream job his father-in-law, Isami, thought he would have liked his own sons to have, but, in truth, Masafumi's work responsibilities were so demanding that he had no home life and little to do with Yōko's upbringing—a situation that Isami would have found peculiar, to say the least.

Like so many other salaried men in postwar Japan, Masafumi put in long hours at the office. He was part of the generation of postwar men driven to put Japan back on its feet and to recoup the career gains he had made before the war. Whenever Masafumi returned to Tokyo from his office in Hiroshima, he invariably arrived home late, after working at the Tokyo main office all day, and, like a deep-sea diver coming up for air, he needed to decompress. Toyo waited on him like a servant. She helped him off with his clothes and fed him in stages, starting with little dishes of delicacies, accompanied by alcoholic beverages, and ending with rice and soup. In Hiroshima he lived in a large, Japanese-style house owned by Mitsubishi and staffed with a housekeeper and a driver who catered to his every need.

Although Masafumi was an experienced manager of the machinery branch of his company's import-export business, he seemed helpless everywhere else. He could not even find the car's cigarette lighter by himself; his chauffeur helped him. Solicitous about my health (if I sneezed, he asked if I was getting a cold and told Toyo to get me a sweater), he was careless about his own physical well-being, and he smoked and drank frenetically. Toyo was on edge as long as he was around; she once told me, "When my husband is not home, I feel relaxed." Fortunately for the couple, Masafumi's work enabled them to live apart, a situation that, ironically, helped save their marriage.[2]

Toyo's youngest sister, Tami, another competent, self-reliant, well-educated Matsuura woman, also had a troubled marriage. In fact, her marriage fell apart almost immediately. Because her husband was still in medical school when she married him, he could not support her and their daughter, Masako. Isami and Kō tried to help their youngest daughter by sending food. But it soon became evident, at least to Tami, that her marriage would not work. For one thing, "he had little to say," she explained. More disconcerting, "he put up a good front, but he did not have the means to earn a living." Tami soon concluded that her husband was more interested in dabbling in archaeology and ancient history than in completing his medical education and supporting his family. She sent their daughter to live with Toyo's family in Hiroshima and worked as a Pilot pen sales representative in the Kyoto branch of the Daimaru department store, a job she managed to secure through an employment agency even though she was older than most of the female employees. Fortunately, she held a degree from a premier Tokyo women's college.

"He had a way of denying reality," is the way Tami explained her husband's failings. Very much the realist, Tami decided before long to leave for good. Without saying good-bye, she took a night train out of her husband's life. Isami, who was also a realist, sent his son-in-law a registered letter telling him he could not see his wife or child until he became a doctor.

The youngest daughter of the family saw her husband one more time in Kyoto in 1951 before deciding to divorce him and live on her own. Although she informed Kō, perhaps to ease her ailing mother's mind, that her husband had only one more year to complete his medical education, in truth her marriage was over. Not all her relatives were sympathetic. "My oldest sister, Mina, was mad at me for a long time," Tami said, "because she had arranged the marriage."

Relocating to Tokyo, Tami moved into her sister Yasu's household after securing a sales job in the main branch of the same department store that had employed her in Kyoto. Yasu helped care for Tami's daughter, who was enrolled in a local primary school. Tami's husband came looking for her in the following year but was told by a family member to return only when he had finished his medical degree. He eventually did become a doctor, and he married an anesthesiologist, but he never saw his daughter again, and she had no wish to see him.[3]

Tami remained single for six years after her separation and eventual divorce. She continued to support herself until one of her brothers-in-law introduced her to a divorced medical doctor, Nakamura Shiro, whom she married in 1956, when she was thirty-two.

Fifteen years older than Tami, Dr. Nakamura was a busy ear specialist on the faculty of Keiō University Medical School. Preoccupied with his professional responsibilities and uninterested in raising a family, he nonetheless agreed to adopt Tami's daughter, Masako. A grateful and relieved Tami willingly took over the management of his household, aided by a seventeen-year-old village girl sent from Yamashiraishi.

Tami's second husband had been among the earliest group of doctors to study in the United States after World War II. His first wife had been unwilling to join him during the three years he spent studying medicine in Iowa and did not even answer his letters. When he returned home, he discovered that she had been living with another man. After he divorced her, she remarried, but her second husband died of a stroke and then she died of breast cancer at about fifty, childless and alone—it was her punishment, Tami seemed to think, for the way she had treated her first husband.

Tami swiftly established herself as an efficient, devoted, and trustworthy wife, thereby earning the gratitude and appreciation of not only her husband and his colleagues and students but also of his relatives, with whom she remained on close terms even after his death. They all knew that Dr. Nakamura had been badly hurt by his first wife and had grown distrustful of people, but after he married her, Tami said, "he brightened up, and everyone noticed the change."

In contrast to her predecessor, Tami viewed her marriage as a job—one with considerable fringe benefits—and she took pride in the way she performed it. Like most Japanese men of that era, her husband was incapable of cooking or shopping for himself. After his divorce, his niece and her husband had moved in with him, but of course, in Tami's mind, "it wasn't the same as having a wife." A niece, for example, would never notice that he did not drink enough liquids; the doctor was too absorbed in his medical research to pay attention to his own bodily needs, and so Tami always brought tea to his study.

Tami was a model wife in other ways as well. She packed her husband's bags. She prepared his evening bath and handed him a glass of beer at night when he came home. She cooked succulent dinners for visiting colleagues and students and handled all household matters, freeing her husband of all of life's practical concerns so that he could concentrate on his work. A visiting professor from the United States whom the couple hosted was so overwhelmed by Tami's hospitality—especially by her way of treating guests like children whose every need was anticipated—that he jokingly said the only thing he was expected to do by himself was to put the food in his mouth. For Tami this was the highest compliment he could have paid her.

Unlike the doctor's first wife, Tami willingly accompanied him on his overseas trips. His professional activities took them to interesting destinations all over the world—Hong Kong, Bombay, Capri, Leiden, London, Boston, New York, and Hawaii—and everywhere they went, they dressed in style and enjoyed comfortable accommodations. Youthful in appearance well into middle age, educated, birdlike in her daintiness but with a quick wit and boundless energy, Tami was an excellent companion to her serious, guarded husband. Photographs of the couple show her in well-tailored two-piece suits and Dr. Nakamura dressed in business suits or wearing slacks with plaid jackets and sunglasses. Tami accompanied her husband when he returned to Iowa to study on a Fulbright fellowship; during their five-month stay, the competent and cheerful Tami made friends despite her limited command of foreign languages and the unfamiliar culture. The strange food ("lots of corn, huge steaks—I threw away half of my portions—and smelly catfish from the Mississippi River") prompted her and a friend to stage a tempura party for twenty-eight guests.

Although Tami's husband appreciated her housekeeping and hostessing skills and showed his respect by entrusting her with his salary, at home they shared little in the way of conversation, common activities, or physical intimacy. Tired from his busy schedule as a medical doctor, teacher, and researcher, after dinner he watched television before going to sleep. He never asked her how she was feeling or expressed any interest in her health, even if she was ill. Although Tami would have liked to have more children, she was unable to conceive. In the early years of their marriage they slept together, but then they built a second story with a bedroom-study for him. She had her own room downstairs. Meiji-type men like him, Tami explained sympathetically, cared only about *gimu*—their duty.

Isami and Kō's children encountered rules of married life quite different from their parents' close relationship. Urban salaried men and professionals were often absent from home, because the demands of the new nation-state occupied their energies either in the business world or at war. The men tended to be emotionally absent too, because family ethics under the modern state downplayed affective ties between them and their wives in favor of devotion to job and nation.

In contrast, Isami and Kō had enjoyed a long life of physical and emotional intimacy. Isami's behavior as a husband reflected the influence of Fukuzawa Yukichi, the late nineteenth-century popular educator who favored a Western-style, conjugal marriage. Great-Grandfather Daisuke's relationship with his second wife, Moto, also served as a model. Using superlatives he rarely, if ever, lavished on anyone else, Isami called them an "uncommonly splendid couple."[4] He used the same word, *couple,* to describe Kō and himself. Kō was not merely the daughter-in-law of the family, or the mother of her husband's children, or the mistress of the house. In his family history, Isami emphasized how he and Kō had attended, "as a couple," the ceremonies celebrating the opening of the new Ishikawa train station in 1935 and how, leaving their youngest children with relatives in Tokyo, they had enjoyed traveling together to the Ishii family wedding in 1934.

Unlike Isami and Kō, few of their children had time to deal with the emotional side of relationships or to repair marital ties that had been frayed by separation and wartime crises and undermined by the country's defeat. They were focused on sheer survival—on regaining their health, their houses, and their financial security—and they concentrated on doing their duty. Not only did the husbands of Toyo and her sisters, from the very beginning of their marriages, work away from home in the new jobs and work-places created by industrialization and empire, but also they were preoccupied by the demands of the world outside their homes. Married men in the transition to urban middle-class life were more like providers than companions to their wives and fathers to their children, and their wives had become the main child-rearers and household managers—a circumstance foreign to Isami, who, even after his children had moved to Tokyo, remained a presence in their lives.

The separation of the worlds of men and women was new to the Matsuura children, who had grown up in a large family where both parents—

as well as many brothers, grandparents, and male and female servants—were ever present in their early years. Isami and his father had done their business in and around their home. The seven daughters of Isami and Kō, living with salaried spouses and in-laws who were essentially strangers to them, preserved close ties among themselves and with their parents. This was their way of smoothing their transition into the urban middle class. When their marriages were in trouble, they turned to their natal family for help.[5]

Strained relationships in family scenarios that Isami had scripted with such care made him even more eager to preserve harmony among his remaining children. Despite the marital difficulties of several of his adult offspring—indeed, perhaps because of them—he remained in close contact with his children to the very end of his life. He sent them gifts of fresh food from the countryside, such as rice cakes and azuki beans. As he grew frail in old age, he enjoined his sons and daughters to help one another all the more. He also urged his children to return home to the village each year to view the tree peonies in blossom, and on his frequent visits to Tokyo he stayed at one or another of his children's homes, where he enjoyed sitting with a grandchild on his lap—the "grandfather with the long white beard," as one granddaughter called him.[6]

The Matsuura sisters, far from railing against the "feudal" or "patriarchal" marriage and family system that had frequently caused them grief, revered the values of their father, Isami, the supreme patriarch. When they complained, it was not about their largely absent husbands or the lack of strong emotional ties with them. Rather, they complained about husbands who failed to do their duty as their father had. Lazy or incompetent men, like some of their brothers, who, lacking ambition, never became *erai* (famous, important) and failed to do "kin work," were also objects of their criticism, whereas husbands who worked hard, provided well, came to the aid of relatives in times of need, and remained faithful won the respect and gratitude, if not necessarily the adoration or passion, of their wives.

Infidelity, however, was strongly condemned. As long as Isami was alive, for example, his daughter Shiki's husband remained civil to her and her family; Isami had lent his son-in-law money to build his medical clinic. After Isami died, however, Dr. Nakao became *urusai* (irksome). The Matsuura sisters suspected that he was unfaithful to Shiki. When she died of a cerebral blood clot in 1980 and he quickly married his nurse, who was forty years his junior, their suspicions were confirmed. The family broke off ties with him.

The women's devotion (more like service) to spouses was tempered by certain realistic considerations or what one might call a quid pro quo; each expected to be granted control over her husband's salary and to inherit his assets, and fought back if another woman entered her husband's life. Even the timid Fuki once chastised her husband for the appearance of impropriety when she discovered he was occasionally having dinner with the daughter of his friend. "He asked me if it would be all right to take her to a movie, and I told him it would be *mazui*" (awkward, unsavory, unadvisable).

Although marriage often involved relationships based on a sense of duty, a few of the members of the twelfth generation did enjoy close affective bonds. Isami's seventh son, Sei, and his wife, Kuniko, probably had the closest emotional and physical relations; she bore three children. "He doted on her. They were a real couple," recalled Toyo's daughter. Also close to their wives were the third and fourth sons: Saburō and Ayako, a childless couple, and the country doctor Yūshirō and Masako, who reared four sons. According to her niece, Masako also doted on her husband. Fumi raised "the best children"—three sons, all Tokyo University graduates who got along well with one another and their own wives and remained loyal to the larger family network. Fumi often took pride in her husband's accomplishments as well. The two "raised the children strictly," said their niece, approvingly, echoing her grandfather Isami's praise of his step-great-grandmother, Moto, who helped raise her stepchildren strictly, and therefore well.

The women of the twelfth generation usually reserved (and volunteered) their strongest criticism not for husbands but for mothers-in-law, women whose behavior was conditioned by a marriage system that, by expecting the eldest son and his wife to live with and serve his parents, pitted two generations of women against one another in a struggle for control of cooking, children, finances, and the attention and support of the male heir apparent. These women also tended to criticize other wives for not performing their domestic roles with sufficient skill and dedication.

All but one of the twelfth-generation sisters—Shiki—outlived their husbands by many years, unlike their mother, Kō. And regardless of how they felt about their husbands, each of them, with the exception of Toyo, nursed her husband literally down to his last breath, staying in the hospital room, feeding him, taking his temperature, and standing by his bed at the moment of his death. At least four husbands and two brothers of this generation died of cancer of the esophagus, stomach, or lungs, possibly related to their heavy smoking habits, and their deaths were drawn out and painful. Nursing their husbands through their final illness was the culminating drama of their married lives; it was an important part of these women's life stories. They faulted any woman who was not at her husband's side at the very end, and had vivid memories of their own performance. Their version of a war story was the tale of how, pushed to the limits of physical endurance, each one stayed the course, keeping her husband company around the clock, bringing his favorite foods to the hospital, removing phlegm from his throat, and waiting on him until the final moment, often with the help of daughters, sisters, or nieces.

Hospital staffs expected family members to participate actively in the care of their patients. Tami recounted being so tired from nursing her husband during his final stage of cancer that she collapsed at one point in the corridor outside his room. Long after Fuki's husband had died of stomach cancer, she vividly remembered the details of his final illness. Because he was head of the hospital where he was being treated, Fuki was able to live in the hospital with him. Her one regret was not giving in to his request for a glass of beer shortly before he died. She also felt sorry for her daughter, who cried when the nurses would not allow her to help care for her father. "The nurses should have let the family help with the nursing," she remarked. "Otherwise, the patients are lonely."

Wives who failed to stay the course—who, like their oldest brother Yatarō's wife, slipped off to the hairdresser or, like Toyo, went home to sleep in her own bed instead of spending the night on a hospital cot in her husband's room—did not qualify as good soldiers. Fuki criticized her older sister Toyo for not staying overnight at the hospital where Masafumi lay dying of lung cancer. He finally died alone during the night, having choked to death on his phlegm. "When Toyo arrived, he was still warm," said Fuki. "Toyo should have stayed, rubbed his back . . . it's lonely at night for patients." Fuki even attributed Toyo's apparent selfishness to her having attended Freedom School: "There's a difference between education at Japan Women's College and Freedom School."

Of course, Fuki, as the wife of the hospital head, had more comfortable accommodations than the standard hospital cot. There were no provisions for family members to stay the night in the large hospital where Masafumi spent his final days, so Toyo commuted every day to the hospital, cooking her husband's favorite food and carrying it on the train. Before his hospitalization, she had cared for Masafumi at home, where he had been mainly confined to bed. Masafumi was in and out of the hospital, coming home when he felt a little better but anxiously returning when he thought he noticed new symptoms. The stress of helping her husband through his final days led Toyo to start smoking again.

This generation of Matsuura women even tended to their mates beyond the grave. They kept the memory of the deceased alive in daily rituals, such as lighting incense and making offerings of favorite foods on the household Buddhist altar. Tami shared the first pot of coffee of the day with her deceased husband, and she also left on the altar a small portion of various delicacies or gifts from others. She regularly brought flowers to his grave site. She lit a lantern on the evening of O-bon in August, to welcome the spirit of the dead, and she instructed her niece Yōko, a Christian, to do the same for her Christian mother, Toyo. She kept in touch with her husband's side of the family, and in other ways acted as though he were still alive. His fine tweeds and leather jacket hung in his upstairs closet for almost two decades after his death, and she continued to use stationery with his name on it. Fuki carried three photographs of her deceased husband in her purse together with his watch and leather wallet and said good morning to him every day. She hoped these mementos would be burned with her when she was cremated.

For a woman whose marriage bond was based on gratitude or respect or pride or economic security, if not a close emotional connection, genuine affection, or physical intimacy, a husband's death brought a certain sense of satisfaction and pride in a job well done. It was comforting to preside over a dignified ending to a long relationship that had yielded benefits in the form of a house, children, food on the table, one or two vacation trips, and status in the community as wife and mother. The husband's reliability in providing well—like a business partner with whom she divided up the work of family well-being—provided sufficient satisfaction in old age. Throughout the years, when the Matsuura sisters found themselves wanting more— entertainment, companionship, sympathy, or help—they had turned to their siblings and their parents.

On the one hand, husbands were powerful; on the other hand, they were like children who needed their meals cooked, their clothes laundered, their suitcases packed, their tea cups or beer glasses refilled. It was a relief when the men were away on business. It was more fun to travel with one's sisters than with a demanding spouse. Once their husbands were gone, the sisters often traveled together around Japan and even abroad.

Their husbands' deaths constituted a kind of retirement from the full-time job of being "on call." Once widowed, the Matsuura sisters visited with one another whenever they wanted, instead of declining invitations to go out if their husbands were in the house that day. When they reached the "retirement" of widowhood, these women were grateful for what they received along with their husband's remaining assets: praise and appreciation from his relatives for their virtuous performances in marriage.

SIXTEEN

Mothering

T OYO WAS HEALTHY AND ENERGETIC when I arrived at her doorstep in the fall of 1963. She was a part-time "leader," as teachers were called, at the Seikatsu-Dan, a progressive kindergarten in Tokyo that employed many Freedom School graduates and followed Hani Motoko's pedagogical principles. With twenty-year-old Yōko in junior college and Masafumi in Hiroshima most of the time, Toyo had finally managed to satisfy her desire to work outside the home and to have money of her own, and she was enthusiastically committed to the kindergarten's goal of teaching children self-reliance at an early age.[1]

After they had returned in 1959 from four years in Rio de Janeiro, Toyo and her husband decided to buy a house in Ogikubo, on the western outskirts of Tokyo, but Masafumi's company sent him back to Hiroshima, and he rarely returned to Tokyo. Their single-story, pink stucco, three-bedroom house was purchased from an American soldier who had been in the occupation. Accustomed to Western amenities from his many years of living abroad, Masafumi liked the two-year-old house's Western fixtures, such as the flush toilet and the stall shower. Only the foyer *(genkan)* and the small tatami-lined room in the front of the house reflected Japanese architectural influence. These had been installed to accommodate the former owner's Japanese wife and mother-in-law. The house did not even have a Japanese-style deep bath, though it did have sliding doors (glass, not wood) opening onto a small lawn (not a rock garden) on the south side. Modern electrical appliances, such as the television and the refrigerator, bore the Mitsubishi trademark, and all the furniture, including beds, couch, and chairs, was Western-style. The large oval coffee table was made of an exotic Brazilian wood. The only item missing (and sorely so, I thought) in this imitation American bungalow was central heating; we used portable kerosene space heaters.

Toyo spoke Portuguese, acquired when she and Masafumi had lived in Brazil, but she seemed to have forgotten the college English she had studied at Freedom School, whereas I had studied Spanish and French and could read Japanese with difficulty, but I was limited to the most rudimentary conversational Japanese, picked up from a Berlitz record shortly before I left the United States. Unfazed, Toyo welcomed me into her home and proceeded, with help from the Matsuura family network, to teach me not only spoken Japanese but everything else I needed to survive in her country, from daily rituals of social interaction to the workings of the intricate transportation system. Forty years later I learned from her daughter that Toyo could speak English at least well enough to interpret for other Japanese wives on shopping and sightseeing excursions in Vancouver during their plane's layover en route to Brazil. I also learned that, while living in Brazil, Yōko had attended a private school run by an American woman. Perhaps because they knew I needed to learn Japanese, neither one spoke to me in English.

Toyo, Yōko, and I took our meals together at a table set under the window at one end of the living room, with our respective dictionaries placed between the plates. I did not know the Japanese names of anything I was eating; indeed, often I did not know *what* I was eating. My vocabulary in Japanese was largely confined to scholarly language. Toyo said I sounded like a missionary, and Yōko, years later, confided that at first I spoke like a man.

Fortunately, a friend from graduate school turned over his language tutor to me. The tutor came to the house with pages of grammatical exercises. Toyo's approach to teaching me to comprehend conversational Japanese was different. She talked—in the rapid speech of busy Tokyoites—about her childhood memories, her interesting overseas experiences, her numerous relatives, or the day's events. Her stories were so riveting, I found myself hanging on her every word, and somehow I understood what she was saying. I remember, for example, how one morning at the breakfast table she told me the story of the Yamashiraishi village priest's lovelorn widow who drowned herself in a well. Once, when I showed her a book of Japanese children's stories I had purchased for a friend's child, she recounted one of her favorites, the story of Momo-san, the little boy found inside a peach by an old couple. On another day, she described, with some amusement, the *nonki* (happy-go-lucky) attitude of Brazilians, so different from the hard-driving Japanese of the 1960s. Although the Japanese wives of other company employees in Brazil had tended to socialize only within their own group, she had ventured out on her own to meet Brazilians and had learned Portuguese from a Brazilian woman introduced to her at the Union Church in Rio de Janeiro.

Toyo never told me that she was in Hiroshima at the time of the atomic bombing. Either out of respect for my sensibilities as an American or because, like other survivors of horror, she was more comfortable not revisiting a painful past, the subject never came up. Besides, when I first met Toyo, she was fully recovered from her bout with tuberculosis and showed no signs of having radiation-related illness. It was only five years later that she and her husband were officially designated *hibakusha,* "atom-bomb survivors." According to a law passed in 1968, all Japanese (but not former subject peoples of Japan, such as Koreans) who were within two kilometers of the epicenter of the bomb on the day it was dropped or immediately afterward were entitled to certain health and financial benefits.[2] In her widowhood decades later, Toyo would receive a monthly pension of twenty-seven thousand yen from the government.[3] But if she bore any physical or emotional scars from her ordeal, she never showed them, at least not to me.

Shortly after I entered her household, Toyo introduced me to several of her nieces and nephews. On the very first day that I met Mina's daughter, Nobu, a college student majoring in English at Aoyama Gakuin, she had the good sense to teach me basic Japanese etiquette, such as what to say to one's hostess at the beginning and end of a meal and how to apologize if late for an appointment. Nobu's buoyancy and her zest for life made her seem almost aggressive in comparison with the more demure Japanese women I thought I would find in Japan. She took me on memorable hiking treks and ski trips in the Japanese Alps—though my skiing skills were even less developed than my ability to converse in Japanese.

Toyo arranged parties at her house for other nieces and nephews and urged me to teach them social dancing—one of the few activities in Japan over which I could claim mastery, especially since Toyo never mentioned that she and her husband had been avid dancers. At these parties I met Yasu's son, Hiroshi, a jolly, slightly rotund young man on his way to becoming an audio engineer, and Fumi's three gentle, friendly, and studious sons, who had escaped with her from Manchuria at the end of World War II and, one after the other, had passed the extremely difficult entrance examinations into the pinnacle of Japan's education system—Tokyo University. To further my own education, Nobu and Yōko dragged me along to tea-ceremony classes at the home of Mina's friend, a descendant of a samurai family. In the

evenings, Yōko and I took walks around the neighborhood, a semisubur-
ban cluster of houses amid a few tiny rice fields, thirty minutes by bus west
of the Ogikubo station of the Chūō railroad line. Before long I was meeting Toyo's sisters and their husbands and having rudimentary conversations
with them. On New Year's Day, a time for dressing in one's best kimono,
going to the neighborhood Shinto shrine, and visiting relatives, Toyo's sister Fumi and her husband and several of Toyo's nephews joined in playing
the traditional New Year's card game, Hyakunin Isshu (One Hundred Poems by One Hundred Poets), kneeling on the floor and snatching one another's poem cards with much laughter and joviality.

In the 1960s Toyo's sisters were all living in or near Tokyo, and almost all
of them, like Toyo, were living well, at least by the standards of the day,
thanks to the economic recovery of the country and the earning ability of
their husbands, who worked long hours five and one-half days a week. Nevertheless, married life meant a daily round of household chores for women
intent on realizing the feminine ideal of "good wife, wise mother."

The primary job for most of the women was caring for their household
members. Domestic work, especially food preparation, occupied much of
their energy. None of the sisters worked at salaried jobs, with the exception
of Toyo's part-time work at the kindergarten. Much of their time was consumed in shopping for and preparing their family's meals.

Most of Toyo's siblings had small families, and, with only a few exceptions, they lived without servants or in-laws. In contrast to Isami and Kō's
extraordinary fertility, only two of their six daughters were able to bear more
than one child; one son was childless; and two daughters, Toyo and Shiki,
each adopted a girl. Nevertheless, keeping even a relatively small family fed,
warm, and clean without central heating, cars, and all the other modern con-
veniences that urban Americans took for granted in the 1960s was a full-time
occupation. With gas a luxury, dishes were washed in cold water. Homes
lacked ovens; cooking was done on two-burner stoves.

Toyo's kitchen—narrow, cramped, and dimly lit—was equipped with
few appliances. Limited to a small refrigerator and scant cabinet space,
Toyo, like other urban housewives, did a daily round of grocery shopping
at small neighborhood stores that were themselves stocked with only minimum amounts of perishable goods. Frozen food was unavailable; besides,
people preferred fresh fruits and vegetables in season. Women bought in
small quantities—an egg, two carrots, one hundred grams of poultry—and
carried home the day's purchases in a small straw or plastic basket hung over
their wrist. On some days Toyo commuted by bus to food stores near the

Ogikubo train station thirty minutes away. Yet, despite these many obstacles, she prepared meals worthy of the finest restaurant.

Delicious, varied, nutritious, Toyo's dinners, which included French and Chinese as well as Japanese cuisine, were mouth-watering adventures that often represented the highlight of my day. Breakfast was Western-style, with coffee, toast, and eggs accompanied by a few lightly fried green vegetables. Toyo would race to the table from the cold kitchen, pull off the scarf that kept her hair in place while cooking, and serve our food piping hot.

In the eyes of Toyo and her youngest sister, Tami, top grades went to housewives who were "fast"—who briskly heated the water for the evening bath, deftly cut the vegetables for dinner with rapid chopping motions, promptly brought out the steaming bowls of rice and hot green tea, and scurried to the door to greet arriving household members and help them off with their wet coats.

Even into the 1960s and among the relatively well-off, urban middle-class Matsuura sisters, there was little time to rest; people hustled, and wives and mothers generated the energy to keep others going. In Toyo's house, I awoke every morning to the sound of her loud voice urging Yōko to wake up. Later (still lying in bed) I heard Toyo consulting with Tami on the telephone about what to feed me. At breakfast Toyo questioned me about my day's schedule. She cheerfully polished my shoes and helped me on with my coat. On rainy days she met me at the bus stop with an umbrella. She washed my laundry in a primitive washing machine, kept outside the backdoor to the kitchen, and hung it on the line to dry. She literally kept me alive.

After their limited diet during wartime and the postwar years, the relatives' greatest pleasure was getting together and eating. The women organized family get-togethers and photograph sessions whenever they had an excuse for one. When Mitsubishi transferred Toyo's husband to Brazil in 1950, her sisters and a few of her brothers had gathered for a family portrait, sporting clothing and hairstyles then in fashion in the United States. Even Isami came for the send-off. In 1964, almost fifty family members—the sisters and their spouses, children, and even mothers-in-law—gathered for dinner at a restaurant and had a group portrait taken, and the following year, at Yōko's wedding, more pictures captured the vitality, prosperity, and closeness of this large urban family network.

The most comfortably well-off of the sisters in the 1960s was probably the youngest, Tami, wife of the ear specialist. She could afford to bring expensive Viennese-style pastries to family get-togethers and to modernize her spacious two-story home with a flush toilet and new kitchen appliances.

Having accompanied her husband on several of his research-related overseas trips to Europe and the United States, she was especially au courant when it came to Western-style life.

In clothing fashions as well as cooking, women were important Western innovators, engaged in the process of cultural assimilation in the arena of daily life. In fact, Toyo had taken a course in fashion design during her Brazil years. The women of the family took great pleasure in acquiring Western-style clothing, which, if imported, was very expensive and not made to their physical proportions. They looked closely at how my clothes were made so that they could learn to sew their own, no easy feat considering they were working with unfamiliar materials and sizes. Sartorial features that I took for granted, such as elastic waistbands or turtleneck sweaters, impressed them, and they noticed and even admired everything I wore, viewing me as some kind of fashion trendsetter, an unfamiliar role for me, since I typically modeled what might be called the impoverished graduate student look. I began to fear that jackets with one or two missing buttons would become all the rage in Japan as a result of my influence.

Women of the family also played the major role in their children's upbringing and education. Unlike their parents' generation, when Isami assisted in childcare and chose his children's schools and spouses, the twelfth generation, now solidly citified, witnessed the separation of men from household and childcare duties and the release of women from both farming and paid labor. Where once their father had supervised the children's marriages, it now fell to the women to perform this aspect of kin work as well. In fact, toward the end of 1964, Toyo was in the midst of arranging a marriage for her daughter Yōko, a recent graduate of a two-year women's college that emphasized nutrition and home economics studies.

Strained relations with her own husband were not sufficient cause for Toyo to encourage a so-called love marriage for her daughter. Yōko had never spent time with young men other than her male cousins; she was the typical, proper, middle-class "daughter in a box." Even now, in the family's thirteenth generation, most of the children in the extended family met their spouses through go-betweens. Despite the emphasis on "love" and individualism sparked by American influence in the immediate postwar years, parents placed economic security first, and, like their own parents, Isami and Kō, they did not trust young people to choose their own marriage partners. Besides, even in 1960s Japan there were few opportunities for young people to date. Fuki's only daughter, Setsuko, preferred to rely on her parents' judgment. They matched her with a doctor, like her father, who agreed to live with her parents in their old age as an adopted son-in-law would. Her husband kept his own surname, but the couple's only son assumed her maiden name.

Although I was no longer living in Toyo's household, having moved to Kyoto in the summer of 1964, I continued to think of Yōko as my younger sister, and, perhaps projecting my own feelings onto her, I rashly attempted to stop the ongoing negotiations of her marriage. It was a match that, at first, seemed completely unreasonable to me: not only was the prospective spouse a stranger to Yōko, but also he was eight years older.

Yōko, too, had vague misgivings. At my suggestion we traveled to Hiroshima to persuade her father to intervene, and he agreed that the marriage was moving along too quickly. Toyo herself was a little taken aback by the speed of the arrangements, which she justified to us by explaining that the man's side was hoping to find a wife for him before his company transferred him overseas. Reassurance came from Yōko's aunts, who called to persuade her that she was doing the right thing. When I tried to talk to Toyo about my misgivings, I found that my arguments suddenly made little sense, even to me, in the context of her life and society.

The prospective groom, located in a proper Japanese way through a family member, possessed, like the bride's father, all the right credentials: a degree from Tokyo University and a job with Mitsubishi. His ties to the family, however attenuated, made him seem less a stranger than he really was, for his aunt was the wife of the brother-in-law of Toyo's sister Shiki. To make the deal even sweeter, he was a second son, free of obligations to care for his own parents and available to live with Toyo and Masafumi in their old age. Finally, he came from a family of doctors dating back to a physician for a Sendai *daimyō* in the Tokugawa period, an argument that, in my own youthful innocence, struck me as irrelevant and left me with no comeback, except to murmur that Yōko's future husband did not know anything about her "personality," a word I did not know how to say in Japanese. That argument was as irrelevant to Toyo as her argument about the family of doctors was to me. When Toyo patiently asked me how young people found appropriate spouses in the United States, I shortly realized I had lost the argument, for all I could think of were the experiences of my friends at coeducational colleges, which involved blind dates and chance meetings of strangers at parties. Yōko was married in February 1965.

In retrospect twenty years later, even after her divorce and the painful events surrounding it, Yōko recollected only having welcomed the marriage. "I wanted to have children. I wanted to be a mother." She also remembered feeling inferior because she was not considered pretty, and, having spent several of her formative years in an American school in Brazil, she was also perceived as an outsider in her own conformist society. Then, too, she had been in Hiroshima when the atomic bomb was dropped, with a scar to remind her and everyone else. During the marriage negotiations, one of her fiancé's relatives had even suggested that she might be infertile as a result of exposure to radiation. Ultimately Yōko was relieved that someone wanted to marry her. And when her fiancé told her that he would open a special savings account to set aside money for her parents after Masafumi's retirement, Yōko's heart was won.

Marriage did not mean that Yōko had to leave her parents' home. Rather, with apartments scarce and rents exorbitant, her husband willingly moved into the Ogikubo house while awaiting transfer to his next company assignment. Marriage did mean, however, that Yōko would have to learn about her adoption.

Shortly after her wedding, while visiting her mother-in-law, Yōko heard for the first time that she had been adopted during the war and that she had a biological father who was a university professor still living in Sendai, two siblings, and several nieces and nephews. Her mother-in-law had obtained this information from the marriage go-between and had gained Toyo's reluctant approval to tell Yōko, who, stunned by the news, returned home that same night to find Toyo alone and weeping.

Toyo was afraid she would lose Yōko's love to her biological relatives. Yōko's response, however, was just the opposite; she felt even more grateful to Toyo and Masafumi, essentially two strangers who had rescued her and had been devoted parents. When she finally met her biological siblings twenty years later, she felt even more blessed, for they had been shunted back and forth between their grandmother and their indifferent stepmother, while she had enjoyed her mother's undivided attention. Mother and daughter had even shared a double bed when I lived with them, renting Yōko's bedroom. Nevertheless, the adoption remained such an emotionally fraught subject that Masafumi did not learn about Yōko's awareness of it until she was pregnant with her first child, at which point he asked Toyo what she would say if Yōko asked her about her own presumed pregnancy years ago.

After Masafumi's death and a few years before her own death, Toyo reluctantly agreed to allow Yōko to meet her blood kin, whose whereabouts were known to the friend who had helped arrange the adoption. Toyo's other friends had persuaded her to relent, arguing that, as an only child, Yōko would be all alone after Toyo was gone. Her biological sister, six years old when Yōko was born, had periodically inquired about her and finally, in 1989, sent her a letter that began "I am your older sister." The sister arranged their first meeting on the grave of their birth mother in Tokyo and brought along her husband, two of her children, and the aunt who had cared for Yōko before the adoption, over four decades earlier. Toyo agreed to invite them to her house for dinner afterward but declined to meet Yōko's biological father, who offered to thank her in person for adopting his daughter. Toyo did not covet recognition for rearing somebody else's child, Yōko explained; Toyo had always wanted to have a "natural relation" with her, to be her "real" mother, and if it had not been for Yōko's marriage, the adoption probably would never have been revealed.

One of the few members of the thirteenth generation who did not have an arranged marriage was Tami's talented daughter, Masako, a graduate of an art school. Masako had inherited her mother's beauty and had enjoyed the material comforts provided by her stepfather—fashionable Western clothing, good medical care, and a private college education—but she had wanted a more passionate marriage for herself, sensing that the marriage of her mother and the doctor had been one of convenience.

Reluctantly accepting her decision to marry the photographer with whom she had fallen in love, her parents gave her a lavish wedding at the Imperial Hotel, as befitted a man of Dr. Nakamura's status. Toyo had sided with her niece in this instance and spoken to the doctor on her behalf. After living in Italy with her husband for several years, however, Masako left him and returned to her parents' home; her husband, like the biological father she had not seen since she was a child, had been unable to make a living. Divorced and the mother of a little girl—precisely the plight of Tami herself after her ill-fated first marriage—Masako went to work while Tami raised her granddaughter. Dr. Nakamura, in a sentiment reminiscent of his father-in-law, Isami, pinned his hopes for continuity of his family name not on a male blood relative but on his wife's bright granddaughter, whom he urged to follow in his footsteps as an ear specialist.

The little girl's future, however, held something very different for her. Her mother fell in love again, and again the man was a photographer, only this time he was a married man and her ex-husband's friend. The two couples had socialized with each other. He, too, was struggling to make a living with his one-man wedding photography business. Moreover, his wife was pregnant. Dr. Nakamura, on his deathbed and fearing that his stepdaughter would squander whatever money she inherited, persuaded Masako to relinquish her legal claims to his will, and he left all his money to Tami, her mother and his trusted second wife. Masako secretly kept seeing her lover, who divorced his wife, and one day after her stepfather had died and Tami was away from the house, she moved out, daughter in tow, and remarried.

Left alone in her comfortable home in the upscale Seijo section of western Tokyo, the widowed Tami was free to pursue a busy schedule of hobbies and family social events. Although she had pushed aside her anger and disappointment with her daughter, she refused to allow the couple to move back in with her when they were having financial problems. Romantic love had been lacking in Tami's marriage, but it seemed a small price to pay. In the second-story room where her husband had once studied and slept alone, she enjoyed sitting and listening to the romantic ballads and theme songs from Hollywood movies such as *Love Is a Many-Splendored Thing* and *Love Story.*

Misfortune and tragedy hounded the children of Toyo's siblings despite the material advantages that most of them enjoyed. Mina's zestful and fun-loving only daughter, Nobu, who had befriended me only a few years earlier, died of stomach cancer in the late 1960s, a short while after she had married. Mina never fully recovered. "It is not natural for a child to die before her parents," she would say, and on visits to Nobu's grave, she would talk to her. Because Nobu had embraced Catholicism during her college years at her missionary-run college, Mina converted after Nobu's death in order to be reunited in the afterlife, she said, with the "most interesting" of her three children.

Another Matsuura sister also lost an adult child. In the late 1980s Yasu's only child, Hiroshi, an ambitious, successful sound engineer with many contacts in the entertainment world, collapsed and died of an aneurysm in his forty-fourth year, leaving behind a wife and three children, one of whom was mentally and physically disabled from birth complications.

Each time misfortune struck, the Matsuura family network rallied to the aid of the afflicted. Sisters and brothers contributed money, time, and effort to siblings in need. Kōjirō had helped to pay the medical bills of his niece Nobu, and her cousins had donated blood. Sororal ties were especially strong. Tami moved in with Yasu and her husband during their period of mourning. She and Yasu shopped and cooked for Mina during her husband's illness. It was not simply feelings of obligation that motivated this mutual assistance; the sisters were genuinely fond of one another and stayed in close touch. Once a year they all attended a Kabuki performance. They also traveled together (without their husbands) and made annual visits to their ancestral cemetery.

The siblings also readily came to the aid of their married children and grandchildren, as their own parents had, unless they deemed the requests completely irresponsible, and these usually involved requests for excessive amounts of money. Deserving relatives were another story. Yasu's courageous daughter-in-law remained with her and her husband, Sho, who helped raise and support the grandchildren. Looking aged beyond his years at his son's funeral, Sho soon realized his grandchildren needed him. In particular, his youngest grandchild—a smart, cute, healthy girl, who, like her father, was said to have an ear for music—saved him from his grief. He began a rigorous exercise program of jogging preceded by an elaborate warm-up, to stay healthy and alive long enough to see the children into adulthood. He was still jogging in his ninetieth year.

Tami also found herself in the position of living with her grandchild. At the age of seventy and still healthy, she agreed to take back her granddaughter and to finance her college education, not in medicine, for which she showed little interest or ability, but, like her mother, in the arts, with a major in theater. But despite Tami's generous spending on the girl's clothing, tuition, piano instruction, concert tickets, and room furnishings, which included a large television and state-of-the-art sound system, her grandchild rebelled against what she viewed as Tami's intrusion into her private life and her old-fashioned values, which Tami often tried to impose on members of the younger generation. Instead of a peaceful old age, Tami found herself locked in screaming arguments with her only grandchild and estranged from her only daughter.

Toyo, too, in her later years had to rescue her grandchildren when Yōko and her husband were finally divorced after many years of tension. The couple had lived with her for ten years after marrying; their three children had been born in the nearby Ogikubo Hospital. But then Yōko's husband was transferred to Osaka, where they and the children squeezed into a cramped apartment typical of urban company housing in the 1960s, and the couple started experiencing marital problems. The husband worked the normal long workweek and left all household and childcare matters to Yōko. Troubled by his lack of attention, Yōko did not know whether their seeming estrangement was normal for Japanese couples, never having seen much of a relationship between her mother and father. Seeking succor for her emotional distress, she turned to her mother's religion and converted to Christianity.

Yōko first suspected that her husband was guilty of infidelity in the late 1970s, after another company transfer sent the entire family to San Francisco. She had made an emergency trip to Japan to see her father, who was dying of lung cancer, and upon returning home had found unfamiliar shirts in her husband's closet—a striped pattern that he did not ordinarily wear.

When her husband was transferred back to Japan in 1982, Yōko went ahead with the children while he stayed in San Francisco for another six months to wrap up business, or so he said. On his intermittent trips back to Japan during that six months, Yōko tried to rescue her marriage. She raised the issue of their marital problems and discovered the name of the woman companion who had claimed her husband's affections. His lover was a Japanese woman several years his senior, the former wife of an American and the mother of several grown children. Yōko called the woman's family members to discuss the "problems" the woman was causing. Yōko also responded to her husband's urgent appeal for money to pay off his debts, as he put it, so that he could leave San Francisco. She reluctantly borrowed the money from Toyo and hand carried it on a plane to San Francisco. When six months passed and both he and shipments of the family's household goods never showed up at the apartment that Mitsubishi had provided for them in Tokyo, Yōko managed to locate her husband through the shipping company's records. She confronted him in the middle of the night at the apartment he had taken with his woman companion. He dragged the boxes of missing goods to the door, and Yōko brought them home in a taxi.

Feeling responsible for having arranged an unsuccessful marriage for her daughter, the widowed Toyo took it upon herself to speak with her errant son-in-law, to whom she had lent a substantial sum of money. She learned that he had met his lover in a bar for Japanese businessmen in San Francisco, where she had worked as a hostess after her divorce. Determined to persuade the woman to "give him up," Toyo planned to visit the couple's apartment, uninvited, and she asked me to come along for moral support. As indebted as I felt to her, I was horrified at the thought of placing both of us in such an awkward situation. It seemed like an act of desperation, destined to fail, and it did. After I begged off, Toyo went to the couple's apartment with her niece Masako. A woman opened the door a crack only long enough to say that Toyo's son-in-law was not home.

As late as 1982 Yōko still had hopes of preserving her marriage—even if her husband refused to live with her—in order to protect the children and her financial resources and to avoid the need to move out of company housing. Her husband, however, sought to divorce her by having her sign a divorce decree, which he unexpectedly put on the table at the Tokyo restaurant where she had agreed to meet him. Furious, she said she would not divorce him while the children were still young. "On that day," said the gentle, patient Yōko, "I felt like killing him."

She also felt like killing herself and briefly considered suicide, reasoning in her distressed state of mind that, with her out of the way, her husband could remarry and his second wife would take care of the children. Of course, a different, more likely scenario was also possible: a new wife would not want to care for the children—precisely the situation that had led to Yōko's adoption. What shook her free of suicidal thoughts was her inability to hurt Toyo.

Because she refused to accept the divorce, the couple went to mediation court. Although, according to Yōko, her husband told lies to demean her as a wife and attempted to justify his behavior by accusing her of not having his meal ready when he came home from work, his philandering hurt his case. The judge ordered him to stay married and to pay a fixed amount each month to his family. He continued to live with his companion and allowed his children to visit him only outside his apartment once or twice a year.

Yōko's estranged husband fell heavily into debt while trying to maintain two households and to please his companion, whom he gave expensive gifts, such as a pearl necklace and flights to the United States to visit her children. He also had gambling debts. To cover his expenses he wheedled loans out of companies doing business with Mitsubishi and also borrowed at exorbitant interest rates from loansharks. Once a representative of one of these lenders called Yōko at home. When her husband could not repay these loans, he borrowed money from his sister, who agreed to help him but only with his promise not to remarry.

Matters came to a head when companies from which the philanderer had borrowed complained to Mitsubishi. A high-ranking Mitsubishi official who had known Yōko's father stepped in and forced Masafumi's son-in-law to resign. The company turned over a portion of his retirement bonus and pension to Yōko and used the rest of the money to pay off his other creditors, including his sister, a wealthy woman, who, at the suggestion of the company official, agreed to let Yōko keep the money. Later, she disowned her brother when he reneged on his promise to her and remarried.

The encounter with her husband's creditors was the final straw for Yōko, who now decided seek a divorce from him. Once again she went to court, an experience so stressful that her duodenal ulcer flared up and she had to be rushed by ambulance to a hospital for surgery, which resulted in the removal of half of her stomach. Toyo refused to allow her son-in-law into the hospital room after the surgery because, when she called to tell him his wife had undergone emergency surgery, he neglected to ask about his children. She said she could forgive him for neglecting his wife but not his offspring.

Toyo was devastated by the divorce, and for several years afterward she was extremely disturbed. "Yōko is my life," she would say of this daughter she had daringly adopted during the war. She had lived with and watched over her daughter after she married and had stayed at her side through several crises, including an emergency appendectomy at the time Yōko gave birth to her third child. It was for Yōko's benefit that Toyo had decided not to leave her own husband, who, though a responsible provider, had also clashed with her over his interest in other women and at times had essentially lived a separate life.

Following the divorce, Yōko and her three teenage children once again took up residence with Toyo in the Ogikubo house, where I had lived when I first came to Japan. By this time the house had a second-floor addition, built after Masafumi had retired from his job in Hiroshima and returned to Tokyo to work for another company. A small bedroom and a large living room on the second floor had provided separate space for Masafumi and his collections of Pepsi Cola bottles, Kewpie dolls, wine glasses, golf clubs, and assorted bottles of wine and liquor, including three different kinds of scotch, vodka, and more. Also displayed were a lizard carved out of wood, a beer stein, and three pipes, each on its own marble stand. The living room, furnished with a couch, two armchairs, a television, and a coffee table, was lighted by large glass windows and, in the evening, by several lamps, whose simple, clean-cut design reflected his preference for modern, Western-style living.

After Masafumi's death, Toyo had rented the second story to two students. Now, for Yōko and her children, she had a carpenter divide the upstairs living room into two bedrooms and add a second kitchen and bath. In her seventies in the early 1980s and a widow for the past six years, Toyo was still full of energy, and for the next ten years, she presided over Yōko's family as well as serving as its chief cook while Yōko worked in a downtown office at a job she had found through a friend of Toyo's. In the early 1990s, Toyo claimed she was the only eighty-year-old woman who still prepared meals for her family, though other women of that age in their circle of acquaintances also cooked, if only for their husbands.

Toyo's Christian forbearance did not extend to her son-in-law. Although she thanked her many other family members by name, one by one, moments before she died in 1993, she denounced her daughter's husband with angry words to her dying day: "I will never forgive him." Yōko tried to be more objective about her husband, who had shown so much potential during the marriage negotiations. She attributed his nearly criminal behavior to his troubled childhood, explaining that he had lost his mother at an early age and that his stepmother may have overcompensated by spoiling him. At least one of Yōko's relatives placed some of the blame on Yōko herself, as her husband did, arguing that she was a poor household manager who kept an untidy home and did not impose enough discipline on her children.

Toyo may have given others the impression that her daughter was not self-reliant, telling them that she lacked domestic skills, although she had earned a degree in nutrition. After Toyo's death, when Yōko invited her mother's friends and relatives to the home for dinner, they all seemed surprised at the elaborate spread she had prepared. Telling me this story with amusement, Yōko suddenly started crying, not because she felt her mother had demeaned her, but because she recognized how much Toyo had done to help her and how much she had loved her. Before she died, Toyo had urged her fifty-year-old daughter to remarry if she could find a suitable husband. Yōko was finally on her own.

Kin Work

DURING TOYO'S THREE-MONTH HOSPITALIZATION, her youngest sister Tami's home became a central command post for the network of relatives eager to lend their support. Yōko reported daily to Tami, who then transmitted medical bulletins to her siblings, beginning at eight o'clock in the morning, when the telephone would start ringing. Toyo's siblings and nephews pooled a fixed sum of money for Yōko to use as cash gifts to hospital nurses and pocket money to splurge on taxicab rides to the hospital. When I arrived in Tokyo to see Toyo after Tami had contacted me about her weakened condition, Toyo's siblings each sent a fixed amount of money to Tami (although she did not need it) to cover my expenses, including carfare, postage stamps, small gifts to take back to my friends, long-distance telephone calls, and the thirty-dollar airport exit fee. Thirty different family members phoned me while I was there, and several invited me to lunch or dinner.

The members of Toyo's household—her daughter, Yōko, and her three grandchildren—took turns staying in her hospital room with her day and night. Whenever possible, they assembled in her private room to eat a take-out meal set on top of a cot, while Toyo, attached to tubes that performed most of her physiological functions and fed her intravenously, dozed in her bed, still a part of her household.

There were two nurses on the floor, but they handled only basic medical procedures, such as changing the intravenous tubes and checking bandages and blood pressure. Dressed in starched white uniforms, the nurses handed the thermometer or juice to Yōko and left. Yōko confidently catered to her mother's needs. Garbed in a smocklike apron, her face covered with a surgical mask, she placed ice in the water bottle, changed wet compresses, and spooned out a few tablespoons of rice gruel the way she had seen Toyo nurse her father, and her aunt Tami care for her uncle Shiro. One of the grand-children massaged Toyo's feet.

Although Toyo had told her doctor she did not want further surgery if the breast cancer spread, her doctor had lied about the cause of her intestinal ailment and persuaded her to go through with another operation. She continued to plead with him to let her die. In early March she almost succumbed to pneumonia. Her blood pressure plummeted, and she had no pulse. When doctors inserted a breathing tube, she signaled for a piece of paper and a pencil to write her request that they remove it because it was too painful. Yōko gave her consent, and the tube was removed. Toyo opened her eyes to see her sisters, who had rushed to the hospital to be with her at the end of her life, and she thanked them all: "Thank you, Yasuko. Thank you, Tamiko. . . . " Then she discussed funeral plans with then. But she did not die. By mid-March the oxygen tube and an antibiotic intravenous drip were taped to her nose. When she finally died on April 6, 1993, Yōko and one of her granddaughters were with her. Her other granddaughter wrote to me in English one week later: "I will try my best on everything and try to be a person like her. (I mean she always tried her best on everything and I want to be like that.)"

For Toyo's funeral, nearly one hundred black-clad relatives and friends converged by train on her church and later attended a memorial service. Among them was the seventy-four-year-old widow of her brother Yūshirō, who had traveled alone from Fukushima to Tokyo and fainted in the middle of the service. Tomoji, the oldest nephew and the thirteenth-generation heir of the main house of Matsuura, never came from Yamashiraishi to visit his aunt Toyo at the hospital or to attend her funeral service, which became yet another strike against him. He also failed to join the twenty-two relatives and several friends who assembled at the church in Tokyo for the tenth anniversary memorial service and afterward gathered in a department store restaurant for lunch.

Among the relatives attending the 2003 commemoration of Toyo's death, in addition to her daughter, grandchildren, and great-grandchildren, were her two remaining sisters and several nieces and nephews. Mina's oldest son and his wife came, as did Fuki's daughter and Fumi's three sons. The widow of Toyo's seventh brother was also there, as was the daughter of Toyo's uncle Ishii Itarō, the deceased former ambassador to Brazil. Tami was accompanied by her daughter and Yasu by her husband and widowed daughter-in-law.

Many of the family members whom I had known well were now gone;

others I had not seen for decades. A few, such as Mina's eldest son and Seishichirō's widow, knew of me, and I of them, but we had never met in person, even though I had already written about them in my manuscript. Now, magically, they became real, as though they were stepping off the pages to speak to me, like characters in a play. Like stage characters, too, they brought props to help establish their ties to me. Mina's son brought a framed photograph of his sister, Nobu, and me dressed in kimono for our tea ceremony class in 1964, a few years before Nobu died. I had given the picture to Mina in 1995 as a gift, and as soon as I saw it, I recognized the identity of the man giving it to me, because I knew that Mina had lived with her son and his wife until her death. Fumi's youngest son, whom I hadn't seen for over two decades, presented me with photographs he had taken of the Matsuura house in Yamashiraishi, organized in an album and accompanied by architectural sketches and an article on the house that had appeared a few years earlier in a Fukushima newspaper. Yasu's daughter-in-law dropped off a loaf of bread she had baked and reminded me that I had given her in-laws gifts for her children when I last saw them ten years earlier.

During the meal Yōko asked me, as the "person who had traveled the farthest," to say a few words to the assembled family members and friends. With no time to gather my thoughts, I could manage to say only that Toyo had been like a mother to me, and I regretted not having sufficiently thanked her while she was alive. In response, one of Toyo's nieces blurted out, "But you came to visit her in the hospital. That was enough."

As the niece's comment suggests, Toyo's relatives in the thirteenth generation and several members of the fourteenth generation continued to observe rules of participation in extended family rituals surrounding illness, weddings, and death. Family members are far fewer in number, however, and the younger generations are less willing to be coddled in the same way as I had been or to fall under the scrutiny of their elders and take their advice, though they have remained quite willing to take their money.

Despite the considerable turnout for Toyo's memorial service, the younger urban relatives showed signs that the close social network among the descendants of Isami and Kō was breaking down. In some cases more individualistic than their parents, the members of the fourteenth generation, in particular, are more likely to guard their private lives from judging, prying great-aunts and to avoid the interference and unwanted advice of grandmothers.

And advise they did, these daughters of Isami and Kō, with their parents' clear sense of right and wrong and commitment to kin work. Toyo's

grandson, who dropped out of high school three months short of graduation because he did not like school, became the object of much discussion
when his grand-aunts got together, and even I was asked to talk sense to
him. His grand-aunt Tami, employing a tactic Isami and Kō would have
appreciated, took him to the grave site of Toyo's in-laws. She showed him
the unkempt Ishikawa graves with the tall grass growing around them. "This
is what happens," she said to the young man with the long hair and mo-
torcycle, "when there is no male to continue the family. You are the only
male in both your grandfather's and your father's families." She told him
what her father, Isami, had told numerous other young men in his day: "You
must be more stouthearted." In other words, get your act together. She then
bought him guitar lessons, but he quit after three months.[1]

Grandnieces who slept with their boyfriends also raised eyebrows among
older family members, and so the information was kept from them if possible. Physical appearance was yet another subject of scrutiny for Isami's
daughters. His seventy-year-old daughter thought nothing of bluntly ad-
vising her fifty-year-old niece on how to dress better. Advice often was accompanied by assistance. Two of Yōko's uncles, possibly prompted by their
wives, took the initiative in asking Yōko's employer to give her some time
off to nurse her mother; they did not bother to consult with her first.

Such interference led at least one of Toyo's nieces to steer clear of relatives whenever possible and one of her granddaughters to shout angrily, "It's
none of your business," when probed about her private life. There was gos-
sip about mothers controlling their adult daughters and, conversely, adult
daughters controlling their elderly mothers. Toyo and one of her sisters were
exasperated with another sister for yielding to her daughter's whims. The
sister in point relished the opportunity to visit her siblings at their homes,
where she could talk freely after remaining quiet at home with her daughter and son-in-law (a man whom the sisters considered rude). On such occasions, however, her daughter would think up an excuse to call her back
home, at least in one sister's interpretation, and she would go "even before
finishing her noodles."

Yet, examples of harmony among several generations living under one
roof—the Confucian ideal that Isami espoused—survived. Fumi, Yasu, and
Mina all seemed to have worked out genial living arrangements with their
daughters-in-law, though Mina, in her nineties, said ruefully that she was
like the family dog; her son and his wife couldn't go anywhere without either taking her along or getting somebody to take care of her.

Family members did not always create patrilocal marriages. At least two men agreed to live with their Matsuura in-laws, either immediately after marrying or in their in-laws' later years. Toyo had planned to share her home with her daughter and son-in-law in her old age, and after Fuki was widowed, she built a house to share with her daughter and son-in-law. Tami's financially strapped daughter and son-in-law, far from insisting on their independence, begged to be taken into her house. Living with one's daughter, instead of daughter-in-law, did not necessarily guarantee greater harmony, however. The older women had no illusions about the trustworthiness of the younger generation and kept a tight grip on their savings accounts into their seventies and eighties.

Older women residing with their adult children and grandchildren confronted familial conflicts that one expects to find in many contemporary societies, with the younger generation resenting the interference of the older generation or feeling burdened by the time required to care for them, but Matsuura family members into the twenty-first century accepted these living arrangements, with their inevitable tensions, as both natural and practical. Young mothers had built-in babysitters; grandparents had security, assistance, and the pleasure of watching their grandchildren grow. Young couples unable to afford astronomically high Tokyo housing prices lived rent-free and with expectations of inheriting the house, which, with not too much difficulty, could be renovated periodically to meet changing family needs.

The cushioning effect of three-generational living patterns was apparent when Fumi's oldest son was transferred to Osaka to participate in his company's high-powered research project on genetic engineering. With housing at a premium and their children's schooling a top priority, his wife and two children stayed behind in Tokyo at the home of his parents. Fumi and her husband added a second-floor apartment to the house they had originally built after the war on the Nishigahara property, where Isami had built a house for his children's school days in Tokyo. After Fumi's husband died, she still had a secure family life in the neighborhood where she had lived for most of her adult years.

At least three of the women of the thirteenth generation, owing to divorce or early widowhood, found themselves dependent on their parents for both housing and child care. Toyo's daughter, Yōko, took an office job after her divorce; Tami's divorced daughter also worked outside the home; and Yasu's daughter-in-law, widowed young, learned how to bake bread in order to open her own baking school in their home, which had once belonged to Yasu's in-laws. The assistance of the grandparents in rearing the children was essential.

One option for healthy older women—to live alone—was not necessarily unappealing to the self-reliant, lively, and remarkably long-lived Matsuura sisters. In fact, Toyo used to flee her noisy house, with its three grandchildren, to stay for a few weeks at a small furnished apartment she rented in a resort for the elderly in the countryside two hours by train from Tokyo. Her youngest sister, Tami, relished living alone; if she had chores to do that were beyond her considerable abilities, she called on her reliable longtime handyman, who did everything from taking down the drapes and bringing them to the dry cleaners to mailing heavy packages at the post office. Once infirmity set in, however, these women expected to be cared for by their adult children, and they were.

Even in their old age and living with their children, the women helped around the house. Unlike their rural female ancestors, the Matsuura women did not need to prove their usefulness by weeding in the hot summertime, but they did feel the need to keep busy. Fuki washed and dried the dishes. Toyo cooked for her grandchildren until the day she entered the hospital for surgery, and in her early nineties Mina was sweeping in the garden of the home she shared with her son and daughter-in-law when she tripped on the garden step, fell, and broke her hip. She might have lived even longer had the operation been successful; informed that she would need a second operation if she wanted to walk again, she chose to take the chance on it rather than become immobilized. She died after the second surgery, but not before waking up to ask the children and grandchildren gathered around her hospital bed if she was already dead, and then thanking them all and telling them that she had enjoyed her long life.

Will the contemporary descendants of Isami and Kō be willing to accept arranged marriages and to live with their parents or in-laws? Other than asserting their desire to safeguard their private lives from the eyes of prying relatives, the few women born into the fourteenth generation voice only mild signs of rebellion or feminist consciousness. One area of revolt, however, concerns marriage.

By the 1990s, the great-granddaughters of Isami and Kō were resisting a marriage system that lacked sufficient attention to love, whatever the murky meaning of that word; after all, of the marriages that had been modeled for them in their parents' or grandparents' generation, few were based on physical and emotional intimacy of the sort Isami and Kō had enjoyed. Several of the fourteenth generation had lived in fatherless households because their parents had divorced or their father had died young or their father's work was in another city.

Choosing one's own marriage partner represents a mode of protest against the old marriage system. One of Toyo's granddaughters ignored her advice and chose a husband on her own, a man she had met through an electronic dating service. The other granddaughter, too, found a husband on her own at the office where they both worked, and her grandson also married a woman of his own choosing. Dating, premarital sex, and "love marriages" constitute new ingredients on the social scene for the younger generation of Matsuura women.

In the postwar period, even Isami softened his position on the issue of "love marriage," or individual choice of marriage partner as opposed to arranged marriage. In addition to accepting, however reluctantly, the marriage of his sixth son to a girlfriend, Isami agreed to intervene on behalf of Toyo's sister-in-law, who fell in love with the only child of parents unwilling to accept her because her father was deceased and her family had no money to bring to the union. Toyo was in favor of the marriage and persuaded Isami to mediate, but the man's parents would not be persuaded. Nevertheless, the couple married, and the man's mother, in her widowhood, found herself alone in another city, deprived of her son, daughter-in-law, and grandchildren. One day, the couple found a coffin outside their gate. In it was the widow's corpse. She had apparently left instructions to have her body shipped to her son's house after she died—shocking behavior to equal the shocking behavior of a son who married for love instead of allowing his parents to choose his wife.[2]

Resistance to the traditional marriage system also takes the form of delayed marriage, employment before marriage, and even childlessness after marriage. Typical of the generation at large, young women of the fourteenth generation of Matsuura are postponing marriage until their late twenties and even beyond, and they do not necessarily want to have children. Like their mothers and grandmothers, most, though not all, are college educated, but unlike their female ancestors, they seek careers and are unwilling to give up jobs for marriage. One college student is following in her father's footsteps as a science major, and another enjoys writing fiction. Tami's granddaughter, in her twenties and still living with Tami, is trying to enter the field of commercial photography. Yōko's daughter-in-law, in her early thirties and childless, is training to become a licensed home-care provider for the elderly. The need for professional elder care is itself a sign of changes in the family system.

Toyo's older granddaughter even expressed hopes of working after her children were born, though Japanese society does not provide many opportunities for career-minded mothers. After graduating from a business college in Japan, she worked in a Tokyo office for a few years and then enrolled in a liberal arts college in the United States. Called back to Japan to help nurse Toyo, she never finished her degree. A competent young woman fluent in English, she complained of a "glass ceiling" at her former job and despaired of ever being able to have a fulfilling career. In her late twenties, she married the white-collar worker she had met at her place of employment and settled down in company housing to raise a family. By the time her third child was born, she was resigned to being a full-time urban mother and the wife of a "salary man" preoccupied with his job, like her mother and grandmother before her. In this sense, she was unwittingly fulfilling her great-grandfather Isami's dream for his daughters: to become stay-at-home, financially secure, middle-class "good wives and wise mothers." But it was not her own dream. As her children grew older, her discontent resurfaced. Her husband, too, was unhappy and had gone through a period of depression. He had considered quitting his job, but he had no other options for supporting his family. When her youngest child entered kindergarten, she wrote in a letter to me, "Now I have more time to spend, and I'm lost. I don't know what to do."

Somehow the women of her grandmother Toyo's generation, despite the misfortunes that befell them, always knew what to do—or had other family members tell them. Moreover, the Matsuura sisters were proud of the jobs they had done as wives and mothers; they believed in playing by the rules. Many of these rules they had learned from their parents, especially from their father.

The Matsuura sisters admired those who worked hard, stayed active, and focused on admirable goals—whether these involved careers, professions, paid jobs, or childrearing—and did their jobs well and purposefully. These women appreciated competence, family loyalty, and, if not intellectual brilliance, at least studiousness and ambition: a go-getter personality. Toyo praised me for being able to read and write Japanese, and Tami lauded my dedication to scholarship, but the sisters also complimented Yasu's daughter-in-law for opening a baking school, and Tami thought highly of her husband's efficient, energetic niece, who put her children in daycare in order to return to her salaried job. The six Matsuura sisters themselves never stopped studying; into their eighties they took classes of one sort or another—English conversation, tea ceremony, yoga—studying with private teachers in small group settings.

Such purposefulness paralleled their husbands' hard-driving dedication to their managerial jobs or professions and reflected the government's focus on promoting Japan's economy and place in the world. Throughout the era of modern nation building, the period of empire, the trials of war and defeat, and the drive to recover after the war, the goals for everyone had been clear. But at the turn of the twenty-first century, with networks of relatives smaller and less cohesive and with the excessive dedication to the work ethic in question now that the country has achieved affluence, a sense of common purpose, shared values, and a fixed path eludes not only the younger generation of Matsuura but also, one suspects, Japan itself.

NOTES

PROLOGUE

1. Gary D. Allinson, "From Bureaucratic Imperium to Guardian Democracy: The Shifting Social Bases of Japanese Political Power, 1930–1960," in *The Social Construction of Democracy, 1870–1990,* ed. George Reid Andrews and Herrick Chapman (Washington Square, NY: New York University Press, 1995), 144.

2. Matsuura Isami, *Yamashiraishi mura o kataru* (Telling about Yamashiraishi village) (Tokyo: Bunshōdō, 1961), 1; hereafter cited as Isami, *Yamashiraishi.*

INTRODUCTION

1. Steven J. Ericson, "The Engine of Change: Railroads and Society in Meiji Japan," *KSU Economics and Business Review* 21 (May 1994): 55–56.

2. Isami, *Yamashiraishi,* 26.

3. The official was the former Asakawa intendant Watanabe Hironobu.

4. Isami, *Yamashiraishi,* 25.

5. Ann Bowman Jannetta, *Epidemics and Mortality in Early Modern Japan* (Princeton, NJ: Princeton University Press, 1987), 165–68.

6. Isami, *Yamashiraishi,* 26.

7. Ibid., 29.

8. Ibid., 25. For the Meiji school system, see *Encyclopedia Nipponica,* vol. 6 (Tokyo: Shogakkan, 1985), 797. From 1886 to 1907 students typically attended four years of public compulsory elementary school *(shogakkō)* starting at age six. The next level of (non-compulsory) public school was either the three-year upper elementary school *(kōtō-shogakkō),* or a lower vocational school, or, for college-bound male students, the five-year middle school *(chūgakkō).* Henry D. Smith, *Japan's First Radical Students* (Cambridge, MA: Harvard University Press, 1972), 2.

9. In 1889, a Kōriyama businessman noted that a toy he had seen in Tokyo in March of that year appeared in the Kōriyama area a month later. "That a fashionable item should spread this quickly to the provinces is really nothing but a result of the opening of the Tōhoku line," he said. See Ericson, "The Engine of Change," 55–56.

10. Isami, *Yamashiraishi,* 37.

11. Ibid., 2.

12. Matsuo Bashō, *Narrow Road to the Interior,* trans. Sam Hamill (Boston: Shambhala, 1991), 5.

13. Herman Ooms, *Charismatic Bureaucrat* (Chicago: University of Chicago Press, 1975), 155. Located in Iwaki province, Shirakawa was a *fudai* (vassal) domain (14).

14. The mode of payment for tax quotas consisted of rice itself but also other farm produce, money, labor corvée, or a combination of all of these.

15. Asakawa Chōshi Henkan Iinkai, ed., *Asakawa chōshi* (History of Asakawa township) 3 vols., vol. 2: *Shiryōhen* (Compilation of historical materials) (Asakawa: Fukushima-ken, Ishikawa-gun, Asakawa-machi, 1997), 964–65; hereafter cited as *Asakawa chōshi,* 2. A *koku* is a unit of measure equaling approximately five bushels. Used as the basis on which the tribute was calculated, however, it referred not only to rice production but also to the estimated yield of all products, converted into rice equivalents. Yamashiraishi's assessed yield in this period was 1,446 *koku.* See *Kadokawa Nihon chimei daijiten* (Kadokawa encyclopedia of Japanese notables), vol. 7: *Fukushima-ken* (Fukushima prefecture) (Tokyo: Kadokawa shoten, 1971), 830.

16. *Asakawa chōshi,* 2:642–44.

17. Edward E. Pratt, *Japan's Protoindustrial Elite: The Economic Foundations of the Gōnō* (Cambridge, MA: Harvard University Press, 1999), 57. For forced loans in the 1860s, see also William Chambliss, *Chiaraijima Village* (Tucson: University of Arizona Press, 1965).

18. The Dutch, confined to a small artificial island off Nagasaki, had been the only Westerners allowed to trade with Japan.

19. Shibusawa Eiichi, *The Autobiography of Shibusawa Eiichi: From Peasant to Entrepreneur,* trans. Teruko Craig (Tokyo: Tokyo University Press, 1994), 17.

20. Peter Duus, *Modern Japan,* 2nd ed. (Boston: Houghton Mifflin, 1998), 71.

21. F. G. Notehelfer, ed., *Japan through American Eyes: The Journal of Francis Hall, 1859–1866* (Boulder, CO: Westview Press, 2001), 329.

22. Ibid., 325–26.

23. *Asakawa chōshi,* vol. 1: *Tsūshi Kakuronhen* (Compilation of survey histories—itemized discussions) (Asakawa: Fukushima-ken, Ishikawa-gun, Asakawa-machi, 1999), 609–15; hereafter cited as *Asakawa chōshi,* 1.

24. Pratt, *Japan's Protoindustrial Elite,* 142.

25. Stephen Vlastos, *Peasant Protests and Uprisings in Tokugawa Japan* (Berkeley: University of California Press, 1986), 142–43. See too Shiba Gorō, *Remembering Aizu,* ed. Ishimitsu Mahito, trans. and with intro. and notes by Teruko Craig (Honolulu: University of Hawaii Press, 1999); and Diana E. Wright, "Female Combatants and Japan's Meiji Restoration: The Case of Aizu," *War in History* 8, no. 4 (2001): 396–417. The Aizu *daimyō* was Matsudaira Katamori.

26. *Asakawa chōshi,* 1:609–15.

27. Ibid., 2:1091–92, from Jinsuke's report to Asakawa officials.

28. Ibid., 1:613–15. Jinsuke was renamed Kōemon, the third Matsuura patriarch to carry that name. (Daisuke also took it in his adult years.) To avoid confusion, I will

continue to refer to the eighth generation head as Daisuke and the ninth generation as Jinsuke.

29. At first the newly created prefecture was called Old Fukushima; in 1876 it became simply Fukushima. Also in 1876, Asakawa became part of Fukushima, after its control as an administrative office had been transferred to the new imperial government in 1868.

30. Kerry Smith, *A Time of Crisis: Japan, the Great Depression, and Rural Revitalization* (Cambridge, MA: Harvard University Press, 2001), 26.

31. Isami, *Yamashiraishi,* 25.

32. Ibid.

33. *Kadokawa Nihon chimei daijiten,* vol. 7: *Fukushima-ken,* 830.

34. Isami, *Yamashiraishi,* 31.

35. Robert W. Bowen, *Rebellion and Democracy in Meiji Japan* (Berkeley: University of California Press, 1980), 8–9, 10–20, and passim.

36. The Three New Laws (Sanshinpō), announced in 1878, established a new system of local administration, covering the organization of counties, districts, towns and villages, prefectural assemblies, and local taxes. See Kurt Steiner, *Local Government in Japan* (Stanford, CA: Stanford University Press, 1965), 30–32. County chiefs were given supervisory power over the village and township assemblies.

37. *Asakawa chōshi,* 1:492–94.

38. Neil Waters, *Japan's Local Pragmatists: The Transition from Bakumatsu to Meiji in the Kawasaki Region* (Cambridge, MA: Harvard University Press, 1983), 83–87. See too James C. Baxter, *The Meiji Unification through the Lens of Ishikawa Prefecture* (Cambridge, MA: Council on East Asian Studies, Harvard University, 1994).

39. James C. Baxter, *The Meiji Unification through the Lens of Ishikawa Prefecture* (Cambridge, MA: Harvard University Press, 1994), 183.

40. Waters, *Japan's Local Pragmatists,* 89.

41. James L. McClain, *A Modern History of Japan* (New York: W. W. Norton, 2002), 193.

42. Isami, *Yamashiraishi,* 32.

43. Ibid.

44. Ibid. In later years he served a four-year term as a high-ranking officer in the Fukushima Agricultural-Industrial Bank.

I. THE HOUSE ISAMI BUILT

1. Isami, *Yamashiraishi,* 37–38.

2. Jukichi Inouye, *Home Life in Tokyo* (London: Pacific Basin Books, 1985; orig. pub. in Tokyo, 1910), 40–41. Tatami are like straw mattresses, about an inch and a half thick and bordered with cloth. Because tatami are all uniform in size, rooms are built in reference to the number of tatami they will contain.

3. *Fukushima minkō* (Fukushima people's well-being), August 23, 1999, 3.

4. Isami, *Yamashiraishi,* 1.

5. Isami, *Yamashiraishi*, 28. Yoshi died at the age of fifty-five. Isami wrote that the name of Jinsuke's second wife did not appear in the family registry, implying his grandfather may not have officially remarried.

6. Ibid., 56.

7. Isami wrote that Yajibei was accompanied by his older sister and "Asakawa mother-in-law." I am assuming he mistakenly wrote the character for older sister rather than wife, because later in his account he refers to the fine penmanship of Yajibei's wife but makes no further reference to a sister.

8. The population of the Tōhoku district overall appears to have increased in the seventeenth century, however. See James W. White, *The Demography of Sociopolitical Conflict in Japan, 1721–1846* (Berkeley: Institute of East Asian Studies, University of California, 1992), 16.

9. Isami, *Yamashiraishi*, 7. The assessed rice yield was 1,355 *koku* in 1594. See *Kadokawa Nihon chimei daijiten*, vol. 7: *Fukushima-ken*, 830.

10. Ooms, *Charismatic Bureaucrat*, 157.

11. Vlastos, *Peasant Protests and Uprisings*, 33. Vlastos reports that the first comprehensive surveys of Fukushima were conducted in 1590 by Toyotomi Hideyoshi. Subsequent surveys raised the amount of estimated yield for tax purposes. In the Shindatsu (northern) part of Fukushima, "frequent surveys during the seventeenth century raised productivity estimates substantially" (30). Peasants from the Shirakawa village of Nakahata in 1712 complained in a petition to the *bakufu* that four times in the past thirty-four years, officials had carried out new cadastral surveys. Over that period, the population had dropped from 900 to 712 residents.

12. Ooms, *Charismatic Bureaucrat*, 156.

13. *Asakawa chōshi*, 1:443–52, describes Honda's "notorious system of strict land tax collection."

14. Ooms, *Charismatic Bureaucrat*, 157–58.

15. *Asakawa chōshi*, 1:443–47.

16. Yamashiraishi in Toyotomi's time was in Aizu domain. It then fell under Shirakawa rule. In 1662 Yamashiraishi became part of the domain of Asakawa, but by the time of Yajibei, it once again was part of Shirakawa, this time under a new lord, Matsudaira Tadahiro.

17. *Asakawa chōshi*, 1:452.

18. Isami, *Yamashiraishi*, 9; and *Asakawa chōshi*, 1:471.

19. *Asakawa chōshi*, 1:464. The new governor was Matsudaira Tadahiro.

20. *Asakawa chōshi*, 1:466–68.

21. Ooms, *Charismatic Bureaucrat*, 160, mentions another village in Shirakawa—Yumoto—that complained about Honda's land survey as late as 1868.

22. Isami, *Yamashiraishi*, 1.

23. *Asakawa chōshi*, 1:471 and 1332; and Isami, *Yamashiraishi*, 1. In the Tokugawa period, village heads were called *shōya* in the Kansai, or southwestern, part of Japan and more commonly *nanushi* in the east and north. After the Tokugawa period, new terms were introduced. The surviving members of the Matsuura family use the term *shōya*, whereas an article about the family published in 1929 called them *nanushi*.

24. Isami, *Yamashiraishi,* 9; interview with Kawaoto Shohei, in Asakawa, 1993; and *Asakawa chōshi,* 1:1332.

25. Herman Ooms, *Tokugawa Village Practice* (Berkeley: University of California Press, 1996), 79. Ooms gives arson and thievery as examples of crimes punished by execution (224). Anne Walthall describes execution of peasants by decapitation, in *Peasant Uprisings in Japan* (Chicago: University of Chicago Press, 1991), 64.

26. Isami, *Yamashiraishi,* 9.

27. Ibid. The ninety representatives were probably the househeads of the landowning households in the village.

28. Uezawa Kenji, "Yon fūfu jūyon jikka hanjōki, Fukushima ken no yamaoku ni Toyotomi Taikō jidai kara renmen to shite sakaeru Matsuura-shi o otonaou" (A record of a prosperous family of fourteen children and of four couples [i.e., generations] living together), *Fujin no tomo* 23, no. 1 (1929): 62. Toyotomi took over the part of Date's territory that is present-day Ishikawa-gun.

29. Uezawa does not provide documentation for the Matsuura claim of descent from warrior ancestry. It is possible that the family's account was a fabrication. Village headmen typically claimed to have samurai ancestry. On the other hand, Asakawa town historian Kawaoto Shōhei found the title of *gōshi* listed next to Yajibei's name in a document in his possession. The *-ji-* in Yajibei's name suggests he was the second son.

30. Isami, *Yamashiraishi,* 10.

31. Ibid.

32. Ibid.; and *Shishin shōbanshō* (Record of all memorable events), compiled by Asakawa-chō chūō kōminkan kobunsho kyōshitsu hen (Asakawa: Henshu Iinkai Iinchō, 1991), 31, item no. 28.

33. Isami, *Yamashiraishi,* 1.

34. Village heads and their staffs were paid salaries. Isami suggests that Yūya did not take his. Yūya may have drawn from a special community tax to pay office expenses, however.

35. Isami, *Yamashiraishi,* 32.

36. Ibid., 31; and *Kadokawa Nihon chimei daijiten,* vol. 7: *Fukushima-ken,* 830.

37. Marius B. Jansen and Gilbert Rozman, "Overview, " in *Japan in Transition, from Tokugawa to Meiji,* ed. Jansen and Rozman (Princeton, NJ: Princeton University Press, 1986), 24.

38. Interview with Oteru, Yamashiraishi, 1993.

39. *Kadokawa Nihon chimei daijiten,* vol. 7: *Fukushima-ken,* 830.

40. Baxter, *The Meiji Unification,* 194–95.

41. Atsuko Hirai, "The Legitimacy of Tokugawa Rule as Reflected in Its Family Laws," *Hōgaku kenkyū* 65, no. 11 (November 1992): 15–16.

42. Isami, *Yamashiraishi,* 12. A high percentage of married people at the time actually lived to age seventy, according to data from the period of 1721–1846. See Hayami Akira and Kurosu Satomi, "Regional Diversity in Demographic and Family Patterns in Preindustrial Japan," *Journal of Japanese Studies* 27, no. 2 (Summer 2001): 311.

43. *Daimyō* governments often offered lower taxes for several years as incentive for

land reclamation. Patricia Sippel, "Chisui: Creating a Sacred Domain in Early Modern and Modern Japan," in *Public Spheres, Private Lives in Modern Japan: Essays in Honor of Albert M. Craig,* ed. Gail Lee Bernstein, Andrew Gordon, and Kate Nakai (Cambridge, MA: Harvard University Press, 2005), 160.

44. Isami, *Yamashiraishi*, 12.

45. *Shishin shōbanshō*, 111, item no. 57. Original plans called for building the administrative office *(jinya)* in Ishikawa, but owing to a tendency for the Ishikawa river to flood, Asakawa was chosen instead.

46. *Shishin shōbanshō*, 92, item no. 50.

47. See Vlastos, *Peasant Protests and Uprisings,* ch. 3. In one instance in 1720, a crowd of several hundred marched to the intendant's office in the town of Tajima, west of Shirakawa, with a petition addressing five grievances, including the high tax, and calling for the abolition of the office of chief headman (51).

48. *Asakawa chōshi*, 1:481–84 and 492–94; and Kobayashi Seiji and Yamada Akira, eds., *Fukushima-ken no rekishi* (A history of Fukushima prefecture), vol. 7 of *Kenshi shirizu* (Prefectural history series) (Tokyo: Yamakawa shuppansha, 1975), 130.

2 . KISSING COUSINS

1. Isami, *Yamashiraishi*, 38. The marriage was registered several months later.

2. Information on Kō's marriage comes from a 1937 published article featuring the Matsuura family and found in Toyo's house. The source is unknown but is probably a women's magazine. The article, which appears to be one in a series on childrearing, is illustrated by photographs of Isami, Kō, and their fourteen surviving children. Kō had most likely been in a "higher school," which, for women, was the equivalent of middle school. In the mid-1890s, there were only seven women's higher schools in Japan. By 1900, there were forty-five, one for each prefecture, with a total of ten thousand enrolled students. The entrance requirement was six years of primary school education. The course of study was four years, though some girls took less time and others more. Girls usually graduated at seventeen. See, Byron K. Marshall, *Learning to Be Modern* (Boulder: Westview Press, 1994), 63.

3. Hayami and Kurosu, "Regional Diversity in Demographic and Family Patterns in Preindustrial Japan," 305–6; and Harald Fuess, *Divorce in Japan: Family, Gender, and the State, 1600–2000* (Stanford, CA: Stanford University Press, 2004), 135.

4. For Fukuzawa's views on women, see Eiichi Kiyoka, trans. and ed., *Fukuzawa Yukichi on Japanese Women* (Tokyo: Tokyo University Press, 1988).

5. Marius B. Jansen, *The Making of Modern Japan* (Cambridge, MA: Harvard University Press, 2000), 470; Ian Nish, *Origins of the Russo-Japanese War* (London: Longman, 1985), 2.

6. John K. Fairbank, Edwin O. Reischauer, and Albert M. Craig, *East Asia: The Modern Transformation* (Boston: Houghton Mifflin, 1965), 481. The Japanese public was disappointed with the treaty provisions, however, and protested.

7. Unnamed 1937 published magazine article found in Toyo's house.

8. Private correspondence with Anne Walthall, October 11, 2000.

9. For this reason, female educator Tsuda Ume added *ko* to her name in 1902, when she established her own independent household. See Yoshiko Furuki, *The White Plum: A Biography of Ume Tsuda, Pioneer in the Higher Education of Japanese Women* (New York: Weatherhill, 1991), 107.

10. Interview with Yasu, 1993. All interviews with Matsuura family members took place in 1993, 1995, and 2003. Although I have presented a year with each interview citation, in some cases the information referenced is actually a consolidation from interviews with that person in one or both of the other years, when he or she was asked to elaborate on a certain question.

11. Interview with Mina, 1995.

12. Hayami and Kurosu, "Regional Diversity in Demographic and Family Patterns in Preindustrial Japan," 306, using records from Nihonmatsu and Aizu domains.

13. *Asakawa chōshi*, 2:486, figures for 1754.

14. Isami, *Yamashiraishi*, 12–13.

15. Ann Waswo, *Japanese Landlords: The Decline of a Rural Elite* (Berkeley: University of California Press, 1977), 14–15.

16. *Shishin shōbanshō*, 35, item no. 31. Herman Ooms, *Tokugawa Village Practice* (Berkeley: University of California Press, 1996), 132, reports that as late as the 1820s, only 44 commoners from 266 villages in one domain were granted the privilege of using their surname, and in another domain, only 2 out of 871 village officials were granted the privilege.

17. Isami, *Yamashiraishi*, 16–17.

18. *Asakawa chōshi*, 2:1152. Isami does not mention the adoption of Mitsu. I am assuming that she is the (unnamed) wife of Yūemon, whom he briefly mentions, though there is an age discrepancy between his reference to the wife and the recorded age of Mitsu in the documents.

19. Atsuko Hirai, "The Legitimacy of Tokugawa Rule as Reflected in Its Family Laws," 164 (29)–165 (30).

20. Anne Walthall, personal correspondence, October 11, 1998.

21. Anne Walthall, "The Family Ideology of the Rural Entrepreneurs in Nineteenth Century Japan," *Journal of Social History* 23, no. 2 (Spring 1989): 463.

22. Only rarely did father and eldest son bear the same personal name at the same time. This happened in the fifth generation, when Yūemon's adopted son-in-law, first called Sōemon, later took the name Yūemon, written with the same characters as the name of the fourth-generation patriarch and with the added name of Jinsuke to distinguish him even more clearly from his adoptive father.

3. FATHER OF THE VILLAGE

1. Uezawa, "Yon fūfu jūyonji ikka hanjōki," 60–61. Portions of this chapter were originally published in Gail Lee Bernstein, "Matsuura Isami: A Modern Patriarch in Rural Japan," in *The Human Tradition in Modern Japan,* ed. Anne Walthall (Wil-

mington, DE: Scholarly Resources, 2002), 137–53. Permission for use has been granted by Rowman & Littlefield, of which Scholarly Resources is now a part.

2. Uezawa, "Yon fūfu jūyonji ikka hanjōki," 65.

3. Ibid.

4. Fukuzawa Yukichi, "The New Greater Learning for Women," in *Fukuzawa Yukichi on Japanese Women,* trans. and ed., Kiyoka, 221.

5. Fukuzawa, "Early Marriage or Late Marriage," ibid., 133–34.

6. Interviews with Tami, Yasu, and Fuki, 1995.

7. Uezawa, "Yon fūfu jūyonji ikka hanjōki," 64.

8. Ibid., 65.

9. See Harald Fuess, "Men's Place in the Women's Kingdom: New Middle-Class Fatherhood in Taishō Japan," in *Public Spheres, Private Lives,* ed. Bernstein, Gordon, and Nakai, 270–71.

10. Interview with Tami, 1995.

11. Interview with Yasu, 1995.

12. Fukuzawa, "The New Greater Learning for Women," 220–21.

13. A distinction is made in Joelle Bahloul, *The Architecture of Memory: A Jewish-Muslim Household in Colonial Algeria, 1937–1962* (Cambridge: Cambridge University Press, 1966), 57, in regard to the Jewish father in Algeria, who was both authoritative and oppressive.

14. Matsuura Kōjirō, *Indoneshia sanjūnen* (Indonesia: thirty years) (Tokyo: Jigyō no nihonsha, 1977), 5. Hereafter, Kōjirō, *Indoneshia sanjūnen.*

15. This is how Yamazaki Fumio, the Buddhist priest of Chōtoku Temple, spoke of Isami as late as the summer of 1995, when I interviewed him in Yamashiraishi.

16. Interview with Oteru, 1993.

17. Smith, *A Time of Crisis,* 22.

18. Conrad Totman, *Early Modern Japan* (Berkeley: University of California Press, 1993), 239–40.

19. John Whitney Hall, *Tanuma Okitsugu* (Cambridge, MA: Harvard University Press, 1955), 126.

20. *Asakawa chōshi,* 1:520–21; and Hall, *Tanuma Okitsugu,* 122.

21. Ooms, *Charismatic Bureaucrat,* 56.

22. Totman, *Early Modern Japan,* 244. Totman writes that Matsudaira diverted rice from other needy places such as Sōma, adding to that domain's famine.

23. Isami, *Yamashiraishi,* 15. Isami's estimates differ slightly from statistics in *Kadokawa Nihon chimei daijiten,* vol. 7: *Fukushima-ken,* 830, which lists Yamashiraishi in 1802 as having 107 households and a total population of 506.

24. Isami, *Yamashiraishi,* 15.

25. *Asakawa chōshi,* 2:613.

26. Ibid., 2:484.

27. Ibid., 2:486; and Anne Walthall, *The Weak Body of a Useless Woman: Matsuo Taseko and the Meiji Restoration* (Chicago: University of Chicago Press), 65. In the first half of the eighteenth century, the average number of children per family in Nihon-

matsu domain was even fewer; many couples had fewer than three. See Hayami and Kurosu, "Regional Diversity in Demographic and Family Patterns in Preindustrial Japan," 306. These authors also report an extremely low age at marriage in this region: age thirteen for women and age nineteen for men during the first half of the eighteenth century, increasing to age seventeen for women toward the end of the Tokugawa period (305–6).

28. Isami, *Yamashiraishi*, 14–15.

29. Isami writes that in 1769 Yūemon signed a document with only his given name, but a document dated 1775 bears the surname Matsuura (ibid., 15).

30. Walthall, *Weak Body*, 11, quoting Marius B. Jansen, "The Meiji Restoration," in *The Cambridge History of Japan*, vol. 5: *The Nineteenth Century* (Cambridge: Cambridge University Press, 1989), 320.

31. Isami, *Yamashiraishi*, 14.

32. Ibid., 70. The three other villages, in addition to the previously mentioned Itabashi and Satoshiraishi, were Fukisaku, Minami Yamashiraishi, and Kita Yamagata, in each of which the population barely reached two hundred.

33. Herman Ooms, *Tokugawa Village Practice: Class, Status, Power, Law* (Berkeley: University of California Press, 1996), 7.

34. Uezawa, "Yon fūfu jūyonji ikka hanjōki," 65.

35. Ibid., 63.

36. From photograph albums in the Matsuura family farmhouse.

37. Isami, *Yamashiraishi*, 31–32.

38. Ishii Itarō, *Gaikōkan no isshō* (My life as a diplomat), reprint (1950; Tokyo: Taihei shuppansha, 1974), 15.

39. Barbara J. Brooks describes the "aristocratic" style of career diplomats in *Japan's Imperial Diplomacy: Consuls, Treaty Ports, and War in China, 1895–1938* (Honolulu: University of Hawaii Press, 2000), 51.

40. Interviews with Yōko, 1993, and with Kawasaki Fumio, 1993.

41. Vlastos, *Peasant Protests and Uprisings*, 78.

42. *Asakawa chōshi*, 1:504–11.

43. Bowen, *Rebellion and Democracy*, 75.

44. *Asakawa chōshi*, 2:1014.

45. Ibid., 1:509.

46. *Asakawa chōshi*, 1:562, lists eighty-two horses in Yamashiraishi in 1809.

47. Karen Wigen, *The Making of a Japanese Periphery, 1750–1920* (Berkeley: University of California Press, 1995), 50.

48. Isami, *Yamashiraishi*, 19–20.

49. Suggested by Anne Walthall in private communication, October 11, 1998.

50. *Asakawa chōshi*, 1:510–11. The full version of the original text, "Asakawa sōdō nōmin ikki no kiroku" (A record of the Asakawa disturbance and farmers' uprising), dated January 1798, appears in *Asakawa chōshi*, 2:1014–36. The author is unknown.

51. *Asakawa chōshi*, 1:506.

52. Ibid., 1:504–11.

53. Chambliss, *Chiaraijima Village*, 143. Examples include permission to conduct official business, often on a monopoly basis.

54. *Asakawa chōshi*, 1:507.

55. Ibid., 1:504–511, 559.

56. Pratt, *Japan's Protoindustrial Elite*, 2.

57. *Asakawa chōshi*, 2:830. Available records do not indicate how the Matsuura village head ruled on this request.

58. *Shishin shōbanshō*, 80–90, item no. 48, from an eleven-page diary written between the eighth and the eleventh months of 1805.

59. Ibid.

60. Brett L. Walker, "Commercial Growth and Environmental Change in Early Modern Japan: Hachinohe's Wild Boar Famine of 1749," *Journal of Asian Studies* 60, no. 2 (May 2001): 346.

61. *Asakawa chōshi*, 2:842.

4. STRONG WIVES

1. Interview with Tami, 1995.

2. Isami, *Yamashiraishi*, 42.

3. Recollections of Kō and the household are from interviews with Tami, 1993 and 1995.

4. Isami, *Yamashiraishi*, 20.

5. Hayami and Kurosu, "Regional Diversity in Demographic and Family Patterns in Preindustrial Japan," 306. In two northeastern villages studied by Noriko O. Tsuya and Saomi Kurosu, the average age that women stopped giving birth was around thirty-three. See "Reproduction and Family Building Strategies in Eighteenth- and Nineteenth-Century Rural Japan: Evidence from Two Northeastern Villages," quoted in Hayami and Kurosu, ibid., 307.

6. Isami, *Yamashiraishi*, 20.

7. *Asakawa chōshi*, 2:796.

8. Ibid.

9. Isami, *Yamashiraishi*, 20.

10. Vlastos, *Peasant Protests and Uprisings*, describes the plight of six villages in northern Shindatsu in 1857, when the *bakufu* assumed direct control over their villages (79).

11. *Kadokawa Nihon chimei daijiten*, vol. 7: *Fukushima-ken*, 830. The text says, "The Matsuura, being *shōya*, became *ōjōya*." This is confusing, because the Matsuura, according to another text, were already *ōjōya*. Possibly the meaning is that Yūemon Jinsuke was asked to continue in his adoptive father's footsteps as league headman.

12. Isami, *Yamashiraishi*, 22–23.

13. It is unclear whether the family chronicler was using the Japanese or Western practice for determining age. There is also a discrepancy in Teizō's year of birth: 1805 or 1807.

14. *Asakawa chōshi*, 1:1337. As previously discussed, one of his descendants, the tenth-

generation patriarch, Yūya, was memorialized for having introduced tobacco, so possibly these earlier efforts of Yūemon Jinsuke did not take hold.

15. Ibid., 2:616–18. It isn't clear whether he founded the granary in 1824. Documents simply report a village collection in that year.

16. There is a discrepancy between Isami's account and the account in *Kadokawa Nihon chimei daijiten*, vol. 7: *Fukushima-ken*, as to whether the *bakufu*'s direct rule began in 1809 or in 1823, and, therefore, it is unclear in which of these two years Yūemon Jinsuke first had to deal with changes in the transport of the rice tribute.

17. *Asakawa chōshi*, 1:575–85.

18. Ibid., 1:586.

19. Isami, *Yamashiraishi*, 20–22.

20. Ibid., 22–24.

21. Walthall, *The Weak Body of a Useless Woman*, documents the dowry and trousseau of wealthy peasant women around 1830 (64).

22. Isami, *Yamashiraishi*, 24.

23. Ibid., 24–25.

24. Akira Hayami, "Population Changes," in *Japan in Transition*, ed. Jansen and Rozman, 295.

25. *Asakawa chōshi*, 2:637.

26. E. S. Crawcour and Kozo Yamamura, "The Tokugawa Monetary System: 1787–1868," in *Economic Development and Cultural Change*, Part I, 18, no. 4 (July 1970): 507.

27. Susan B. Hanley, *Everyday Things in Premodern Japan: The Hidden Legacy of Material Culture* (Berkeley: University of California Press, 1999), 20–21. Hanley's information comes from a tenant farmer's budget in the 1840s.

28. Isami, *Yamashiraishi*, 22–23.

29. Ibid., 24.

30. Ibid., 22–24.

31. Ibid., 24.

32. Ibid., 27. The firstborn daughter was married into the Inoue family, with whom the Matsuura had longstanding ties through marriage and adoption.

33. "Matsuura Kōemon Nikko-Edo dōchū nikki" (Matsuura Kōemon Nikko-Edo travel diary), in *Asakawa chōshi*, 2:955–68. Hereafter cited as "Matsuura Kōemon nikki."

34. Private correspondence received from Barbara Ambros, April 24, 2000.

35. Robert S. Ellwood and Richard Pilgraim, *Japanese Religion: A Cultural Perspective* (Englewood-Cliffs, NJ: Prentice-Hall, 1985), 14.

36. The couple was probably traveling without a religious guide, or *oishi*, the low Shinto priest who ordinarily provided lodgings for pilgrims, distributed shrine charms, offered prayers, and led pilgrims to the shrine sanctuaries. See Sokyo Ono, *Shinto: The Kami Way* (Rutland, VT: Charles E. Tuttle, 1967), 94–95.

37. George Wilson, "Pursuing the Millennium," in *Conflict in Modern Japanese History*, ed. Tetsuo Najita and J. Victor Koschmann (Princeton, NJ: Princeton University Press, 1982), 178–79.

38. Isami, *Yamashiraishi*, 24.

1. Article about the family found in Toyo's home, published 1937. Source and page numbers unknown. Hereafter cited as 1937 article.

2. Ibid.

3. Ibid.

4. David R. Ambaras, "Social Knowledge, Cultural Capital, and the New Middle Class in Japan, 1895–1912," *Journal of Japanese Studies* 24, no. 1 (1998): 6–7.

5. Margit Nagy, "Middle-Class Working Women," in *Recreating Japanese Women,* ed. Gail Lee Bernstein (Berkeley: University of California Press, 1991), 201.

6. See Fuess, "Men's Place in the Women's Kingdom," 280–85.

7. See Jordan Sand, *House and Home in Modern Japan: Architecture, Domestic Space, and Bourgeois Culture, 1880–1930* (Cambridge, MA: Harvard University Press, 2003).

8. Marshall, *Learning to Be Modern,* 137–38. The figure is for 1935. Marshall explains that the definition of "higher education" varies. In the same year, there were approximately 384,000 students in girls' "higher schools," the level before college. The proportion of the population enrolled in the tertiary level of education in the 1930s was only 0.3 percent, but was still twice as high as the proportion in Britain and France.

9. As quoted in Christine R. Yano, "Defining the Japanese Nation in Popular Song," in *Japan's Competing Modernities: Issues in Culture and Democracy, 1900–1930,* ed. Sharon A. Minichiello (Honolulu: University of Hawaii Press, 1998), 253.

10. Figures for the fatalities vary. The Bureau of Social Affairs estimated 200,000 dead. Bureau of Social Affairs, *The Great Earthquake of 1923* (Tokyo: Home Office, 1926), ii. Edwin O. Reischauer estimates fatalities at 130,000 in his *Japan: The Story of a Nation,* 4th ed. (New York: McGraw-Hill, 1990), 144. Still others list the total dead as 91,000. Edward Seidensticker writes that the death toll is not known, but the highest estimates for Tokyo alone are around 100,000. See his *Low City, High City, Tokyo from Edo to the Earthquake: How the Shogun's Ancient Capital Became a Great Modern City, 1867–1923* (Cambridge, MA: Harvard University Press, 1991), 4. Reports on the magnitude of the earthquake also vary. *The Japan Times International,* August 19–25, 1991, claimed the Great Kantō Earthquake registered 7.9 on the Richter scale. The initial shock waves knocked out the seismograph at Japan's Central Weather Bureau.

11. Interviews with Fuki, 1993, 1995.

12. Seidensticker, *Low City, High City,* 4.

13. Interviews with Fuki and Tami, 1995.

14. Sally Hastings, "Atomi Kakei (1840–1926) and Women's Education in Japan," unpublished manuscript, 11.

15. Ronald P. Dore, *Shinohata* (New York: Pantheon Books, 1978), 135.

16. Ibid.

17. Marshall, *Learning to Be Modern,* 77.

18. Jonathan Sand, "At Home in the Meiji Period: Inventing Japanese Domesticity," in *Mirror of Modernity: Invented Traditions of Modern Japan,* ed. Stephen Vlastos (Berkeley: University of California Press, 1998), 191–207.

19. Sharon Sievers, *Flowers in Salt* (Stanford, CA: Stanford University Press, 1983), 164–65.

20. Hani Gyo, quoted by Teresa Watanabe, "Aptly Named Freedom School Goes against Scholastic Grain," *Los Angeles Times,* Sunday, June 24, 1990, D11.

21. Interview with Horiuchi Yōko, August 2003. Hereafter, her interviews are cited with her given name only.

22. A catalog of Wright's designs shows the school name as Giyu Gakuen rather than Jiyū Gakuen and translates it as "the School of the Free Spirit"; the date of the design is listed as 1921. Paul Laseau and James Tice, *Frank Lloyd Wright: Between Principle and Form* (New York: Van Nostrand and Reinhold, 1992), 193. Hani contacted Wright through his associate Endō Arata. Endō's design for a model middle-class house appeared in a volume entitled *Risō no katei* (The ideal home), which accompanied a home exposition to which Hani Motoko contributed model room interiors in 1915. See Sand, "At Home in the Meiji Period," 206.

23. Eleanor M. Hadley, *Memoir of a Trustbuster: A Lifelong Adventure with Japan* (Honolulu: University of Hawaii Press, 2002), 25.

24. Interview with Yōko, 2003.

25. Interviews with Toyo's classmates Shiba Miyoko and Sugiura Sugako, 1993.

26. Gael Graham, "Exercising Control: Sports and Physical Education in American Protestant Mission Schools in China, 1880–1930," *Signs, Journal of Women in Culture and Society* 20, no. 1 (Autumn 1994): 34.

27. Interviews with Shiba Miyoko and Sugiura Sugako, 1993.

28. Ibid.

29. Hadley, *Memoir of a Trustbuster,* 28. By the late 1930s, however, Hadley found a greater sense of intellectual freedom at Tsuda (29).

30. The term *Taishō chic* derives from the Honolulu Academy of Arts exhibition titled "Taishō Chic: Japanese Modernity, Nostalgia, and Deco," in 2002. See the book of the same title published by the academy in 2001 in conjunction with the exhibit.

31. Interview with Yōko, 2003.

32. The number of female white-collar workers employed in government offices, for example, increased from sixteen thousand in 1920 to thirty thousand in 1930. Between 1911 and 1926, the number of female nurses increased more than fourfold, from thirteen thousand to fifty-seven thousand. The greatest increase in the employment category of "public servant" was in female teachers, especially at girls' schools. See Nagy, "Middle-Class Working Women during the Interwar Years," 201–3.

33. Interview with Yōko, 2003.

34. Ibid.

6. THE MARRIAGE PIPELINE

1. Interview with Matsuura Masako, Yūshirō's widow, 1995.

2. *Seijika Jinmei Jiten* (Japanese statesmen: a biographical dictionary) (Tokyo: Nichi-

gai Asoshietsu, 1990), 44. Ishiwata Eijirō studied under Katsu Kaishū, a leader in the modernization of the Japanese navy. See also Ishiwata Sōtarō denki hensenkai, ed., *Ishiwata Sōtarō* (Tokyo, 1954).

3. Interview with Mina, 1995.

4. Correspondence with Tami, 2003.

5. Information on Masafumi is drawn from Toyo's conversations with me in 1963; and interviews with her youngest sister, Tami, in 1993 and 1995; with her daughter, Yōko, in 1995 and 2003; and with her friend Ibuka Yuriko in 1993.

6. Interview with Fuki, 1995.

7. Edward Seidensticker, *Tokyo Rising: The City since the Great Earthquake* (Cambridge, MA: Harvard University Press, 1990), 68ff.

8. Interviews with Fuki, 1993 and 1995, provide the information on her marriage.

9. Ibid., 1995.

10. Isami, *Yamashiraishi,* 41.

11. Seidensticker, *Tokyo Rising,* 40.

12. Ibid., 46.

13. Interview with Mina, 1995.

14. Interviews with Tami, 1993 and 1995.

15. Interview with Fumi, 1993.

16. Interviews with Matsuura Masako, 1993 and 1995, provided the information about Yūshirō and Masako's marriage arrangements.

17. Ibid.

7. FRUGALITY AND FANCY SCHEMES

1. Ishii, *Gaikōkan no isshō,* 214; and Isami, *Yamashiraishi,* 41–42.

2. Isami, *Yamashiraishi,* 42.

3. Ibid., 12–13.

4. Ibid.

5. Pratt, *Japan's Protoindustrial Elite,* claims that *gōnō* (wealthy farmers) had to engage in interregional trade and moneylending to succeed (10). My direct evidence for the scope of the Matsuura family's trade is only Daisuke's business transactions in Edo in 1863, as recorded in his journal.

6. "Matsuura Kōemon nikki," in *Asakawa chōshi,* 2:955ff., quotation from 962.

7. Duus, *Modern Japan,* 68–69.

8. Shibusawa, *Autobiography of Shibusawa Eiichi,* xiv.

9. Pratt, *Japan's Protoindustrial Elite,* describes the taxing of breweries (174).

10. In 1877, the total rice production dropped to 1,115 *koku*—even below the production during the 1830s, a troubled decade of famine.

11. *Kadokawa Nihon chimei daijiten,* vol. 7: *Fukushima-ken,* 830.

12. Isami, *Yamashiraishi,* 28.

13. Information about family holdings comes from interviews with Kawaota Shōhei, 1993, and Matsuura Tomoji, 2003. Estimates of the Matsuura family's holdings are nec-

essarily approximate, because the amounts not only varied over time but also depend on the reliability of my informants' knowledge about the family's holdings in other villages. Several people interviewed agree that Isami himself overestimated his holdings at the end of World War II.

14. Isami, *Yamashiraishi*, 38.

15. Ibid., 40–41.

16. Ibid., 38–39.

17. Ibid., 41.

18. Ibid., 39.

19. Waswo, *Japanese Landlords*, 76, 79.

20. Isami, *Yamashiraishi*, 45.

21. Ibid., 39.

22. Ann Waswo, *Housing in Postwar Japan* (London: RoutledgeCurzon, 2002), 40.

23. Isami, *Yamashiraishi*, 40. Isami owed a hundred thousand yen. This was an enormous amount. In contrast, the average debt of cultivators in 1927 was 545 yen, while tenant farmers owed, on average, 426 yen. See Kozo Yamamura, "The Japanese Economy, 1911–1930: Concentration, Conflicts, and Crises," in *Japan in Crisis: Essays on Taishō Democracy*, ed. Bernard S. Silberman and H. D. Harootunian (Princeton, NJ: Princeton University Press, 1974), 306. According to other estimates, in 1930 the average rural household had a deficit of seventy-seven yen. See Thomas R. H. Havens, *Farm and Nation in Modern Japan: Agrarian Nationalism, 1870–1940* (Princeton, NJ: Princeton University Press, 1974), 137.

24. The other character in the seal was *hin* (tools or utensils).

25. Ibid.

26. Approximately three hundred thousand poor tenant farmers resettled in Manchukuo in the 1930s. Many came from the impoverished Tōhoku district.

27. See Smith, *A Time of Crisis*, chs. 3 and 4.

28. See Stephen Vlastos, "Agrarianism without Tradition: The Radical Critique of Prewar Japanese Modernity," in *Mirror of Modernity*, ed. Vlastos, ch. 6.

29. Kōjirō, *Indoneshia sanjūnen*, 10.

30. Isami, *Yamashiraishi*, 41.

31. Ibid., 38.

32. Ibid., 38 and 52.

33. Ibid., 40.

34. Ibid., 41.

35. Ibid., 42.

36. Ibid., 30.

8. OUTPOSTS OF MODERNITY

1. Interview with Kawai Ikuko, 1995.

2. The term *privileged interlopers* comes from Mark R. Peattie, "Japanese Treaty Port Settlements in China, 1895–1937," in *The Japanese Informal Empire, 1895–1937*, ed. Peter

Duus, Ramon H. Myers, and Mark R. Peattie (Princeton, NJ: Princeton University Press, 1989), 187.

3. Fairbank, Reischauer, and Craig, *East Asia,* 472–73.

4. Alfred Schinz, *Cities in China* (Berlin: Gerbruder Borntraeger, 1989), 123.

5. Interview with Tami, 1995.

6. Interview with Ibuka Yuriko and her husband, 1995.

7. Chalmers Johnson, "The People Who Invented the Mechanical Nightingale," in *Showa, the Japan of Hirohito,* ed. Carol Gluck and Stephen R. Graubard (New York: W. W. Norton, 1992), 75.

8. Schinz, *Cities in China,* 123. Figure is for 1930.

9. Population of Japanese nationals is from Peattie, "Japanese Treaty Port Settlements in China," 170; information about the residents' association and schools is from Seng Heng Teow, "Re-thinking Japanese-Chinese Cultural Relations in the 1930s," in *Public Spheres, Private Lives,* ed. Bernstein, Gordon, and Nakai, 333.

10. Interview with Ibuka Yuriko and her husband, 1995.

11. Interview with Yōko, April 2003.

12. Interview with Ibuka Yuriko, 1995.

13. Gotō Ken-ichi, "The 'Question of the Netherlands East Indies': Japanese-Dutch Relations, 1900–1942," in *Bridging the Divide: 400 Years The Netherlands-Japan,* ed. Leonard Blusse, Willem Remmelink, and Ivo Smits (Leiden: Hotei Publishing, 2000), 203–4.

14. Kōjirō, *Indoneshia sanjūnen,* 8–9.

15. W. G. Beasley, *Japanese Imperialism, 1894–1945* (Oxford: Clarendon Press, 1987), 223. The amount from the Indies increased to 25 percent by 1936.

16. Gotō, "The 'Question of the Netherlands East Indies,'" 204.

17. Ibid., 204.

18. Ibid., 201.

19. Elsbeth Locher-Scholten, "So Close and Yet So Far: Indonesia," in *Domesticating the Empire: Race, Gender, and Family Life in French and Dutch Colonialism,* ed. Julia Clancy-Smith and Frances Gouda (Charlottesville: University Press of Virginia, 1988), 133. Other Dutch opinions were less generous. Many Dutch colonial residents viewed the Javanese as primitives and traced their illiteracy to "congenital stupidity." See Frances Gouda, "Good Mothers, Medeas, or Jezebels: The Dutch East Indies," ibid., 248.

20. Kōjirō, *Indoneshia sanjūnen,* 9–11, quotation from 9.

21. Ibid., 9–10.

22. Ibid., 12–13.

23. Ibid., 11.

24. Ishii, *Gaikōkan no isshō,* 47.

25. Ibid.

26. Peattie, "Japanese Treaty Port Settlements in China," 188.

27. Brooks, *Japan's Imperial Diplomacy,* 51.

28. Ishii, *Gaikōkan no isshō,* 215.

29. Ibid., 215–16.

30. Ibid., 214.

31. Louise Young, *Japan's Total Empire,* describes the evolution of this sense of Manchuria as Japan's "lifeline" (ch. 3).

32. Interview with Fumi, 1995.

33. Paul H. Clyde, *The Far East,* 3rd ed. (Englewood, NJ: Prentice-Hall, 1962), 545.

34. Young, *Japan's Total Empire,* 261.

35. Ibid., 249–50.

36. Ibid., 250.

37. David D. Buck, "Railway City and National Capital: Two Faces of the Modern in Changchun," in *Remaking the Chinese City: Modernity and National Identity, 1900–1950,* ed. Joseph W. Esherick (Honolulu: University of Hawaii Press, 2000), 65.

38. Ibid., 76–77.

39. Ibid., 86.

40. Koshizawa Akira, *Manshūkoku no shuto keikaku: Tōkyō no genzai to mirai o tou* (Capital planning in Manchukuo: inquiring about Tokyo's present and future) (Tokyo: Nihon keizai hyōronsha, 1988), 171. There were 324,000 Chinese, 13,000 Koreans, and approximately 1,000 Europeans and Americans. These numbers grew precipitously after 1940; in 1942 the total population was 655,000, with a combined Japanese-Korean population of 148,000 and a Chinese population of 507,000.

41. Interview with Fumi, 1995.

42. Peattie, "Treaty Port Settlements in China," 209.

43. Young, *Japan's Total Empire,* 265.

44. Buck, "Railway City and National Capital," 86.

45. Ibid., 86–87.

46. Ibid., 86.

47. Ibid., 88.

48. Bruce Cumings, "The Legacy of Colonialism," in *The Japanese Colonial Empire, 1895–1945,* ed. Ramon H. Myers and Mark R. Peattie (Princeton, NJ: Princeton University Press, 1984), 493, citing Chong-sik Lee, *Counterinsurgency in Manchuria: The Japanese Experience, 1931–1940* (Santa Monica, CA: Rand Corporation, 1967).

49. Ishii, *Gaikōkan no isshō,* 173–74, quoted in Barbara J. Brooks, "The Gaimushō's China Experts, 1895–1937," in *The Japanese Informal Empire, 1895–1937,* ed. Duus, Myers, and Peattie, 389.

50. Isami, *Yamashiraishi,* 44; and interview with Tami, 1995.

51. Young, *Japan's Total Empire,* 263.

52. Interview with Tami, 1995.

9. ISAMI'S CHILDREN IN HARM'S WAY

1. Kōjirō, *Indoneshia sanjūnen,* 15.

2. Interview with Matsuura Masako, 1995.

3. Peter Williams and David Wallace, *Unit 731: Japan's Secret Biological Warfare in World War II* (New York: Free Press, 1989), 14.

4. Interview with Masako, 1995.

5. Williams and Wallace, *Unit 731,* 38–39.

6. Ibid., 34–35.

7. Isami, *Yamashiraishi,* 43.

8. Kōjirō, *Indoneshia sanjūnen,* 18.

9. Gouda, "Good Mothers, Medeas, or Jezebels," 244–45.

10. Yuki Tanaka, "'Comfort Women' in the Dutch East Indies," in *Legacies of the Comfort Women of World War II,* ed. Margaret Stetz and Bonnie B. C. Oh (Armonk, NY: M. E. Sharpe, 2001), 44.

11. Remco Raben, "The War Issue: History and Perception of Japanese Rule in Indonesia," in *Bridging the Divide,* ed. Blusse, Remmelink, and Smits, 213.

12. John Toland, *The Rising Sun: The Decline and Fall of the Japanese Empire, 1936–1945* (New York: Random House, 1970), 418.

13. E-mail communication from Jan van Bremen, Centre for Japanese Studies, University of Leiden, June 18, 1997, H-Net list for Asian History and Culture.

14. Raben, "The War Issue," 215.

15. Ibid.

16. Ibid., 218.

17. Tanaka, "'Comfort Women' in the Dutch East Indies," 64.

18. Raben, "The War Issue," 218.

19. Kōjirō, *Indoneshia sanjūnen,* 23–24, 27, and 48.

20. Estimates of the number of Japanese lives lost on Guadalcanal range from nineteen thousand to twenty-five thousand. See Charles W. Koburger Jr., *Pacific Turning Point: The Solomon Campaign, 1942–43* (Westport, CN: Praeger, 1995), 75.

21. Toland, *The Rising Sun,* 418.

22. Ibid., 430–31.

23. Interview with Tami, 1995.

24. Ishii, *Gaikōkan no isshō,* 214.

25. Joshua A. Fogel, "The Japanese Residents' Association of Shanghai," *Journal of Asian Studies* 59, no. 4 (November 2000): 927–95. See also Donald A. Jordan, *China's Trial by Fire: The Shanghai War of 1932* (Ann Arbor: University of Michigan, 2001).

26. Peattie, "Japanese Treaty Port Settlements in China," 205.

27. Brooks, "The Gaimushō's China Experts," 389–90.

28. Ibid., 392.

29. John Hunter Boyle, "Peace Advocacy during the Sino-Japanese Incident," in *China and Japan: A Search for Balance since World War I,* ed. Alvin D. Coox and Hilary Conroy (Santa Barbara, CA: ABC-Clio Books, 1978), 257, quoting Ishii.

30. Brooks, *Japan's Imperial Diplomacy,* 192–93.

31. Hadley, *Memoir of a Trustbuster,* 33.

32. Peattie, "Japanese Treaty Port Settlements in China," 208–9.

33. Ishii, *Gaikōkan no isshō,* 282. There was newspaper speculation at the time about why he was transferred, but journalists did not know he had tried to resign. Ishii Itarō was ambassador to Brazil from September 1940 to August 1942.

34. Ienaga Saburō, *The Pacific War: World War II and the Japanese, 1931–1945* (New York: Pantheon Books, 1978), 195.

10. HARD TIMES ON THE HOME FRONT

1. Isami, *Yamashiraishi,* 45.

2. John W. Dower, *Embracing Defeat* (New York: W. W. Norton/Free Press, 1999), 90.

3. Ienaga, *The Pacific War,* 194.

4. Peter Duus, "Presidential Address: Weapons of the Weak, Weapons of the Strong—the Development of the Japanese Political Cartoon," *Journal of Asian Studies* 60, no. 4 (November 2001): 990.

5. Fairbank, Reischauer, and Craig, *East Asia,* 806–7.

6. Isami, *Yamashiraishi,* 43.

7. Interview with Mina, 1993.

8. Photograph in possession of Matsuura Tomoji.

9. Isami, *Yamashiraishi,* 43.

10. Fairbank, Reischauer, and Craig, *East Asia,* 808; and Dower, *Embracing Defeat,* 91.

11. Interview with Matsuura Masako, 1995.

12. Isami, *Yamashiraishi,* 43.

13. Interview with Mina, 1995. Tokyo Imperial University was renamed Tokyo University after the war.

14. Others of their generation, however, went on to become the "bedrock of postwar recovery," dedicated company men and mothers devoted to their children's education. In popular imagination, they "had managed the psychological divide and social chaos that was the transition to peacetime." See William W. Kelly, "Finding a Place in Metropolitan Japan: Ideologies, Institutions, and Everyday Life," in *Postwar Japan as History,* ed. Andrew Gordon (Berkeley: University of California Press, 1993), 197.

15. Isami, *Yamashiraishi,* 43.

16. Correspondence from Yōko, September 5, 2003.

17. Interviews with Yōko, 1995 and 2003.

18. Toshikazu Kase, *Eclipse of the Rising Sun* (London: Jonathan Cape, 1951), 78, reissued as *Journey to the Missouri.*

19. Isami, *Yamashiraishi,* 45.

20. Gordon Mark Berger, *Parties Out of Power in Japan, 1931–1941* (Princeton, NJ: Princeton University Press, 1977), 116 and 117n.

21. Herbert P. Bix, *Hirohito and the Making of Modern Japan* (New York: Harper-Collins, 2000), 178.

22. Ibid., 478.

23. Robert J. C. Butow, *Japan's Decision to Surrender* (Stanford, CA: Stanford University Press, 1967), 37.

24. Kido Kōichi, *The Diary of Marquis Kido, 1931–45* (Frederick, MD: University Publications of America, 1984), 398–99.

25. Isami, *Yamashiraishi,* 45.

26. Fairbank, Reischauer, and Craig, *East Asia,* 808; and Marius Jansen, *The Making of Modern Japan* (Cambridge, MA: Harvard University Press, 2000), 650.

27. Toland, *The Rising Sun,* 850.

28. Frank Gibney, ed., *Sensō: The Japanese Remember the Pacific War: Letters to the Editor of* Asahi Shimbun (Armonk, NY: M. E. Sharpe, 1995), 204.

29. Isami, *Yamashiraishi,* 45.

30. Interview with Tami, 2003.

31. Interview with Fuki, 1995.

32. Kōjirō, *Indoneshia sanjūnen,* 23–24.

33. Isami, *Yamashiraishi,* 46.

34. John Keegan, *The Battle for History* (New York: Vintage, 1995), 27.

35. Fairbank, Reischauer, and Craig, *East Asia,* 808.

36. Isami, *Yamashiraishi,* 46. According to John Toland, *The Rising Sun,* thirty-seven thousand small distillation units throughout the country were each producing three to four gallons of crude oil daily, and production reached seventy thousand barrels a month, but refining it was so difficult, only three thousand barrels of aviation gasoline were produced by the end of the war (746n).

37. Kido, *The Diary of Marquis Kido,* 432.

38. Bix, *Hirohito and the Making of Modern Japan,* 497–98, quoting William L. Shirer, *The Rise and Fall of the Third Reich: A History of Nazi Germany* (New York: Simon and Schuster, 1960), 1139.

39. Kido, *The Diary of Marquis Kido,* 433–35.

40. Jansen, *The Making of Modern Japan,* 651.

41. Interview with Fumi, 1993.

42. Ienaga Saburō writes that reservists were ordered "to defend the area as the Kwantung army evacuated officers' dependents by train." In Korea the Imperial Army seized the railroad line for military use only. See Ienaga, *The Pacific War,* 191.

43. Isami, *Yamashiraishi,* 46.

44. Interview with Fumi, 1995.

II. SURVIVING HIROSHIMA

1. Col. Paul Tibbetts, *The Bomb,* from World at War documentary film series (Thames, 1973), reissued in video (Ontario: Thorn EMI, 1984), vol. 8.

2. John Hersey, *Hiroshima* (1946; New York: Vintage Books, 1989), 5 and 8. Those directly underneath the exploding bomb heard nothing; they only saw a lightning flash. Those farther away heard the blast that followed moments later. All but a few buildings were destroyed in the two-mile radius around the epicenter.

3. Quoted in Robert Jay Lifton, *Death in Life* (orig. pub., New York: Random House, 1967; Chapel Hill: University of North Carolina Press, 1991), 29.

4. Nikolay Palchikoff, "The Nuclear August of 1945," *New York Times,* Op-Ed., August 6, 2001.

5. Butow, *Japan's Decision to Surrender,* 215.

6. Toland, *The Rising Sun,* 839. There are numerous versions of where the recorded disks were hidden. Robert J. C. Butow, *Japan's Decision to Surrender,* writes that the bag was put in a safe concealed behind an old Chinese scroll in a chamber set aside for officials-in-waiting to the empress (216). William Craig claims that the disks were taken by Court Chamberlain Tokugawa Yoshihiro, who hid them in a wall safe in his own room in the administration building in the center of the palace grounds (*The Fall of Japan* [New York: Penguin Books, 1979], 189).

7. Butow, *Japan's Decision to Surrender,* 216; and Leonard Mosley, *Hirohito* (Englewood Cliffs, NJ: Prentice-Hall, 1966), 328. Mina claims that Ishiwata had been entrusted with the recording. Toshikazu Kase says only that Ishiwata and Kido, the lord privy seal, "hid all night by the safe." Kido, in his memoirs, describes going "to the vault with Mr. Ishiwata." He writes that he was told of the "riot" by a chamberlain, whereas Mosley writes that Ishiwata was the one who told him of the revolt.

8. Butow, *Japan's Decision to Surrender,* 216fn.

9. Dower, *Embracing Defeat,* 34.

10. Isami, *Yamashiraishi,* 46.

11. Ibid.

12. Jansen, *The Making of Modern Japan,* 660.

13. Donald Ritchie, quoted by Howard W. French, "An Expatriate Who Can't Resist Telling His Mount Fuji Story Again," *New York Times,* August 8, 2001, B1.

14. Richard Pyle, "Its Empire Lost, Japan Had to 'Bear the Unbearable,'" *Arizona Daily Star,* August 15, 1985, 11.

15. Interview with Tami, 1995.

16. Interview with Yōko, 2003.

17. Estimates vary on the number of people who died from the atomic bombing of Hiroshima. In *The Pacific War,* for example, Ienaga quotes a Japanese report of 200,000 persons (202). John Toland gives the same figure, citing the first curator of the Peace memorial in Hiroshima (790n). Duus gives a range of 78,000 to 140,000 (*Modern Japan,* 2nd ed., 246). These discrepancies are explained in part by the difference between the initial estimates and subsequent ones that take into account bomb-related deaths that occurred later.

18. John W. Dower, "Hiroshimas and Nagasakis in Japanese Memory," *Diplomatic History* 19, no. 2 (Spring 1995): 278–79. Peter Duus gives a figure of "total Japanese war dead" as 2,694,322. In addition to military fatalities, this includes civilians in Okinawa and Saipan as well as civilian families killed in air raids on major Japanese cities, prisoners of war in the Soviet Union, and the 100,000 soldiers and civilians who died in Manchuria in the winter of 1945–46. Millions more were reported ill or injured as of 1945. See Duus, *Modern Japan,* 249. The death figure for American military men is 400,000, as reported in J. David Singer and Melvin Small, *The Wages of War, 1816–1965: A Statistical Handbook* (New York: John Wiley, 1972), 67–68, which lists Japanese military casualties as 1 million between 1941 and 1945 and 250,000 more for the Sino-Japanese War between 1937 and 1941. Duus and Dower say there were 1,740,955 Japanese military fatalities.

19. Isami, *Yamashiraishi,* 46.

20. *Kadokawa Nihon chimei daijiten,* vol. 7: *Fukushima-ken,* 830.

21. It is unclear whether the dam was built to irrigate the mountain plots or constituted a separate project.

22. Gary Allinson, *Japan's Postwar History* (Ithaca, NY: Cornell University Press, 1997), 48.

23. Dower, *Embracing Defeat,* 56.

24. Kurt Steiner, *Local Government in Japan* (Stanford, CA: Stanford University Press, 1965), 102.

25. Isami, *Yamashiraishi,* 33.

26. Kido was arrested as a class A war criminal on December 6, 1945, and indicted on fifty-four charges of war crimes. He pleaded not guilty but was found guilty and sentenced to life imprisonment. After serving ten years, he was released on parole in December 1955 and was unconditionally released in April 1958. Before Kido was imprisoned, Ishiwata was in contact with him. The two men discussed plans to reform the peerage system. Ishiwata also reported to him on plans to abolish the Office of the Privy Seal and on other matters affecting the Imperial family. Ishiwata seems to have been the conduit through which Kido learned of his chief secretary's resignation and of plans to abolish his own position. Kido, *The Diary of Marquis Kido,* reported that Ishiwata "said the president of the Privy Council and the premier consented to the move" (463). Ishiwata may have also participated in plans to transform the emperor from a god-ruler to an ordinary human being. A diary entry for December 23, 1945, made by Kinoshita Michio, recorded the names of several men, including one identified simply as Ishiwata, as having participated in the drafting of the Declaration of Humanity. See Nakamura Masanori, *The Japanese Monarchy: Ambassador Joseph Grew and the Making of the "Symbol Emperor System," 1931–1991* (Armonk, NY: M. E. Sharpe, 1992), 110.

27. Isami, *Yamashiraishi,* 48; and interview with Tami, 1995.

28. "A Frightening Comeback for TB," *Japan Times Weekly,* International Edition, October 5–11, 1998, 20.

29. Isami, *Yamashiraishi,* 49.

30. Interview with Yōko, 2003.

31. Interview with Tami, 1995.

12. MISSED FORTUNES

1. Isami, *Yamashiraishi,* 47.

2. Ibid., 52.

3. Ibid., 52; and Steiner, *Local Government in Japan,* 98–99. The original purge directive of January 4, 1946, applied only to "government service," which included "all positions in the central Japanese and prefectural governments and all of their agencies and local branches, bureaus, and offices." An accompanying memorandum stated that the purge would be extended to the local government level at a later time. See also Ronald

P. Dore, *Land Reform in Japan* (London: Oxford University Press, 1959), 316, which describes results of a survey of thirteen villages that showed that twenty-eight of the thirty-nine persons driven from office had been the most influential local leaders before Japan's surrender.

4. Dore, *Land Reform in Japan*, 316.

5. Steiner, *Local Government in Japan*, 101–2.

6. Allinson, *Japan's Postwar History*, 56.

7. Isami, *Yamashiraishi*, 52–53.

8. Ibid., 59.

9. Ibid., 59–62.

10. Ibid., 56.

11. Ibid., 58.

12. Ibid., 53.

13. Ibid., 60.

14. Ibid., 55 and 57; and interview with Tami, 1993.

15. Correspondence from Yōko, September 5, 2003.

16. Isami, *Yamashiraishi*, 55.

17. Ibid., 56.

18. Ibid., 57.

19. Ibid., 58. According to Tami, Isami never officially moved into the cottage. He seems to have stayed in the main house and possibly even retained his legal headship of the family until his death.

20. Isami, *Yamashiraishi*, 71.

21. Ibid.

13. MAKING HISTORY

1. *Fukushima minpō*, August 23, 1999, 3.

2. Interview with Matsuura Tomoji, 2003.

3. Isami, *Yamashiraishi*, 50.

4. Ibid., 42.

5. Ibid., 2.

6. Ibid., 68.

7. Ibid.

8. Ibid., 69.

9. Ibid., 72.

10. Ibid., 71.

11. Ibid., 74.

12. Ibid., 71.

13. Ibid., 74.

14. Interview with Tami, 1993.

15. Ibid.

16. Isami, *Yamashiraishi*, 68.

17. Called the seventh-year anniversary of the death, *nanakai no hi* actually occurs in the sixth year. Thus, Kō died in 1955.

18. Isami, *Yamashiraishi,* 49–61, describes Kō's last years.

19. Ibid., quotations from 60 and 61.

20. Ibid., 57–61.

21. Interview with Kawasaki Fumio, 1995.

22. Isami, *Yamashiraishi,* 69.

23. Interview with Tami, 1993.

14. ABSENT HUSBAND

1. Kōjirō, *Indoneshia sanjūnen,* 73.

2. Ibid.

3. Ibid., 71.

4. The Dutch tribunal in Jakarta was the only one that sentenced Japanese officers to severe punishments for forcing Dutch women into prostitution as "comfort women." It did not concern itself with native Indonesian women's similar sexual servitude, however. See C. Sarah Soh, "Japan's Responsibility toward Comfort Women Survivors," *Japan Policy Research Institute Working Paper* 77 (May 2001): 1.

5. Raben, "The War Issue," 221.

6. Kōjirō's assessment of Imamura is shared by John Toland, who calls him "one of the most respected figures in the (Japanese) Army" and confirms that Imamura's "liberal methods" at one point jeopardized his career in the army. See Toland, *The Rising Sun,* 418. A Dutch source says of the trials, "justice was administered with remarkable bias," arguing that the "prosecution often failed to build a solid case and many verdicts were based on circumstantial evidence." See Raben, "The War Issue," 221.

7. Kōjirō, *Indoneshia sanjūnen,* 47. Kōjirō also successfully aided the defense of two members of the Kenpeitai, the Japanese military police, by arguing that their Indonesian accusers feared they would be implicated as collaborators for having befriended the Japanese men during the war.

8. Ibid., 27.

9. Blusse, Remmlink, and Smits, eds., *Bridging the Divide,* 242.

10. Kōjirō, *Indoneshia sanjūnen,* 48.

11. Ibid., 31–32.

12. Ibid., 32.

13. Isami, *Yamashiraishi,* 40.

14. Ibid., 50 and 53.

15. Interview with Tami, 1993.

16. Ibid.

17. Isami, *Yamashiraishi,* 54.

18. Kōjirō, *Indoneshia sanjūnen,* 54.

19. Ibid., 55–56.

20. Ibid., 59.

21. Ibid.

22. Ibid., 64.

23. Ibid.

24. Interview with Tami, 1993.

25. Ibid., 74–75.

26. Ibid., 77–78.

27. Ibid., 92.

28. Ibid., 90.

29. Ibid., 4.

30. Interview with Tami, 1993.

15. COUPLES AND UNCOUPLINGS

1. Interview with Yōko, 2003.

2. Information on Toyo and Masafumi comes from interviews with Tami and Yōko, 1993, 1995, and 2003; from Isami, *Yamashiraishi,* 51; and from my own recollections.

3. Information on Tami comes from interviews with her, 1993, 1995, and 2003; and from Isami, *Yamashiraishi,* 52–55.

4. Isami, *Yamashiraishi,* 24.

5. I describe the intricate family network in "Social Networks among the Daughters of a Japanese Family," in *Public Spheres, Private Lives,* ed. Bernstein, Gordon, and Nakai, 293–317.

6. Recollection of Tami's daughter, 1993.

16. MOTHERING

1. Information in this chapter, unless otherwise noted, comes from Yōko and from my own recollections.

2. Seiitsu Tachibana, "The Quest for a Peace Culture: The A-bomb Survivors' Long Struggle and the New Movement for Redressing Foreign Victims of Japan's War," *Diplomatic History* 19, no. 2 (Spring 1995): 337–39; and John W. Dower, "Three Narratives of Our Humanity," in *History Wars: The Enola Gay and Other Battles for the American Past,* ed. Edward T. Linenthal and Tom Engelhardt (New York: Henry Holt, 1996), 66.

3. The equivalent value of this amount in U.S. dollars has fluctuated between 270 and 200, depending on the exchange rate.

EPILOGUE

1. Interview with Tami, 2003.

2. Interview with Yōko, August 2003.

biological warfare unit (Songo), 138
Brazil: Ishii Itarō in, 144, 260n33; Toyo in, 205–6, 218–19
brides: age of, 36, 250–51n27; wedding customs of, 98
brothels, 103, 104
B-25 bombers, 147
B-29 bombers, 145, 154, 155, 159
Buddhism: black lacquer altar of, 22; death anniversary rite of, 187, 266n17; Yamashiraishi temple of, 29–30, 59, 72
butsudan (Buddhist altar), 22

cadastral surveys, 25, 26, 246n11
children of Isami: childhood activities of, 48–49; education of, 57–58, 83–85, 87–88, 89; as family disappointments, 108, 114, 173–76, 177, 178–80; health care for, 49–50; infertility problems of, 126, 151, 210, 220; marriage arrangements for, 97–100, 151; as mutual support network, 221, 226–27, 233; parental discipline of, 50–51; postwar resettlement of, 163–64, 165–66, 167–68; from Shōwa era, 150, 261n14; sleeping arrangements for, 22; toys of, 49; urban middle-class marriages of, 211–12, 222; wartime survival of, 162. *See also* daughters of Isami
China: devalued scholarship of, 1–2; Japanese diplomats in, 131–32; Japanese occupation of, 127–28, 142–43; nationalist movement in, 143; Shanghai Incident in, 100; in Sino-Japanese War, 134–35, 143–44, 263n18; Westernized port cities of, 123–24
Chinese language characters, 39, 58
Chise (Daisuke's mother-in-law), 40, 73–74, 75, 76
Chise (Isami's sister), 39, 41
Chiyo (Yutarō's wife), 100, 148, 177–78, 179, 186
Chōsh domain, 10
Chōtoku Temple (Yamashiraishi), 29–30
Christian converts: academic influence of, 93; Ishii Itarō as, 132; in Matsuura family, 95, 199, 203, 205–6, 226, 227;

in Tokugawa era, 34; Tokyo mission schools of, 89
Civil Code of 1898, 52
clothes: at Christian mission schools, 89; classes in sewing, 92; of Japanese diplomatic corps, 131; rural/traditional, 57–58; Western influence on, 95, 222
Confucian ideals, 3, 50, 182, 185, 236
currency devaluations, 75, 110–11

Daimaru department store (Kyoto), 208
daimyō. See domain officials
Daisuke. *See* Matsuura Daisuke
dancing bans, 101, 124
Date, House of, 28, 247n28
daughters of Isami: adoptions by, 151–53, 220, 224–25; as caregivers of spouses, 213–15; domestic practical skills of, 68–69, 238; education of, 57–58, 85, 88–91, 92–95; elder advice from, 235–36; elder living arrangements of, 236–38; infertility problems of, 126, 151, 210, 220; marriage arrangements for, 97–99; meal preparation by, 220–21; traditional values of, 212–13, 240–41; urban middle-class marriages of, 211–12, 222; weddings of, 98, 101–2, 103; widowhood experience of, 215–16, 226
demokurashi (democracy), 170, 184
Depression, 114, 115, 257n26
Diet elections, 116–17, 169–70
divorce: of Isami's granddaughter Masako, 225; Kōjirō's desire for, 198–99; Masafumi's desire for, 126; of Tami, 208–9; of Tatsugorō, 175; of Tomoji, 190–91; of Yōko, 227–30
domain officials *(daimyō):* land reclamation incentives of, 247–48n43; of Shirakawa, 25; special tax levies of, 7–8, 244n15; tax assessments by, 25–27, 34, 246nn11,21; village headmen's relations with, 6, 62, 63–64, 257n57
Doolittle, James H., 147
Dutch colonialists: Sukarno's imprisonment by, 202; treatment of Japanese

troops by, 197; treatment of natives by, 129–30, 140, 258n19; war crime tribunals of, 164, 196, 266nn4,6,7

Dutch East Indies (Indonesia): defeated Japanese troops in, 197; description of, 127; electric power in, 195; Japanese exploitation of, 128–29, 258n15; Kōjirō's activities in, 127, 129–40, 139, 140, 141, 200–201, 202; nationalist aspirations of, 139–40, 197; status of natives in, 129–30, 140, 258n19; war crimes trials in, 164, 196, 266nn4,6,7

East Asia Common Culture Institute (Tō-A Dōbun Shoin), 59

East Indies. *See* Netherlands East Indies

Echigo-Takada domain, 34, 55, 72

Edo (Tokyo), 63; Daisuke's business dealings in, 110–11, 256n5; foreign trade pressures in, 8–10; renaming of, 11; Tokugawa expansion of, 78. *See also* Tokyo

education: Daisuke's promotion of, 13–14, 57; of Isami, 2–3, 4, 243n3; of Isami's children, 57–58, 83–84; of Ishii Itarō, 58–59; of Ishiwata men, 98–99; as marital prerequisite, 99, 100; Meiji system of, 4, 243n8; middle-class competition for, 84–85; at Tokyo public universities, 87–88; at Tokyo women's schools, 88–94, 255nn29,30; of village children, 59; of village heads, 29, 56–57; wartime pursuit of, 149–50, 261n14; Western impact on, 1–2; of women, 85–86, 248n2, 254n8; Yūya's promotion of, 3–4, 58

elections: of postwar candidates, 169–70; of Seiyūkai candidate, 116–17; women voters in, 188

electric power, 52, 113, 195

Endō Arata, 134, 255n22

English language, 4, 89, 90, 91, 218

famines: Great Tenmei Famine, 54–55, 250n22; of 1680, 25; of Tenpō era, 72–73

firearms *(teppō)*, 65, 73

fire dangers, 21, 61, 118–19

food shortages: in famine of 1680, 25; in Great Tenmei Famine, 54–55, 250n22; in Manchuria, 135; as postwar concern, 162–63, 165; in Tenpō era, 72–73; in wartime Japan, 146–48, 149, 150–51

foreign trade: with Dutch East Indies, 128–29, 258n15; inflation effects of, 110–11; shogunal policy on, 8–10, 244n18

Formosa (Taiwan), 127, 130, 142

Freedom School (Jiyū Gakuen, Tokyo), 89, 106, 152, 214; architectural design of, 91, 255n22; Christian influence at, 93; educational philosophy of, 92–94, 255nn29,30; Isami's selection of, 90; student graduates from, 95–96, 151; and Toyo, 90–96, 126, 12, 205, 207, 214

Fudō (Buddhist deity), 79

Fujin no tomo (Woman's Friend) magazine, 48, 91, 94, 95–96, 101

Fuki. *See* Akakura Fuki

Fukushima: cadastral surveys of, 246n11; during Depression, 115, 257n26; location/map of, 5; peasant uprisings in, 10–11; popular rights movement in, 14; prefecture of, 12, 245n29; preparatory school in, 4

Fukushima City, 12, 15, 16

Fukuzawa Yukichi, 2, 85; childrearing philosophy of, 49, 52; marriage ideal of, 37, 211; poem by, 118; school founded by, 88

Fumi. *See* Sugai Fumi

furoshiki (cloth squares for carrying books), 57

fusuma (sliding wall panels), 23

Germany, 123–24, 156

geta (wooden clogs), 58, 67

Ginza, the (Tokyo), 86, 105, 108

gold coins *(ryō)*, 55, 71, 74, 79, 110–12

gōonin-gumi (five neighboring households), 34. 64, 65

Ise Shrine, 79, 109
Ishii Bungorō (Isami's uncle), 109
Ishii Itarō (Isami's cousin/brother-in-law), xviii, 100, 109; Brazil assignment of, 144, 260n33; education/career of, 58–59; and Japanese Army, 135; as Shanghai consul-general, 131–32, 142; on Sino-Japanese War, 143, 144; U.S. postings of, 130–31
Ishii Moto (Isami's sister/Itaroō's wife), 39, 41, 58, 59, 100, 109, 131, 132
Ishikawa, 32; 1879 population of, 15; Kō's relocation to, 167; railway line to, 117; Toyo's recuperation in, 205; Yūshirō's medical practice in, 166
Ishikawa Ikuko (Toyo's sister-in-law), 123, 124, 135
Ishikawa Masafumi (Toyo's husband), 135, 224; background of, 100–101; death of, 214–15; employment of, 125–26, 164, 207; in Hiroshima bombing, 159, 161–62; personal traits of, 126, 208; wedding of, 101–2; Western-style home of, 217, 230; wife's treatment by, 124–25, 126, 205–7
Ishikawa Masayoshi, 100–101
Ishikawa Toyo (Isami's second daughter), 23, 51, 87, 136, 164, 175; adopted daughter of, 151–53, 224–25; author's visits with, xi–xii, xiv, 217–19; Christian conversion of, 205–6; and daughter's husband, 228, 230–31; education of, 90–95; elder advice from, 235–36; elder living arrangements of, 230, 238; employment of, 217; funeral/memorial for, 234–35; granddaughter of, 239–40; in Hiroshima bombing, 159, 161, 219; as husband's caregiver, 214–15; illness of, xii–xiii, 205, 233–34; infertility of, 126, 151; marriage arrangement role of, 222, 223; marriage of, 97, 100–102, 125, 126, 206; on marriages of family members, 178, 225, 239; meal preparation by, 220–21; personal traits of, 96, 126, 207; Qingdao experience of, 124, 134; Tokyo residence

of, 217; Western influence on, 95, 101, 217, 230
Ishiwata Bin'ichi (Toshikazu), 99
Ishiwata Eijirō, 98, 255–56n1
Ishiwata Fumimaro, 99
Ishiwata Mina (Isami's first daughter), 41, 102, 107, 135, 155, 190; birth of, 38; death of child of, 226; education of, 88–89, 90; elder living arrangements of, 236, 238; and Hani Motoko, 91; husband of, 98–99; in-laws of, 106; on Isami, 57, 83, 149–50, 171; on Kō, 51; and marriages of family members, 199, 201–2, 208; signification of name, 40; son of, at Toyo's memorial, 234–35; on surrender document, 263n7; Tokyo residence of, 165; wartime relocation of, 147; on Yūya, 53
Ishiwata Nobu (Isami's granddaughter/Mina's daughter), 219, 226, 235
Ishiwata Rintarō (Isami's grandson/Mina's son), 149–50, 161
Ishiwata Rokusaburō (Mina's husband), 98–99
Ishiwata Sōtarō (Mina's brother-in-law), 156; education of, 99; and Japanese surrender document, 160–61, 263nn6,7; on Nanjing's devastation, 143–44; and new cabinet formation, 153–54; postwar accomplishments of, 165, 264n26
Isoko (Tomoji's wife), 182, 186
Itabashi village, 11, 55

Japan: air-raid attacks on, 147, 154–55; atomic bombing of, 159–60, 161–62, 224, 262n2; bank moratorium in, 114; in crisis years of 1930s, 115–16, 257n26; diplomatic ostracism of, 124, 127–28; Dutch East Indies interests of, 128–29, 139–40, 258n15; food shortages in, 146–48, 149, 150–51, 162–63; foreign automobile market of, 201, 202; imperialist intentions of, 127, 130; Manchurian interests of, 133–34, 259n40; map of, xxx; in modernity transition, 1–2, 17;

league headmen *(ōjōya):* first Matsuura
   as, 56, 251n32; horse trade practices
   of, 61, 251n46; Isami's praise of, 185;
   tax relief petitions to, 62–63, 251n50;
   Yūemon Jinsuke as, 71, 252n11. *See
   also* village heads
League of Nations, 127
Liaodong (Kwantung) Peninsula, 37, 133
Liberal Party (*Jiyūtō;* Meiji period),
   14, 16

MacArthur, Douglas, 183
Manchuria: Fukushima farmers in, 115,
   257n26; Japanese takeover of, 124,
   127; as marriage to men stationed
   in, 107; modern cities of, 132–34,
   259n40; Russo-Japanese rivalry over,
   37–38, 248n6; during Sino-Japanese
   War, 134–36; Soviet troops in, 157–
   58, 262n42; war crimes in, 138
Manchuria Mining Development
   Company, 107
Manchurian Central Bank Club, 134
maps: of Asia, *128;* of Fukushima
   prefecture, *5;* of modern Japan, *xxx*
marital infidelity: of Kōjirō, 198–99;
   of Shiki's husband, 212; of Toyo's
   husband,126; of Yōko's husband,
   228–29
marriage: age of brides at, 36, 250–51n27;
   caregiver role in, 213–15; companionate type of, 206–7; contemporary
   practices of, 236–37, 238–40; Fukuzawa Yukichi's views on, 37, 211; of
   Japanese men, in United States, 131;
   love marriage type of, 176, 213, 225–
   26; meal preparation duty in, 68,
   220–21; partners for, as problematic,
   107, 166–67; postwar difficulties in,
   203–4; of servants, 67; status benefits
   from, 41–42, 97; of urban middle
   class, 211–12, 222; and wedding cost,
   98, 174. *See also* marital infidelity;
   marriage arrangements
marriage arrangements: for Fuki, 102–4;
   for Fumi, 106–7; for Isami, 37–38;
   Isami's rules on, 97–98, 99–100, 102;

in 1960s, 222–24; resistance to,
   238–39; for Shiki, 106; for Tami,
   166–67; for Tatsugorō, 174; for
   Tomoji, 181–82; for Toyo, 100–101;
   in wartime, 151; for Yatarō, 100; for
   Yūshirō, 107–8
Masafumi. *See* Ishikawa Masafumi
Masako (Isami's granddaughter / Tami's
   daughter), 167, 208, 209, 225–26, 228
Masako (Yūshirō's wife). *See* Matsuura
   Masako
Matsudaira Sadanobu, 54–55, 250n22
Matsudaira Tadahiro, 246n16
Matsuo Bashō, 6
Matsuura Daisuke (Isami's great-
   grandfather): as adopted heir, 43,
   73; adopted son-in-law of, 77, 253n32;
   business ventures of, 110, 256n5;
   death of, 3, 40; education projects
   of, 13–14, 57; and foreign trade crisis,
   9–11; headman responsibilities of,
   74, 75; with Isami, in Tokyo, 1–3,
   154; as marriage model, 211; personal
   traits of, 13, 75; retirement of, 11;
   special tax levies on, 7–8, 244n15;
   travel destinations of, 77–80, 253n36;
   wives of, 75–76
Matsuura house: business offices of, 23–
   24, 30, 247n34; centennial anniversary of, 192; children's activities at,
   49, 57; children's return to, 147, 148–
   49, 163–64, 167; electrical power for,
   52; Isami's calligraphy at, 182; multi-
   generational members of, 40–41,
   75–76, 182; neglect of, by Tomoji,
   190–91; peasant attacks on, 11, 21,
   60–61; preserved documents from,
   191, 235; razed by fire, 21; rebuilding
   of, 62–63; residence areas of, 21–23,
   245n2; retirement cottage of, 24, 192;
   servants' duties at, 67–69; wife's role
   at, 66–67, 68
Matsuura Isami: adult children's ties to,
   212; business ventures of, 112–14, 168,
   171–72; childrearing practices of, 48–
   51, 52–53, 213, 250n13; death / funeral
   of, 189; debt of, in 1927, 114, 257n23;

Matsuura Kōzō (Isami's brother), 41, 115, 143, 156, 163

Matsuura Kuniko (Seishichirō's wife), 150, 175, 213

Matsuura Masako (Isami's daughter-in-law/Yūshirō's wife): caregiver role of, 178; marriage of, 107–8, 213; postwar responsibilities of, 166; at Songo army base, 137–38; on Tomoji's behavior, 190; at Toyo's funeral, 234; wartime chores of, 148–49; on Yatarō's illness, 179

Matsuura Miyo (Isami's mother/Yūya's wife), 58, 66, 67, 115, 162

Matsuura Moto (Isami's step-great-grandmother/Daisuke's second wife), 1, 9, 13, 24, 40, 85, 186; Isami's praise of, 76, 80, 213; as marriage model, 211; travel destinations of, 77–79, 253n36

Matsuura patriarchs: adoption of heirs by, 42, 43–44, 249n18; business ventures of, 31, 33, 63, 72, 109–10, 252n14, 253n15, 256n5; Confucian ideals of, 185; diary practices of, 45; downfall of, xiii–xiv, 186–87, 189–90; education commitment of, 28–29, 56–57, 58–59; founding headman of, 27–29, 247nn27,29; by generation, 46; grave sites of, 108, 150, 162, 192; household size of, 55, 250–51n27; inheritable surname of, 43, 56, 249n16, 251n29; Isami's chronicle of, xiii, 182–84, 185–86; land reclamation by, 33, 42–43, 247–48n43; land reform's impact on, 170–71, 183, 184; marriage arrangement practices of, 41–42, 97–98; under Meiji reform, 12–13, 14–16, 32, 111, 245nn29,36; naming practices of, 44, 45–47, 249n22; official headman duties of, 63–65, 252n57; paternalistic headman role of, 53–54, 55, 59–60, 185, 250n15; peasant protests against, 10–11, 60–63; retirement cottage of, 24, 192; rice landholdings of, 112, 256–57n13; in rice land scandal, 118–

19; special tax levies on, 7–8, 244n15. See also Matsuura Isami

Matsuura Ryoko (Isami's great-grand-child), 182

Matsuura Saburō (Isami's uncle), 3

Matsuura Seishichirō/Sei (Isami's seventh son), 39, 150, 165, 166, 174–75, 213

Matsuura Shinrokurō/Shin (Isami's sixth son), 39, 144–45, 150, 164, 172, 176

Matsuura Sōemon (Yajibei's son), 32–34, 35, 109, 247n42

Matsuura Sōemon II, 41, 42–43, 110–11

Matsuura Tatsugorō/Tatsu (Isami's fifth son), 150, 161, 165, 172, 173–74, 175

Matsuura Tazuko (Kōjirō's wife), 100, 141, 195; Kōjirō's treatment of, 198–99, 202–3

Matsuura Teru (Isami's sixth daughter), 50, 52, 95

Matsuura Tomoji (Isami's grandson/Yatarō's son), 234; inadequacies of, 181, 186–87; marriages of, 181, 190; Matsuura family house of, 190–91, 192

Matsuura Toshisaburō/Saburō (Isami's third son), 144, 164, 199–200; business venture of, 171–72; career difficulties of, 166, 173; education of, 88; marriage of, 100, 213; military draft of, 142; prewar concerns of, 115

Matsuura Yajibei, 25, 27–30, 55, 246n7, 247nn27,29

Matsuura Yatarō (Isami's first son), 102; birth of, 37; in business ventures, 113, 156; education of, 88; illness of, 50, 179; in multi-generational household, 40–41; personal inadequacies of, 108, 114, 173, 177, 178–79; as village head, 169, 179–80; wife of, 100, 177–78

Matsuura Yoshi (Isami's grandmother/Jinsuke's first wife), 1, 24, 40, 77, 246n5

Matsuura Yūemon (Sōemon II's grand-son): adopted heir of, 43–44, 249n18; business ventures of, 110; death of, 70; education of, 56–57; elite status

education of, 83, 87, 89, 90; elder advice from, 236; elder living arrangements of, 226, 238; employment of, 208, 209; financial status of, 221–22; generosity of, 226–27, 233; on Great Kantō Earthquake, 155; as husband's caregiver, 214, 215; infertility of, 151, 210; on Isami, 52–53, 86, 265n19; on Kō, 51; Manchurian holiday of, 136; marriages of, 166–67, 208–10; on marriages of family members, 125, 178, 205; and Miyo's stroke, 66; on retirement cottage, 192; on rural transporation, 67, 117; signification of name, 40; on wartime meals, 150–51; on *yukata* maintenance, 68–69

Nakao Shiki (Isami's fourth daughter), 98, 112, 135, 150; adoption by, 220; education of, 90–91, 95; husband of, 106, 212; infertility of, 126, 151; stylishness of, 102, 103

Nakao Shin (Shiki's husband), 106, 165, 173, 212

Nakoso Beach property, 114, 156, 169

naming practices: for daughters, 39–40; to honor ancestors, 24–25, 37; of identifying women, 73–74; of inheritable surname, 43, 56, 249n16, 251n29; purposes of, 39; of recycling personal names, 44–47, 249n22

Nanjing (Nanking), 143–44

Naruse Jinzō, 89, 90

Natsume Sōseki, 57

New Woman's Association, 90

Nichol, Captain, 141

Nihonbashi district (Edo/Tokyo), 86, 87, 110

Nihon Joshi Daigakkō (Japan Women's College, Tokyo), 89–90, 100, 214

Nihonmatsu domain, 12, 250–51n27

Nikko, 78, 154

Ninomiya Sontaku, 32, 57

Nishigahara property (Tokyo), 101, 102; in Kantō Earthquake, 86, 114; postwar family homes on, 165, 174, 175; for students' residence, 83–84; during Tokyo air raids, 154, 155

Nishin Trade Company, 201

Nobu (Isami's granddaughter/Mina's daughter), 219, 226, 235

Nogi Maresuke, 102

North China Development Company (Kitashina Kaihatsu, Beijing), 144

occupation. *See* Allied occupation

ōjōya. See league headmen

Okinawa, battle of, 156–57

Oyamadō highway, 78

Pearl Harbor attack (1941), 135, 136, 137, 139, 146–47

peasants: domainal regulation of, 34; legal recourse by, 27, 35, 247n25; mediation petitions by, 63–65, 252n57; naming practices of, 44–47, 249n22; with parental respect virtue, 32–33; protests against headmen by, 10–11, 35, 60–63, 248n47; stored documents of, 24; with surname privilege, 43, 249n16; tax relief petitions by, 62, 251n50; urbanization of, 86; village head's status as, 28

Peers School (Tokyo), 99

Perry, Matthew C., 8

petitions to headmen: for mediation, 63–65, 252n57; for tax relief, 62, 251n50

pilgrimages, 78–79, 253n36

pine oil production, 155–56, 262n36

political parties, 14–15, 116–17

population trends: in Edo, 78; during Great Tenmei Famine, 55, 250n23; in Harbin, 138; in Japan, 1834–1840, 75; in Shinkyō, 134, 135, 259n40; in Tokyo, 86; in Yamashiraishi, 25, 31, 55, 111, 163, 246n8, 250nn23,27; in Yūemon's villages, 56, 251n32

prefectures, 12, 14–16, 245nn29,36

premarital sex, 236, 239

primogeniture right of inheritance, 42

Qingdao (China), 123–24, 126, 134

Qingdao Japanese Residents' Association, 126

railway lines: in Fukushims, 4, 116–17, 243n9; of Meiji period, 1, 13; in Qingdao, 123; in south Manchuria, 133, 134, 135
retirement cottage (*inkyō*), 24, 30, 177, 178, 192, 265n19
rice crop: during Depression, 115; granary for, 72, 253n15; petitions for inspection of, 62–63, 251n50; production of, in 1877, 111, 256n10; of Tōhoku region, 5; for tribute purposes, 7, 25, 27, 72, 244nn14,15, 253n16; volcanic destruction of, 54–55, 250n22; wartime requisition of, 146, 147–48. *See also* rice land
rice husker invention, 189
rice land: assessments of yield from, 25–27, 34, 246nn11,21; *bakufu* administration of, 70–71, 72, 253n16; land reform's reallocation of, 170–71, 183, 184; Matsuura holdings of, 112, 256–57n13; Meiji taxation of, 30, 111; 1937 scandal over, 118–19; reclamation of, 33, 42–43, 247–48n43. *See also* rice crop
rock quarry project, 171–72
rōnin (masterless samurai), 28
Russians: Manchurian development by, 133–34, 138; Siberian labor camps of, 164, 167–68; in wars against Japan, 37–38, 157–58, 262n42
Russo-Japanese War, 17, 37–38, 101, 116, 133, 248n6
ryō (gold coins), 110–11
ryōsai kenbo ("good wives, wise mothers"), 85

Saburō. *See* Matsuura Toshisaburō/Saburō
Sagawa Kō. *See* Matsuura Kō
Saionji Kimmochi, 99
Saipan (Mariana Islands), 153, 154
sake brewery, 33, 109, 111
salmon preservation, 68
samurai status, 28, 247n29
San Francisco, 131
Sano Akemi (Tatsugorō's wife), 174
satarii man (white collar worker), 195
Satoshiraishi village, 55, 60
Satsuma domain, 10

schools. *See* education
sea salt harvesting, 156
Seikatsu-Dan kindergarten (Tokyo), 217
Seishichirō/Sei. *See* Matsuura Seishichirō/Sei
Seito (Bluestocking) literary journal, 90
Seiyūkai Party, 116–17
Sekison Shrine (Mt. Oyama), 79
servants: manager of, 66–67; sleeping arrangements for, 22; tasks/skills of, 67–69; wartime draft of, 148
Shandong (Shantung) Peninsula, 123–24
Shanghai, 131–32, 134, 142–43
Shanghai Incident (1932), 100, 142
Shibusawa Eiichi, 9
Shiki. *See* Nakao Shiki
Shindatsu district, 10, 12, 246n11
Shinkansen high-speed line (Bullet Express), 117, 203
Shinkyō (Changchun, Manchuria), 133–34, 135, 157, 259n40
Shinobu district, 12
Shinrokurō/Shin. *See* Matsuura Shinrokurō/Shin
Shirakawa domain: famine in, 54–55, 250n22; Meiji's replacement of, 12; split of, in 1741, 34; tax levies on, 25–26, 246n11; as Tokugawa checkpoint, 6, 244n13; Yamashiraishi in, 246n16
shogakkō (compulsory elementary school), 243n8
shōji (wood-paneled sliding doors), 22
Shōwa generation, 150, 261n14
shōya. See village heads
Siberian Expedition (1920), 101
Siberian labor camps, 164, 167–68
silkworm cultivation, 31
Sino-Japanese War, 85; food shortages of, 146; Ishii's role prior to, 142–43; Japanese casualties in, 162, 263n18; Manchuria's status in, 134–36; Nanjing's destruction in, 143–44
sleeping arrangements, 22, 224
soba noodle, 148
Sōemon III. *See* Matsuura Yūemon Jinsuke
Solomon Islands, 141

Sōma domain, 12, 55, 250n22
sonchō (mayor), 32
Songo army base (Manchuria), 137–38
Songo fever, 138
South Manchuria Railway, 133, 134, 135
Soviet Union, 157–58
soy sauce, 110
streptomycin, 167
Sugai Fumi (Isami's fifth daughter), 112,
    164, 175; children of, 213, 219; edu-
    cation of, 90–91, 92; illness of, 95;
    Manchurian experience of, 133–34,
    157–58; marriage of, 106–7, 213; in
    multi-generational home, 236, 237;
    son of, at Toyo's memorial, 235;
    Tokyo residence of, 165
Sugai Kanji (Fumi's husband), 107, 133, 164
Sugiura Chiyo (Yatarō's wife), 100, 148,
    177–78, 179, 186
Suharto, T. N. J., 202
suicide, 168, 203
Suigun railway line, 117
Sukarno, Achmed, 129, 140, 202
Sumida River (Tokyo), 155
Surabaya (Dutch East Indies), 127
surnames: inheritability of, 43, 56, 249n16,
    251n29; women identified by, 73–74
surrender document, 160, 263nn6,7
Sydney (Australia), 130

Taira train station (Tokyo), 154
Taishō chic (term), 94, 255n30
Taishō period (1912–26), 84–85
Tami. See Nakamura Tami
tatami, 22, 23, 245n2
Tatsugorō/Tatsu. See Matsuura Tatsugorō/
    Tatsu
taxes: centralized administration of, 70–71,
    72, 253n16; domainal assessments for,
    25–27, 34; headmen's relief of, 55; land
    reclamation's impact on, 43, 247–48n43;
    Meiji system of, 30, 111; modes of
    payment, 244n14; nonpayment of, in
    1847, 75; peasant protests against, 35,
    248n47; petitions for relief of, 62,
    251n50; as special levies, 7–8, 244n15
Tazuko. See Matsuura Tazuko

tearooms (kissaten), 106
Teizō/Kōemon. See Matsuura
    Kōemon/Teizō
Tenmei Famine, 54–55, 250n22
Tenpō famine, 72–73
Teru (Isami's sixth daughter), 50, 52, 95
Tō-A Dōbun Shoin (East Asia Common
    Culture Institute), 59
tobacco crop, 31, 72, 110, 252–53n14
tobacco pipe (kiseru), 37
Tochigi prefecture, 108
Tōgō Heihachirō, 38
Tōhoku region (Northeast Japan): charac-
    teristics of, 5–6; population trends in,
    246n8; railway line of, 1, 243n9
Tojo Hideki, 146, 147, 153
tokonoma (alcove for displaying art
    objects), 23, 24
Tokugawa period (1600–1868): centralized
    tax system of, 70–71, 72, 253n16;
    domainal tax assessments of, 25–27,
    34, 246nn11,21; elite residences of, 22;
    end of, 11–12; foreign trade policies of,
    8–9, 244n18; Great Tenmei Famine
    in, 54–55, 250n22; parental respect
    policy of, 32–33; peasant uprisings of,
    10–11, 35, 60–63, 248n47; political/
    social system of, 6–7; population
    trends in, 55–56, 78, 250nn23,27;
    regulatory ordinances of, 34–35; Shira-
    kawa domain of, 6, 244n13; special
    tax levies of, 7–8, 244n15; terms for
    village heads in, 246n23
Tokyo (Edo): air-raid attacks on, 147, 154,
    155; Asakusa district of, 103, 104;
    destruction of, 161, 163; food short-
    ages in, 147, 165; in Great Kantō
    Earthquake, 86–87, 254n10; Isami's
    real estate deals in, 83, 114, 165–66;
    as Meiji capital, 11; military coup
    attempt in, 116, 137; postwar return
    to, 165–66; public universities in, 87–
    88; Western influence in, 1–2, 86,
    104–5; women's private schools in,
    88–91, 92–94. See also Edo
Tokyo Imperial University, 87–88, 99, 100,
    107

Tomita Kōkei, 32
Tomoji. *See* Matsuura Tomoji
Toshisaburō/Saburō. *See* Matsuura
    Toshisaburō/Saburō
Toyo. *See* Ishikawa Toyo
Toyotomi Hideyoshi, 28, 246nn11,16,
    247n28
toys, 49
trade. *See* foreign trade
trains. *See* railway lines
Tsingtao Beer brewery, 123
Tsukioka Hiroshi (Isami's grandson/Yasu's
    son), 151, 219, 226
Tsukioka Sho (Yasu's husband), 151, 164,
    167–68, 227
Tsukioka Yasu (Isami's seventh daughter),
    50, 139, 147; as caregiver, 165; death
    of child of, 226; education of, 89, 90;
    elder living arrangements of, 236, 237;
    husband of, 151, 167–68; illness of,
    167; signification of name, 40; West-
    ern influence on, 95
tuberculosis: of Fuki, 167; Kōjirō, 196; of
    Kō's son, 167, 187, 188–89; of Kōzō,
    168; of Toyo, 205, 219; of Yasu, 167

uchikowashi ("house-smashing"), 60
udon (wheat noodles), 52, 68
Uemura Masahisa, 95
Uemura Tamako, 95
Ueno district (Tokyo), 98
Ueno Station (Tokyo), 1, 13
Unit 731 (Manchuria), 138
United States: in battle of Guadalcanal,
    142; in battle of Okinawa, 156–57;
    Hiroshima bombing by, 159–60, 161–
    62, 262n2, 263n17; Ishii's impressions
    of, 130–31; Japanese medical students
    in, 209; Manchukuo policy of, 127–
    28; status of Japanese in, 131; Tokyo
    air-raid attacks by, 147, 154, 155. *See
    also* Allied occupation; Western
    influence
urban workers: marriage roles of, 211–
    12; rural migration by, 115, 257n26;
    as share of workforce, 84; women as,
    94, 255n32

Veterans Association (Yamashiraishi), 146
village heads *(shōya):* business offices of,
    30, 247n34; class status of, 28; house
    architecture of, 22; with inheritable
    surname, 43, 249n16; under Meiji
    reform, 12–13, 14–16, 32, 111,
    245nn29,36; occupation's purge of,
    169, 264–65n3; official duties of, 6,
    34–35, 63–65, 252n57; peasant upris-
    ings against, 10–11, 35, 60–63, 248n47;
    punishment of, for tax fraud, 27,
    247n25; qualifications for, 27–29,
    247n29; residences of, 22, 245n2;
    retirement accommodations for, 24;
    salary of, 33; special tax levies on, 7–
    8, 244n15; terms for, 246n23. *See also*
    league headmen; Matsuura patriarchs
villages. *See* peasants; Yamashiraishi village

war crimes: Dutch military trials on, 164,
    196, 266nn4,6,7; of Japanese Army,
    157; Kido's indictment for, 165,
    264n26; at Songo facility, 138
Watanabe Hironobu, 79–80, 243n3
wedding kimono, 98
weddings, 98, 101, 103, 174. *See also*
    marriage
Western influence: at Christian mission
    schools, 89; on clothing, 89, 95, 222;
    on education, 1–2, 4; on female
    athletics, 93; on female's official role,
    85, 90; on foreign trade policy, 8–9,
    244n18; at Hani's Freedom School,
    92–94, 255n30; on imperialist agenda,
    130; and individualism, xiv, 184, 235–
    36; and industrialization, xiii–xiv,
    113–14; Japanese reaction against, 101,
    124; in Manchuria, 133–34, 138; on
    Meiji policies, 12–13; in Qingdao port,
    123–24; in Tokyo, 86, 104–5; on Toyo,
    95, 101, 217, 230
White Crane Castle (Aizu-Wakamatsu
    domain), 10
widowhood, 215–16, 226
wives: age of, at marriage, 36, 69, 250–51n27;
    care of dying spouses by, 213–15; child-
    bearing years of, 69, 252n5; contem-

porary marriages of, 236–37, 238–40; from influential lineages, 41–42; meal preparation by, 68, 220–21; traditional wedding customs of, 98; urban middle-class role of, 85, 90, 211–12, 222; of village heads, 66–67, 68; widowhood experience of, 215–16, 226. *See also* marriage

women: athletics training for, 93; child-bearing years of, 69, 252n5; customary naming of, 39–40; education statistics on, 85–86, 248n2, 254n8; identified by surname, 73–74; official middle-class role of, 85, 90; on pilgrimages, 78–79; schools/curriculum for, 88–91, 92–94, 255nn29,30; as urban workers, 94, 255n32; voting rights for, 188. *See also* wives

Women's Sacred Learning Academy (Joshi Seigakuin, Tokyo), 89

women's suffrage, 188

World War II: censorship during, 142; Dutch East Indies occupation of, 139–41; food shortages of, 146–48; Guadalcanal battle of, 141–42, 260n20; Hiroshima bombing of, 159–60, 161–62, 262n2, 263n17; Isami's war efforts during, 155–56, 262n36; Japanese casualties of, 263n18; Midway battle of, 147; new cabinet formation in, 153–54; Okinawa battle of, 156–57; Pearl Harbor attack of, 135, 136, 137, 146–47; surrender announcement of, 160, 263nn6,7; Tokyo air-raid attacks of, 147, 154, 155

Wright, Frank Lloyd, 91, 105, 134, 255n22

Yajibei (founding Matsuura ancestor), 25, 27–30, 55, 246n7, 247nn27,29

Yamashiraishi mura o kataru (Telling about Yamashiraishi village). *See* Matsuura Isami's chronicle

Yamashiraishi village: centralized taxation of, 70–71, 72, 253n16; domainal tax assessments of, 25–27, 246n16; electric power in, 52; executed village heads of, 27, 247n25; first Matsuura headman of, 27–29, 247nn27,29; first primary school in, 14; during Great Tenmei Famine, 55, 250n23; headman's relationships in, 53–54, 59–60, 183–84, 185, 250n15; horse trade in, 61, 251n46; household size in, 55, 250–51n27; location/climate of, 5; Meiji consolidation of, 15–17; occupation's impact on, 184–85; population trends in, 25, 31, 55, 111, 163, 246n8, 250nn23,27; postwar food preparations in, 162–63, 264n21; postwar return to, 163–64, 167–68; in prefectural system, 12, 15, 245n29; rice crop yield of, 244n15; rice granary of, 72, 253n15; rice requisitions from, 146, 147–48; Zen Buddhist temple of, 29–30, 72

Yamashiraishi Women's Association, 155

Yamazaki Fumio, 59, 189nn20,21, 250n15, 251n40

Yasu. *See* Tsukioka Yasu

Yatarō. *See* Matsuura Yatarō

yōiku hin ("child support money"), 84

Yokohama, 8, 9, 86

Yōko. *See* Horiuchi Yōko

Yoshi (Isami's grandmother/Jinsuke's first wife), 1, 24, 40, 77, 246n5

Yoshiwara district (Tokyo), 104

Young People's League (Yamashiraishi), 171

Yūemon. *See* Matsuura Yūemon

Yūemon Jinsuke. *See* Matsuura Yūemon Jinsuke

yukata (kimono), 67, 68–69, 98

Yukijinushi Company, 175

Yūshirō. *See* Matsuura Yūshirō

Yūya. *See* Matsuura Yūya

Zen Buddhist temple (Yamashiraishi), 29–30, 59, 72

Zero planes, 145

Compositor: Integrated Composition Systems
Text: 11/13.5 Adobe Garamond
Display: Adobe Garamond
Printer and binder: Edwards Brothers, Inc.